T0140110

Human–Computer Interaction Series

Editors-in-chief

Desney Tan
Microsoft Research, USA

Jean Vanderdonckt
Université catholique de Louvain, Belgium

More information about this series at http://www.springer.com/series/6033

Gilbert Cockton • Marta Lárusdóttir
Peggy Gregory • Åsa Cajander
Editors

Integrating User-Centred Design in Agile Development

 Springer

Editors
Gilbert Cockton
School of Design
Northumbria University
Newcastle upon Tyne, UK

Marta Lárusdóttir
School of Computer Science
Reykjavik University
Reykjavik
Iceland

Peggy Gregory
School of Physical Sciences and Computing
University of Central Lancashire
Preston, UK

Åsa Cajander
Department of Information Technology
Uppsala University
Uppsala, Sweden

ISSN 1571-5035
Human–Computer Interaction Series
ISBN 978-3-319-81211-3   ISBN 978-3-319-32165-3   (eBook)
DOI 10.1007/978-3-319-32165-3

Printed on acid-free paper

This Springer imprint is published by Springer Nature
The registered company is Springer International Publishing AG Switzerland

Foreword

Software thinking is broken and it is not easily fixed. Agile sailed in about a decade and a half ago, but it fell short in many ways. It turned out that the users were completely left out and the customer was brought in as the major source for innovative ideas and creative thoughts about the end-user needs and desires. The software industry was too busy fixing the problems generated by engineering thinking dating back several decades. Yes, we have acknowledged now that big systems cannot be defined in detail upfront and we need to be flexible as we go along. In one way, the agile movement has been a success as, for example, today agile thinking penetrates also to the design of safety critical systems. On the other hand, despite hundreds of studies, we still lack a clear definition of what agile is and what agile is not. Luckily this book does not attempt to answer this definition-related question but addresses something much more fundamental and an important issue, namely, why is it so hard to put together a way of developing software that delivers creative, fun, friendly and easy-to-use software.

This book is rooted in the user-centred design (UCD) field and ultimately wants to combine the great things in agile development with the great things in UCD but does it in an intriguing way that makes the reader wonder: why had I not thought about that before? I have a strong background in software process improvement and in agile software development fields. I have published dozens of industrial studies trying to understand why and how agile works like it does. I thought I could guesstimate upfront the solutions that this book set out to deliver. The authors of this book surprised me very positively. They have opted not to attempt to deliver a single solution that easily fixes all or most of the current problems. Authors share years and years of lessons learned and take a critical standpoint on contemporary thinking. The authors' own field receives a healthy dose of criticism as well as agile development. The book forms a foundational understanding on the complexities surrounding UCD in agile contexts and does it well.

The book has a number of audiences that will benefit for the authors' efforts. I personally will use this book next year when I teach software engineering to 2nd-year undergraduate students of informatics and computer science. The concrete hints, practices and techniques about the user-centred work will benefit students who think that ultimately Scrum is sufficient for all their needs. Academics more broadly will benefit from the wide angle of perspectives and the critical tone that the book takes when discussing how to make UCD work within agile development. For industrial readers, the book contains a great deal of concrete empirical guidance, as it is based on a large number of industrial case studies in various contexts, companies and cultures.

If I were to interpret the book's solution in making UCD work in agile contexts, it would be its acknowledgement of the fact that no existing methods provide a comprehensive solution in any particular situation, but rather a mixed-method approach is required: companies need to develop their own ways of working, supported by professional training and coaching. The result is a method or a way of working that only works in one organisational setting, since each development situation and the people therein are unique, and that software development is a predominantly intellectual activity where classical engineering methods and tools have proven to only work suboptimally.

Personally, I enjoyed reading especially the forward-looking chapters and tend to agree with the authors that design research and creative thinking would have a lot to give to software developers and researchers. I would have loved to see the authors commenting on the newly formed SEMAT initiative (Software Engineering Method and Theory; see http://semat.org/), which is said to form the new theoretical grounding for software development. Although I can understand that SEMAT presents an overly engineering type of thinking, it may not be radical enough to change the status quo in industrial practice.

Is software thinking still broken after having read the book? Perhaps yes, but to a lesser extent. This book shows that there is room for innovative thinking in the field, and I hope readers will agree and find the book as valuable as I have.

Department of Computer and Information Science   Pekka Abrahamsson
Norwegian University of Science and Technology, NTNU
Trondheim
Norway
May 2016

Book Overview

This book originates from a NordiCHI 2014 workshop [1]. Six workshop position papers have been updated and expanded for this book: five case studies (Chaps. 2, 3, 4, 5 and 6) and a proposed new framework (Chap. 9). One position paper [2] was updated for publication elsewhere [3]. The other is available from the workshop's website [4]. Five additional chapters were prepared for this book: the introduction (Chap. 1), the report on the workshop (Chap. 8), a sixth case study (Chap. 7) and two forward-looking analyses (Chaps. 10 and 11). Half of the case studies have industrial authors, with the other half authored by academic researchers working in close collaboration with commercial and public organisations.

The editors' introduction (Chap. 1) begins with the workshop's context; then reviews topics across chapters, position papers and workshop activities; and lastly presents agendas for further research into the effective integration of user-centred design (UCD) and agile development methodologies (Agile).

After briefly overviewing UCD, Agile and their integration (Agile UCD), the introduction surveys four major topics from the workshop and book chapters:

- *Cultures* across the development of digital products and services
- *Teams*: roles, responsibilities, communication, boundaries and capabilities
- *Tasks*: process, sprint and activity-level issues and ideas
- *Research approaches*: human science rigour and creative design research practices

Culture is discussed via values that materialise through people, practices, places and artefacts. *Team factors* are discussed in terms of the following: range of observed roles and associated responsibilities; team boundaries and communication practices; and nurturing cross-functional capabilities. *Task factors* are reviewed across three scopes: processes, iterations and activities. The book's case studies resolve several tensions between Agile and UCD by adapting process and iteration structures, supported by innovative approaches and resources for Agile UCD.

High-quality appropriate research approaches are a major strength of all chapters. Human science traditions within UCD are reflected in rigorous systematic qualitative and quantitative research. Creative design research practices are also in evidence. These are not all currently common in applied Agile or UCD research but have been applied in several guises to make innovative contributions to Agile UCD practice.

These main topics cover a range of successes and challenges within Agile UCD, as well as future research opportunities. The introduction's first research agenda is practice based and tactical. It can be advanced through professional action research, potentially supported by academic collaboration. The second is more wide ranging, open-ended and foundational. Challenges, issues and questions here reflect the broadening scope of development and operational support for digital products and services, which now are coming close to being the backbone of contemporary commercial and public organisations, rather than simply being internal systems that support work within them. The second research agenda looks beyond Agile and UCD to the wider contexts of digital economies and digitally enabled social and cultural innovation. Chapter 1 recognises the scale of challenges here: collaboration across professions and disciplines is needed to meet them. Fortunately, case study chapters offer good foundations for meeting these future challenges, supported by the forward-looking chapters.

Chapter 2 reports the first of six case studies: *User Integration in Agile Software Development Processes: Practices and Challenges in Small- and Medium-Sized Enterprises* (Oliver Stickel, Corinna Ogonowski, Timo Jakobi, Gunnar Stevens, Volkmar Pipek and Volker Wulf) reports findings on Agile UCD from in-depth case studies within three German SMEs. The research collected data using interviews and observations, which were analysed thematically, drawing on grounded theory. Findings identify three main themes that characterise how SMEs integrate UCD into Agile work:

1. Roles
2. Channels and tools
3. Filtering and interpretation

   Chapter 2's recommendations include:

- Understanding the importance of agile and organisational culture
- Holistic consideration of roles, channels and tools
- Awareness of the challenges of filtering and interpreting user feedback

Chapter 2 reveals the diversity of successful Agile UCD, with each SME exploiting a range of roles and practices, especially in relation to customer and user feedback. The mass market orientations of all three SMEs create strong user-focused cultures. All made effective use of shared media and tools, but this was not without challenges.

Chapter 2 balances positive attitudes towards UCD with the recognition that, even in companies with strong user-centred cultures, UCD needs to change. UCD is seen as addressing real users' needs and wants, but not necessarily with clarity on how users should actually be involved and how this fits into established development processes. UCD is not yet mature, because optimal combination of methods is still not well understood. UCD is not the sole source of user-focused practices: good contributions can be made using management research on innovation, as well as established brand evaluation practices such as Net Promoter Scores.

Chapter 2 identifies where unmodified agile practices such as user stories [5] and daily stand-up meetings support UCD work. Conversely, some innovation practices such as a lead user group have not worked well previously with one SME, and another has concerns about their test households becoming blind to some issues. Overall, this chapter reports sophisticated integrative practices for Agile UCD that allow optimism in the face of more superficial analyses of incompatibility. There are challenges, especially with the product owner role. While the diversity across the three SMEs may obstruct generalisation, Stickel and colleagues rightly argue that the insights from the SMEs' practices can still be helpful.

Chapter 3 presents the second case study: *Templates: A Key to Success when Training Developers to Perform UX Tasks* (Tina Øvad and Lars Bo Larsen) reports the iterative development of curricula and method templates for training developers to carry out UX tasks. Companies often lack staff who are trained in UX and usability methods or do not have enough UX staff to avoid UX teams being perceived as a bottleneck (plus there are also issues about how time consuming UCD work can be). Øvad and Larsen trained developers from three companies with the overall goal of developing a toolkit that was suitable for use within Scrum sprints and would also develop a shared language within development teams. Developers received 1 day of training for each method and were provided with templates that describe how to conduct UX tasks. These templates supported a 'fill in the blanks' approach to UX work. Three methods were covered: focused workshops, AB testing and contextual interviews.

Chapter 3 draws on long-standing UCD research from the 1990s on training developers (especially novices, who need structure) and more recent research within Agile contexts, including work by the authors and collaborators. Agile contexts need to integrate UX work on a daily basis, which was not considered in related 1990s UCD research. A rigorous empirically informed iterative process was followed over 2 years, with up to four iterations for one method. The limitations of 'observe and learn' tactics soon became apparent, so existing template usage, which had been observed in use for documentation in agile development, was transferred to method training materials. Experiences led to continuous changes to templates and guidance documentation.

The effectiveness of the training was rigorously monitored using a mixed methods research approach. Developers were interviewed before and after training and a third time after independent use of the method. Training sessions were observed and recorded for later analysis. Meaning condensation was used for qualitative analysis.

The materials are not intended for stand-alone use but require prior formal training. Introduced in this way, the materials were highly valued by developers, who developed confidence and a secure trust in their capabilities for independent use. However, not all suggestions and requests from trainees were acted on. Iterative improvements were focused on performance before preference. Requests for examples were not acted on, because of a risk of superficial learning leading to inappropriate copying.

Chapter 4 provides the third case study: *Integrating Scrum and UCD: Insights from Two Case Studies* (Alvaro Aranda Muñoz, Karin Nilsson Helander, Thijmen de Gooijer and Maria Ralph) presents two case studies showing how UCD can be integrated with Scrum. The first case study reports on how a UCD-focused research team proactively and independently adopted and adapted Scrum in two-week sprints to develop a 3D prototype for improving information visualisation for manufacturing.

Team members in the authors' company typically work on more than one research and development (R&D) project. This gave the authors access to other R&D projects for their second case study, which reviewed Agile UCD practices in three other teams. Knowledge, insights and experiences from the two case studies inform the authors' recommendations for future Agile UCD practices:

- Configure physical space to support collaboration, synchronisation and shared understandings across the extended project team, as well as to recognise contributions to ongoing and completed tasks.
- Synchronise resources to support advance planning.
- Plan for UCD's need for extra planning and communication relative to Scrum.
- Plan for external UCD dependencies, especially relating to user research and testing.

Based on the above, the authors propose to modify Sy's approach [6, 7] for Agile UCD, as well as to further adapt Scrum practices:

- Contextual inquiry is restricted to Sprint 1, and completed there, with no requirements for new features collected after that.
- Design chunks (concept groups [6, 7]) can be implemented across a few sprints.
- Anticipating resource needs and aligning these with availability, with some planning several sprints ahead to reduce postponement of UCD tasks.
- Variable sprint lengths.
- Dropping the closed window rule [5] to add tasks to the backlog when developers finish early ('bottomless sprints'), and also when tasks needed to be reprioritised, even within short two-week sprints.
- Use of persistent media to include team members who work part-time on a project, and thus cannot attend all meetings, plus adaptations to Scrum boards to recognise the contributions of all team members (not only developers).

Overall, much of the focus and effort in this case study was directed towards ensuring that all team members were included and valued. Another predominant focus was on being realistic about the uncertainties of creative UCD work in an R&D environment while at the same time anticipating and heading off scheduling problems.

Chapter 5 presents a fourth case study: *Integration of Human-Centred Design and Agile Software Development Practices: Experience Report from an SME* (Carmelo Ardito, Maria Teresa Baldassarre, Danilo Caivano and Rosa Lanzilotti) presents a planned integration of Scrum and human-centred design (HCD, which unlike UCD, does not see users as design's only stakeholders).

Ardito and colleagues' previous experiences of integrating HCD into a waterfall process created positive expectations, as did principles common to Agile and UCD: iterative design, user involvement, continuous testing and prototyping. While not common to all UCD or Agile, these nevertheless indicate potential for integrating complementary approaches, which was explored collaboratively with experienced project managers from an Italian SME. Thorough literature research on Agile UCD spanning almost a decade of studies identified sources of opportunities and challenges:

1. Upfront tasks, with HCD needing sufficient time here for stakeholder research
2. Prototyping for rapid evaluation and communication
3. User stories, potentially extended to cover usability and acceptance criteria
4. Inspection evaluations of paper prototypes in support of design refinement
5. User testing of interactive prototypes, possibly as part of acceptance testing
6. One sprint ahead for the first few sprints only

HCD could benefit from Agile's high iteration frequency, constant customer involvement and incremental development. Knowledge of opportunities and challenges informed co-design of an agile HCD methodology with points of difference from Scrum:

1. A *customer committee* supports the product owner (PO), increasing customer and user involvement in planning.
2. Multidisciplinary research during project *inception* (UCD, market, technical).
3. An initial *Sprint n.0* resulting in a high-level prototype and basic software services in place, drawing on earlier multidisciplinary research.
4. Physical *Scrum Islands* sitting two developers, visual interaction designer and PO together, removing need for daily stand-up meetings and formal sprint end reviews.
5. Predefined very short one-week sprint cycles, with tasks carrying over to next sprint.
6. Continuous *(IN)Sprint Reviews* supported by customer committee testing.
7. *Multidisciplinary project retrospective* after project completion, covering product quality and customer satisfaction and opportunities for the SME to improve strategy, management and software and process quality.

Customer feedback was gathered throughout the project from the earliest stages, with customers actively engaged at multiple points throughout, including acceptance testing for both usability and internal software quality. The extensions here were experienced as a positive integration of HCD into Scrum-based practices.

Chapter 6, *Communication Breakdowns in the Integration of User-Centred Design and Agile Development* (Silvia Bordin and Antonella De Angeli), reports the fifth case study of the large university-based Smart Campus project. This was moved to Scrum from an initial iterative participatory design (PD) process. PD is a form of UCD where 'the people destined to use the system play a critical role in designing it' [8]. This happened almost 1 year into the project, forcing dynamic adaptation of Agile and PD practices, adding to the challenges for Agile UCD. The corresponding position paper's title was *Catch Me If You Can: Reconciling Agile and UCD*, which refers to the challenge of reconciling PD with Agile at a fast pace in the context of a high volume of feedback from a large user community.

Smart Campus aimed to develop mobile apps to support a student community. A pervasive PD approach was expected, supported by multiple feedback channels. Before Scrum was introduced, extensive upfront work had preceded app development. However, the unanticipated introduction of Scrum made it difficult to fully follow PD principles. To understand the difficulties encountered, and how to overcome them, two interview studies were planned and carried out. A researcher external to the project conducted the interviews, which were then transcribed and analysed, controlling for coding bias. A literature review in conjunction with the interview studies revealed how UCD work practices can be obstructed by Agile; the authors benefitted from two 2014 literature surveys that covered 76 [9] and 71 [10] papers, which highlight the topicality of the chapters in this book.

Three themes emerged from the combined literature and interview data analyses:

1. Differences in how user involvement is understood across roles in the project team
2. Differences in how documentation was valued by project team roles
3. Coordination of design and development work

The nature and funding of Smart Campus resulted in management approaches different to those advocated by Scrum: a wider range of stakeholders were actively involved and forced breaches of the Scrum principle of self-organising teams [5]. Similar breaches are reported in other case studies, without evidence of any negative impact. However, PD involving a large user community significantly adds to the challenges for UCD within Scrum. Bordin and De Angeli thus advocate adopting participatory development [8] and design thinking [11, 12] alongside Scrum to promote an organisational culture receptive to innovative software design for communities.

Chapter 7 presents the last study: *Towards Understanding How Agile Teams Predict User Experience* (Kati Kuusinen, Heli Väätäjä, Tommi Mikkonen and Kaisa Väänänen). It is an inventive study of how accurately different roles with an agile team can predict a system's UX from users' perspectives. As with the training courses and materials developed by Øvad and Larsen (Chap. 3), the motivating practical goal is to reduce UX specialists (UXSs) being (perceived as) a bottleneck. If developers can perform more UCD work, then faster design iterations based on UX evaluation are possible, and meaningful UX goals can be set for sprints. For example, another study for the projects involved [13] indicated that developers did not participate in user tests or identifying and defining target user groups.

Team members from six enterprise software development projects in five companies participated. All six used Agile with release cycles under 6 months long and released software in use. The application contexts were work-based enterprise systems. Software had graphical user interfaces, requiring UX design work that was underway.

Each participant rated their enterprise application against 16 UX dimensions and also gave it an overall UX rating and rated how well it responded to needs. Need fulfilment ratings by team members correlated most strongly with users' ratings for non-instrumental UX, e.g. 'aesthetic' or 'presentable'. Only users' ratings for 'useful' correlated significantly with their assessment of need fulfilment. Team members rated their released software twice: once from their own perspective and once from the users. Ideally, these ratings should match, but the former was more critical than the latter. However, PO and UXS ratings from the users' perspective were closer than developers' to users' actual ratings.

The results show that team members can predict instrumental aspects of UX but are less able to predict hedonic quality, with POs and UXS performing better than developers. To better predict UX ratings, developers need to better understand users. Chapter 7 identifies the use of personas as one possible tactic here. Without better knowledge of users, making use of developer ratings of achieved UX could be harmful.

The remaining four chapters are forward looking and authored by academic researchers but all draw on industrial case studies. Chapter 8 uses the combined input of workshop attendees. Chapters 9 and 10 use retrospective analyses of several case studies. Chapter 11 uses secondary sources from research into creative design.

Chapter 8 reports on the NordiCHI 2014 workshop from which this book originates. It describes its motivation, the approach used, its eight position papers and analysis and discussion of its themes. Six position papers were Scrum case studies. The others focused on Kanban [4] and Scrum and Lean [2].

Agile-style techniques were used to run the workshop, including time-boxed increments to workshop analyses, a small group discussion approach and a persistent shared visual workspace. During the workshop, post-it notes were collected from all participants about 'challenges and obstacles' and 'interesting points' that they had identified during position paper presentations. Post-its were then organised into two affinity diagrams. The smallest affinity groups for 'challenges and obstacles' were 'tools/toolboxes' and 'synchronisation', indicating that tools and high-level process issues were modest concerns (even though synchronisation issues dominate the Agile UCD literature). The smallest post-it groups for 'interesting points' were 'tools' (again), 'documentation' and 'UX team' (does that reflect attendees' UX credentials?). Large groups for 'interesting issues' formed around user involvement and feedback, pair working and internal communication. Chapter 8 presents results from a phased affinity diagram analysis of the post-its. Eight final themes were formed:

- People and roles
- Teams and communication
- Culture ('challenges and obstacles' only)
- Methods and practices
- Time and synchronisation

- Artefacts and tools
- Research and problems ('interesting points' only)
- Miscellaneous

The largest theme by post-it count, 'Methods and practices', highlighted the practicalities of integrating UCD into Agile and the practices that make that possible. Two people-centred themes, 'Teams and communication' and 'People and roles', came next. Both are key to improving integration. The smallest theme, 'Artefacts and tools', was nevertheless the focus of some novel solutions presented at the workshop. These themes reflect the scope and breadth of discussions, with much focus on fitting together the big picture of agile theory and methods with the lower-level detail of day-to-day practices. Potential links between theory and practice provided a focus for considering innovative new practices to ameliorate persistent challenges to effective Agile UCD. However, despite the workshop's focus on research and innovation as well as challenges, discussion focused on familiar unresolved issues, despite many presented examples of progress. Nevertheless, some new challenges and innovative solutions do not figure prominently in current surveys:

- Power relations in Agile
- Training developers in UCD ('Developers doing UCD' was the largest initial 'interesting issues' group)
- Filtering and interpretation of user feedback

Chapter 9 presents Kati Kuusinen's *BoB: A Framework for Organizing Within-Iteration UX Work in Agile Development*. This new framework seeks to combine the 'best of both' worlds of UCD and Agile. BoB uses an initial upfront activity for early product definition, which includes a workshop and results in a clickable version of an initial product. After this important enabling milestone (similar to Chap. 4's Sprint 1 and Chap. 5's Sprint n.0), a sequence of sprints requires a cross-functional team to work together, thus avoiding difficulties with the one sprint ahead approach [6, 7], which tend to result in inescapable mini-waterfalls across sprints. The BoB framework is based on four mixed methods studies spanning 4 years and involving over 300 respondents from 9 companies in 10 countries (7 in Europe and 3 in Asia), working across IT services, engineering, middleware, mobile enterprise applications and industrial systems (including safety critical). The BoB framework is supported by guidelines on people, process, tasks and tools. It shifts the focus from roles (as in Scrum) to analysis and design tasks, which are carried out by small cross-functional teams. It reduces the emphasis on 'definitions of done' (as in Scrum [5]) with an acceptance of trial and error, with the need to iterate user interface designs [14].

Elements of the BoB framework are already in use by some companies involved in the underpinning studies. It is too early to judge whether BoB will overcome challenges for Agile UCD, but Kuusinen expects cross-functional teams to work together better and that faster feedback from customers and users will result. BoB is expected to halve the feedback cycle time for a feature compared to one sprint ahead

Agile UCD, since design and development are concurrent instead of sequential. Thus, it should take one iteration instead of two to receive and act on feedback based on real use.

Chapter 10 provides a refreshing change from UCD criticisms of Agile's shortcomings. *Challenges from Integrating Usability Activities in Scrum: Why Is Scrum So Fashionable?* (Marta Lárusdóttir, Åsa Cajander, Gudbjörg Erlingsdottir, Thomas Lind and Jan Gulliksen) instead investigates the positive reasons why organisations choose Scrum. The attractiveness of Agile is contrasted with that of UCD, which is not as fashionable. As with Chap. 9 by Kuusinen, this chapter is based on retrospective analysis of existing case studies, in this case data from five survey and interview studies involving 110 respondents from over 40 companies in mainly two countries. The results of these studies are interpreted through the twin lenses of Abrahamsson's theory on management fashion [15] and Roger's diffusion of innovations theory [16]. For much of UCD's history, it has held the moral high ground [17], insisting that we must put users' needs and comfort first. The respondents in the five studies did not all always do so. While there is no doubt that Scrum benefits from its fashionability (much of this of its own making [5]), Abrahamsson's theory on management fashion [15] requires rational and progressive motives for adopting new innovations, and the respondent's positions in the case studies make it clear that, to them, Scrum adoption is both rational and progressive. Scrum also has advantages in relation to Roger's diffusion of innovations theory [16]. The future fortunes of UCD in most software development contexts thus depend on understandings of management fashions and diffusion of innovations. UCD's moral high ground has clearly not won the majority of hearts and minds since the 1980s, so alternative approaches to dissemination and uptake are needed that focus on UCD's worth as a favourable balance of benefits over costs and risks. Both UCD and Agile have understandably focused on promoting their benefits while downplaying or ignoring their costs and risks. Balanced approaches are required.

Chapter 11 introduces a third element to the methodology mix. *Integrating Both User-Centred Design and Creative Practices into Agile Development* (Gilbert Cockton) argues for the integration of creative design practices as well as UCD within agile methodologies. The expectation is that the benefits arising from a more balanced and integrated design process will increase by knowingly adding key creative design practices (rather than assuming that Agile UCD is creative enough). Also, costs and risks will decrease. Cockton draws on almost half a century of secondary literature from design research to identify three key insights on the nature of creative design work:

• Creative design work co-evolves problem and solution spaces.
• Design materials talk back.
• The best design work is generous in scope and intent.

The first insight guides Agile and UCD to fully break away from the constraints of idealised rational engineering design and its rigid segregation of problem and solution spaces via a thick wall of requirements specifications [18]. The second insight defends the use of UCD and creative design 'documents' (as in Chap. 6), which are to be understood in the broadest sense of persistent media rather than Agile's preferred face-to-face conversations. Such documents are expected to change and this is not wasteful. Instead, this is one of the primary ways through which problem and solution spaces co-evolve in creative design work. The third insight challenges UCD and Agile practices to look beyond the 'requirements of others' and let designers add their subjective generosity to the objective needs and wants of users (UCD) or a product owner's user stories and associated business value (Agile). Acting on these three insights will provide opportunities to balance and integrate creative, engineering and user-centred design and, in doing so, be guided and shaped by designers' generosity. The result here is a design process that is BIG [19]: balanced, integrated and generous.

Overall, this book's chapters present a comprehensive survey of progress and continuing challenges in the integration of Agile and UCD. The quality and depth of the case study research is impressive. The forward-looking chapters propose novel broader futures for Agile UCD. There are good grounds for optimism now in the face of the initial shock of Agile reversing many UCD gains. These reversals are temporary, and we can look forward to the best of both worlds, or perhaps the best of several worlds, combining to improve the development of digital products and services.

Newcastle upon Tyne, UK   Gilbert Cockton
Reykjavik, Iceland   Marta Lárusdóttir
Preston, UK   Peggy Gregory
Uppsala, Sweden   Åsa Cajander
May 2016

References

1. Lárusdóttir M, Cajander Å, Gulliksen J, Cockton G, Gregory P, Salah D. On the integration of user centred design in agile development. In: Proceedings of NordiCHI'14. ACM, pp 817–82
2. Law ELC, Lárusdóttir MK (2014) User Experience (UX) design: agile or lean?. In: Proceedings of the workshop: on the integration of UCD and agile development, NordiCHI 2014, Helsinki, Finland. Available from https://ucdandagile.wordpress.com
3. Law ELC, Lárusdóttir MK (2015) Whose experience do we care about? Analysis of the fitness of Scrum and Kanban to user experience. Int J HCI 31(9):584–602
4. Lindell R (2014) Attending experiential qualities in system development. In: Proceedings of the workshop: on the integration of UCD and agile development. NordiCHI 2014, Helsinki, Finland. Available from https://ucdandagile.wordpress.com
5. Meyer B (2014) Agile! The good, the hype and the ugly. Springer
6. Sy D (2007) Adapting usability investigations for agile user-centered design. J Usability Stud 2(3):112–132
7. Sy D, Miller L (2008) Optimizing agile user-centred design. In: CHI'08 extended abstracts on human factors in computing systems, CHI EA'08, ACM, pp 3897–3900

8. Schuler D, Namioka A (eds) (1993) Participatory design: principles and practices. Lawrence Erlbaum, Hillsdale
9. Jurca G, Hellmann TD, Maurer F (2014) Integrating agile and user-centered design: a systematic mapping and review of evaluation and validation studies of agile-UX. In: Agile conference (AGILE), 2014, IEEE (2014), pp 24–32
10. Salah D, Paige RF, Cairns P (2014) A systematic literature review for agile development processes and user centred design integration. In: Proceedings of 18th International conference on evaluation and assessment in software engineering, 5. ACM
11. Brown T (2005) Strategy by design, fast company, June 2005. http://www.fastcompany.com/52795/strategy-design
12. Brown T (2009) Change by design: how design thinking transforms organizations and inspires innovation. Harper Business, New York
13. Kuusinen K (2015) Task allocation between UX specialists and developers in agile software development projects. In: Proceedings of INTERACT 2015, LNCS 9298. Springer, pp 27–44
14. Gould J, Lewis C (1985) Designing for usability: key principles and what designers think. CACM 28(3):300–311
15. Abrahamsson E (1996) Management fashion. Acad Manag Rev 21(1):254–285
16. Rogers EM (2003) Diffusion of innovations, 5th edn. Free Press, New York
17. Cooper G, Bowers J (1995) Representing the user: notes on the disciplinary rhetoric of human-computer interaction. In: Thomas PJ (ed) The social and interactional dimensions of human-computer interfaces. Cambridge University Press, Cambridge, pp 48–66
18. Gram C, Cockton G (1996) Design principles for interactive software. Chapman and Hall, London
19. Cockton G (2013) Design isn't a shape and it hasn't got a centre: thinking BIG about post-centric interaction design. In: Proceedings of MIDI'13. ACM, Article 2, 16 pages. doi:10.1145/2500342.2500344

Acknowledgements

We would like to thank the NordiCHI 2014 workshop chairs, our workshop participants, the authors of chapters, our reviewers and colleagues at Springer for making this book possible. The workshop merged two separate proposals, improving the balance of expertise across the organisers. The COST TwinTide Action IC0904 (www.twintide.org/) provided a context for collaborations between three of the editors.

Contents

Part II   Future Directions

Contributors

Carmelo Ardito Dipartimento di Informatica, Università degli Studi di Bari Aldo Moro, Bari, Italy

Maria Teresa Baldassarre Dipartimento di Informatica, Università degli Studi di Bari Aldo Moro, Bari, Italy

Silvia Bordin Department of Information Engineering and Computer Science, University of Trento, Trento, Italy

Danilo Caivano Dipartimento di Informatica, Università degli Studi di Bari Aldo Moro, Bari, Italy

Åsa Cajander Department of Information Technology, Uppsala University, Uppsala, Sweden

Gilbert Cockton School of Design, Northumbria University, Newcastle upon Tyne, UK

Antonella De Angeli Department of Information Engineering and Computer Science, University of Trento, Trento, Italy

Thijmen de Gooijer ABB Corporate Research, Västerås, Sweden

Gudbjörg Erlingsdottir Lund University, Lund, Sweden

Peggy Gregory School of Physical Sciences and Computing, University of Central Lancashire, Preston, UK

Jan Gulliksen KTH Royal Institute of Technology, Stockholm, Sweden

Karin Nilsson Helander ABB Corporate Research, Västerås, Sweden

Timo Jakobi University of Siegen, Siegen, Germany

Kati Kuusinen Tampere University of Technology, Tampere, Finland

Rosa Lanzilotti Dipartimento di Informatica, Università degli Studi di Bari Aldo Moro, Bari, Italy

Lars Bo Larsen Aalborg University, Aalborg, Denmark

Marta Lárusdóttir School of Computer Science, Reykjavik University, Reykjavik, Iceland

Thomas Lind Department of Information Technology, Uppsala University, Uppsala, Sweden

Tommi Mikkonen Tampere University of Technology, Tampere, Finland

Alvaro Aranda Muñoz ABB Corporate Research, Västerås, Sweden

Corinna Ogonowski University of Siegen, Siegen, Germany

Tina Øvad Radiometer Medical, Copenhagen, Denmark

Aalborg University, Aalborg, Denmark

Volkmar Pipek University of Siegen, Siegen, Germany

Maria Ralph ABB Corporate Research, Västerås, Sweden

Gunnar Stevens Bonn Rhein-Sieg University of Applied Sciences, Augustin, Germany

Oliver Stickel University of Siegen, Siegen, Germany

Kaisa Väänänen Tampere University of Technology, Tampere, Finland

Heli Väätäjä Tampere University of Technology, Tampere, Finland

Volker Wulf University of Siegen, Siegen, Germany

Chapter 1
Integrating User-Centred Design in Agile Development

Gilbert Cockton, Marta Lárusdóttir, Peggy Gregory, and Åsa Cajander

Abstract Integrating user-centered design (UCD) into software development methodologies has always been a challenge. In the first two decades of UCD, structured methodologies provided a process where UCD methods could be clearly integrated, at least in principle, and thus integration challenges were not primarily due to process structures. This changed with the spread of agile software development approaches, which differ substantially from structured development. While there has been progress in combining UCD and agile approaches, many problems remain. In response to this, at NordiCHI 2014, a workshop on *Integrating User Centred Design in Agile Development* brought together researchers and practitioners at the leading edge of combining these two potentially complementary approaches to software development. The chapters in this book update and extend the position papers that were presented and discussed at the workshop. Six authors developed their position papers into chapters for this book. Five additional chapters introduce the book, report on the initial workshop, and provide three additional studies. The case studies in this book cover a very wide range of organizational sizes (from 8 to 135,000) in over 15 countries, operating in consumer, Small and Medium Enterprises (SME), large Business to Business (B2B), public sector and non-profit markets across a range of around 20 application domains. Some chapters synthesise several studies that were conducted over a number of years. This introduction presents the context for the workshop, identifies common themes with regard to cultures, teams and tasks in agile UCD development, and discusses future trends and a research agenda for adapting UCD to agile development contexts.

G. Cockton (✉)
School of Design, Northumbria University, Newcastle upon Tyne NE1 8ST, UK
e-mail: gilbert.cockton@northumbria.ac.uk

M. Lárusdóttir
School of Computer Science, Reykjavik University, Reykjavik, Iceland

P. Gregory
School of Physical Sciences and Computing, University of Central Lancashire, Preston, UK

Å. Cajander
Department of Information Technology, Uppsala University, Uppsala, Sweden

© Springer International Publishing Switzerland 2016
G. Cockton et al. (eds.), *Integrating User-Centred Design in Agile Development*,
Human–Computer Interaction Series, DOI 10.1007/978-3-319-32165-3_1

Keywords User-centered design • User experience • Participatory design • Design thinking • Agile software development • Scrum • Future trends

1.1 User-Centred Software Development

Integration of User-Centred Design (UCD) within agile systems development processes (Agile) can be problematic. Although some persistent difficulties predate Agile, its evolving contexts continue to constrain possibilities for integrating UCD activities. Even so, there has been much progress over the last decade. The number of papers considered in systematic literature reviews about this topic has risen from 35 to 83 across 2010, 2011, 2014 [1] and 2015 (See Chap. 8 for references). These papers identify the conditions under which Agile and UCD can work together. Agile claims to consider the users' perspective, but this is not always the case. There are still opportunities for innovation, research and discussion.

The integration of UCD with software development processes such as 1980s structured methods was challenging, but for different reasons to those currently associated with Agile. As software engineering (SE) developed in the 1970s, it focused on software artefacts, much as older engineering practices focused on their artefacts too, such as bridges, dams, manufacturing lines and power generators. Waterfall processes dominated, which were based on a fixed sequence of development phases, from problem analysis and requirements specification, through design, implementation and verification, to software installation and operation [2].

UCD was initially developed and advocated to improve software usability. As hardware costs plummeted in the 1980s, more people had access to computer equipment, but did not have access to the extensive training previously given to specialist computer operators. After effective usability methods were developed, in the 1990s UCD's scope broadened to quality in use. Satisfaction, effectiveness and contextual fit were added to speed, and ease of use and learning as foci for UCD work. In the 2000s, UCD's quality in use foci further extended to include positive user experience (UX). With each extension of UCD's scope, the aim has been to improve quality in use, both by reducing costs and risks and also by better addressing users' experiences, needs and wants. Today, UCD's benefits can convincingly deliver on a wide range of values, including effectiveness, efficiency, satisfaction, wellbeing at work, brand loyalty, health and safety, employee retention, respect for human dignity, and competitiveness. Given this, in theory UCD should be attractive to software development.

When attempts were first made to introduce UCD into software development in the 1980s, the main challenge was gaining acceptance for UCD practices across all development phases. UCD aligned well with waterfall processes, but the strength of the case for UCD was often not enough to extend UCD activities beyond evaluation. UCD activities such as contextual research fitted into the problem analysis phase, and user testing fitted into the verification phase. However, UCD required development phases to be repeatedly iterated [2] until the software under development satisfied user needs for both functionality and usability. This required time to be set aside for regular communication and decision-making with stakeholders. Not all software methodologies were capable of being made iterative and consultative [2].

Agile developed as a reaction against the constraints of waterfall software development methodologies. Some of its key characteristics were compatible with UCD: evolving requirements iteratively across a series of iterations, incremental development to allow early delivery of working software, and introducing close collaboration with customer representatives. Other characteristics were less favourable to UCD, such as reduced opportunities for user testing and less upfront planning before software implementation. These adverse factors can almost exclude UCD from the most popular agile practices [3, 4], or have UCD responsibilities transferred to business analyst roles. However, there are several different agile methodologies [3, 4], so it is important to avoid generalizations that do not apply to all of them. Furthermore, development practices descriptions are (knowingly) unavoidably underspecified, so all methodologies must be contextualized and completed in use. Thus neither positives nor negatives that are apparent in published descriptions of a methodology will inevitably emerge in practice. Project teams have to work at achieving potential positives, and they can also work to avoid potential negatives. What actually happens during software development is more important than what a methodology advocates or what detractors say will happen. It is thus important to go beyond published accounts to understand how agile development is managed, and how this impacts the ability to integrate UCD activities. Nevertheless, published methods do set the tone and expectations for practice. The limitations that we see in published methods are often not overcome in practice.

1.1.1   Position Papers and Chapters

This book presents case studies and forward-looking analyses of the potential for improved integration of UCD activities within Agile. Most of the chapters began as position papers for a NordiCHI 2014 workshop [5]. The call for participation for this workshop invited position papers on:

- Case studies and work in progress related to UX and Agile.
- Success stories and best practices from integrating UCD and Agile.
- Challenges from working with UCD in Agile
- Integration of UCD and Agile in different domains such as games and healthcare.
- Values and perspectives underpinning UCD and Agile in theory.
- Theories and methods relevant to research on Agile and UCD.
- Discussion of future trends for UCD and Agile research.

There is an overview of the position papers in Chap. 8, which summarizes the results of the NordiCHI 2014 workshop. Two position papers presented at the workshop were not developed into chapters for this book: one by Lindell [6] and one by Law and Lárusdóttir [7]. In [6], the design process of a music creativity app was described. Workshop discussion of this paper identified issues with breaking down the 'big idea' for the app into manageable and meaningful small units for development in a single agile 'sprint' (iteration). Such issues, which compound the impact of limited upfront design of architectures, are a known problem with the most popular agile methodologies [4]. At first in [6], design and implementation work focused on technology, but this left many design questions unanswered. Lindell argued for a quality-driven open-ended artisan approach to software development, with careful attention to the experiential qualities of the design.

The position paper by Law and Lárusdóttir [7] presented and discussed an analysis of whether agile software development, exemplified by Scrum, is more compatible with UX work than lean development, exemplified by Kanban. The comparison between Scrum and Kanban, using a rather lean and agile analysis process, led the authors to make a preliminary conclusion that Kanban fits UX better, given its greater flexibility. Subsequently the authors conducted a more comprehensive study on the same subject [8], but the results of empirical studies were ambivalent. Neither Kanban nor Scrum support UX effectively.

There are summaries for each chapter in the Book Overview before this introductory chapter. Two case study chapters report on first time use of Scrum in a UCD context, and contain useful tutorial material for readers who are new to Scrum: Chap. 4 (Sect. 4.2.2) and Chap. 5 (Sect. 5.3.1). For readers new to UX, Chap. 7 (Sect. 7.2) provides similar tutorial material in relation to its study of agile teams' ability to predict users' evaluations of UX and need satisfaction.

The overall objective of the workshop was to provide a venue for researchers and practitioners, from within and outside of Human-Computer Interaction (HCI), to begin to shape the future of Agile and UCD research. The workshop had two goals:

1. Identifying future trends for research on Agile and UCD
2. Identifying challenges and success stories when working with UCD and Agile.

Most accepted position papers responded to the second goal. Six workshop position papers have been revised, extended and strengthened to provide detailed case studies for this book (Chaps. 2, 3, 4, 5, 6 and 9). For example, Chap. 3 extends its initial position paper with the outcomes of six additional iterations of UCD training materials for use in Agile contexts (doubling the underpinning evidence since the workshop). Chapter 7 is an additional study by a workshop attendee and her colleagues.

The extensive study of diverse Agile UCD practices is a distinctive strength of this book. The workshop summary (Chap. 8) benefits from this breadth, as do other forward-looking chapters (Chaps. 9, 10 and 11). Chapter 9 updates a future oriented position paper on a new framework for Agile UCD. Chapters 10 and 11 from three of the editors and their colleagues add two analyses that reflect critically on the futures of both UCD and Agile (from the positions of Management Fashion and Creative Design respectively). Chapters 9 and 10 draw extensively on several existing case studies by their authors. Chapter 11 draws on creative design research literature to challenge the position that a simple combination of UCD and Agile is sufficient for software innovation. All chapters are informed by the workshop, which at least one author of each chapter attended.

The case studies across the book's chapters span a very wide range of organizations. The smallest has eight employees, with most in the range of 100–500 or 500–2000. The largest range from 10,000–20,000 to 135,000 worldwide. The case study companies have staff in over 15 countries, operating in consumer, SME, large B2B, public sector and non-profit markets across a range of over 20 application domains, including:

> home and SME finances, home technologies and appliances (including smart homes), automotive technologies, mobile technologies (especially apps), telecommunications, energy and power systems, manufacturing systems, enterprise software (including customer process monitoring and licensing), banking, e-commerce, healthcare, music technology, nursery schools, higher education, local community systems, web portals for information aggregation, web infrastructure software for sign-on and app launching, data integration/visualization, embedded systems, cross platform systems, and software testing tools.

As noted in Chap. 8 (workshop summary), the breadth of application areas here indicates that Agile is now mainstream. Many case study applications were business critical and a few were safety critical. Some participating companies were bespoke system developers for external customers, whereas others developed in-house and consumer systems. Several involved hardware as well as software development. Around 450 respondents in total participated in the case studies reported and analysed in this book. All case studies (Chaps. 2, 3, 4, 5, 6 and 7) involve Scrum users, with Chaps. 4, 5 and 6 reporting projects using Scrum for the first time.

Chapter 8's themes, which emerged from the workshop presentations of position papers, are thus well grounded in current UCD practices within Agile. These themes are extended and deepened by the additional breadth and detail of the book chapters. However, the value of breadth here does not just lie in convergence on repeated themes, but also in the distinctive practices that were unique to projects and/or organisations. These distinctive practices resist simple generalisations and demand an open contextual approach to understanding relationships between UCD and Agile.

The breath across some aspects of the position papers did however allow some common themes to be identified at the workshop. These have been reinforced and extended by this book's chapters. They relate to both current and past agile UCD practice, and also to future possibilities for research and practice. The next section presents themes for current and past agile UCD practice. Sect. 1.3 discusses future trends.

1.2 Main Common Themes for Current and Past Agile UCD Practice from the Workshop and Chapters

The chapters in this book update and extend the position papers from our NordiCHI 2014 workshop. The chapters let us revisit, strengthen and extend observations made during the presentations of position papers. As reported in Chap. 8 (workshop summary), position papers reported on best practice, ongoing challenges, and future opportunities. These provided items for an affinity diagram that was simplified after the workshop into eight themes across two groups: "challenges and obstacles", which have been experienced and will persist into the present; and "interesting points" which can be in the past (e.g., as best practice to adopt) or future (e.g., as opportunities). Themes can thus orient towards either the past or future.

Chapter 8 reviews the identified themes in detail. In this section, we use a higher level overview based on Chap. 9 (novel framework for Agile UCD), which recommends a shift of focus from *team roles* to *tasks* when improving Agile UCD. Chapter 8's themes from the workshop are thus further consolidated into observations about *teams* and *tasks*. These are alternative but overlapping lenses on software development, one focusing on how development teams are organized and managed, and the other focusing on how development *work* is organized and managed. The two are highly interdependent and in reality they are largely inseparable. However, some issues and opportunities are best approached from a team perspective and others are best approached from a work perspective. There are some loose couplings here, in that some aspects of process structure can be common to several team structures, and vice versa.

Table 1.1 associates example workshop themes and chapter topics with *teams* and *tasks*. Three workshop themes are not included: "miscellaneous"; *Culture*

Table 1.1 Team and task topics across chapters

Chapter	Team topics	Task topics in chapter
2	Roles	Channels and tools usage
		Filtering and interpretation
3	Training	Hands-on use
4	Team	Artefacts (within tasks)
		Activities
5	Customer Committee	Inception
	Scrum Islands	Sprint n.0
		One-week sprint
		(IN)Sprint Review
		Project retrospective
6	User involvement	Document use
		Synchronisation
7	PO, UX specialists and developers	UX assessment
8	*Post workshop themes:*	Artefacts and tools
	People and Roles	Methods and practices
	Teams and Communication	Time and synchronisation
9	People	Process
		Tasks
		Tools
10	Insiders and Outsiders	Activities
11	Generosity	Talkback
		Problem-solution co-evolution

("challenges and obstacles"); and *Research and Problems* ("interesting points"). The latter two are respectively covered before and after team and task factors. This section thus gathers workshop themes under the headings of:

1. Culture
2. Teams
3. Tasks
4. Research

The fourth theme was not a major focus at the workshop, but it is addressed in detail across the chapters in this book, as summarised in Sect. 1.2.4 below.

1.2.1   Culture

In 2002, Elden Nelson interviewed Kent Beck ("the father of XP") and Alan Cooper (inventor of Goal-Directed Design and Personas) [9]. The aim was to find the common ground and the points of difference between the agile approach of XP and the UCD approach of Goal-Directed Design. Relatively little common ground emerged during the interview, with points of major differences throughout. Ambler's reading of this interview was that "our thought leaders may be a bit too extreme" [10]. It is a clear example of a common tendency to exaggerate and entrench the culture clash between Agile and UCD. This clash can make integration of Agile and UCD appear to be impossible, but it is clear from the case studies in this book that this is not so, although no-one is claiming that a perfect marriage has yet been achieved. It has proved impossible for many projects and organisations to fully integrate UCD into agile practices. Chapter 8 notes the tensions between designer and developer cultures that surfaced at the workshop. Chapter 7 (study of agile team roles predictions of users' UX evaluations) captures some of these tensions: UCD does not trust developers to understand users, but developers do not trust users to know what they want.

Underpinning values and perspectives were a focus in the workshop call, and can continue to obstruct worthwhile innovations, both at the level of specific projects and in the wider professional communities where developers and designers form their identities and allegiances. While many synergies between Agile and UCD are being successfully exploited, remaining areas of conflict need to be identified, understood and (where possible) effectively addressed. This has to be related to the wider context of digital products and services, and related to other professional cultures such as Participative Design and Design Thinking (Chap. 6).

Cultures can only manifest themselves through people's practices in specific places. Our behaviours, built environments and material artefacts manifest meanings, and thus values (Chap. 10 focuses on why Agile is valued). Manifestations of culture in turn shape people's expectations and behaviours. Organisations that wholly base development work on Agile or UCD can readily appear to have practices that could never be compatibly combined, as they take different positions on:

- what constitutes a valid problem or issue and what can be ignored
- what resources are provided and how they are allocated
- adequacy and excellence in design work

Values across the chapters that can underpin incompatible practices, create synergies, or even both, are now reviewed.

1.2.1.1 Agile and UCD Values

Book chapters present value systems that are disjoint, but not automatically incompatible. Agile values (in the sense of things that are valued) across chapters include:

- self-empowered independent autonomous teams of interacting individuals
- working software that satisfied customers accept for the value that it delivers
- customer collaboration, with acceptance of changing requirements
- flexible practices for rapid reaction to customer feedback
- velocity evidenced in early delivery of initial working versions, speed to market, and speed of communication within a project with on-time delivery
- visibility, awareness and accountability
- productivity: ability to focus without interruption
- a sense of achievement in relation to clear roles and short term goals (in contrast, developers can see usability as vague and fuzzy)
- ease of development with low waste, preference for informal lightweight methods
- being fashionable

These are values as communicated in the chapters. They are not necessarily all orthodox for all agile methodologies. For example, speed is not promoted as a value in the Agile manifesto [11]. What is valued there is as the highest priority is "early and continuous delivery of valuable software." Similarly, being fashionable is not mentioned in the manifesto either. In contrast, UCD values expressed across the chapters include:

- iterative processes and tools that support planning of comprehensive user-focused research and objective empirical evaluation, maintaining a user focus at all times
- human science values evidenced through well documented evidence and data analysis in user research and usage evaluation, removing 'games of chance' from design
- understanding the user before meaningful software development begins
- a coherent holistic picture of what will be developed
- superior expert knowledge of human-computer interaction (HCI)
- attention to detail: few usability problems should be left behind!
- satisfied users, due to hedonic and instrumental quality in use (UX values)

The above two lists of worthwhile practices and attributes from this book's chapters go well beyond the Agile Manifesto's [11] compact four pairs of more and less favoured phenomena of:

1. Individuals and interactions over processes and tools
2. Working software over comprehensive documentation
3. Customer collaboration over contract negotiation
4. Responding to change over following a plan

Two things are important to note here. Firstly, the manifesto begins: "we are uncovering better ways of developing software by doing it and helping others to do it". The manifesto is a contribution to a process, not a last word. However, this is not how it is always read, especially after 15 years. Secondly, there are no inherent value clashes here, since the manifesto states that "while there is value in the items on the right, we value the items on the left more" [11]. The manifesto itself thus does not outlaw the processes, tools, documentation, contracts or plans "on the right". Rather, it does not want them to get in the way of the things "on the left": individuals' interactions, working software, customer collaboration or responding to change. Tensions between Agile and UCD are due to the *extent* to which interpreters of the manifesto value items on the left more than the items on the right. The manifesto takes no position on what this extent should be, and therefore tensions between Agile and UCD are at best only partially due to the manifesto, but are mostly a question of interpretation and degree.

Agile's potential for sidelining UCD practices is thus not due to the manifesto as written, but instead to further turning the left hand side of the four clauses into crude rules and then banning the values on the right, e.g.:

1. Just have individuals and interactions: you do not need processes and tools.
2. Just make working software and no documentation.
3. Just collaborate with your customer: you do not need to negotiate a contract.
4. Just keep responding to change: you do not need to follow a plan

Some interpretations may thus devalue UCD to the point of its suppression, but this does not apply to all twelve agile principles that complement the manifesto [11]:

1. Our highest priority is to satisfy the customer through early and continuous delivery of valuable software.
2. Welcome changing requirements, even late in development. Agile processes harness change for the customer's competitive advantage.
3. Deliver working software frequently, from a couple of weeks to a couple of months, with a preference to the shorter timescale.
4. Business people and developers must work together daily throughout the project.
5. Build projects around motivated individuals. Give them the environment and support they need, and trust them to get the job done.
6. The most efficient and effective method of conveying information to and within a development team is face-to-face conversation.

7. Working software is the primary measure of progress.
8. Agile processes promote sustainable development. The sponsors, developers, and users should be able to maintain a constant pace indefinitely.
9. Continuous attention to technical excellence and good design enhances agility.
10. Simplicity–the art of maximizing the amount of work not done–is essential.
11. The best architectures, requirements, and designs emerge from self-organizing teams.
12. At regular intervals, the team reflects on how to become more effective, then tunes and adjusts its behavior accordingly.

Over half of the principles above should not block good support for UCD (i.e., Principles 2, 4, 5, 8, 9, 11 and 12). Conflicts however could arise from Principles 1, 3, 6, 7 and 10. Principles 1, 3 and 10 could all curtail UCD work, and perhaps eliminate it ('Early', 'shorter', 'work not done'). Principle 6 devalues documentation, which UCD uses to evidence its scientific values ("what do you mean by documentation?", Chap. 6). Principle 7 potentially conflicts with Principle 1: 'working' could just mean 'running' and not 'valuable' 'for the customer's competitive advantage'. Chapter 5 notes Agile's focus on functional requirements in relation to this.

A further problem arises if the only values considered in software development are only ones *interpreted* to come from the Agile Manifesto or its principles. Core UCD values and principles appear in neither. Agile values take precedence, whether these are orthodox or imagined, and thus Chap. 4 (proactive use of Scrum in a research and development setting) reports that the easiest and fastest to implement features would get implemented first and then demonstrated without prior user testing. Chapter 6 (imposition of Scrum on a university Participative Design project) reports a project team's dissatisfaction with the impact of Agile on its user community, who were effectively replaced as the customer by the project funder. Even so, integrating UCD with Agile is most challenging when UCD cannot adjust to Agile values. For example, Chap. 4 reports difficulties of estimating the time required for UCD work. Chapter 6 reports that developers could prototype faster than UX specialists, who were slowed down by the volume of community feedback. In fights between 'faster' and 'better', 'faster' won. The highest priority of Agile is "to satisfy the customer through early and continuous delivery of valuable software", and therefore 'better' should win. Unfortunately, Agile in practice can value speed more than value!

Comprehensive, effective and reliable integration will require relaxation of some of both UCD and Agile values some of the time. Agile holds up a valuable mirror to UCD, which must deal with valid issues that predate Agile (Chaps. 2, 4, 5, 6 and 7): UCD methods can lack transparency, be very time consuming, and result in inconsistent outcomes. For example, users can ask for different things (Chap. 8), which may be incompatible or irrelevant (Chap. 2), and UX specialists can be wrong (Chap. 7). One strength of this book's chapters is that authors recognize the need to rethink some key UCD practices and are willing to adapt them to make their use possible in Agile settings. For example, in Chap. 3 (UX training courses and materials for developers) data analysis requirements for Contextual Inquiry are relaxed, and iterative development of training and developer support materials, resulted in time spent on A/B testing being halved.

Agile can make UCD better, and vice versa. Kuusinen's novel BoB framework for Agile UCD (Chap. 9) relaxes both UCD and Agile values, as is clear in the guidelines for using BoB (Table 9.3): designs need to be good and complete enough to be tested; early user feedback is better than late perfection; user interfaces will need to be refactored; and user expectations will need to be managed. Kuusinen's novel BoB framework also shows how UCD can make Agile better: 'working software' can be a clickable prototype, a working user interface with no functional back-end, a full working prototype, or a fielded version in use. UCD can thus hold up a valuable mirror to Agile, and a spirit of compromise can make both faster and better able to react effectively and wisely to change, build common understandings, and increase communication. Similarly, Chap. 2 balances positive attitudes towards UCD with the recognition that, even in companies with strong user-centred cultures, UCD needs to change. UCD is not seen as curretly mature, because optimal combination of methods is still not well understood. UCD is seen as addressing real users' needs and wants, but not necessarily with clarity on how users should actually be involved and how that fits into established development processes. UCD is positioned as an evolving normative ideological practice, with a primary focus on users, which is similar to Agile's focus on customers. Chapter 2's authors view process as a secondary concern in Agile and UCD, and Agile is seen to better promote a culture of self-evaluation. However, UCD is not the sole source of user-focused practices: good contributions can be made using management research on innovation, as well as established brand evaluation practices such as Net Promoter scores. There are thus important values and associated practices beyond UCD and Agile.

1.2.1.2 Values Other than Agile and UCD

There is more to software development than UCD and software implementation. Values from Agile and UCD are not the only ones encountered in this book. Chapter 6 (imposition of Scrum on Participative Design project) rightly argues that some tensions between Agile and UCD have to be resolved at organizational level, where decisions have to be made between conflicting values. There are also values of importance to specific application domains and markets that are supportive of Agile UCD integration. For example, organizations in Chap. 3 (UX training for agile developers) value:

- innovation from simple systematic consumer insights
- safety
- security

Chapters 2, 4, 5 and 7 contain further examples of companies' values including:

- experimentation (one SME had experience of both waterfall and PD practices)
- inclusive workplaces
- strongly phased hardware engineering practices, with early development of wireframes and systematic testing
- close collaboration with customers and suppliers, supported by transparent continuous communication
- high quality UX
- well-timed testing of feature groups (and not just what the last sprint delivered)
- democratic design driven by user-focus
- coherent synergetic product and service portfolios
- competitive advantage
- market intelligence, including price guidance

Interestingly, the Chap. 3 values of safety and security, as well as performance and accessibility, can get foregrounded to gain approval for what are really UX fixes (Chap. 10). Such 'passing off' is less common in organisations that develop safety critical and consumer products, with their associated 'testing' and 'insight' cultures. Every case study introduces domain values that favour some forms of integration over others for UCD and Agile. Mass market companies in Chaps. 2 (SME use of Agile) and 3 (UX training for developers) need high levels of confidence in UX before they release new products to market (one has a usability laboratory). Healthcare equipment in Chap. 3 is subject to usability and other requirements from the U.S. Food and Drug Administration (hence use of A/B testing). Projects in Chaps. 2 and 6 benefitted from Living Labs. Hardware produced in Chaps. 2, 3 and 7 organisations cannot be iterated or incremented as easily as pure software products or services. Research and Development (R&D) contexts in Chaps. 4 (proactive UX R&D use of Scrum) and 6 (imposed use of Scrum) allow more flexible self organisation than many other settings. In Chap. 4, only an R&D prototype was needed as a deliverable. Chapter 6's educational setting enabled open source practices, bonds of community, interns, student evaluations and other important participative practices. However, the funder's values introduced hierarchy and formality that limited the extent and form of participation. The project management team retained overall control and steered the direction of the project, appointing "champions" for each of the eight apps developed. In Chap. 7, agile teams had value expectations for enterprise software users that turned out to be incorrect: users' values were not predominantly instrumental. In short, each development context brought values that shaped both Agile and UCD practices.

The Smart Campus research project (Chap. 8) aimed to develop mobile apps to support a student community. A pervasive PD approach was expected, supported by multiple feedback channels. Before Scrum was introduced, activities completed had included community engagement and workshops, focus groups, diary studies, online ethnography, benchmarking university mobile apps, conceptual design, service infrastructure, research on online student communities, personas, scenarios, storyboards and sketches; in short, extensive upfront work preceded application development. However, the unanticipated introduction of Scrum obstructed further PD practices. To understand the difficulties encountered, and how to overcome them, two interview studies were planned and carried out by a researcher external to the project. A literature review in conjunction with the interview studies revealed how Agile can obstruct UCD work practices; the authors benefitted from two 2014 literature surveys that covered 76 [12] and 71 [1] papers, which highlight the topicality of the chapters in this book.

These difficulties, which may obstruct integration of UCD and Agile when the 'user' is actually a community and is therefore not uniquely defined, contributed to the project not being fully appreciated by university management, even though the eight mobile apps were used and positively evaluated by the users: in fact, two of these apps had been developed by the student community, and there were 2000+ posts in the online project forum.

The case study chapters are particularly valuable in providing examples of organizational culture and values in context. In addition to the two sets of Agile and UCD values, a third set of organisational values must underpin Agile and UCD values to let them be acted on. Chapter 2's SMEs' practices do more than simply combine Agile and UCD: much broader ranges of values are involved, including those underlying business inputs to product and service development such as innovation and marketing [13, 14]. Chap. 2 also describes how user support and marketing contribute evaluation data and ideas for improvement. Similarly, success for Chap. 3's companies also involves more than Agile and UCD values, which may have to be relaxed to enable success. Chapter 2 thus suggests that UCD may have to relax on its scientific values in fast-paced market-driven environments.

Equally, organizational values may impede Agile. To adopt Agile, an organization has to value: trusting employees; self-organisation; continuous reflection and learning and being able to adapt when necessary. Many organisations have hierarchical cultures that are driven by top-down management. These cultures find it hard to adopt Agile until they embrace agile culture beyond their IT function.

Chapters 4 and 5 (first uses of Scrum in UCD contexts) demonstrate how well-motivated teams can resolve some tensions between Agile and UCD bottom up. As well as Agile, UCD and organizational values, there are values of importance to development team members, who are the source of a fourth relevant set of values. Chapters 5 and 6 recognise the contributions of established SE work and associated values [15–18]. Some of these values may be shared with employers, but others are professional values specific to roles, or reflect personal goals related to current achievements and aspirations. Examples include:

- meeting deadlines
- technical achievement
- internal software qualities such as maintainability, reliability, portability, efficiency and security
- professional distinctiveness
- creative exploration through trial and error: knowingly playing a 'game of chance'

- aesthetics, both visual and technical (e.g., beautiful code [6]).
- confident and personally secure integration of UX tasks within development
- highly directive prescriptive methods
- open flexible methods that maximize use of personal expertise

Chapter 7 correlated development teams' overall assessment of UX with their ratings on particular UX dimensions for software that they had developed in Agile UCD contexts. Significant correlations between their overall rating of UX and their specific ratings for 'good', 'desirable', 'innovative' and 'recommendable' indicated that development teams saw these attributes as major determinants of UX quality. These attributes correspond to market oriented values that align developers with their companies, valuing brand equity and competitive advantage. They are not primarily UCD values.

An important developer value is seen in personal responsibility for the consequences of design decisions. Chapters 3, 4, 5 and 6 all refer to Product Owners or project managers either generously adding to user sourced requirements (as advocated in Chap. 11), or more often overriding these. Not everything that customers or users want is desirable or possible. As feedback channels mushroom, it is simply not possible to take every customer or user suggestion on board, especially when many conflict.

Designers are a fifth source of values for development projects. Their designerly values are the sole focus of Chap. 11. Chapter 6 also advocates Design Thinking [19, 20] and thus designers' professional values (e.g. keeping up to date with Android look and feel guidance). Interestingly Chap. 6 is the only one to celebrate success, despite the funder having issues with the project: its Smart Campus apps were popular with users. In contrast, Chap. 7 displays UCD's ancestral distrust of designers [21], and disapproves of "designers' creativity and originality and ... ability to break design conventions" [22]. Breaches of "design conventions" are seen as bad design decisions, when often conventions do need to be broken, as evidenced in recent debates on 'hamburger menus' for apps [23]. Similarly, Chap. 9 argues that "good UX should not be a game of chance, but it requires deliberate work," reflecting UCD's initial engineering values.

Agile comes close to creative practices, and thus has less overt distrust of creative designers than UCD. Chapter 11 presents a broad overview of creative design and notes how Agile has embraced some creative practices, but remains constrained by some engineering ideals. For example, although requirements can change, Scrum requires them to be clear at the start of a sprint [24]. Even so, Agile has softened up UCD to accept the creative design characteristic of problem-solution space co-evolution when integration with Agile is achieved. Chapter 9 thus accepts that we cannot know in advance what a system under development should be like and how it should be implemented [25], motivating a fundamental Agile principle of welcoming late change [11, 26].

Designers' creative inspiration is never completely down to Chap. 9's "game of chance", but creative designers expose themselves to influences in ways that cannot be completely deliberate. Often these influences, inspirations and opportunities arise from their own work, which unexpectedly 'talks back' to them (Chap. 11). It is important here to distinguish designers' craft mastery from their creative inventiveness. The former is the material expression of ideas from the latter. Craft mastery can be exercised at will as required, but ideas that are repressed or suppressed may be lost forever. Historically, UCD has posed more of a threat to creative designers' values than Agile has, although both embrace idealized engineering design values that can repress or suppress creative practices. However, Kuusinen's 'design debt' in Chap. 9 reasonably expects designers to relax the production values associated with their craft mastery to allow rapid deployment and testing.

Chapters 4, 6 and 8 accept the uncertainties and generous opportunities of creative design. Chapter 6 refers to [27], which describes a 1-day design studio that was used to bridge between UCD and Agile. This was a sensible compromise a decade ago, but has now been superseded by Google's week long *Design Sprints* [28], which can provide a firm foundation for Agile UCD at the point of project inception or within upfront activities. As with all similar innovation approaches (including Design Thinking [19, 20]), Design Sprints combine design, UCD, technology and business perspectives in a single process where, with skill and will, these can be balanced against each other. A similar mix of technical, art and design perspectives was advocated in a position paper [6].

Customers are a sixth source of project values. Customers' values in Chaps. 2, 3 and 5 drive the integration of UCD and Agile. In Chap. 5, an Agile UCD methodology was co-designed between a software developer and a university. Otherwise, customers are given limited detailed attention in the case studies, as are users' values. Chapter 8 reports concerns that were raised at the workshop about UCD values being overlooked in the commissioning process.

Users are a seventh source of project values. If UCD goes to plan, users' needs and wants should always be understood and responded to. However, Agile contexts are forcing UCD to reconsider the ideal that if users have a need, then software must meet it. A focus on the user at all times must relax to consider other equally important considerations from business and engineering. Also, the ability of UX specialists to know users' priorities, even when they have worked with them on a project, is called into question in Chap. 7, where users were asked to rate overall and specific UX dimensions for products developed by Agile teams. Associated project teams were also asked to rate their product for overall and specific UX, but from both their own and from their users' perspective. Overall ranking of UX dimensions was not possible (i.e., how users and teams valued some dimensions more than others), since the products differed. However, comparisons between each specific UX dimension and each product's overall UX rating did reveal significant correlations, but these differed for each comparison (users, teams' own, teams' predicted). These differences indicate that that users' value systems are not what Agile teams think they are. For enterprise software, instrumental dimensions should logically better predict overall UX, but this was not so. Analysis by role indicated that no team roles were particularly accurate, although POs and UX Specialists (UXS) could better predict user ratings than developers. Commitment to UCD values does thus not translate automatically into accurate user empathy.

At the workshop, a danger was noted that HCI knowledge can be seen as 'common sense' that everyone knows. HCI expertise needs to be appropriately valued, otherwise customer or user preferences could take precedence over specialist HCI knowledge that indicates better design options. Users and customers should not always be given what they want. Thus in Chap. 3, requests for fully completed example templates were not acted on. It is important to bridge across (and adjudicate between) the cultural values that rendezvous in digital product and service development.

Agile and UCD values are thus not the only ones in play when integrating their practices and associated cultures. Instead, integration always occurs in contexts where five further sources of values are in place, i.e., organizational values, which mediate across four specific role values for developers, creative designers, customers and users. Cultures manifest lived values through material and social practices (e.g., documentation and meetings respectively). However, in Chap. 2, the individual organizational cultures are not homogeneous. Different roles within organisations bring different values with them, and in the largest SME "heated conversations can happen". If these are well managed, design quality will benefit.

While values may appear to be logically incompatible, cultures only actually clash through incompatible material and social practices. Thus claims made for irreconcilable differences between Agile and UCD cultures have to be evidenced by practices and not values. Such practices are shaped by methodologies and their associated team and task structures.

1.2.1.3 Cultures and Methodologies

Workplaces and projects are focal points for the convergence of scores of values from at least seven distinct sources. Only two are methodologies, which Chap. 2 states are normative and ideological, i.e., they are primarily prescriptions supported by descriptions of required practices. Methodologies signal what matters to practitioners, either directly through manifestos or indirectly via their practices. Ideologies thus become inscribed in people, places and things, e.g., respectively through Scrum's roles, stand up meetings or Scrum Boards. Work practices, environments and artefacts need to be compatible with a methodology's values, but methodologies in turn must be compatible with organizational and project roles' values.

Cultures are complex. Simplistic shoot outs between Agile and UCD ignore other sources of values, to which methodological ideologies are subordinate. Important enablers and obstacles lie outside of Agile and UCD, within the organisations that work on integrating Agile and UCD. Many current organizational enablers increasingly favour Agile, hence its fashionability (Chap. 10). The maturity of much IT has changed its role from a 'service' function to being the 'driving' function of business. New business ideas often only come into being when they are realized through IT. Business and IT are thus merging, giving rise to challenges for organisations that vary in magnitude. For some organisations, the challenges are substantial, and major difficulties with managing these challenges impede successful adoption and integration of Agile and UCD. At the same time Agile has been widely embraced because it addresses these challenge for business. In many ways Agile isn't just a methodology. Instead, many of its concepts are enablers for organisational transformation through new ways of configuring 'work' in modern businesses. Agile can be applied in many different settings. This book's case studies span organisations at different stages of maturity in terms of their readiness to exploit Agile UCD.

Agile methodologies have undoubtedly become very dominant recently. As IT has transformed from a 'service' function to the 'driving' function of business, IT development has grown from 'one off projects' to continuously developed 'online products'. Agile approaches and concepts have helped IT departments to change their approach in order to deliver what businesses need. However, as Agile is adopted, it is not just specific practices that need to change, but the wider cultures within which practices occur. Such changes can be difficult, especially in large organisations.

The case study chapters provide a broad understanding of culture, with balanced accounts of how organizational and professional cultures combine to support integration of Agile and UCD. While not perfect, and thus potentially disappointing to UCD and PD (Participative Design) ambitions, the quality of integration is at least reasonable, and organisations are finding ways to make further progress, in contrast to the workshop's "challenges and obstacles" focus on culture.

Cultures are not deterministic, nor do value preferences bestow competences. For example, a Chap. 2 SME valued home-based testing, but had no role in place with responsibilities for engagement and liaison with test households. Nor had this SME worked out how much contact developers should have with users. Values can only be lived through material and social practices. Until these are in place, values will remain frustrating aspirations.

The case studies are particularly valuable in demonstrating that a methodology's values cannot completely constrain software development. While values may be clearly advocated in manifestos and seminal publications, their impact plays out in complex dynamic contexts that can balance one set of values against another, and Agile values do not always win (either orthodox or imagined). Scrum is by far the most popular agile methodology currently [29]. However, all of the 'Scrumish' practices in this book's case studies breach key Scrum rules. There is extensive up front activity, breaches of the closed window rule [4], tasks running across sprints, involvement in sprint planning beyond the core development team (PO, Scrum Master, developers), many roles that do not exist in Scrum, stand up meetings involving roles outside of the core development team, and missing sprint reviews and retrospectives. For example, despite Scrum's preference for face to face meetings, extensive electronic documentation and project records are common (Chaps. 2, 4, 5 and 6). Electronic documentation in a software tool can be rapidly accessed and updated, reducing some drawbacks of documentation assumed by the Agile manifesto.

Much of the dogma associated with Scrum has been neutralized in this book's case studies. This corroborates Meyer's view that development teams have to interpret and adapt Agile, and that they sensibly do so in ways that avoids dogmatic damage [4]. For example, until fairly recently, Scrum distinguished the 'committed pigs' in the core development team from 'involved chickens' of customers, users and other outsiders, but this has now been relaxed [30]. In Chaps. 2, 4, 5, 6 and 9, decision making is shared by the core team (PO, Scrum Master, team members) of developers with other roles, avoiding the restrictions of Scrum dogma.

The ability to adapt agile methodology can be attributed to pervasive values of agile culture such as self-organisation, continuous reflection and learning, and methodology adaptation. All the case studies contain examples of how agile teams have adapted their approach to achieve their aims, exemplifying the strengths of agile culture that may indicate why Agile has become so popular and fashionable.

The following positions on culture and Agile UCD thus emerge from the workshop and the chapters:

- UCD and Agile's values are largely disjoint but not inherently incompatible. Dogmatic rules from either side are more likely to be a source of tensions. Truly flexible and collaborative responses however can minimize tensions.
- Systems development takes place in a large soup of values. Agile and UCD only contribute some of the values in play. Most come from other organizational and professional sources (e.g., marketing, creative designers, customer support, security and safety experts). These may be disjoint sources of either conflict or synergies. In principle, UCD should consider user values, and Agile should consider customer values. Even so, specific values from each cannot guide UCD or Agile work until they are understood and acted on (as above, value preferences do not bestow competences). User and customer values are best understood by giving them their own place in the 'soup of values', not by being represented indirectly by UCD or Agile.
- Conflicts and synergies are manifested in teams and tasks in work contexts, where the ideologies of methodologies meet the realities of software development work.

Methods require knowledge, orientations and expertise for effective application. Development teams must collectively have appropriate values, knowledge and expertise. In practice, methodologies shape development work indirectly via:

- Divisions of labour as required roles and their associated responsibilities within development *teams*
- Development *tasks*, via prescribed and proscribed practices.

These two further themes, teams and tasks, are next discussed. What makes teams and tasks 'good' relates to values associated with Agile UCD in specific contexts. Teams on tasks deliver on values, hence the workshop focus on fitting together the big picture of agile theory and methods with lower levels detail of day-to-day practices.

1.2.2   Software Development Teams

Team work requires a division of labour and some form of leadership. Both are usually supported by named roles with specified responsibilities. Role names may not fully reflect or even match responsibilities. Responsibilities may arise that existing team members are poorly equipped to deal with. This may be due to disciplinary or professional background, or to relative inexperience. To thrive, all organisations must learn, and thus teams have dynamic aspects that must be considered alongside static organistional structures. Key themes in the workshop and chapters related to teams that will now be discussed are:

- Roles and responsibilities
- Team boundaries and communication practices
- Cross functional capabilities of teams and individuals

1.2.2.1   Roles and Responsibilities

The third largest group of post-its at the workshop was "Roles and people" (Chap. 8). A people focus was seen as key to addressing integration challenges for Agile UCD. The most popular agile method [29], Scrum, allows only three roles: Product Owner (PO), Scrum Master and multiple team members [4]. There must be no differentiation of rank or expertise within team members. They should all be capable of carrying out all development tasks. Such simple teams never appear in any chapter. For example, Chap. 2 has multiple roles across its three studies:

> Sole/multiple differentiated POs, social media manager, support team, developer, customer lab, independent tester, functional tester, design and verification and testing, quality management, user contact, feedback categorizer, feedback manager, user, market analyst, coordinator & project manager, creative director, senior art director, customer.

Chapter 2 thus reveals the diversity of successful Agile UCD practices, with each SME exploiting a range of roles and practices, especially in relation to customer and user feedback. One SME had a dedicated social media management group, evidencing their strong commitment to user and customer feedback. Although all used 'Scrum like' methodologies, these were significantly extended and complemented with additional roles and externally facing activities. One organization collaborated with third party suppliers, extending product development teams beyond, for example, Scrum's preferred roles of developers, Scrum Master and Product Owner (PO). All three SMEs had mass market orientations that create strong user-focused cultures.

The 'Scrumish' nature of most agile development (Chap. 10, i.e., not fully compliant orthodox Scrum) is clearly indicated by an order of magnitude difference in role count across case studies. Chaps. 3, 4, 5, 6, 7, 8, 9 and 10 add to Chap. 2 roles, e.g.:

> mechanical engineer, proxy product owner, senior researcher, graphic designer, customer committee member, student, intern, architect, user experience specialist (UXS).

The existence of further roles such as junior researcher and hardware engineer can be inferred. Interestingly, while Scrum has only three roles, the DSDM agile methodology, has a dozen [31]. However, only four appear above (some in specialized forms).

In several case studies, the PO role was filled by either an existing role (e.g., UXS, project manager), a pair of roles, or a group (Chap. 5's customer committee comprises a PO, a development team member and two customer representatives, ideally one user and one business representative). Role complexity partially reflects the size and maturity of the organization, but as roles increase, teams become more clearly cross-functional. As team size increases, the need to split into subteams with leaders increases. Role complexity also reflects skill specialization.

Agile methodologies rarely distinguish users from customers, but every case study does. Chapter 6's Participative Design (PD) context required the student community to be the customer, but the university as project funder effectively took this role. Customer-user distinctions vary between software vendors (who develop then sell) and software development services (who are paid to develop). For the latter, customers may limit or prevent access to *their* users. Also, stakeholder roles beyond users and customers come into consideration for specific projects (Chap. 4 thus writes not of UCD but HCD – Human-Centred Design).

Clear effective positions, policies and practices are needed with regard to roles, responsibilities and relationships of customers and users in Agile UCD. The issues associated with roles are largely to do with their adequacy, which in turn depends on the responsibilities for each role, and how they can communicate with each other. In the case studies, if a role was needed, it had usually been created.

UCD values are relevant to UXS, PO, Scrum Master, developer, customer and user roles, but other sets of values take precedence for other roles. The range of roles associated with software development reflects the spread of values within the organization. The appropriate division of labour across roles is contextual. There can be no universal optimum, nor will Agile or UCD values always dominate. Chapter 2 thus argues against fixed roles. Instead, a full set of roles needs to be considered holistically on case by case basis for each organization and/or project. Holistic considerations of the division of labour are also important to ensure that someone is responsible for UX overall (Chap. 10). This is clearly important in relation to UCD values.

The existence and names of roles impacts less on development work than do actual responsibilities and the ability to discharge them, and power and a lack of responsibility. Responsibilities can be sources of tensions and controversy. Professionals may not have only one role on only one project, but several across several projects. This is especially so for UXSs in a central team, as opposed to a dedicated UXS per project. Similarly, Chap. 4 argues that Scrum cannot work well with part-time staff who are not fully allocated to a single project. Scrum Masters found it difficult to ensure that projects were appropriately resourced as staff were (partially) reallocated to other projects. Part-time team members are not always on site and available for stand up and other meetings. Chapter 6 also noted a similar problem: differences in shift work meant that some interns and students could not attend regular face to face meetings.

In Chaps. 5 and 9, people are allocated to both tasks and roles. Tasks may be shared, especially by a pair of a developer and a UXS. Figure 9.4 in Chap. 9 proposes sharing of responsibilities across four roles, with all roles being responsible for product vision and understanding the user. This requires developers to be involved in UCD/UX tasks, and preferably to have some contact and interaction with users. Chapter 9's BoB Framework supports its flexible division of labour with guidelines for people (e.g., co-operate, respect others) and tasks (e.g., task allocation should respect professional expertise). There is clear recognition here of the diversity of values in play for software development, and the need to support the right values at the right times.

Some degree of collective responsibility is preferable. The resulting management challenges should be worth it. In Chaps. 4 and 5, teams decided to proactively apply Agile and took a bottom-up collaborative approach to Agile UCD. Within their emergent processes, role specific responsibilities were added to those for pairs and teams. For example, POs added to requirements when they saw gaps in elicited user and customer needs and preferences. In Chaps. 2 and 6 (as part of the customer committee), POs had to exercise judgement, and took responsibility for avoiding neglect and resolving conflict in the face of incomplete and conflicting user requirements. Avoiding neglect is an example of the creative design principle of *generosity* (Chap. 11), with customers and users receiving more than they envisage. Rigid UCD that restricts software capabilities and qualities to what customers and users ask for can obstruct high quality design work.

POs thus shared responsibilities with customers (as Agile requires) and users. This is an example of a more common phenomenon, where the scope of the PO's role expands and contracts on a case by case basis as a result of internal and external consultation. Cumulatively, this can make it almost impossible for POs to live up to their responsibilities, especially within the constraints of Scrum. Chapter 2 presents examples of breaking these constraints, with positive outcomes, through multiple POs and through customer involvements in thematic focus groups, where they fed back on quality in use and internal software quality. Similarly, Chap. 5 describes the responsibilities of a customer committee that includes the PO.

In Scrum, the PO should represent the customer. However, customers work directly as project team members in some case studies: customers as funders were directly involved in top down decision making in Chaps. 2 and 6, which constrained the autonomy of the PO and the development team. In Chap. 2, customers organized beta testing and also carried out user testing independently of the development team (Chap. 10 also refers to user testing by customers). The design, verification and testing role for a SME in Chap. 2 organized the user panel and user testing, and also filtered problem reports in the Bugzilla tool.

Developers' responsibilities were in focus at the workshop. Agile empowers developers. UCD's longstanding distrust of designers and developers [21, 32] was sometimes in evidence at the workshop. For example, bias was a concern when developers are responsible for evaluating the quality of their UX work. At the same time, measures to improve developers' UX capabilities attracted much interest, with 20 post-its for the 'developers doing UCD' affinity group being the largest group within 'interesting points'. In Chap. 3, 'developers doing UCD' is supported by a training role, with responsibility for deep learning, maintaining the requirement for learning by doing, and rejecting requests for detailed examples that could undermine this.

Developers need training and support to take on UCD work. Chapter 6's PD context created a high volume of user feedback. Project management initially reviewed and prioritized user feedback, but left it to the development team after the move to Agile. Developers would proactively review postings on the project forum, and later the Github tool, when they needed to, but did not feel responsible for letting users know whether and how their feedback was being acted on. Developers did not have time for this. However, users wanted more transparency through feedback about their suggestions. PD advocates felt unease about not taking needs from the student community fully into account.

Training can also determine how roles are allocated. The Scrum Master role in Chap. 6 was filled by the project's Chief Technology Officer (CTO), who read up on Scrum and introduced it to the development team through a sample Scrum planning meeting.

Managing user feedback is a common issue across this book's chapters. Chapter 2 presented the very wide range of channels that are now possible for user feedback, and the challenges in creating and allocating associated roles. For example, there were uncertainties over the need for, and nature of, a new household testing role in Chap. 2. Chapter 6 draws on the PD literature to contrast informative, consultative and participative forms of user involvement. The PD focus in Chap. 6 led to conflict here, with researchers and educators wanting their technically skilled computing students to be participants, but developers and management wanting them to be mostly informative. Student users themselves were mostly informative, with only 27 % of forum comments suggesting improvements rather than simply reporting problems (67 %). Students thus mostly became app testers, rather than sources of requirements for apps.

A lack of responsibility or power is the main challenge for UCD roles, especially when other roles cannot or do not pick up uncovered UX responsibilities. Gaps here are often reflected in team boundaries and communication practices.

1.2.2.2 Team Boundaries and Communication Practices

Team work requires co-ordination and collaboration, and both require communication. The second largest post-it group at the workshop was "Teams and Co-ordination", indicating its importance. Communication is an important focus in Chaps. 2 and 6.

Roles who can fully meet their responsibilities on their own are not part of a team. Teams who can fully meet their responsibilities on their own are working for themselves. Communication, collaboration and co-ordination are thus required for effective software work, since team work requires collaboration and co-ordination and customers require communication. Developing software for customers requires interactions with stakeholders who may not be part of the project team, which may correspond to the development team, or extend beyond them. Some roles can feel excluded, especially UXS roles who cannot participate in routine development team meetings such as daily standups (Chap. 10). At the workshop, it was remarked that UXS roles can be seen solely as a service team for research (before development starts) and analysis or evaluation (after an iteration). This may not involve UXSs enough, as it excludes them from interaction design and may also limit their access to the PO (as noted at the workshop, Chap. 8). Furthermore, it restricts UXS support for problem-solution co-evolution, a key characteristic of creative design (Chap. 11), since UX expertise is excluded from framing problems and solutions within sprint planning, progression and retrospectives. Pair designing can avoid this, with a UXS working closely with a developer during a sprint (recommended in Chap. 9, and practiced effectively in Chaps. 6 and 10 projects).

Teams may nest like Russian dolls, i.e., an agile development team within a project team within a virtual organization of stakeholders. Team membership can vary. For example, in Chap. 2, a social media manager and UXSs from a 'customer lab.' would be invited as needed to sprint meetings (adding to the responsibilities of the PO or Scrum Master). Also in Chap. 2, one PO decides on a case by case basis how to involve external partners who are part of an extended development team. The resulting virtual organization requires upfront design and subsequent co-ordination.

Chapter 9 argues that the whole team should be involved in user communications, which requires feedback channels to be in place. While this could mean a broad project team or a development team within it, the intention is that developers are involved. Chapter 10 observes that developers can be 'protected' from customers, which becomes difficult when developers access communication tools that let customers and users contribute comments. In Chap. 6, some developers chose to ignore some "kinds of users" based on their online behaviors. Even so, the online forum for Smart Campus did host some good discussions and created a mature sense of ownership. Some workshop participants felt that disagreements that are managed openly and inclusively can result in better design decisions and more effective team working (Chaps. 2 and 8). An alternative approach, also in Chap. 2, frames open fora as 'users helping users', lowering expectations for the SME to make active contributions (while still being able to monitor comments). However, this is specific to a single user feedback channel, and would not generalize to all project communication.

The extent and nature of developer contact with customers remained unresolved in one of the Chap. 2 case studies, where hearing opinions and problems was thought to be useful for forming understandings of users, but has "to be channelled in some way", which is likely to require some form of tool.

Agile's preference for face to face communication is not met in most of the case studies. While the Scrum Islands in Chap. 5 are so continuously face to face that they remove the need for daily stand ups and sprint reviews, multiple asynchronous online communication channels were nevertheless in use for this case study. For example, the PO used the Redmine tool to formalise backlogs, classify issues and assign them to development team members. In Chap. 6, remote workers made use of dropbox for sharing documents, and Google Hangouts for design discussions. Chap. 2 (Table 2.3) lists dozens of communication channels and associated media (e.g., face to face, documents, online). The quality of communication channels, and of access to them, can either enable or obstruct roles in meeting their responsibilities. In Chap. 6, only the Scrum Master, who was the Chief Technology Officer (CTO), could write into the developer wiki, thereby creating a hierarchy that goes against Scrum principles. Also, it was noted in the workshop (Chap. 8) that customers may not be used to online communication but send feedback through 'snail mail'.

Although Chap. 4 concludes that Agile requires full time team members, they developed an innovative two sided Scrum Board, with inventive use of coloured post-its of different sizes, to involve and acknowledge part-time team members. A planning whiteboard and display space on two walls further communicated the big picture, supporting synchronisation and making visible the work of non-Scrum roles such as UXS and Architect. However, such uses of physical space require routine co-location (as do Chap. 5's Scrum Islands and Chap. 9's BoB framework).

Chapter 3 advocates training developers to give them a common language as a foundation for aligning design and development within sprints, but adequate tool support is needed to support communication across all stakeholders. Chapter 6 reports problems with communication within a PD project, where the lack of notifications in its online forum reduced developer feedback to users. Along with users' initial inability to track problem tickets, this lowered expectations that did not improve once the use of GitHub did make problem tickets visible. Also, developers could not easily search GitHub.

Online tools for communication with users and customers are becoming vital to effective development of digital products and services. A quality infrastructure needs to be in place before any development sprint releases a version to customers. This is not an area where difficulties can simply be refactored out in a later sprint. Once created, low expectations are hard to undo. Poor PD infrastructure in Chap. 6 also made the volume of content from the multiple feedback channels difficult to manage, slowing down design work and making it very difficult for designers to work one sprint ahead of developers. Formal, semi-formal and informal communication approaches were experimented with, but none proved to be fully satisfactory for integrating design and development.

The range of communication tools and media across the case studies indicates the impact of Web 2.0 and its social media on Agile UCD. Workshop attendees were struck by the range of media and the purposes that tools were used for. Such tools and media can bring companies much closer to their customers and users, but exploiting opportunities here is not straightforward. At the workshop, integration and consolidation of different needs and desires was identified as a challenge. The volume of content can become a torrent. Current tools do not always provide good support for searching, filtering or responding. A SME in Chap. 2 has developed its own review aggregation tool. It is important to frame expectations for users and customers to avoid disappointment or frustration. As tools become more capable, users can expect more from them.

Online tools are also used across the case studies within development teams, despite the Agile preference for face to face meetings. One can wonder what a new Agile Manifesto for 2016 would look like, 15 years after the original [11]. Many teams are not co-located and cannot be, due to part-time or shift working on projects, or essential cross-site development, sometimes global and 24/7.

Agile UCD thus depends on adequate access to a broad range of well managed inclusive communication channels across different media. Agile's preferred face to face meetings are thus extensively complemented by persistent physical and asynchronous online media. However, a team needs a shared language to use these effectively, especially as teams become more cross functional. The training in Chap. 3 aims to develop this, for teams with 4–5 years' experience of Scrum. Similarly, a SME in Chap. 2 "encourages everybody working on a project to constantly take a step back and actively try to view the product through the eyes of a customer as well as a user". The Art Director for this SME had a strong UCD orientation. This leads into the observation that the social practices associated with roles and team boundaries, and the material and social practices associated with communication, depend on specific individual capabilities, which are next briefly considered.

1.2.2.3   Cross Functional Capabilities of Teams and Individuals

One of Agile's strengths is its focus on learning, e.g., through Scrum's Sprint Retrospectives. Chaps. 4, 5 and 6 present clear evidence of experiment and invention (including independent adoption of Scrum by UXSs), although the unplanned imposition of Scrum in Chap. 6 (apart from the CTO attending a Scrum Master course) made it hard to fully resolve issues of user involvement, documentation and communication. The case study in Chap. 5 benefitted from the company's existing initiatives on Learning Organisation and Experience Factory Models, which had already established favourable support for learning before adopting Agile.

The workshop (Chap. 8) noted the importance of team building and support and facilitation for key design practices. This cannot be achieved by specialised roles alone. Instead T-Shaped People [19] are required, for example developers with design literacy or designers with coding literacy (workshop discussion of position papers for Chaps. 6 and 9). Chapter 9 notes a need for UXSs to understand large scale software development. POs must be as T-Shaped as possible (Chap. 2), but not impossibly so!

Team capabilities for Agile UCD need to be sustainable and scalable (Chap. 8). Continuous education and development, where people learn from each other, needs to be part of Agile UCD practices, resulting in a virtuous circle of learning (Chap. 9). The Scrum backlog concept could be extended to training here, with a training backlog running across projects.

The position papers for Chaps. 3 and 7 drew considerable comment at the workshop, with 16 % of "interesting issues" post-its focused on "Developers doing UCD", which was generally seen as "a very good idea" that attracted "great interest", although one attendee wondered if there is "enough time for developers to also do UCD duty" and another felt that this form of Agile UCD integration would depend on company type. Although Agile has no overt focus on users, the case studies reported that developers were, or became, willing to carry out UCD work, but are initially held back by a lack of competence and thus confidence. Chapter 3 thus reports on the development of formal UCD training for developers that avoided 'observe and learn' education in favour of independent hands-on project specific cases within 3 months of the training. The pair development advocated and reported in Chaps. 6, 9 and 10 is an informal approach to building UX skills in developers. Both formal and informal approaches address the UX as bottleneck problem by providing additional UCD resource through developers.

In summary, Agile UCD needs adequate teams. Roles and communication practices matter, but the foundations for success lie in individuals' attitudes and capabilities.

1.2.3   Software Development Tasks

Much of the focus during the workshop was on fitting the big picture of agile theory and methods together with the lower level detail of day-to-day practices. This book's chapters present innovative practices that can make progress on remaining challenges for Agile UCD. While there is a fine line between how a development team is structured and how work is assigned and completed within the team, the lower level detail of day-to-day practices is primarily focused on development *tasks*, albeit within the context of organizational structures. Chapter 2 argues that issues concerning Agile UCD are more practical than conceptual and celebrates Agile's focus on learning. Sect. 1.2.1 above supports Chap. 2's position: there are few value conflicts and conceptual mismatches between Agile and UCD. There are gaps in each methodology, but as Chap. 5 argues, this lets Agile and UCD complement each other. The challenges lie in creating practices that integrate both methodologies, for example through the training regime in Chap. 3 or the BoB framework in Chap. 9.

Issues and ideas in chapters in this book related to tasks are discussed below at the levels of processes, iterations (e.g., sprints) and low level activities.

1.2.3.1   Process Level Issues and Ideas

In the most minimally extreme form of Scrum, there would only be sprints that implement user stories. While Scrum appears to be such a form, there are always activities prior to the first development sprint. The key questions for Agile UCD are what these upfront activities should be and how much time and resources should be allocated to them. Agile values favour minimal upfront activities [11], whereas UCD ones require comprehensive planning. Chapter 10 argues for a big picture being established from the outset through a thorough pre-study. However, UCD is not an obvious part of Agile and can be deprioritized and passed over. At the same time, agile practices are flexible, with the case studies in this book providing extensive evidence that UCD can be integrated into Agile. Where there are difficulties, this can be due to UCD. For example, UCD costs and/or timescales can be difficult to estimate, which can make it difficult to systematically integrate UCD into Agile (Chap. 4). However, a lack of supporting documentation from initial contextual studies will compound this problem (Chap. 8).

The more specific process challenges for Agile UCD thus concern: upfront activities; transitions between sprints; types of sprints and their synchronization; and constraints on the overall process.

Upfront activities prior to the first development sprint are sometimes referred to as Sprint 0 [33, 34], but Chap. 5 also has an *Inception* stage prior to this. UCD tends to overlook Inception, where project sponsors develop an initial brief and vision. Much can already be in place as regards software and hardware platforms, key features, design purpose and target market at this point, but UCD is typically envisaged as starting with a clean sheet. UCD's 'no designing before users and tasks are thoroughly understood' rule [21] displays a remarkable ignorance of how business decisions on new products and services are made [35]. Both Agile and UCD have to situate themselves in the wider contexts of customers, designers, developers and organizational sponsors. Chapter 5 is unusual in acknowledging the Inception phase. Agile and UCD both need a good awareness of how and where projects really start, which is usually before any project team meets for the first time. Some agile approaches however do take these factors into consideration. DSDM [36] has a Pre-project phase (for the development of a proposal in line with strategic goals), a Feasibility phase (which looks at project viability and a high-level investigation of potential solutions, costs and timeframes) and a Foundations phase (to develop a high level view of how the project will meet business needs and who will be involved). RUP [37] has an Inception phase similar to DSDM's Foundations, during which the business case and high-level requirements are developed as well identifying people who will be involved.

Good initial plans for product development are important when responding to user feedback. In Chap. 2, an extra feature was regularly requested by users, but was not implemented because it "would make other, quite specific, long-term plans for the software impossible on a technical level."

Sprint 0 can take many forms, but it is seen as vital for establishing a baseline understanding of users and their needs. Chapter 9 also advocates design activities, with a clickable prototype as a final outcome of an early product definition workshop, with the product/service vision and the most critical user stories also established as an initial backlog. Agile UCD can build on DSDM's Workshop Facilitator role here [31, 36] to combine business, design and UCD perspectives. In Chap. 5, Sprint n.0 lasted 40 days (20 % of the elapsed budget at the time of writing). Chapter 9 advocates minimizing the time spent on upfront activities. However, what is minimal will depend on what is needed.

Insights developed during Sprint 0, and decisions made there and during inception, need to be preserved during the transition to the first development sprint, and in all subsequent transitions between sprints. Chapter 9 notes that sprints can stop developers from thinking ahead, which carrying a common vision forward can support. The big picture from a common vision can support other activities such as chunking features within sprints to support UCD activities, or planning two or more sprints ahead (Chaps. 4 and 5). Both example activities here rely on being able to decompose the big picture into manageable chunks of work, an issue flagged at the workshop [6].

Transitions between iterations such as Scrum sprints also depend on the types of sprint in a development process. When completely focused on development, Agile typically has regular feature development and refactoring iterations, which address internal software quality [2] and add no new features. However, 'design refactoring' can address external software quality (Chap. 9). Also, the most common approach for Agile UCD is one sprint ahead [38, 39], which can add design and testing sprints alongside development ones (Chap. 9). This can result in synchronisation challenges, but there were only 5 (out of 145) post-its related to synchronization at the workshop (and a further 13 related to more general time issues). Also, the Chaps. 4 and 5 case studies worked (at least) one sprint ahead and reported no issues, but both were using Scrum for the first time in a mature UCD setting (as at Autodesk, where one sprint ahead originated [20, 21]).

Synchronisation challenges can be eased in two ways. Chapter 4 allowed bottomless sprints, which need the capability to look a few sprints ahead. Case studies in Chaps. 2 and 4 also let some UCD activities cut across sprints. User testing can be a source of difficulties here, as user tests may not fit easily within a sprint, and when they do, it can be hard to respond to test feedback before the end of the sprint. Even so, Chap. 10 notes that usability techniques can be fitted into Scrum [40]. In Chap. 3, Contextual Inquiry interviews were carried out one at a time, and thus there was no need for time consuming data consolidation. However, some challenges are not so easily overcome, for example, working across time zones (Chap. 4) or torrents of user feedback (Chap. 6): "one of the most disruptive elements in effective synchronization."

Process level issues are above the iteration level. Managing them well makes it possible to get the best out of each iteration. Exact planning is not possible in creative work (Chap. 11), so Agile must be flexible enough to accommodate this. Ad hoc interventions in Chap. 2 were noted at the workshop. Chapters 4 and 9 advocate chunking groups of tasks. Chapter 4 reports difficulties in accessing users for UCD work within the constraints of sprints. In response, a longer time frame was adopted, with a calendar showing availability of team members over the next 3 months. This made it possible to look ahead when planning future sprints.

1.2.3.2   Iteration Structure Issues and Ideas

Agile iterations such as Scrum's sprints are timeboxed development tasks for specific goals. The most straightforward way to integrate UCD and Agile is to incorporate the former into the day to day work of the latter, i.e., into the iteration structure of an agile methodology. UCD difficulties with Scrum are often attributed to the length of sprints, but this book's Scrum case studies used a range of flexible sprint lengths, and ran some activities in parallel for more than one sprint ahead. It makes sense to fit as much as possible within the main sprint structure and backlog. In principle, all forms of development activity can have their own backlog (Chap. 11), or be combined into a single one (Chap. 9). The sketch wall in Chap. 4 could be regarded as an extension of the Scrum Board.

Chapter 8 refers to Agile's design/develop conundrum, i.e., an intricate difficult problem that has only a conjectural answer, in this case the question as to when to design and when to develop. Pair working (Chaps. 5, 6 and 9) can achieve day to day integration of both design and development. As well as reducing synchronization problems, it lets sprints vary their balance between designing and developing. For example, UCD activities can run one or more sprints ahead alongside code refactoring, or new feature implementation could pause to allow design refactoring in response to user or customer feedback. Both 'technical debt' and 'design debt' must be accepted (Chap. 9), i.e., leaving a feature or its UX at a (very) basic initial standard to allow more rapid deployment and customer/user feedback.

Chapter 5 reports a simplified sprint structure that required no end of sprint review or retrospective. This was made possible by a customer committee and Scrum Islands, with the latter providing continuous feedback and the former being able to continuously plan ahead. This should reduce concerns about rigid sprint structures as obstacles to UCD. Chapter 4 reports interesting restrictions on actions arising from sprint retrospectives that allowed manageable changes to be made to sprint practices within the overall process. The case study here was particularly innovative. Methods that did not work, such as Agile's Planning Poker were replaced with a simpler resource: different sized post-its on the scrum board.

Some work will not fit into a standard iteration, although every effort should be made to make this possible when needed, and to deliver working designs as part of this (Chap. 9). Where this is not possible, then developers may be forced to work ahead of supporting UCD work (Chap. 6). However, the lengths of iterations can vary, which can be to the benefit of UCD work. Case studies report ad hoc interventions that breach required Agile practice, e.g., relaxing the closed window rule for essential iterative development (e.g., Chap. 4, which also let developers work ahead of the current sprint), although the closed window rule is reported as a problem in Chap. 10.

Iterations can be planned more than one ahead. Chapter 4 planned 5 sprint milestones ahead (initially for 1 week sprints), which allowed UX work in advance, bringing UX and feature implementation as close as possible, but not absolutely in parallel. Availability of part-time team members had to be factored into planning.

1.2.3.3 Low Level Activity Level Issues and Ideas

While processes can span months and even years, and iterations weeks and sometimes months, activities within sprints may last only days or hours. It is at this level of design, implementation and evaluation tasks that Agile UCD is actually delivered. Process and iteration structure may potentially enable or obstruct, but the enablers and blockers here only become real in the context of actual development work.

Tasks or activities are supported by *resources*, which may be grouped into *approaches* and named as re-usable methods [41]. Approaches are incomplete, and resources can be too. Approaches become methods through development work, which adds, completes and adapts resources. Both UCD and Agile methods and practices may have to be adapted for Agile UCD. Chapter 3 thus adapted three UCD methods through two to six iterations of training materials to fit its industrial development contexts. For example, contextual interview notes can be indexed using sequence models (contextual interviews and sequence models are resources for Rapid Contextual Design [42]), fusing analysis and data collection activities for quicker work.

The workshop and chapters contain some very good examples of appropriation and adaptation. The largest group of post-its at the workshop (91 or 37 %) was "Methods and Practices" ("Artefacts and Tools" comprised 16 of these). This identifies activity level resourcing as a key focus for Agile UCD. Roles and responsibilities are enabled or obstructed by the quality of their access to resources. However, expectations or preferences can result in ineffective use of resources. The desirability of formal prescriptive methods was discussed at the workshop, despite the common understanding (e.g., Chap. 10) that informal methods work best for agile [40]. Even formal methods cannot be 'followed' to the letter [41].

New resources are becoming available for Agile use. Chapter 2 provides evidence of the Internet of Things providing new resources in support of UCD activities, with SMEs tracking data from their software and hardware products. This complements web-originated customer and user information. However, Chap. 2 notes that good ideas remain hard to come by, so judgement in design management remains irreplaceable. A PO in one of the chapter's case studies makes use of simple heuristics based on frequency. A single suggestion or report of a problem is not enough, but 2–3 may be, but it may be that he: "stay[s] with [his] opinion". The extent of digital data and information here is still often filtered by a "feeling for", as well as by the road map for products and services.

Interaction Design support and tools are becoming more capable. Support is needed for keeping up to date with platform style guidance (Chap. 6) and rapid prototyping tools. The production quality and functional capabilities of these tools is increasing, and they can deliver code for development (e.g., HTML, CSS – Chap. 9). This makes it possible for UX work to 'keep up' with the pace of an agile project. High fidelity 'just in time' prototypes are now possible, and quicker to create than by drawing. Chap. 9 recommends progression from a clickable prototype, via a shell application with a partially functioning or no back end, to a fully functioning version released and in use: "it is … actual usage that really validates the viability of the system."

User research and evaluation are the core contributions of UCD to software development. UX evaluation is often regarded as poor value for the time and resources expended. Agile can change this, and is doing so, by early release of software for evaluation in use. This may be initially a restricted release [10], for example to living labs in Chaps. 2 and 6, or for release approval by a customer committee (Chap. 5). Once in full use, evaluation of digital products and services can draw on user support teams and marketing and business resources such as Net Promoter Scores (Chap. 2).

In summary, all development tasks are completed within or alongside iterations, which in turn form parts of an overall software development process. Support for tasks depends on resources, including the scheduling resources associated with sprints and processes. Ultimately, an extensive effective integration of Agile and UCD depends on the resources and approaches needed to support it. There are many examples of effective innovations here in this book's chapters, and many opportunities for further work, which are discussed in Sect. 1.3.

1.2.4 Research Methodologies

The topics listed in the call for participation for the NordiCHI workshop from which this book originates included theories and methods relevant to research on Agile and UCD. There was limited discussion of research methods at the workshop, where only three post-its related to research (within a larger group of' "research and problems", Chap. 8). However, collectively, this book's chapters make use of a wide range of research methods, which include:

- Literature surveys
- Theoretical analyses
- Surveys
- Interviews
- Observation, including participant observation
- Material culture studies (e.g., collection and analysis of Agile UCD arefacts such as user stories or bug/usability reports)
- Autobiographical reflection
- Grounded Theory, Meaning Consolidation, and other qualitative analyses
- Principal Components Analysis.
- Building mid-range theories, constructs and propositions from case studies
- Case studies
- Collaborative reflection
- Action Research (and Research through Design as a specific form of this)

Some of the above research methods, particularly case studies, are appropriate for early exploration of human practices that are still not well understood. Case studies can involve multiple methods: method mixes have been applied across multi-stage research projects and programmes lasting from 2 to 4 years in case study chapters.

There is no immediate clear pattern of groups across these methods. However, just as Kuusninen's distinction between teams and tasks (Chap. 9) provided a structure for the two previous sections, we can draw on a framework from design research to support analysis of research approaches in this book's chapters. Although, the research methods above are largely associated by chapter authors with human science and action research practices, they way that they have been applied and combined is almost identical to well established design research practices.

Over 20 years ago, Frayling transferred a distinction between education *into* art and education *through* art to art and design research [43]. The former is the study of art, learning about its history and contemporary institutions. The latter is learning through the practice of art. Frayling thus contrasted *research into art and design*, with its historical and contemporary studies using humanities and human science methodologies, with *research through art and design*, with creative practices as the backbone of research methodology. Frayling also added a third mode of research in art and design, research *for* art and design. This mode developed knowledge and practices for use in art and design, e.g., knowledge of materials and design methods. Frayling also distinguished between 'Research' and 'research', i.e. original and significant academic *Research* in contrast to routine *research* within a professional practice (e.g., traffic surveys, epidemiology, food testing, market research). Focusing on art, Frayling found it difficult to come up with examples of *Research* for art, but found ready examples of artists' preparatory studies. He nevertheless referred to examples of *Research* for design (knowledge of materials and design methods), but failed to recognise these as original and significant academic research that could support future design practice and research.

The chapters in this book can be contrasted on the basis of Frayling's three modes of art and design research:

- *into*: studies of the agile development practices of *others*
- *through*: case studies based on researchers' *own* agile development practices
- *for*: research that results in guidance and practices for future design practice and research, e.g., in the form of knowledge, procedures, practices, principles or tools

In a study of design research PhDs, Yee concluded that Frayling's research modes are not mutually exclusive, but typically combine [44]. For example, chapters in the book could be classified as:

- research *into* design *for* design: studies of the agile development practices of others from which guidance and practices for future design practice and research are derived (e.g., Chap. 2)
- research *for* design *into* and *through* design: case studies based on secondary literature and researchers' own agile development practices from which guidance and practices for future design practice and research are proposed (e.g., Chap. 4)
- research *into* design *through* design *for* design: case studies based on researchers' own agile development practices and secondary literature from which guidance and practices for future design practice and research are derived from data and materials collected during a case study (e.g., Chap. 5)

Chapter 2's approach is *research into design for design*, i.e., existing SME practices are studied as a basis for offering suggestions for better integration of UCD and Agile. Stickel and colleagues positioned UCD as an evolving normative ideological practice, with a primary focus on users, similar to Agile's focus on customers. However, their studies of Agile UCD 'in the wild', focused on what does happen rather than what should happen. Disparities between theory and practice in the literature make it important to study actual practice. They thus prefer a realist position over a normative one, and so draw on extensive qualitative research expertise to apply well established methodologies from design research to software contexts. The predominant research into design research mode here is essential for well-grounded understandings of when UCD and Agile can or cannot be successfully integrated. Differences exposed via research into design can explain disparities in the literature. For example, the two smaller SMEs studied in Chap. 2 are effectively part of larger virtual organisations in integrated value chains. Analysis here must consider the culture of the SME in focus, the cultures of their customers and partners, and the emergent dynamic culture of the embracing virtual organization.

Chapter 3's approach is *research for design through design*, i.e., it is research with the aim of developing support for design practice through iterative development of training materials and courses. New forms of support for Agile UCD were developed through practice-led iterations of curriculum and template design, with assessment through pre- and post-tests (after training, after independent use). Overall, Øvad and Larsen report the results of sustained critical sensitive informed and imaginative responses to developers' training experiences. The authors sensibly see their training suite as only one form of intervention in support of Agile UCD. Even so, it offers a highly effective strategy for addressing some outstanding challenges for Agile UCD.

Chapter 4's approach is *research for design through and into design*, where prototype development ('through design') is used to gain experience in Agile UCD, supplemented by a study ('into design') of agile practices in other teams in the same company, where team colleagues often worked on more than one project. This let the authors investigate the agile UCD practices of three other teams: two were working on the prototype development and other projects; the other was a UX team servicing several projects. Chapter 4 illustrates the advantages of experimental creative research through design practices. Sprint lengths were varied, 'invisible' UCD activities spanning sprints were actively supported, and Scrum Board configurations were iterated to adapt a well-established Agile resource to communicate the project's 'big picture' (in combination with two walls of a project space). These experimental creative research through design practices were *more agile than Agile*, in that they could change the rules in Scrum rather then be constrained by them. The results of these experiments were combined with the studies of three other teams to support research *for* design i.e., the researchers used the experience of their and other teams to offer guidance on running Scrum for future UCD focused projects, e.g.:

- conduct initial field studies in the first sprint, and develop infrastructure in the second sprint alongside user evaluations of lo-fi prototypes
- run UCD work one sprint ahead from Sprint 1 onwards, combining further field studies, lo-fi prototyping and user evaluations

- adopt 'design chunking' of closely related product features for implementation together in one sprint to let design and development activities manage dependencies. Design chunking addresses a known major issue with Scrum when dependencies between features are poorly managed. Costly refactoring of code can be required to correctly manage feature interactions
- do not have part-time staff on projects

Chapter 5 combined *research into and through design for design*. The initial research *into* design used secondary sources *for* co-designing an Agile HCD methodology that was suitable for the case study company and project. Positive experiences and best practices reported in this literature meant that Agile was not wholly negatively framed as obstructing HCD. An action research methodology supported the research *through* design in two ways. Firstly, the design of the web portal advanced the action research (above: creative practices as the backbone of research methodology). Secondly, the co-designed Agile HCD methodology also structured the action research process. In short, both the *product* and *process* of design were the means through which action research was carried out.

Chapter 6's approach is research *into* design *for* design, i.e., Smart Campus practices provided experiences that were studied retrospectively (*into*) to advocate improving an organisation's Agile UCD capabilities through PD and Design Thinking approaches (*for*). To understand the difficulties encountered in preserving PD practices, and how to overcome them, two interview studies were planned: the first occurred several months after the adoption of Scrum, the second one after over one year.

The imposition of Agile at a specific point in the project prevented early planning for integration (as was achieved by co-design in Chap. 5), which would have allowed a research through design methodology. Instead, the authors began with research into design, where they complemented their own project experience with interviews, which supported collaborative reflection to reduce bias, along with a researcher external to the project conducting the interviews, which were then transcribed and analysed, controlling for coding bias. A literature review in conjunction with the interview studies revealed how UCD work practices had failed following changes in the work situation; the authors benefitted from two 2014 literature surveys that covered 76 [12] and 71 [1] papers, which highlight the topicality of the chapters in this book.

Chapter 6 thus combines case study analyses, a literature survey, and collaborative reflection with software professionals. Grounding, analysis, modelling and guideline derivation were meticulous and reflect the strong empirical basis of almost all chapters in this book. The difference between design research and practice is evidenced by a project retrospective that was more rigorous, detached and systematic than any routine agile sprint or project retrospective could be.

In each case study for Chaps. 4, 5 and 6, Scrum-like processes were being used for the first time. In Chap. 4, Muñoz and colleagues decided to experiment, as a UCD focused team, with a Scrum process. In Chap. 5, Ardito and colleagues co-designed a Scrum inspired process and then applied it in an action research project. In contrast in Chap. 6, Bordin and De Angeli found Scrum imposed on their research project. We thus see differences in autonomy in these three practice-based case studies. Chapters 4 and 5 case studies were largely under the researchers' control. Chapter 2 presented three SME case studies without action research interventions. Chapter 3 reported on the progress and outcomes of training interventions with agile developers.

Chapter 7 also addresses the capabilities of agile developers by assessing the potential for developers taking on more UCD work, as in Chap. 3. This research *into* design study focused on the capabilities of specific roles in a project team, rather than on the broad context of agile development, as in Chap. 2's qualitative study, but Chap. 7 uses a quantitative method, principal component analysis of data from UX rating scales. This straightforward research *into* design *for* design investigates opportunities for using UX ratings in Agile UCD. It does not lead to clear guidance, since the results are somewhat surprising and the sample of specialist roles is very small in comparison to developers and users. Although UXS and PO roles were better than developers at predicting users' ratings of product UX for case studies, they were not good enough to recommend using professional's ratings (even when taking the users' perspective) as a substitute for empirical evaluation involving end-users. However, the study is valuable for two reasons. Firstly, it calls the empathy of UXS and PO roles into question. UXS are meant to be the users' advocate, and POs are meant to be the customer's advocate, but the small sample do not appear to be well enough equipped for this role (moreover, perfect empathy may well be impossible for anyone). Secondly, it suggests that users' UX ratings could provide useful support for iteration (sprint) planning. Further research is required to: establish whether the reported results will change with a larger sample of UXS and PO roles; and explore the value of users' UX ratings in Agile UCD.

Chapter 8 reports a short collaborative research *into* design workshop that provides a future research agenda for a range of mixes of research *into*, *through* and *for* design.

Chapter 9 uses a co-ordinated sequence of research *into* design studies to develop a research *for* design output: the BoB framework, ending with collaborative reflection to reduce bias. The BoB framework is based on four mixed method studies spanning 4 years and involving over 300 respondents from 9 companies in 10 countries (7 in Europe and 3 in Asia), working across IT services, engineering, middleware, mobile enterprise applications, and industrial systems (including safety critical).

Chapter 10 takes a similar research *into* design to suggest some novel tactics *for* improving the diffusion of UCD. Chapters 9 and 10 have both passed through the first stage of the research programme methodology proposed in [41]: detailed, well-structured case studies of usability work. They both reach the second stage: metareviews of case studies of usability work. Chapter 9 has reached the third stage: modeling the interaction design process across a complete project life cycle, based on the results of a meta-review. The stages of the proposed research programme structure in [41] are designed to support each other, with the aim of reaching a fourth stage where well-grounded and theorized conjectures about the impact of resources and approaches can be formulated and tested. The BoB framework makes formulation and testing of such conjectures possible. Its supporting guidelines (Chap. 9 Table 9.3) can be read as a first outline of a coherent set of related conjectures.

Chapter 11 is a research *into* design study using secondary sources that moves to research *for* design by outlining how Agile UCD can expand its current scope via BIG (Balanced, Integrated and Generous) design [45]. Collectively, the case studies span much of the scope of BIG design, but no single case study explicitly set out to span this scope, nor did any cover the full scope in isolation.

Action research practices in case studies (research *through* design [43]) have proved effective and have created a range of resources that can be adopted and adapted for Agile UCD. These include training materials, workplace layouts, process structures, and sprint practices (research *for* design [43]). Development and assessment of new approaches in practice is a research methodology that is suitable for applied projects in universities and industry, where it can benefit from collaborative reflection (e.g., Chaps. 2 and 9). Frayling's modes of art and design research thus provide a useful framework for contrasting the high level research strategies taken in each of the book's chapters, which significantly improve on the workshop position papers in their coverage of theories and methods relevant to research on Agile and UCD. The framework provides a structure that can make sense of the diverse range of research methods applied in each chapter. Frayling's research modes also provide a basis for identifying future methodological work for Agile UCD, as well as framing best practice. For example, future action research methodologies for Agile UCD could combine the planning of Chap. 5 with the systematic iteration of resources in Chap. 3.

1.3 The Future of Agile UCD Practices and Research

There has been successful Agile UCD work for over a decade, which chapters in this book augment with new successes from ambitious resourceful and innovative software development teams. Nevertheless, the previous section has identified continuing challenges. Many challenges can be addressed via a combination of professional innovation and applied academic research. Some challenges however require more focused fundamental research, which could further develop methodologies at the leading edge of Agile, UCD and creative design research.

Two topics are addressed in this section: the continuing challenges for Agile UCD; and future trends for research on UCD and Agile.

1.3.1 *Continuing Challenges for Agile UCD*

Novel approaches and resources developed in this book's case studies will not transfer to all development contexts. Some will not scale to larger teams who are not co-located, so the current solutions are not viable in all agile contexts. Chapter 6 also raises issues of transfer to Open Source contexts, which remain a challenge for Agile.

Domain values give rise to specific needs [46]. Some application domains are not addressed in this book, or example, no chapter addresses games. Challenges for Agile here include the need to completely implement a game's narrative for adequate gameplay. Similarly, at least a few game levels need to be in place for the first release of a game. This need for comprehensive capabilities at first release may reduce the benefits of following Agile in games and perhaps other domains such as healthcare, once systems significantly exceed the complexity of focused specialist products (such as those developed by a Chap. 3 SME).

There are thus continuing challenges of extending Agile UCD to further application domains, application complexity, team sizes and open source contexts. The case studies also indicate a need to develop better tool support to improve Agile UCD work. When widely available tools (as in Chaps. 2, 4, 5, 6 and 9) are used for new Agile UCD activities ('appropriation'), this will improve diffusion, as will use of (improved) open source tools.

Some continuing challenges are specific to organizational settings. A workshop post-it in response to Chap. 5's position paper: can an action-research-based approach be used to alter the 'call for tenders'? What is interesting here is the reframing of a longstanding UCD issue as an action research problem. However, experimental interventions here would be limited to IT service companies and their customers. For mass market product and services, this is a question for project inception. Either way, action research here must involve suppliers and customers.

Some continuing challenges are specific to UCD. Chapter 9 suggests using personas [47] to develop shared user empathy. These could be co-created by designers and developers, building on Chap. 3's preference for independent hands-on creation of project resources over observe and learn. Support for estimation beyond feature implementation is also required. In Chap. 4, the existing agile practice of Planning Poker did not transfer successfully to an experimental Agile UCD context. Similarly, iteration (sprint) planning must expand beyond a feature focus to reduce constraints on creativity and flexibility (Chap. 6), but this is a joint challenge for Agile and UCD. Such multi-functional iteration (sprint) planning will better align design and development, by improving support for novel approaches to sprint management, as in Chaps. 4, 5 and 9.

Some continuing challenges are more general and are all linked to Agile becoming more mature and mainstream. Scaling and sustainability are still concerns. A single methodological or process success on a small project that is intended for general use must translate into sustainable success on larger projects. Also, the whole development process needs to be covered. Chapter 5 shows awareness of life before upfront development activities (i.e., project inception), pointing to a need to research process planning from cradle to grave, and not just from kick-off to product launch. Strategic visions exist in some form before kick-off workshops, but these are not well integrated into either UCD or popular agile approaches. Chapter 9's BoB framework has an early product definition workshop, and Chap. 5 outlines its lengthy Sprint n.0. Research needs to provide details and examples to better support Agile UCD from project inception onwards. For example, User Stories [48, 49] need to be linked to a holistic big picture that puts them in a strategic context. A big picture can also support Chap. 4's chunking of feature groups to support of UX quality [33, 34]. Similarly, an overall project vision and roadmap is vital for strategic filtering of user and customer feedback (Chap. 2), since a major problem for UCD is that users' needs aren't all the same, even for a largely coherent subgroup represented by a persona archetype [47]. Upfront activities are thus vital to creating and documenting this big picture, e.g., as a vision or roadmap.

Merging, interpreting and filtering user feedback was a challenge that was in focus in Chaps. 2 and 6. Given that customers want user feedback (and suppliers want customer feedback), users and customers must be motivated to provide feedback, and to keep doing so, especially in Participative Design contexts (PD: Chap. 6). Feedback on feedback is thus another Agile UCD practice that requires further applied research in practitioner and research contexts. To be able to provide feedback on feedback, feedback needs to be effectively collected and efficiently analysed, which is becoming a major challenge with the development of a wide range of crowdsourcing channels (e.g., web, social media, instrumentation, user support, living labs) alongside formal evaluation activities (which may be out-sourced). An initial research agenda here includes investigating appropriate balances of quantitative and qualitative data, making use of existing CSCW and Mobile HCI research (e.g., [50, 51]) and associated tools (e.g., the open source Shake tool from Chap. 2's authors and colleagues: http://github.com/UniSiegenCSCW/Shake).

In summary, challenges remain with Agile UCD for some application domains:

- larger project teams;
- open source contexts;
- tendering;
- estimation;
- multi-functional iteration (sprint) planning;
- whole process planning;
- creating and maintaining a project vision and keeping development activities focused on it, and efficiently and effectively managing increasingly complex user feedback.

These continuing challenges can be largely addressed by action research within Agile UCD, with or without the support of academic researchers, using hybrid practice-based design research methodologies that combine Frayling's modes [43], as in this book's case studies. Chaps. 3, 4 and 5 provide inspiring examples of invention and reflection that can be emulated in further practice-based research on process planning and management, on multi-channel evaluation data, and on documentation. Future research in these areas needs to report: tactics (e.g., developer training); example novel and adapted resources and approaches (e.g., extranet Scrum Boards, triangulation of customer/user feedback, kick-off workshops, design sprints [28], pair working); and systematic research reports on Agile UCD experience.

Careful record keeping and critical collaborative reflection are needed to ensure high research quality. Rigorous reflective experience reports need to be able to identify the separate contributions of team composition and work structure, and how these combine in practice. Support and impedance from organizational cultures needs to be identified, along with the role of Agile, UCD, developer, designer, customer and user values. It is important to contextualize experience reports so that readers can assess how they match their own development contexts. Alongside this, following Chap. 3, experimental studies also need to aim to develop agile research for agile practice (and following Chaps. 4, 6 and 11, to develop creative research for creative practice).

1.3.2   Future Trends for Research on Agile and UCD

Some challenges for Agile and UCD, both integrated and in isolation, require sustained research interventions across multiple projects with the involvement of academic researchers, professional communities and key customers. Successful research here will require research methodologies with sophistication beyond those used in this book's chapters. The case study methodologies in this book do not lack sophistication, but the research challenges for some future work are substantial.

Practices are always changing and developing, so continued empirical research is essential: good ideas can come from academics and practitioners working together. Variety in research methods gives different insights, academic rigour is helpful, and academics are prepared to look at failures as well as successes (both are limitations of the many experience reports in the agile literature). Theoretical views also help to move understanding forward, and reframe discussions. However, pragmatic outputs such as models, templates, process descriptions and techniques are helpful for practitioners. Most importantly, researchers need to get better at getting their findings and insights back out to the practitioner community so that they can learn from and use them. The latter applies to all of the recommendations on future research below, which are not exhaustive. There is no 'definition of DONE' for Agile UCD research. There will always be new challenges and new issues to explore, but maybe one of the most important challenges is to maintain collaboration between researchers and practitioners. With these pervasive challenges in mind, more challenging research areas include:

1. the focus and quality of surveys on Agile, and their ability to accurately represent trends and actual practices
2. length of experience with Agile and openness to integrating UCD and other practices such as creative design and innovation processes
3. longitudinal studies of customer value and UX from Agile UCD
4. managing a broad range of non-functional requirements beyond UX
5. adapting Agile UCD to novel technologies and application domains

The 'Scrumish' nature of practices across all the case studies suggest that the results of key surveys such as VersionOne's [29] must be interpreted in the context of what is most probably very loose self-reporting. Two respondents reporting themselves as Scrum users may well have very different agile work practices. Knowing what is actually happening at an appropriate level of detail will not be revealed by large quantitative surveys. Qualitative literature surveys [1, 12] are currently better at revealing the detail and nuances of Agile UCD practices. However, follow up interviews with an appropriate sample of respondents to large online questionnaires could well improve on current literature surveys that are likely to be a few years behind current practices.

Balancing quantitative surveys with qualitative interviews can better answer question about what is actually happening in Agile, beyond self-reporting of methodology names. A question raised by one position paper [7] was: is Scrum going out of fashion and being replaced by Lean methodologies such as Kanban? This is not an easy question to answer. However, what is happening is that organisations are creating their own Agile mixes, which may lower barriers to UCD. The case studies all use local Agile mixes rather than one specific exclusive 'branded' methodology. However, there is a sense for some researchers currently that elements of Lean or Kanban are making inroads into Scrum practices, but respondents to large surveys may still report that they are just using Scrum. If Lean or Kanban are becoming more common, in whole or in part, then future research needs to focus on integrating UCD here as well as with Scrum.

As Sect. 1.2.1.2 above (Values other than Agile and UCD) has noted, understanding 'what is happening in Agile UCD' involves more than just understanding contemporary Agile and UCD. What appears in this book's case studies is not simply openness to Agile or UCD, in fact it is much simpler, i.e., simply openness. There is evidence of openness to approaches from creative design, innovation, business and SE (software engineering), with examples of each integrated into agile practice.

A further drawback on annual quantitative surveys is that they only provide a snapshot in time, as do qualitative case studies. However, given that method mixes constantly evolve, a question follows as to whether there are points in an organisation's experience with Agile or UCD that are more favourable to integrating other practices. In the case studies in this book, novice use of one approach is supported by experienced use of another. Thus experienced UCD teams' first use of Scrum with UCD, with local adaptations, was generally successful in the Chaps. 4, 5 and 6 case studies (although Chap. 6 reports frustrations related to Participative Design). Conversely, in Chaps. 2, 3, 7 and 9, organisations with years of Agile experience successfully integrated UCD practices. There is thus no broad evidence that commitments to Agile completely obstruct UCD practices. UX roles are not in charge, and may feel excluded from sprint and similar meetings, but the issue here is one of degree, i.e., how, when and to what extent ideal UCD practices are not possible. The question of maturity and readiness is thus not straightforward, and asking it may currently be premature. Instead, exploratory longitudinal studies are required to track the evolution of method mixes in organisations that initially primarily use Agile or UCD, and those that start with both or neither at similar stages of development.

Organisations need to combine perspectives and approaches from SE, UCD and business to deliver the customer value that Agile aims at. Research is needed to establish how UX and customer value do or do not develop post release. This also requires sophisticated longitudinal research methodologies. At organizational level, consumer market SMEs in Chap. 2 already have practices to track this. For example, one PO shares his phone number with experts in their user community. However, research needs to look for patterns across larger samples of organisations.

SE has always been challenged by non-functional requirements [2] such as UX and customer value. A research question on the development of UX and customer value can be extended to more non-functional requirements, e.g., security, sustainability, maintainability, privacy and other ethical concerns. Chapter 5 described how non-functional requirements for internal software quality were monitored in its case study. Chapter 10 reports how external software qualities [2] such as security and accessibility are used as 'trojan horses' to sneak in usability requirements. UCD has often taken a moral position, but Chap. 10 shows that this is not as fashionable as Agile's values.

As smart, transmediated and pervasive technologies support workplace users and become a key to efficient organisations, ethical issues such as work-life balance become more important. Emerging digital technologies and the complex landscape of the many application domains where they can be used make UX work more complex, and increase the challenges of conducting high quality research in these areas. Chaps. 2, 3, 6 and 9 cover extensions of Agile UCD to mobile technologies and hardware based ('embedded') systems. In technical terms, Agile has extended into new application domains using novel technologies, but UCD may not be keeping up. The training regime in Chap. 3 can help companies catch up here, but new approaches are needed for non-functional requirements in contexts for new applications of novel technologies.

This concludes discussion of elements of a future collaborative practice-based research agenda. Other research needs to be more academic in nature, as it relates to one workshop call focus: theories and methods relevant to research on Agile and UCD. This section closes with a discussion of each.

One of the current limitations of the Agile literature is that much of it consists of 'experience reports' where rigour is typically weak. There is also a tendency only to publish 'success stories' rather than failures. Research approaches such as single and multiple case studies, action research, and ethnography should improve rigour, especially when these are integrated through adoption and adaptation of methodologies from research through design (also known as constructive design research [52]).

Documentation is key to rigorous research through design, which offers an experimental setting that can be used to develop practices that can be transferred to practitioner contexts. Documentation, preferably created, maintained and accessed via shared extranet tools, underpins the underdeveloped areas of Agile UCD, i.e., process planning, aligning design and development, feedback management, and communication within project teams. Experimental research needs to develop tactics, resources and approaches. Mixed media documentation practices (Chaps. 4

and 6) are required that can curate code, sketches, architectures, prototypes, text, data, and images.

Future methodological directions for foundational Agile UCD research can thus benefit from developments in design research that combine appropriate documentation, critical reflection and creative practice for rigour in open ended experimental studies. This is primarily an area for academic research until methodological issues are resolved, particularly in relation to appropriate documentation and critical reflection.

Explicitly framing of Agile UCD research projects as hybrid forms of design research will guide researchers to draw on relevant theories, results and methodologies from design research. For example, a range of research through design methodologies is covered in [52], and HCI and design research conferences regularly update this with new work on practice-based methodologies.

Existing UCD research can also contribute to improving Agile UCD research. Chapter 2 describes how one PO used a heuristic similar to any two agreement [53], but this is known to risk missing severe problems [54]. Similarly, Chap. 2 argues that crowdsourcing approaches to evaluation can exploit "concepts from HCI and CSCW, such as comprehensive situated user feedback and engagement mechanisms right inside of products, or leveraging modern mobile devices to facilitate relatively lean, event-contingent qualitative and quantitative data collection".

Another advantage of academic research in this area is that we can use theory to help to understand and hence improve practice. Theories relevant to research on Agile UCD in the chapters are largely drawn from the business and innovation literature. Chaps. 6 and 11 draw on Design Thinking (as did [6]). Chapter 10 draws on Management Fashionability and Diffusion of Innovation. Chapter 11 draws on design research, which underpins much innovation work [13, 19, 20, 22, 27, 45]. These are not mainstream theories in HCI or SE. They evidence a shift from seeing software development as solely a concern for Agile and UCD, and extend the scope of challenges to a broader range of disciplinary practices. Theories from Organisational Science, Psychology, Sociology and Communications Science are also likely to be relevant to improving our understanding of Agile UCD in its broader organizational, professional and business contexts. Also, theories from design research are relevant.

A simple question has been asked since the dawn of UCD, and was asked at the workshop in relation to a position paper [7]: "What is good and bad in different methods?" This question is simple to ask, but very difficult to answer. Even harder to address is a need expressed at the workshop following the position paper for Chap. 3: a method for validating UCD methods, including their adapted forms. Given that the methods communicated in the training materials were revised for each iteration, this in some ways was a surprising question. The position paper celebrated agile research for agile practice, and a requirement for rigorous validation would significantly reduce agility here. Even so, the pre- and post-tests methodology applied in Chap. 3 did show improvements with each iteration of each method, but this was largely in terms of developers' perceptions and not whether each version of each method delivered 'correct' results when it was applied.

A need to validate and evaluate methods reflects engineering and human science values. However, there is a fundamental error in regarding methods as independent variables that have fixed effects in highly variable contexts. Less demanding assessments of method innovation and adaptation in Agile UCD can however be on the research agenda. Chaps. 2, 3 and 6 use qualitative research methods that reveal practices, but without attempting to assess their validity for every development context. There is scope for methodological improvement here, but an important body of theory in design research [41, 45] strongly advises against any attempt to 'prove' that 'methods' are valid. This is because 'methods' are an inappropriate unit of analysis for design and evaluation work. It is possible to establish reliable impacts for resources, at a lower level of analysis, and project level factors at a higher level. However, methods are too underspecified for there to be reliable 'method effects'. Methods are the result of development work, and not inputs to them [41]. The nature of creative work is such that methods cannot be systematically followed. Chapter 11 presents the underlying theory here.

Future research on Agile UCD can apply a framework from design research [45] to research *into* design studies such as Chap. 2's case studies. The framework in [45] replaces the resource *types* in [41] with resource *functions* that can identify work done at specific points in activities. For example, a resource can be informative or inquisitive, or it may direct work (e.g., Chap. 3's templates). Resource function analysis was used in [55] to identify the reasons for the success of an unplanned evaluation approach, Creative Sprints. The hybrid design research approach here was thus research *into* design *for* design. It identified organisational requirements for effective application of Creative Sprints.

Resource function analysis can also be used to support collaborative reflection. Chaps. 6 and 9 benefitted methodologically from collaborative reflection, and resource function analysis guided collaborative reflection in [55]. The results of resource analyses such as [41] can inform training approaches (as in Chap. 3) to improve evaluation performance in Agile UCD via relevant research.

There are thus many opportunities for improving the methodological and theoretical support for Agile UCD research.

1.4 Conclusions

The chapters developed after the NordiCHI 2014 workshop make substantial contributions in relation to all topics in the workshop's call for participation:

- Case studies and work in progress related to UX and Agile.
- Success stories and best practices from integrating UCD and Agile.
- Challenges from working with UCD in Agile systems development
- Values and perspectives underpinning UCD and Agile in theory.
- Integration of UCD and Agile in different domains such as games and healthcare.
- Theories and methods relevant to research on Agile and UCD.
- Discussion of future trends for UCD and Agile research.

In conclusion, some key observations can be offered. Firstly, Agile UCD requires give and take. Both Agile and UCD can learn from each other, and from other approaches from design, engineering and business. Chapter 2 argues that Agile provides better support for work-based learning than UCD does. UCD's origins in the human sciences tend to favour library-based learning.

Secondly, UCD can be difficult, but so can SE in agile and other guises. Agile UCD by extension is even more difficult. In such circumstances, the good natured collaboration between UCD and SE professionals in most of the case studies (most of the time) is at least as important to research success as methodological rigour.

Thirdly, Agile UCD is going to get even more difficult as it becomes better interfaced with design thinking and business strategy. The big picture will get bigger. Progress on tactics will always be needed, but strategic capability will become the dominant goal. Interactive systems are no longer just supporting workers on tasks. They now underpin enterprises and services. In some senses, IT systems are becoming *the* business, rather than just supporting it. Narrow foci will not be sustainable, whether these foci are on UX or internal software quality: both respectively represent legitimate UCD and SE concerns that have to co-exist with, and take their direction and goals from, the wider enterprise contexts within which contemporary IT systems are developed. Both Agile and UCD will have to face both inward and outward: inward towards their professional and disciplinary concerns, and outward to the value and experiences that they aim to deliver. Agile UCD is only one step in a larger process of integrating software development and business functions in support of the digital economy and digital social and cultural innovation.

References

1. Salah D, Paige RF, Cairns P (2014) A systematic literature review for agile development processes and user centred design integration. In: Proceedings of the 18th international conference on evaluation and assessment in software engineering, vol 5. ACM, New York
2. Gram C, Cockton G (1996) Design principles for interactive software. Chapman and Hall, London
3. Boehm B, Turner R (2003) Balancing agility and discipline: a guide for the perplexed. Addison-Wesley, Boston
4. Meyer B (2014) Agile! The good, the hype and the ugly. Springer, Switzerland
5. Lárusdóttir M, Cajander Å, Gulliksen J, Cockton G, Gregory P, Salah D (2014) On the integration of user centred design in agile development. In: Proceedings of the NordiCHI '14. ACM, New York, pp 817–882
6. Lindell R (2014) Attending experiential qualities in system development. In: Proceedings of the workshop: on the integration of UCD and agile development, NordiCHI 2014, Helsinki. Available from https://ucdandagile.wordpress.com
7. Law ELC, Lárusdóttir MK (2014) User Experience (UX) Design: agile or lean?. In: Proceedings of the workshop: on the integration of UCD and agile development, NordiCHI 2014, Helsinki. Available from https://ucdandagile.wordpress.com
8. Law EL-C, Lárusdóttir MK (2015) Whose experience do we care about? Analysis of the fitness of scrum and kanban to user experience. Int J Hum Comput Interact 31(9):584–602

9. Nelson E (2002) The Beck-Cooper interview: extreme programming vs. interaction design. Available from http://www.id-book.com/downloads/beck_vs_cooper_debate.pdf
10. Ambler SW (2008) Tailoring usability into agile software development projects. In: Law E, Hvannberg E, Cockton G (eds) Maturing usability. Quality in software, interaction and value. Springer, London
11. Beck K, Beedle M, Van Bennekum A, Cockburn A, Cunningham W and 12 other authors (2001) Manifesto for Agile Software Development. http://www.agilemanifesto.org/
12. Jurca G, Hellmann TD, Maurer F (2014) Integrating Agile and user-centered design: a systematic mapping and review of evaluation and validation studies of Agile-UX. In: Agile Conference (AGILE), 2014, IEEE (2014), 24–32
13. von Hippel E (2005) Democratizing innovation. MIT Press, Cambridge, MA
14. Keiningham TL, Cooil B, Andreassen TW, Aksoy L (2007) A longitudinal examination of net promoter and firm revenue growth. J Mark 71(3):39–51
15. Basili VR, Caldiera G, Rombach HD (2002) Experience factory. In: Encyclopedia of software engineering. Wiley, New York
16. Schneider K, von Hunnius J-P, Basili V (2002) Experience in implementing a learning software organization. IEEE Softw 19(3):46–49
17. Gartner S, Schneider K (2012) A method for prioritizing end-user feedback for requirements engineering. In: 5th International workshop on Cooperative and Human Aspects of Software Engineering (CHASE), IEEE 47–49
18. Lee MJ, Ko AJ (2012) Representations of user feedback in an Agile, collocated software team. In: 5th International Workshop on Cooperative and Human Aspects of Software Engineering (CHASE), IEEE 76–82
19. Brown T (2005) Strategy by design, fast company, June 2005. http://www.fastcompany.com/52795/strategy-design
20. Brown T (2009) Change by Design: How Design Thinking Transforms Organizations and Inspires Innovation. HarperBusiness, New York
21. Gould J, Lewis C (1985) Designing for usability: key principles and what designers think. CACM 28(3):300–311
22. Lavie T, Tractinsky N (2004) Assessing dimensions of perceived visual aesthetics of web sites. Int J Hum Comput Stud 60(3):269–298
23. Wang K (2015) The ultimate guide to hamburger menus and their alternatives. http://apptimize.com/blog/2015/07/the-ultimate-guide-to-hamburger-menus-and-alternatives/
24. Sutherland J (2003) SCRUM: get your requirements straight before coding. https://www.scruminc.com/scrum-get-your-requirements-straight/
25. Cockburn A, Highsmith J (2001) Agile software development: the people factor. IEEE Comput 34(11):131–133
26. Highsmith J, Cockburn A (2001) Agile software development: the business of innovation. IEEE Comput 34(9):120–127
27. Ungar JM, White JA (2008) Agile user centered design: enter the design studio – A case study. In: Proceedings of the CHI 2008. ACM, New York, pp 2167–2177
28. Knapp J (2016) Sprint: how to solve big problems and test new ideas in just five days. Simon and Schuster, New York
29. VersionOne (2015) State of Agile™ Survey. www.versionone.com/pdf/state-of-agile-development-survey-ninth.pdf
30. Porter S (2011) Chickens and pigs, scrum.org community publications Article 90, https://www.scrum.org/About/All-Articles/articleType/ArticleView/articleId/90/Chickens-and-Pigs
31. Plonka L, Sharp H, Gregory P, Taylor K (2014) UX design in agile: a DSDM case study. In: Agile processes in software engineering and extreme programming: 15th International conference, XP 2014, Lecture Notes in Business information processing, Springer
32. Cockton G (2008) Revisiting usability's three key principles. In: Czerwinski M, Lund AM, Tan DS (eds) CHI 2008 extended abstracts 2473–2484
33. Sy D (2007) Adapting usability investigations for agile user-centered design. J Usability Stud 2(3):112–132

34. Sy D, Miller L (2008) Optimizing Agile user-centred design. In: CHI '08 extended abstracts on human factors in computing systems (CHI EA 08), ACM, 3897–3900
35. Cockton G (2012) UCD: critique via parody and a sequel. In: Proceedings of the CHI 2012 extended abstracts on human factors in computing systems (CHI EA '12). ACM 1–10
36. DSDM Consortium (2014) The DSDM Agile project framework. DSDM Consortium Ebook: https://www.dsdm.org/resources/dsdm-handbooks/the-dsdm-agile-project-framework-2014-onwards
37. Shuja AK, Krebs J (2007) IBM Rational unified process reference and certification guide: solution designer (RUP). Pearson Education, Indianapolis, IBM Press
38. Brhel M, Meth H, Maedche A, Werder C (2015) Exploring principles of user-centered agile software development: a literature review. Inf Softw Technol 61:163–181
39. da Silva T, Martin A, Maurer F, Silveira M (2011) User-centered design and Agile methods: a systematic review. In: Proceedings of the agile methods in software development (Agile 2011)
40. Jia Y (2012) Survey on scrum and UCD. Master thesis, Uppsala University
41. Woolrych A, Hornbæk K, Frøkjær E, Cockton G (2011) Ingredients and meals rather than recipes: a proposal for research that does not treat usability evaluation methods as indivisible wholes. Int J HCI 27(10):940–970
42. Holtzblatt K, Wendell JB, Wood S (2005) Rapid contextual design: A how-to guide to key techniques for user centered design. Elsevier, San Francisco
43. Frayling C (1993) Research in art and design. RCA Res Pap 1(1)
44. Yee JSR (2010) methodological innovation in practice-based design doctorates. J Res Pract 6(2), Article M15. http://jrp.icaap.org/index.php/jrp/article/view/196/193
45. Cockton G (2013) Design isn't a shape and it hasn't got a centre: thinking BIG about post-centric interaction design. In: Proceedings. MIDI '13. ACM, Article 2, p 16
46. Cockton G (2015) Domain Values and Method Transferability: an Initial Framework. In: Christou G, Zaphiris P, Law ELC (eds) 1st European workshop on HCI design and evaluation, IRIT Press, p 85–90. www.irit.fr/recherches/ICS/projects/twintide/upload/427.pdf
47. Adlin T (2010) The essential persona lifecycle: your guide to building and using. Morgan Kaufmann, San Francisco
48. Cohn M (2004) User stories applied. Addison-Wesley Professional, Boston
49. Kaczor K (2011) 5 common mistakes we make writing user stories. Scrum Alliance Member Article. https://www.scrumalliance.org/community/articles/2011/august/5-common-mistakes-we-make-writing-user-stories
50. Yetim F, Draxler S, Stevens G, Wulf V (2012) Fostering continuous user participation by embedding a communication support tool in user interfaces. AIS Trans Hum Comput Interact 4(2):153–168
51. Dax J, Ludwig T, Meurer J, Pipek V, Stein M, Stevens G (2015) FRAMES – a framework for adaptable mobile event-contingent self-report studies. In: Diaz P, Pipek V, Ardito C, Jensen C, Aedo I, Boden A (eds) End-user development, LNCS, 9083. Springer, Dordrecht, pp 141–155
52. Koskinen IK, Zimmerman J, Binder T, Redström J, Wensveen S (2011) Design research through practice: from the lab, field, and showroom. Morgan Kaufmann, Waltham
53. Hertzum M, Molich R, Jacobsen NE (2014) What you get is what you see: revisiting the evaluator effect in usability tests. Behav Inform Technol 33(2):143–161
54. Woolrych A, Cockton G (2001) Why and when five test users aren't enough. In: Vanderdonckt J, Blandford A, Derycke A (eds) Proceedings of the IHM-HCI 2001, Joint AFIHM-BCS Conference on human-computer interaction vol II, Cépadès Éditions
55. Garnik I, Sikorski M, Cockton G (2014) Creative sprints: an unplanned broad agile evaluation and redesign process. In: Proceedings of the NordiCHI '14. ACM 1125–1130

Part I
Case Studies

Chapter 2
User Integration in Agile Software Development Processes: Practices and Challenges in Small and Medium Sized Enterprises

Oliver Stickel, Corinna Ogonowski, Timo Jakobi, Gunnar Stevens, Volkmar Pipek, and Volker Wulf

Abstract HCI and CSCW research as well as practice has strongly indicated the value of integrating (end) users in software development processes. Such integration can help address actual needs and wants, to avoid undesirable developments and to strengthen the User Experience of a product. A user-focused approach to software development has some conceptual overlap with agile software development practices, such as quick and iterative (user) testing. However, out in the wild, organisations seem to have difficulties actually mapping user-centered development with agile processes for a variety of reasons ranging from organisational or hierarchical aspects up to financial issues. This problem seems specially prevalent in Small and Medium sized Enterprises (SMEs) where such constraints can be even tighter than in larger organisations. To help understand those problems and to identify possible solutions, we turned to three quite different German software SMEs, varying in size, market focus and organisational structure. By way of qualitative field studies, we were able to identify key roles and tools as well as methodological, organisational and analytical practices and challenges in integrating (end) users into agile software development.

Keywords Agile software development • User centered design • User feedback • Case study • Qualitative study

O. Stickel (✉) • C. Ogonowski • T. Jakobi • V. Pipek • V. Wulf
University of Siegen, Siegen, Germany
e-mail: oliver.stickel@uni-siegen.de; corinna.ogonowski@uni-siegen.de;
timo.jakobi@uni-siegen.de; volkmar.pipek@uni-siegen.de; volker.wulf@uni-siegen.de

G. Stevens
Bonn Rhein-Sieg University of Applied Sciences, Augustin, Germany
e-mail: gunnar.stevens@h-brs.de

© Springer International Publishing Switzerland 2016   49
G. Cockton et al. (eds.), *Integrating User-Centred Design in Agile Development*,
Human–Computer Interaction Series, DOI 10.1007/978-3-319-32165-3_2

2.1   Introduction

Software has become an invaluable part of private and professional life all over the world. This has led to Usability and User Experience[1] becoming increasingly important factors for the success or failure of ICT systems. While this obviously holds true for all sort of systems allowing user interaction, for the purpose of this contribution, we will focus on software systems. For the software world, we have solid research [13] as well as norms such as the DIN EN ISO 9241 suggesting that integration of (end) users in all phases of a development project is one of the most central factors for positive UUX.

Looking at the economically important sector of Small and Medium Sized Enterprises (SMEs) however, we frequently find deficits in the incorporation of UUX methods into software development. Hering et al. [14] indicate factors such as financial, logistical, hierarchical or methodological issues that hold the SME sector back with regards to the systematic integration of users and user feedback in development processes. Furthermore, norms and process models such as the aforementioned ISO 9241 or user-centered design (UCD) often lack clarity regarding the *actual* implementation of user integration and how to fit this into established process models in organisations.

Our contribution addresses this research/practice gap by helping to identify relevant issues for SMEs when dealing with user integration and presenting solutions as well as best practices evolved in these organisations. We grounded our work in a practice-based, socio-technical understanding of Human Computer Interaction (HCI) and Computer Supported Collaborative Work (CSCW) [33]. Consistent with this base, we chose qualitative case studies in three contrasting German software SMEs as our main research instrument:

Foo[2] is one of the largest German SMEs in the software business focusing on end users with quite nuanced processes for the integration of user-centered methods and agile development processes.

Bar is a relatively large SME (if decidedly smaller than Foo) producing software and hardware for end users. Bar's focus on UUX has a briefer history and smaller extent than Foo's.

Qux is a very small, design-driven software company which mainly fulfills orders, i.e. with no direct end user market.

Based on our fieldwork in all three organisations, we were able to identify *Roles, Channels and Media* as well as *Interpretation and Filtering* of user feedback as the three main themes moderating (and moderated by) the success or failure of user integration in agile development processes. In the following sections, we first give

---

[1]From here on, we will abbreviate "Usability and User Experience" as UUX. For the purpose of this chapter, we do not need the distinction between more task-focused and more ludic aspects.

[2]All organisation names as well as all personal names in this contribution are anonymised for privacy reasons.

an overview of the relevant state of the art before reporting our results and discussing them with a focus on these three themes.

2.2   Related Work

In this section, we present an overview of the relevant scientific background and literature, starting with a very brief primer on agile software development, leading up to the relevance of user integration for positive UUX and finally the synthesis of both aspects.

2.2.1   Agile Software Development

Agile software development [2] refers to relatively new paradigms for structuring ICT projects such as Scrum [25] or Kanban [1]. Agile methods differ from classical process models such as the "waterfall" in rejecting the notion of a "heavy", largely predefined and pre-planned project which is then processed step by step. Instead, agile methods take into account changes occuring during software projects and propose to prepare for and embrace them [31]. This results in four central values as codified in the *Agile Manifesto* [2]: (1) Individuals and interactions over processes and tools (2) Working software over comprehensive documentation (3) Customer collaboration over contract negotiation (4) Responding to change over following a plan.

2.2.2   User Integration for a Better UUX

Existing literature provides several reasons for integrating users and customers into the design process including improved UUX as well as political, economical and ethical considerations [34]. For example, Participatory Design (PD), arguably the earliest systematical approach for active user involvement in software development, originates in workplace democracy movements [4, 9], supported by trade unions. However, commercial software companies also discovered and implemented PD, valuing methods such as collaborative storyboarding or group elicitation approaches [11]. *Active* user participation was deemed to be effective since actual users of a product were understood to know their own perspectives and needs best [22]. While most "original" – political – PD approaches do not necessarily consider positive UUX as a core focus, various understandings of PD have evolved with different accentuations. For example, the American school of PD dropped the political framework and rather pursued the development of more efficient products [15], thus taking user integration in a more UUX-focused direction.

Later approaches to user integration in ICT development projects include Integrated Organisation and Technology Development (OTD) [32] as well as STEPS

[12]. Both approaches are normative software development models that involve close collaboration of users and developers. Both are also more focused on their application in organisations. However, as they are designed for a very close and rather intricate collaboration of developers and customers, they are not easily usable for the development of mass-market off-the shelf software – especially not for SMEs, considering their often limited resources [13]. Looking at the earlier stages of ICT projects, we should also mention von Hippel [30], who has long focused on User Driven Innovation and its benefits. However, the focus on early phases also limits this approach.

Current trends include Design Case Studies which involve significant user integration [33] as well as Infrastructuring as a more holistic perspective on how to understand the development of socio-technical systems [23]. Managing user integration in ICT projects also increasingly relates to user-centered design (UCD). UCD, as codified in ISO 9241-210 can be seen as a normative design and development model that argues for user integration in all phases of a development process. Consequently, the UCD ideology specifically views the user as an asset of the product development process. Furthermore, unlike older models, it explicitly focuses on generating a positive UUX as well. Within a UCD process, users should be included in early phases (ideation) and user research should be conducted. This covers everything that helps to understand who the users are, what their system of values and requirements are and so on. Further on in the process, users can participate in mock-up generation or evaluation and similar activities before finally being consulted in the evaluation of releases. Since UCD was developed to be adaptable to existing software engineering approaches, its specification leaves room for tailoring to a local context which in turn needs interpretation and negotiation in the form of interaction between users, designers, engineers and other stakeholders.

2.2.3 Synthesis and Research Gap

Agile methods favour 'customer'-focus [2] while UCD and UUX obviously address 'users'. Especially in corporate settings, the customer does not usually coincide with the end user. However, both ways of thinking highlight stakeholders and their needs instead of favouring a process-focused view. In this regard both approaches share quite relevant characteristics [6]. It is, however, much less clear how to integrate them on a practical than a conceptual level:

There are multiple positive reports on adaption and integration attempts of UCD and UUX. Isomursu [16], for example, presents a single case study on a multinational corporation and its shift to agile methods. Also, Sy [29] reports on beneficial effects on a product's UUX in the case of a big corporation through the combination of two measures: firstly, the development process was restructured in favour of a more agile procedure, and secondly, the reporting of usability testing activities were modified to match the agile cycles. However, it has also been noted quite frequently [10, 19, 21] that the actual implementation of UCD – and more generally, the optimal combination and positioning of different UUX methods – is not yet well understood in practice. Hence, there have been different scientific workshops and tutorials, e.g. [18] as well as suggestions for procedural models or frameworks to facilitate integration. Silva et al. [26], for example, base their framework on an Interaction Design Lifecycle and specifically include design cycles into the agile process. Beyer [3] focuses on UUX professionals and how to integrate them in agile environments, not least by facilitating understanding for UUX development strategies. Scrum roles themselves are also regarded as relevant for the successful integration of UUX and Agile. Singh [27] identifies the Product Owner (PO) as the most crucial role for such attempts and states that POs are often overwhelmed since they have to coordinate many stakeholders, artifacts and ceremonies and are not necessarily qualified in UUX. This leads the authors to propose the appointment of two POs, one of which focuses on more traditional responsibilities in the Scrum model while the other one's responsibilities lean towards UUX [27].

Overall, literature suggests manifold thematic relations between UCD/UUX methods and agile software development. There have also been investigations and practical attempts to integrate both approaches, leading to some beneficial results in practice as well as some more theoretical concepts. However, prior work strongly indicates that the understanding of UCD/UUX and agile still leaves many gaps, especially regarding the systematic understanding of the actual practices and challenges faced by organisations *in the wild* [8, 10]. This contribution is an attempt at helping to fill this gap by way of three comparative case studies with a focus on the domain of SMEs.

2.3   Cases

In the following sections, we will first describe our three cases in more detail before summarizing them in a tabular form.

2.3.1   Foo: A Very Large SME with Established UUX Practices

Foo is a large SME with about 500 employees and a strong corporate focus towards UUX and user integration. Actively pushed by the company's management, this culture has evolved over many years. During those years, Foo has experimented with different approaches towards development and/or user integration, ranging from traditional waterfall models to Participatory Design projects (explicitly framed as such). Foo's product portfolio is centered on software systems for end users with an emphasis on personal and organizational finance administration and management tools. We mainly worked with one project team within Foo which is responsible for iFin, a tool for personal finance management. iFin is a mass-market product, cross-platform (mobile and desktop, multiple operating systems) and is developed in an agile fashion, utilizing Scrum. iFin has settled on 4-week sprint cycles and the agile team consists of developers and designers. Some other roles we will be referring to later are not part of the Scrum team – they are asked to work with the Scrum team as needed. Hence those roles do not have to work in fixed sprint lengths but – given the need to collaborate with the 'core' Scrum team – they are aware of the sprints and their work is moderated by those cycles and other agile practices developed by the Scrum team.

2.3.2   Bar: A Big SME with Emerging UUX Practices

Bar is a large SME with about 200 employees. Until recently, Bar focused on customer home electronic components. Especially in the area of home network components, Bar has developed nuanced processes and competences. However, more recently, the company decided to develop a line of Smart Home components which were about to be launched on the market at the time of our study. This led Bar to focus more strongly on software development in general and interface design in particular. Due to the increased amount of user interaction with smart home devices in comparison to more passive network electronics, UUX was explicitly addressed, too. Originally a hardware-developing and engineering company, Bar is used to managing projects with a strongly phase-oriented process model. However, at micro level, at least the software team reportedly self-organizes using Scrum. Studying the case of iHome development, we found several more ways in which Bar departed from the phase-oriented path and tended towards more agile methods. The complexity of a Smart Home system, the multitude of (also external) parties involved and the stronger emphasis on interaction components led to a mixture of milestones and agile ways of completing them. Integrating end users into the evaluation of iHome prior to market launch was deemed especially important by Bar. Our work with Bar focused on the smart home team, their emerging agile development processes as well as their in-house user test sample for working with and evaluating prototypes, both in terms of functionality and UUX.

2.3.3   Qux: A Small, Design-Driven Software Company

Qux is a growing but still quite small software developing company of just 11 employees. They offer development and consultancy services and design of innovative software and mobile apps as well as digital products in areas such as the Internet of Things, smart home, energy and e-mobility. Being a service company, Qux's focus is less on selling to end users directly but rather on projects for their customers, who provide the products and services to end users. The company has successfully established a flat team hierarchy. It is only divided in two units: design and development, which are supplemented by the functions of both CEOs (Scrum Master/Project Manager and Creative Director) and Social Media Marketing. One of the CEOs, who is responsible for project management, also manages the commercial tasks of the company and hence does not carry the title of Product Owner. Related to the company's hierarchy, Qux has a corporate culture and image with a strong focus on communication and exchange between all employees; design-driven development; UUX and decision making. Their agility is reflected in the management of their projects. Projects were conducted using 2- to 4-week sprints, depending on the project's size. Customers play an active role in the design and development process. In regular sprint reviews they have to provide additional feedback about the design process and results with respect to current developments of the market or internal strategical decisions in order to keep project progression flexible and close to market trends. Transparency and continuous communication with customers is a key issue for Qux too.

2.3.4 Comparative Overview of Three Cases

For a comparative overview of the three cases and their characteristics. Table 2.1 provides details and summarizes data with respect to size, study focus, agility and peculiarities of the SMEs.

2.4 Method

In this section, we will explain our methodology and our analytical process. Subsequently, we will provide an overview of our data and coding scheme.

2.4.1 Study Design and Data Collection

How does [Foo | Bar | Qux] integrate user input and feedback into their agile software development process and how does this relate to UCD?

This was the basic research question motivating our study. It is important to note that we did not approach the field with a focus on up-front theory but rather based our approach on open, field-driven research, inspired by Grounded Theory (GT) [28]. Therefore in each case, we went quickly into the field where we iteratively developed our understanding of the company's practices as well as our research strategy according to our findings. We deemed a (field-)data-driven approach to be important given the disparities between theory and practice and the ambiguities described in the state of the art.

Table 2.1 Case summaries

	Foo	Bar	Qux
Size	About 500 employees	About 200 employees	11 employees
Product portfolio	Wide variety of software products for mobile and desktop, focused on finance administration on the personal level as well as for the SME and nonprofit sectors	Variety of products concerned with home networks. More recently soft- and hardware for the smart home including heavy coordination with third parties	Software solutions focusing on mobile applications, front and back end applications for the domains of energy, smart home, renewable energies, e-mobility and the Internet of things
Study focus	iFin, a cross-platform personal finance management tool	iHome, a soft- and hardware ecosystem for smart homes	No specific project, lateral study through the company
Agility	Scrum team utilizing 4- week sprints. Core Scrum team (mostly developers) is supported by other teams such as e.g. an inhouse usability lab who do not work in formal sprints – however, the Scrum team sets the overall pace	Complexity led away from sprints to milestone- oriented development. Requirements engineering upfront, but highly iterative within three main phases: proof of tech-concept in the wild, proof of combination of HW and UI concept, beta testing	Scrum-oriented project management with 2- to 4-week sprints based on project size. Company's philosophy follows principles of user-centered design. Active integration of customers in design and development by regular sprint reviews
Peculiarities	Long company history and company culture of user-centricity (established over years). Three product owners instead of one for iFin	Established their own in-house testbed, semiprofessionalised. Project manager with sole direct contact to users, defines usability concepts	Mainly business to business but target is often mass-market. Project manager is not framed as project owner. High transparency to customers

In total, we conducted 15 interviews. Seven of them were at Foo and four at Bar and Qux respectively. Within the iFin team at Foo, we conducted interviews with a Product Owner (PO), Social Media Management (a one-person team), the head of the support team[3] for all products (not just iFin), a member of the support team specialised in iFin and a developer as well as two members of the in-house usability lab. We also conducted participant observations during usability tests in the in-house lab (3h) as well as during a Scrum planning meeting (4h). At Bar, we conducted interviews with the heads of the development team, the Design and Verification and Testing (DVT) team, the product marketing team as well as the responsible PO. At

---

[3]To be clear: Foo's support team is the user support department, i.e. the staff responsible for helping customers with issues. The name 'support team' is actually an in-vivo code from the fieldwork at Foo.

Table 2.2 Data index

ID	Description	ID	Description
I-F-01	Product owner	I-B-01	Product manager
I-F-02	Social media officer	I-B-02	Head of development
I-F-03	Chief of support	I-B-03	Head of design, verification and testing
I-F-04	Customer lab	I-B-04	Head of marketing
I-F-05	First level support	I-Q-01	CEO 01: scrum master & head of project management
I-F-06	Software developer	I-Q-02	CEO 02: creative director
I-F-07	PO other project	I-Q-03	Senior art director UI/UX
O-F-01	Scrum sprint planning meeting	I-Q-04	Mobile developer
O-F-02	Two usability tests		

Qux, we conducted interviews with two of the three CEOs who also acted as Scrum Master/Head of Project Management (PM) and Creative Director (CD) respectively. Similar interviews were conducted with a Senior Art Director UI/UX and a Mobile Developer.

In Table 2.2, we have indexed all interviews and observations. For clarity: I-F-04 was an interview with two participants (the full staff of Foo's in-house usability lab); I-F-07 was an interview with a PO for a different product team than iFin since this PO was referred to us as one of the central experts in regards to agile software development and UCD in the company[4]; and in cases such as I-B-03 and I-Q-01, one person fills multiple roles.

The interviews lasted between 60 and 120 min and were recorded as well as transcribed pragmatically, i.e. full verbatim transcriptions utilising only markers for salient events such as laughter, peculiar facial expressions or breaks. However, we did not include micro-expressions, precise break times, detailed pitch analyses, etc. since we did not deem such data necessary for our research interest in practices and challenges. All interviews utilised a guideline which evolved in the field, led by the field. The interview language was German in all cases, the quotations in this contribution are translated. Transcripts were supplemented by handwritten field notes and memos (about 25 pages). Furthermore, we gathered artifacts such as user stories, bug reports or usability reports, mainly at Foo because of its bigger size and the availability of many such artifacts as well as the fact that Foo was our first case study and the data helped us to open up the field. Finally, we supplemented our interviews by multiple further inquiries to the interview partners via Skype, phone and email during the analytical process whenever relevant questions arose. Brief descriptions of the data sources can be found in Sects. 2.3.1, 2.3.2, 2.3.3 and an index in Table 2.2.

---

[4]At this point in the analytical process, it had already become clear that the intersection of those two topics would be central to our study.

2.4.2   Data Analysis

All data and artifacts were subsequently coded axially and selectively using a GT approach [28]. However, we do not claim to have established a 'Theory of UCD and Agile' – we feel that such an encompassing theory would necessitate multinational and even more contrasting cases as well as a longer period of time. Rather, our analytical process followed GT methodology and can serve as one of many pieces in a more comprehensive puzzle towards a theory. To clarify even more: we oriented ourselves on Thematic Analysis [5] which, essentially, is GT without the overhead of extensive theory building but with the option to add that on top iteratively. The coding process started immediately after the first interview and was continued and evolved throughout the research activities. During the field research phases, we held weekly discussion and mirroring meetings regarding the coding activities in our research group. This also included researchers who were not active in the field, some not even in our research project at all. These researchers helped by asking questions those working in the field did not think of, forcing the latter to explain a significant amount of tacit information. The coding structure continued to change up to the point when the gathered data no longer added significant new insights (saturation). This also helps to explain the different contents of data collected in the three cases – with the evolution of a denser coding scheme, (transferable) insights led to saturation points more quickly as per the intention of GT-inspired approaches.

Table 2.3 provides an overview of the theme structure as well as examples of sub-codes for each case. The three central themes boil down to "Roles", "Channels and Media" and "Filtering and Interpretation". Our report on results which follows in the next section is also oriented on this structure.

2.5   Results

In this section, we will report on the three most important themes as listed in Table 2.3 as well as their interrelations, starting with the *Roles*, leading up to *Channels and Tools* and finally, aspects of *Filtering and Interpretation*.

2.5.1   Roles

2.5.1.1   Foo

With Foo, we found multiple roles to be in contact with users. The support team obviously has most points of contact since they are confronted with a wide variety of user issues on a daily basis. However, they are not only trained to solve those issues but also to try and understand where they come from and ask for more feedback than strictly necessary to solve the issue in order to provide input for

Table 2.3 Examples of analysed sub-codes

Themes	Foo	Bar	Qux
Roles	PO, multiple POs, Social media management, support team, developer, role empowerment, differentiation of POs' skills, in-house usability lab	PO, DVT, development, user contact, categorising feedback, managing feedback, market analysis, in charge of usability, functional tester, coordinator	Project manager, creative director, senior art director, social media manager, developer, quality management, testing by noninvolved employees
Channels & tools	Email, chats, phone, letter, forums, facebook, twitter, TFS, bug tracker, daily stand-up, Scrum, sprint, user story, facebook, daily stand-up, sprints, open and honest communication, channels towards the user, channels from the user, app stores, blogs, grapevine, coffee corner	Bug-tracking, office grapevine, technical proof of concept, PO as field tester, friendly user testing, product specification tool, employee participation, missing standard tools, wireframing, outsourcing user studies, gap user value – integration, iterative development, milestones, chat, phone, virtual seminars	Bug-tracking, test cases, user story, daily stand-up, coffee corner, friendly user testing, app stores, market research customer sprint review, third-party services, email, phone facebook, missing standard tools, (non) filtered feedback, integration in management software, taking a step back as designer
Filtering & interpretation	XYZ (long-planned feature preventing certain feature requests from being implemented), what does the customer actually want? Company culture, grapevine, discussions, database, lead users, conflicts, mood	Prioritisation via frequency, ticket-system, expenditure processing feedback to make it useful, log files, text-data, pictures, video-data, limits of outsourcing feedback, sharing feedback with third parties in the project	Frequency, missing metadata, feedback requests, sorting & editing, communication with customers, ticket-system, testers' aptitude, reliability in third party services, lab tests as stress situation, environment control

product development. To this end, Foo has kept their support team in-house, located near the development, management and other teams. They are also actively trying to foster a culture of deep and long-term engagement with, as well as knowledge about, Foo's products. To let a first level support employee speak for himself:

> I've been working for Foo for about ten years now. I can use the software blindfolded. I can find problems and difficulties while standing on my head. I-F-05

Foo also has an in-house 'customer lab', which is a traditional usability lab, staffed by two UUX-experts. They carry out structured user testing at the request of the iFin team and report to the Product Owner. However, the customer lab is not part of any team as such – in essence, they offer a service to all of Foo's development teams. Furthermore, Foo also has a defined role for Social Media management (SMM). The SMM tries to engage with users by way of providing them with information, monitoring discussions, trying to mediate if necessary and very consciously tries to get a "feeling for the mood" (I-F-02) on Social Media in regards to Foo's own products as well as the competition. Like the support team, the SMM is not part of the Scrum team as such and also has some other duties in the company (such as maintaining blogs not connected to iFin). However, the SMM's main focus is iFin and by far the majority of her work time is spent on this project.

As in established Scrum doctrine, we found the role of the PO to be the central hub within the different approaches of user integration and user contact in Foo. There are two notable observations in regards to Foo's PO structure for iFin: First, there are actually three POs. One manages daily affairs such as codifying user stories; the second one focuses on the epics and the third has a background in design. The PO-team's skills compliment each other; however, they also consult with internal experts (such as the SMM) on a case-by-case basis. Second, while it is certainly in the Scrum-spirit for the PO to represent end-users (and hence, to engage with them as well), some of iFin's long-term users even have the PO's phone numbers and call them occasionally, especially when something in the product changes in a way they do not like. Software developers themselves do not usually have user contacts in Foo.

2.5.1.2   Bar

Bar has a product-oriented organisational structure based on Business Units. The company's software development teams are familiar with Scrum methods and use sprints when working with their core product line of home networking systems. However, the general process of developing a product is not iterative:

> The usual procedure here is the so-called phase model. We divide this into five parts: Evaluation, conception, planning, and prototyping [and finalisation] phase - that's where you can see we have a background in hardware. [..] Within the development division we principally organise ourselves using Scrum. Not textbook-style, but tailored a little to Bar's needs. We do daily stand-ups, though, and plan our sprints with items. (I-B-02)

The specific requirements and the heavy software focus of iHome, however, have influenced the general project management and development process of Bar towards a more agile and iterative development, which is reflected by the emerging roles, tools used and integration of user feedback. The latter is generally rarely surveyed or integrated into Bar's development cycles, as user interaction with its products, especially via software, is only an optional feature. Therefore, with the decision to develop iHome, Bar enters new territory. For a better understanding of existing feedback practices, it is worth noting that our interviews focused on the development process of iHome before market launch. At this point, Bar had no experience in handling customer feedback after rollout but had only begun to specify strategies.

Direct user contact with a friendly user group is limited and structured in clear channels through a fixed sample of users as well as internal testing (more on this below). During development, Bar's 'Design, Verification and Testing' division was the central role responsible for testing and validating new software releases with regards to bugs and completeness compared to the requirements:

> Since the DVT is our last line of defense, they have to check somehow what has been developed ...Meaning they always compare the requirements with the result [result = a release] (I-B-01)

At the time of writing, Bar has also established a support team structure intended to work closely with users with the explicit goal of feeding back to product development. Like Foo, Bar also utilises Social Media as well – however, with Bar, Social Media work is co-located within the marketing division, whereas Foo has a separate, explicit organisational role for Social Media management. Bar also planned to hold web based seminars to explain possible usage scenarios to customers and has included a direct chat feedback mechanism in their software. Furthermore, the software also features classic support options via mail and phone. Bar's development team is more distributed than Foo's, including more external partners, with the in-house development team focusing on coordination and conception. As with Foo, Bar's central role for UUX is the business unit's PO. He handles all reports and user feedback and makes all decisions in regards to UUX. During the user testing phase, he mainly drew feedback from the office grapevine and the bug tracking system used by test households:

> [...] Then, they [user feedback and feature requests, consolidated by the DVT] came to me. [...] and I had to go back to the wireframe or make clear how this and that is intended [...]. (I-B-01)

The PO consults with external companies on a case-by-case basis. He has direct user contact, mainly for concrete, deeper enquiries and user problems within the test sample. This approach, however, is rather unstructured and is either prompted by a specific problem description via the bug tracking system or by friendly users directly approaching the PO. In addition to the PO with his quite direct channel, DVT sometimes has contact with friendly users, but less frequently and only when clarification is needed on a bug reported. While these structures have proven successful for the beta test, up to this point, Bar has not yet decided which department should take responsibility for handling feedback from real customers after the launch, nor how to manage underspecified feedback.

2.5.1.3   Qux

Qux has a very flat hierarchy which splits up into a Design- & Development unit, Social Media Marketing as well as the roles of both CEOs who act as Scrum Master & Head of Project Management (PM) and Creative Director (CD), respectively. The PM is responsible for internal quality control of concepts and releases while the CD and the Senior Art Director UI/UX (AD), located within the Design & Development unit, manages all UUX aspects. Hence Qux has formed a structure where the PM takes on what might be called the more managerial aspects and the AD the user-focused ones, in comparison to Foo and Bar who subsume both aspects under the role of their respective POs.

In contrast to the typical role of a PO, in Qux the PM takes the responsibility not only for these tasks but also for additional functions of the company. Besides the project management of all projects realised by the company, he manages commercial tasks which is why they framed his role as PM. Based on the number of employees, there is still no need for several Product Owners, who are responsible for single projects or markets. This might change if the company grows further.

A central distinction of Qux as a software company in comparison to Foo and Bar is that their customers are generally not their end users. Hence, we find roles such as support teams and product-specific social media engagement not within Qux but rather within their portfolio of customer organisations. Wider user tests (and hence roles with user contact) are also outsourced to third parties or the respective customer organisation takes charge of those activities itself. Qux also actively asks the customer organisations for feedback after each sprint.

Furthermore, this structure brings with it a certain fluidity of roles. On a case-by-case basis, Qux leverages all of its staff as well as friends and family for ad-hoc testing and feedback. This culture is illustrated quite well by the actual Senior Art Director UI/UX:

> [...] my father, who has no affinity for such things [ICT]...I really like to just hand him stuff [beta versions] – just to see what he does. (I-Q-03).

The dynamic feedback loops between roles and units all converge on the PM. This approach of internal testing is based on a quite explicit corporate culture focused on user-centered design which encourages everybody working on a project to constantly take a step back and actively try to view the product through the eyes of a customer as well as a user:

> I think we are quite good in putting ourselves into those roles [users] [...] When somebody is working on a project, we also try to put him together with a colleague working on a different project [...], to get a different view. I think that's really important. (I-Q-02)

2.5.2   Channels and Tools

2.5.2.1   Foo

Central to Foo's agile Process is Microsoft's TFS which is used as a code repository as well as for handling and prioritising the backlog and supplementary data such as technical logs and feature requests as well as usability test reports. The developer especially, in addition to the POs, utilise TFS to manage and track iFin's development.

The support team utilises email, phone, fax, letters and chat as well as product-specific web-forums to engage with users directly, although the forums are focused on a *"customers help customers"* (I-F-03) approach. User feedback is taken from the support-specific ticket system and is put into the TFS if deemed valuable (more on this distinction in Sect. 2.5.3).

The Social Media manager mainly utilises Facebook and Twitter and, to a lesser extent, Blogs as channels to interact with and include users. Notably, she does not use any special Social Media management tool. She tries to contextualise user feedback as much as possible by utilising the rich data provided by Social Media. Subsequently, she directly engages with the POs in about feedback via email or face-to-face conversations. It is notable that she does not use the TFS even though she has access to it. Furthermore, regular surveys utilising the Net Promoter Score [17, 24] are carried out. When problems occur such as server outages, known bugs or similar issues, the Social media management informs customers via available channels and, more importantly, keeps them up to date. An example from I-F-02 was a bug occurring after an update which crashed the app immediately after starting it. A bug-fix was implemented and submitted to the app store very quickly but due to the approval process in the store concerned, the update needed time to be made available to the customers. The SMO kept the customers informed every step of the way which received positive feedback.

The customer lab's main channels and tools are traditional user tests with Thinking Aloud and sometimes Heuristic Evaluations and Cognitive Walkthroughs, although they also use methods such as Contextual Inquiry-inspired approaches, even in users' homes. The CL usually utilises series of tests with 5–20 participants and frames the results as comprehensive reports in a structured format. These are subsequently put into the TFS for the POs. Notably, it is also possible for everybody in the development team to tune into live video feeds from the usability testing sessions, although it has been expressed in I-F-04 and I-F-06 that developers do not usually do this, stating that the *"reports are enough"* (I-F-06). Tests in the CL are only carried out by request of the POs, the management or other decision making roles.

Apart from the TFS, the POs also have product-specific email accounts for free-form feedback which can be reached by the users from within iFin. Furthermore, the POs actively monitor as many app stores and similar places on the Web where users leave feedback of some sort. Foo even developed an in-house tool, specifically for the purpose of aggregating such reviews and making them manageable. As mentioned before, lead users sometimes contact the POs in person, utilising phones as well as email. Foo's POs also receive a certain amount of automated use tracking data. However, this is reserved for very specific and heavily debated cases due to privacy concerns. In line with Scrum practice, one of the most central tools for Foo's POs are User Stories which are built, maintained and utilised without any company- or project-specific peculiarities.

Central channels and media in Foo also include sprint review and planning meetings, meetings and discussions among the POs as well as daily stand-ups. As already indicated, only the Scrum team itself is included in those activities by default. Other roles such as the customer lab or the SMM can and will be asked to join specific meetings on request. However, a significant amount of coordination, discussion and other (meta-)work is also done without any formal media or channel: *All* interviewees in Foo talked about the importance of *"Flurfunk"* (I-F-01) (literally "corridor radio"– the office grapevine), coffee corners and informal meetings for coordination, sharing and discussing user feedback and user perspectives.

2.5.2.2   Bar

Within the unit we worked with, software development was initially structured in sprints, whereas the overall project plan featured three main phases: technological proof of concept, bringing UI and hardware together and, finally, beta testing with friendly households and bugfixing. Due to the complexity of both the system and the project itself, Bar switched to a rather milestone-driven development cycle, in which iteration was promoted. In particular, Bar decided to test its system in the wild during its hardware development, rather than relying on lab testing only. To our understanding, this was already a major difference compared to the usual development processes, which can be perceived as one example of acknowledging the need to involve users in earlier stages of development. Regarding the product specification, Bar utilises a custom in-house database system geared towards product management in which all requirements and properties of the product are held and maintained. Generally, the main features and style of the product were defined up front in this database which is used for all Bar products. Wireframes of the final system were developed quite early in the development process of iHome and can be understood to be similar to traditional target specifications for internal purposes as well as coordinating artifacts with external contractors. While usually static for Bar's other products, it turned out that the requirements specification of iHome called for much more flexible handling compared to typical products in the system, where there are fewer user interfaces. Central documents like wireframes were therefore included in the specification system, but were frequently updated throughout the whole project.

> [...] Meaning they [the DVT] always compare the requirements with the result [a release] and can refer to the wireframe [...] [interviewer asks how the wireframes changed during the development process] Well, they stayed relatively stable in scope [...] here and there, there were adaptions [...] (I-B-01)

While testing the technical proof of concept was limited to members of the software development division, systematic user testing regarding the UI is only applied when all desired features, as specified by the wireframes, have already been implemented. The focus in this phase is not on finding innovative new features or investigating end-user appropriation but rather to purposefully shape UI-components and interaction flows. To this end, Bar has joined forces with an external partner in order to establish a Living Lab [20] infrastructure as a test bed: About 30 households are given the product a few months before rollout in order to test it in their homes. These tests take place without instruction or rules apart from a commitment to actively use the system and test specific features after updates. Bugzilla has been implemented as a channel where users can input tickets. This is supplemented by occasional informal exchanges face-to-face. During the Living Lab phase, Bar also recognised that users did not always seem to log all their problems into Bugzilla, especially when the problems in question did not relate to hard and evident bugs:

> [...] If somebody had an issue beyond hard problems, they did not necessarily put it in [into Bugzilla]. There are many kinds of problems [...] like nice-to-haves, problems with understanding things or other issues like that. (I-B-01)

Additionally, comprehensive automated logging of use data is conducted in the background with the goal of making issues reproducible. After commercial rollout, Bar's plans are to have the support as well as the marketing divisions report directly to the PO on user feedback.

2.5.2.3   Qux

Qux uses Jira and Confluence as basic infrastructure in order to scaffold agility in their development process. These tools are utilised for internal coordination, especially for the PM. Furthermore, Qux's intention is also to establish customer-facing transparency. Hence, customers can also issue tickets and feedback (depending on the project structure agreed upon with the customer).

As regards active user feedback and participation, Qux employs different methods. In some cases, customer organisations carry out their own beta testing and feedback acquisition, select and aggregate it and send it to Qux. In other cases, all data from such tests is handed over to Qux without aggregation. Another option is to rely on direct user feedback via email generated from feedback-buttons and similar options integrated into applications, without the involvement of customer organisations. Qux's employees are aware of a wide variety of tools and systems to facilitate user feedback such as TestFlight or crowdsourcing systems, but on various occasions throughout the interviews, it becomes clear that they are still searching for an optimal system, especially one that meshes with agile development and more easily supports the handling of user feedback:

> [...] In each release in Scrum, there is one functional area, which gets completed and released, so to speak [...] there's always this wish, we are looking for a suitable platform [...] so we can say: 'you don't have to send me an email, you don't have to write down anything, you don't have to call me [...] then they could just hit a button, rate it [the specific result of a sprint/release], write a short text, Twitter-style at most [...] which would then just be sent to us so we could look at it. (I-B-01)

Apart from users, the customer organisations themselves are also actively queried as sources for feedback. Qux's PM puts it like this:

> [...] obviously, we also collect feedback from our customers. When we present something [...], we ask them quite in a quite focused way: '[...] please look at this'. We have them take responsibility, which is a good thing, since basically it is their project... Which is why I expect them to care and not just complain in the end, after a release [...] They have to give feedback frequently. (I-Q-01)

Furthermore, Qux frequently employs app store reviews and ratings as feedback channels, similarly to Foo. For more qualitative evaluations regarding UUX and UI, Qux has no formal tools or channels in place. Here, they rely on a user-focused and agile company culture as described above as well as ad-hoc feedback in meetings with customers and beta testers. Internally, user/customer and/or peer feedback is not only shared via Jira but also via daily stand-ups which are emphasised as an important tool:

> [...] we meet at 9:00 and everybody explains what he did the day before and what he plans to do today [...] you don't put things off[...] (I-Q-03)

This ritualistic form of informal exchange is supplemented by the grapevine, as it is at Foo. Like Foo, Qux then utilises User Stories and Bugs according to Scrum to codify and work with user feedback. Both artifacts are primarily input and maintained by the PM. To be clear, the PM is not the only *source* of such data, as explained above, but he *maintains* it.

2.5.3   Filtering and Interpretation

In the previous sections, we reported how and with the participation of which roles customer feedback is gathered and passed along through Foo, Bar and Qux. There is, however, one step missing – what emerged as *filtering and interpretation.*[5] This is the process of analysing and assessing user feedback as well as matching it with other feedback and/or internal goals. It also encompasses the challenge of identifying what the user *really* means or needs.

2.5.3.1   Foo

Foo has a long history of experimenting with the incorporation of user feedback in their development cycles and within this history, there have been failures, too. One example from the interviews (I-F-01, I-F-03, I-F-05) is a former experimental project grounded in Participatory Design in which the development of a software product relied heavily on a selected group's input and co-design. The members of this group were considered lead users in their domain. However, as it transpired, the product became much too specialised and thus did not appeal to many potential customers. Experiences like this reinforced Foo's focus on filtering as well as diversifying user feedback structures – as outlined in the previous sections, customer feedback is sampled through a wide range of channels, representing an attempt to level the playing field and keep specialisation appropriate to the product. What this means is that in the example of iFin, which has a very widespread and heterogeneous

---

[5]This is actually an in-vivo code. A PO at Foo used those exact words.

user base, specialisation has to be kept at a much broader and shallower level than for some of Foo's other products, e.g. those targeted at landlords and this much smaller and more focused group's specific needs.

The most important decision makers in relation to the filtering process are the POs. They consciously try to match their vision of the product with the customer input, adapt, prioritise and, if deemed necessary, modify or reject specific feedback. These decisions are grounded in the work performed by the roles described above. The customer lab does not engage in filtering per se but rather reports comprehensively, based on proven methods. The Social Media manager engages in partial filtering – she tries to match every piece of incoming input with previous decisions made by the POs. If the input is identical or very similar, she *"informs the customer accordingly"* (I-F-02), meaning notifications such as "request denied", "request in development" and so on. In such cases, she does not alert the POs. Should she hand a specific piece of new user feedback to the POs, she usually annotates it and states her opinion about it, i.e. actively enriches the user feedback based on her long-term experience with iFin. Notably, the support team filters actively. Customer feedback is gathered and discussed by the leader of the support team for the respective product and the chief of support, and filtered. Thus some feedback may never even reach the POs:

> If a person wants a new feature, the support employee checks the database weather the feature has already been requested by someone else. If so, the customer's ID is added to the incident. If not, the request is inserted in the database, which triggers a message to the team leader who assesses it. If he decides that the request is useful, the entry is set to 'visible' for the PO and the development team. (I-F-03)

Throughout all interviews with Foo, the exact operationalisation of the filtering processes remains somewhat vague but can be categorised broadly into two classes: *Qualitative* and *Quantitative* filtering. Quantitative filtering concerns the frequency and intensity of a specific type of feedback. The support team seems to utilise quantitative filtering which is also easy to do for them since the customer feedback from each 'call'[6] is recorded in their database. Quantitative aspects are, however, no guarantee for the feedback to get implemented – an often cited example (I01, I02, I03, I04, I05) from our interviews is that of a feature requested by a significant number of customers. However, this feature would make other, quite specific, long-term plans for the software impossible on a technical level. Hence, it is not implemented. The opposite constellation, i.e. individual or occasional cases of feedback seem more straightforward: (very) specific features which get requested by very few people usually get filtered out.

Qualitative filtering is a 'softer' aspect and seems primarily associated with experience, and a certain 'artfulness' rather than just hard data. It was next to impossible for all interviewees to really describe techniques and methods for qualitative filtering. Instead, in nearly every interview, it was stated explicitly or

---

[6]Terminology taken from the interviews – a 'call' should be understood as any kind of communication with users, not just telephone calls.

implicitly that a *lot* of knowledge about and a *"feeling for"* (I-F-01, similarly phrased also in I-F-03 and I-F-05) the product has to be developed over time in order to 'get it right'. A need to actually be a user of the product oneself has also been mentioned. All in all, Foo's Social Media management is the role with the deepest engagement in qualitative filtering procedures.

Qualitative and quantitative filtering mechanisms are reported to compliment each other well, e.g. within I-F-01 and I-F-04 and none of both aspects is viewed as sufficient by itself.

2.5.3.2 Bar

Like Foo, Bar's PO has a key function in the process of filtering and interpreting user feedback. He exclusively classifies and judges incoming information and notes from a range of roles through different channels. He has to decide and to match the pieces of information with the long-term goals for the product. On a quantitative, heuristic level, Bar judges feedback as relevant if it comes in 2–3 times in similar form:

> I give the thing [iHome] to 10 people and get 10 different opinions when I ask a specific question. That's rather difficult. At the moment, my strategy is that I look deeper into things after I hear issues 2–3 times. [...] Well, I always look at all the things [feedback], but when A says A, B says B and C says C, I stay with my opinion. (I-B-01)

While, so far this has proven effective, Bar's PO is also aware of the pitfalls of such an approach:

> But usually, you feel a bit like, well, the father of such a system. That makes each [...] feedback which is not exactly the same as your view of the system a critique and you have a certain defensive position. It is difficult to be neutral. (I-B-01)

Filtering and categorising feedback coming in from Bugzilla is managed by the DVT. They decide when and if something gets bumped up to the PO for decision making or directly to the development team for implementation. Our interview partners at Bar stated that informal, ad hoc (coffee corner-)talks between DVT, developers and the PO are central instruments in discussing, judging and triangulating feedback. Hence, we can also categorise filtering and interpretation mechanisms in Bar in quantitative and qualitative aspects. However, the structures are less complex and less differentiated than in Foo's case.

It is notable that Bar has yet to establish formal structures for who actually takes responsibility for the liaison and engagement with their test households, leading to difficulties in regards to filtering and interpreting feedback coming from those households:

> [...] there is the question if the developer should have frequent contact? I just don't know. Partially, sure, so he can hear opinions face-to-face and hear users' problems – just to understand. [...] [the users] all have their opinions. That has to be channeled in some way. Can you categorise such things? (I-B-02)

Lastly, Bar's PO is unsure if the test users might not become blind to certain issues due to routine and debates weather the user sample should be regularly changed, at least partially:

> [...] you just breeze over certain issues [after engaging with the product becomes routine]
> [...] if the beta-tester is at the point [where an issue arises] for the second time, he just skips it [referring to ignoring issues or finding workarounds]. (I-B-01)

In this regard, the PO consideres the potential limitations of outsourcing feedback collection and management to a service provider. While generally managing feedback is a burden, having an external mediator between users and decision makers within Bar was also deemed problematic. The close contact with the user and the PO's more or less direct and uncomplicated channels for approaching them for specification and further questions were valued very much, which led to the installation of the friendly user test set.

2.5.3.3   Qux

The situation for Qux is quite different from that of the other two SMEs with regards to filtering and interpretation of feedback. Based on their role as a service provider, they face the dichotomy of having to engage and negotiate with their customers as well as having to discuss and judge user and customer feedback internally. Qux's open communication between the CEOs and the units is helpful in providing a lean and agile structure to quickly engage with such feedback. The strings of such decision making processes all converge on the PM but subsequently have to be debated with the customer who makes the final decisions, sometimes forcing Qux into less than optimal decisions:

> For the most part, it is not very good if the customer selects [test] users itself but it's just the way it is; we don't have the target audience on board. It's a shame but it's the way it is. (I-Q-03)

Yet, Qux's employees voice rather unequivocal support for user-centered design, UUX and customer integration and – as mentioned before – reflect on those topics frequently. The Creative Director puts this in simple, decisive words:

> [Question about what would speak against a strong UCD-motivated process] "Just ignorance. If you do UCD, you put the user or the user group in your focus [...] which is logical. We don't build things for animals or for little grey men but for people." (I-Q-02)

Given their company structure, current practice in Qux's development process is to utilise as many automated use tracking, bug-tracking and data gathering tools as possible since those can be integrated easily and quickly (and cheaply) into their products. Data can thus be gathered in the background without disturbing users. This quantitative feedback is then triangulated with qualitative information which mainly comes in through email, either directly from users or aggregated from customers. This practice meshes well with Qux's agile process, in so far, as it can be considered during the task planning of further sprints. Quantitative heuristics similar to Bar's case are employed to speed the process up but Qux's sentiment is that qualitative information gathered by direct exchange and engagement with users would be more valuable. However, limited staff resources as well as Qux's customer relationship make it hard to implement and also limit the possibility for Qux's staff to pose questions to users if they arise about qualitative data aggregated by Qux's customers. Trust in the validity of such data is critical but Qux has no first-hand way of ensuring this. In addition to that, handling qualitative user feedback is currently done based on the number of similar issues are reported. If things are mentioned more than twice, feedback is worth discussing further internally discussion as well as with customers.

2.6 Discussion

Based on the three contrasting case studies, we see a growing awareness of the need to integrate users into soft- and hardware development. Even a classically non-iteratively operating company such as Bar either plans user integration from the beginning or learns about the value of iterative development and feedback during the process of developing products which rely heavily on user interaction and thus on a positive UUX. Our studies also show that the number of users a company can engage with as well as the differentiation of channels and tools can scale alongside the company's size. This is problematic since small companies like Qux who perceive the need to engage more with users simply cannot do so adequately. It is certainly possible to utilise internal testing, using ad-hoc methods such as convincing friends to give feedback or put a mental emphasis on a user perspective. However, it seems that the more people actually try to do this, the more they realise that such methods are inadequate and have pitfalls such as too much introspection or blindness to certain aspects. Such concerns become especially obvious when a second web of entanglements, i.e. external customers, becomes part of the process. A possible solution to such problems might be working with external, specialised partners for certain aspects of user engagement, such as Crowd-Testing platforms or testing *as a service*.[7] Through economies of scale, such services can be offered more cheaply than building complex infrastructures for user engagement and feedback internally and might be an entry point for more in-depth work with users, as witnessed in Bar's case.

The differentiation of roles is a highly interesting factor. It, too, can – and maybe even has to – scale alongside the size of the company itself. With Foo, we have an exceptional example where, over the course of many years, a very intricate web of different roles has emerged. Those roles and their different perspectives compliment each other well and eliminate many of the insecurities and problems we saw in the other cases, such as Bar's issues with responsibilities for certain aspects of working with users or Qux's problems with data validity.

---

[7]An example might be Living Labs as a service, see e.g. [20].

However, different roles do not just magically compliment each other – they also clash and Foo shows how to facilitate this in a purposeful manner. Company culture is the keyword here. Foo's Social Media management might, for example, disagree *very* strongly with a PO's vision for something since she actively tries to take on a qualitatively grounded user perspective. Heated discussions can happen – and, according to Foo, they should. All roles need to be empowered enough not to fear personal or other negative consequences yet still be able to get behind the overall product vision. Agile development can help here because it facilitates constant, quick engagement within teams and provides structures in which things can be explored and tested without great risk or cost (and hence, usually personal consequences). UCD can help as well because a common denominator in developing products *for users*, not 'for oneself' can put things into perspective, especially in regards to company culture. In Qux's case, we see that even a small company can form a very strong user focus in its culture. We also see that this has significant impact on the products (if not as much as a combination with a strong base in resources and differentiated roles, tools and channels).

With regards to channels and media, careful diversification also seems advisable. Again, Foo serves as the example of a large SME but it is much less the diversity of their tools and channels but rather their project-specific usage and focus which make them successful. For example, Foo's internet forums do not require much maintenance because they are framed as 'users help users'. Foo knows that their chat option enabling users to talk to the support team is not used all that much and could be cut without too much damage should the need ever arise; but they also know that they should probably not change PO's phone numbers lest they lose the engagement with their long-term expert users who freely offer them very valuable feedback. Certainly, smaller SMEs might not reach Foo's level of diversification but they *can* and should put careful, product- and user-specific thinking into which tools and channels they actually use, how they frame them and what they do with them.

Looking at more Scrum-related channels and media, it should be noted that diversification also seems relevant here: For example at Foo, roles such as Social Media manager or the support team do not participate by default in Scrum activities such as sprint planning meetings or daily stand-ups. At Bar, we found that only software development organises itself in a Scrum fashion. On the one hand, this leaves some room for different paces (customer support, for example, simply cannot happen in sprint cycles due to its mostly reactive nature) and 'outside' perspectives.[8] On the other hand, such diversification also induces friction and can make it hard for teams or even individuals to relate to each others' work practices such as pace, focus, long-term view, technical vs. social aspects and so on. This can be moderated by establishing and fostering informal exchanges and including non-members of the Scrum team into Scrum events, tools and channels on a case-by-case basis. However, we have our doubts that there can be a one-size-fits-all template on how to do this. It is an individual, highly context-specific process that needs time, intelligent *and*

---

[8] As in outside of sprints and their – by definition – extreme focus.

emphatic people as well as studying examples and constantly evaluating your own approaches as well as being willing to change them. In our opinion, this is actually one of the central advantages of agile processes with regards to UCD and UUX: they cultivate a culture steeped in constant self-evaluation, iterative changes and – crucially – the fact that rollbacks can be necessary and completely acceptable.

There seems to be one central point which can make or break user-centered agile software development in a Scrum project and that is the PO. There is a very great deal of power about the agile process itself as well as about UCD/UUX aspects centralised in one single person. The demands on such a person are very high and, depending on the project, may even be too high. Hedging one's bets in the sense of utilising more than one PO might, consequently, make sense as has already been indicated in literature [27]. We see this in all our cases. It is most visible in Foo's case with three POs, but Bar and Qux also distribute some aspects of what might be construed in strict Scrum doctrine (if there is such a thing) as the PO's responsibilities. Hence, codifying strict roles might not always be advisable and a certain leeway might make sense. For example, appointing a senior member of a UX-design team to a part-time PO assisting a continuous PO might be worth considering if actually employing two full-time POs with complimenting skill-sets is not viable due to project or financial constraints. However, not all agile processes are Scrum and most development processes – in practice – are not textbook Scrum or any other process model but are rather oriented on guidelines and otherwise adapted. Yet, based on our results and our experiences as well as other published research such as [27], we would think it likely that the importance of the PO is generalisable to an extent for processes involving a role similar to a PO.

Concerning the crucial aspect of filtering and interpreting user feedback, we also would like to point to the differentiation of roles, tools and channels as well as to a solid company culture as the main factors for success. Furthermore, making conscious decisions about including qualitative as well as quantitative types of data in the development process seems highly advisable as well as economic. Regarding the operationalisation of filtering and interpretative techniques; quantitative filtering seems to be the more straightforward one: given thorough documentation in database form, user feedback can be quantified and analysed rather easily. This data can supply very valuable intelligence into trends. However, it seems extremely important to supplement the quantitative view qualitatively: a *good* idea is not necessarily the same as an *often requested* one. This makes qualitative filtering a necessity. To use an analogy, in our interviews, we found certain similarities between this kind of filtering and qualitative sciences like ethnography: deep immersion into a product's user base and using the product oneself – getting a *feel* for it and forming *experience* – has been stated as very important and again, different perspectives and their intersections are considered valuable (one could compare this to the concept of inter-coder reliability in qualitative data analysis). Furthermore, a certain distance from possible moderating factors (like budget aspects or other business influences) seems associated with successful qualitative filtering in a manner not unlike the (artificial) naive approach utilised by ethnomethodologists. All in all, both views compliment each other and if possible, neither should be viewed on its own when engaging in filtering and interpretative action.

Thinking into the future, HCI and CSCW might provide help on the intersection of agile development and UCD in certain areas: As indicated by Qux's wishes for lean, almost Twitter-style feedback tools, Bar's utilisation of a partly externalised user testing infrastructure or Foo's quick and easy in-house tool to work with app store reviews, properly (co-)designed tools to support agile and user-centered processes are lacking. There are concepts from HCI and CSCW, such as comprehensive situated user feedback and engagement mechanisms right inside of products, see e.g. [34] or leveraging modern mobile devices to facilitate relatively lean, event-contingent qualitative and quantitative data collection [7]. However, even if we as researchers might not necessarily like it, those concepts can sometimes be unwieldy and are not necessarily suitable for market-driven environments, necessitating collaboration between researchers and professionals.[9]

2.7   Conclusion

We believe that there is no one-size-fits-all template for UCD/UUX and agile software development. The integration of user centered and agile principles is an artful business which necessitates many case-by-case decisions. However, we also believe that case studies such as the ones described in this contribution can help navigate at least parts of this difficulty – which, incidentally, is also why we decided to keep our discussion on a relatively high level. Furthermore, we think that *some* principles might be abstracted and generalised. We would like to close this contribution with a presentation of those principles by way of a concise section on suggestions.[10]

2.7.1   Suggestions for Integrating UCD and Agile Software Development

UCD is important for good UUX (and market success): This is the most obvious point and well-established in the scientific community but given the fact that multiple SMEs do not yet focus on UCD, it needs to be re-iterated.

---

[9]An attempt at an explicitly simple and lean user feedback system similar to what Qux wished for is currently being developed open source led by our research group. It is called 'Shake' and interested parties are welcome to try it out and/or contribute on http://github.com/UniSiegenCSCW/Shake.

[10]However, please keep in mind that those suggestions are grounded in literature and three essentially qualitative case studies. They can make no claim to completeness or applicability in *all* but we believe they are helpful in *many*.

Agile culture: Agile principles such as quick and iterative work (as well as scrapping things if need be) are well suited to be interwoven with UCD methods and user integration. However, there are still open questions (see below) and each case is *individual*.

Company culture: Multiple people with multiple perspectives need to have voices in the process and should to be able to challenge decision-making processes without retribution. Space and opportunity for informal exchanges and the grapevine are vital.

Differentiate roles, channels and tools: A differentiated, yet holistically considered organisational structure is a necessary base for UCD and agile development and should be constantly iterated upon. User integration at (too) isolated points might even be counter-productive. Triangulation is necessary.

Filtering and interpretation are necessary: Not everything that a customer wants can be done or is actually a good idea and vice versa. Good ideas can be hard to come by. Qualitative and quantitative filtering mechanisms should be employed.

Filtering is not trivial: Staff need to be educated, to actually use the product and to develop an appropriate frame of mind. Supportive ICT systems can be useful but are not necessarily available.

The PO is the critical point: A PO needs to make a significant amount of highly relevant decisions, which is why the person filling such a role needs a grounded (multi-stage) base for those decisions and a quite comprehensive skill-set.

Consider more than one PO: It may be sensible to employ more than one PO or at least to treat the role more fluidly. If this is done, it is vital to establish and communicate the different responsibilities of the POs so not to impact the agile process negatively.

Acknowledgements We thank all employees of three SMEs who participated in this study. This contribution has been funded by the German BMWi (Federal Ministry for Economic Affairs and Energy) though the projects CUBES (FKZ: 01MU14001A) and SmartLive (FKZ: 01MU12026A).

References

1. Anderson DJ, Reinertsen DG (2010) Kanban: successful evolutionary change for your technology business. Blue Hole Press, Sequim
2. Beck K, Beedle M, Van Bennekum A, Cockburn A, Cunningham W, Fowler M, Grenning J, Highsmith J, Hunt A, Jeffries R, Kern J, Marick B, Martin RC, Mellor S, Schwaber K, Sutherland J, Thomas D (2001) Agile manifesto. http://agilemanifesto.org/
3. Beyer H (2010) User-centered agile methods. In: Carrol JM (ed) Synthesis lectures on human-centered informatics, vol 3. Morgan & Claypool Publishers, pp 1–71
4. Bratteteig T, Bjerknes G (1995) User participation and democracy: a discussion of Scandinavian research on system development. Scand J Inf Syst 7(1):73–98
5. Braun V, Clarke V (2006) Using thematic analysis in psychology. Qual Res Psychol 3:77–101
6. Chamberlain S, Sharp H, Maiden N (2006) Towards a framework for integrating agile development and user-centred design. In: Extreme programming and agile processes in software engineering, Oulu, vol 4044, pp 143–153

7. Dax J, Ludwig T, Meurer J, Pipek V, Stein M, Stevens G (2015) FRAMES – a framework for adaptable mobile event-contingent self-report studies. In: Diaz P, Pipek V, Ardito C, Jensen C, Aedo I, Boden A (eds) End-user development. Lecture notes in computer science, vol 9083. Springer, Cham, pp 141–155
8. Draxler S, Stickel O, Winter D, Stevens G (2014) Nutzerintegration in softwareprojekte durch multi-channel feedback. In: Butz A, Koch M, Schlichter J (eds) Mensch & computer 2014 – Tagungsband. De Gruyter Oldenbourg, Berlin, pp 175–184
9. Ehn P, Kyng M (1987) The collective resource approach to system design. In: Kyng M, Bjerknes G, Ehn P (eds) Computers and democracy: a Scandinavian challenge. Avebury, Brookfield, pp 17–57
10. Ferreira J, Noble J, Biddle R (2007) Agile development iterations and UI design. In: Proceedings of the AGILE 2007, AGILE '07. IEEE Computer Society, Washington, DC, pp 50–58
11. Floyd C, Mehl WM, Reisin FM, Schmidt G, Wolf G (1989) Out of Scandinavia: alternative approaches to software design and system development. Hum-Comput Interact 4(4):253–350
12. Floyd C, Reisin FM, Schmidt G (1989) STEPS to software development with users. In: ESEC '89: proceedings of the 2nd European software engineering conference. Springer, London, pp 48–64
13. Hansson C, Dittrich Y, Randall D (2006) How to include users in the development of off-the-shelf software: a case for complementing participatory design with agile development. In: Proceedings of the 39th annual Hawaii international conference on system sciences, HICSS '06, Kauai, vol 8, pp 175c–175c
14. Hering D, Kraft X, Schwartz T, Wulf V (2013) Usability-Hindernisse bei Software entwickelnden KMU. In: Boll S, Maaß S, Malaka R (eds) Mensch & computer 2013 – Workshopband, pp 9–18. Oldenbourg Verlag, München
15. Holtzblatt K, Beyer H (1993) Making customer-centered design work for teams. Commun ACM 36(10):92–103
16. Isomursu M, Sirotkin A, Voltti P, Halonen M (2012) User experience design goes agile in lean transformation   a case study. In: 2012 agile conference, Dallas, pp 1–10
17. Keiningham TL, Cooil B, Andreassen TW, Aksoy L (2007) A longitudinal examination of net promoter and firm revenue growth. J Market 71(3):39–51
18. Larusdottir M, Cajander A, Gulliksen J, Cockton G, Gregory P, Salah D (2014) On the integration of user centred design in agile development. In: Proceedings of the 8th Nordic conference on human-computer interaction, NordiCHI '14. ACM, New York, pp 817–820
19. Lee JC (2006) Embracing agile development of usable software systems. In: CHI '06 extended abstracts on human factors in computing systems, CHI EA '06. ACM, New York, pp 1767–1770
20. Ley B, Ogonowski C, Mu M, Hess J, Race N, Randall D, Rouncefield M, Wulf V (2014) At home with users: a comparative view of living labs. Interact Comput 27:21–35
21. Lievesley MA, Yee JSR (2006) The role of the interaction designer in an agile software development process. In: CHI '06 extended abstracts on human factors in computing systems, CHI EA '06. ACM, New York, pp 1025–1030
22. Muller M, Haslwanter J, Dayton T (1997) Participatory practices in the software lifecycle. In: Helander M, Landauer T, Prabhu P (eds) Handbook of human-computer interaction. Elsevier, Amsterdam/New York, pp 256–297
23. Pipek V, Wulf V (2009) Infrastructuring: towards an integrated perspetive on the design and use of information technology. J Assoc Inf Syst 10(5):447–473
24. Reichheld FF (2003) The one number you need to grow. Harv Bus Rev 81(12):46–54
25. Schwaber K (1995) SCRUM development process. In: Proceedings of the 10th annual ACM conference on object oriented programming systems, languages, and applications (OOPSLA), Austin, pp 117–134
26. Silva T, Silveira MS, Maurer F, Hellmann T (2012) Paulo: user experience design and agile development: from theory to practice. J Softw Eng Appl 5:743–751

27. Singh M (2008) U-SCRUM: an agile methodology for promoting usability. In: Proceedings of the agile 2008, AGILE '08. IEEE Computer Society, Washington, DC, pp 555–560

28. Strauss A, Corbin J (2008) Basics of qualitative research grounded theory procedures and techniques. SAGE Publications, Los Angeles

29. Sy D (2007) Adapting usability investigations for agile user-centered design. J Usability Stud 2:112–132

30. von Hippel E (2005) Democratizing innovation. MIT, Cambridge

31. Williams L, Cockburn A (2003) Agile software development: it's about feedback and change. Computer 36(6):39–43

32. Wulf V, Rohde M (1995) Towards an integrated organization and technology development. In: Symposium on designing interactive systems (DIS'95). ACM, Ann Arbor, pp 55–64

33. Wulf V, Rohde M, Pipek V, Stevens G (2011) Engaging with practices: design case studies as a research framework in CSCW. In: Proceedings of the ACM conference on Computer supported cooperative work. ACM, New York/Hangzhou, pp 505–512

34. Yetim F, Draxler S, Stevens G, Wulf V (2012) Fostering continuous user participation by embedding a communication support tool in user interfaces. AIS Trans Hum-Comput Interact 4(2):153–168

Chapter 3
Templates: A Key to Success When Training Developers to Perform UX Tasks

Tina Øvad and Lars Bo Larsen

Abstract Working with usability and UX design in an agile development context such as Scrum has been found challenging. Not all companies have the need or resources for a team of dedicated UX specialists. In other cases the UX team is perceived as a bottleneck. We therefore set out to investigate; how companies can perform UX tasks, when no or little UX expertise exists in the organization; if it is possible to perform this work in line with the Scrum sprints and how such work should be facilitated. To do this and since the Scrum framework states that every team member should be able to perform every work task, we trained software developers in three different companies to perform certain selected UX methods. The training was done as 1-day training sessions. The developers were provided with materials describing UX methods modified to be used in an agile, industrial environment. These consisted of guidelines, templates and cheat sheets. These materials were refined throughout the training sessions based on observations and feedback from the developers. We found that especially the templates were highly valued by the developers. The templates provided a quick overview of the method, guided them in the work and gave them security and confidence in conducting this type of work independently of the researchers. The templates described in the paper have been made publicly available and may be used freely.

Keywords User experience (UX) • Usability • User centred design • Agile software development • Scrum • Templates • Training

T. Øvad (✉)
Radiometer Medical, Copenhagen, Denmark

Aalborg University, Aalborg, Denmark
e-mail: tina@oevad.com

L.B. Larsen
Aalborg University, Aalborg, Denmark
e-mail: lbl@es.aau.dk

© Springer International Publishing Switzerland 2016   77
G. Cockton et al. (eds.), *Integrating User-Centred Design in Agile Development*,
Human–Computer Interaction Series, DOI 10.1007/978-3-319-32165-3_3

3.1 Introduction

Even though a company realizes a need to increase the usability and user friendliness of their products, it might be unable to invest in the resources needed to achieve this [1]. This could be to set up a specialized UX team or assign UX specialists to their product development teams. Furthermore, studies have shown that companies with UX specialists often experience UX work as a bottleneck [2].

In this paper, we address these problems by investigating how a company can perform UX tasks, when no or little UX expertise exists in the organization. We investigate if it is possible to perform this work in line with the Scrum sprints and how such work should be facilitated.

Our approach to alleviate these problems is to leverage already existing resources in the organization – by enabling software developers to perform certain UX tasks. We do not make any claims towards this approach being the best or indeed the only solution – in fact; we believe it should be combined with other initiatives. However, we do make the claim it is a viable solution and in the following sections we will demonstrate how this can be achieved through a number of empirical studies.

Industry has largely adopted agile approaches. In particular, Scrum has become popular [2, 3]. This paradigm states that every team member should be able to perform every work task. Therefore, it seems quite rational to train developers to conduct certain usability and UX tasks. This will utilise the developers' already present domain knowledge [4, 5] and could potentially facilitate a better downstream utility and a shared language within the development team. Thus, to enable developers to conduct UX tasks seems to be a potential solution to the challenge of increasing the presence of UX activities in the development process. This is elaborated and argued further in Sect. 3.2 on related work.

Working with usability and UX design in an agile development context such as Scrum has been found challenging [6–8]. The contrast between the workload of usability work and the simplicity, speed [3], iterative nature, and focus on sprint completion [9] in Scrum is a challenge. One recommendation is to integrate usability work into day-to-day development tasks [10]. A specific suggestion is to investigate how usability work can be conducted on a small scale so the activities can be integrated into each sprint [3]. Informal and lightweight approaches are already commonly followed in industry [11]. Bruun and Stage [12] show how basic usability evaluation training is a fast and cheap approach to provide developers with minimum skills. For example, basic training can provide developers with a better understanding of user perspectives, while not replacing usability practitioners [13]. Instead basic training can strengthen the collaboration between non-technical and technical roles [14].

As stated above, we suggest addressing this problem by using software developers as a UX work resource. To facilitate this, we have selected and modified three widely used UX methods to be tailored to an agile, industrial environment [15–18]. This is described in Sect. 3.3. We will make the case that this approach will facilitate a shared language in the development team while at the same time reduce a potential bottleneck in the organization.

Our approach is empirical: We do in-situ training sessions with software developers from three different companies. We record their attitudes towards UX tasks before and after the training sessions, and monitor their performance, when they apply the acquired knowledge and carry out the tasks independently. During the process, we provide written materials, such as guidelines, templates and "cheat-sheets". We developed and refined these supporting materials in an iterative manner throughout the process, reinforced by observations and developer feedback. This is described in detail in Sect. 3.5, where focus is on the templates, which proved to be the most popular and usable tool. Furthermore, we show examples of the evolution of the templates. The materials developed in this work and described in the following sections have been made available as a freely accessible resource via the Open Publication Licence and can be downloaded from [19].

3.2   Related Work

This section reviews a number of empirical studies concerning developers receiving training to conduct certain UX tasks.

Bruun and Stage [12] introduced eight software developers from a small company (20+ employees) to a 2-day basic training course in a traditional user based usability test with video analysis. As a part of the training, the developers were to analyse five video clips from a previous conducted usability test. After this, five of the developers were asked to conduct a user test on one of their own products and analyse this for usability issues. Two HCI specialists likewise analysed the data. Results showed that the developers were able to identify 48 % of all usability problems compared to a team of HCI specialists, who identified 62 %. A second study focusing on the IDA usability testing method showed comparable results between developers and specialists. A follow up study later revealed that developers had fixed approximately 60 % of the found issues, thereby accepting the usability corrections as a task in their development project [12].

Karat and Dayton [20] reported on two different training programs for education developers in user research and usability methods. The first training program was conducted at an IBM software development lab as a 6-day on-site training session. The training session's purpose was to establish a corps of usability advocates among the developers, by introducing them to contextual inquiry, customer interviews, and design constraints and standards, which they could use in their daily work. The training resulted in the practitioners conducting numerous of user inquiries and establishing effective communication between different parts of the organization. Both the practitioners and the management expressed satisfaction with the training and its outcome, which had increased the general awareness of usability among the employees. The consulting company Bellcore provided the second training program as a service to their customers. The training consisted of a 3-day workshop where the developers were seated in small groups of 6–7 people, with minimum one real end-user among these. The workshop introduced a participatory design framework and focused on task analysis and paper mock-ups. The workshop was split into 10 % formal lecture and the remaining 90 % of the time was focused on the developers applying the methods on their own products. Because the learning environment of the workshop was very similar to a real software development environment, they argue that the participants would have an easy job explaining their methods to other co-workers, and likewise easily be able to apply the methods from the workshop in their real project. However, they did not present any evidence for these positive benefits of the workshop's outcome [20].

Nielsen et al. [21] presents a series of five workshops training all-in-all 27 developers in designing GUIs. Each workshop was designed as a 1-day event and focused on design principles and guidelines for GUIs, and paper mock-ups. The participating developers worked together as a team and used the learned methods for their own GUI designs. Afterwards usability specialists using a heuristic inspection method evaluated each GUI design. Afterwards the results of the inspections were discussed with the participants in order to provide constructive feedback to the developers' design and learning. Seven months after the training, they made a follow-up evaluation on one of the participating teams. They had made a complete GUI prototype for one of their products. The prototype was inspected using heuristic evaluation. The inspection revealed several usability problems but also showed that the developers had been able to apply the leaned methods and design a cohesive GUI [21].

Based on these experiences, as well as requirements made by the participating companies, we decided to apply a number of constraints to the approach:

- The training should be conducted in-situ, both for convenience and for easy access to resources, such as test participants, prototypes and other equipment.
- The cases provided in the training sessions should be real-life and taken from the company's on-going product development process.
- A training session should have a duration of 1 day and include a large proportion of hands-on exercises.
- Training materials such as templates and other documents should be prepared prior to the training and provided at the training session.
- After the training session, the participants should carry out the tasks independently of the researchers, preferably within a 3-month window.

3.3   Method Selection

The constraints mentioned above narrowed down the number of suitable methods, together with the demand that the methods should be suitable to be used in an agile, industrial setting and applied by software developers.

We did not include more explorative user research methods (e.g. ethnographical studies) primarily applied prior to the product development process. Nor did we include the very formal quantitative usability evaluations sometimes performed by the end of the development process. However, Contextual Inquiry was listed, since this approach can be used throughout the development process in order to gain information regarding the use situation and the end-user.

These decisions were based on the fact that software developers are typically not involved at these phases of the product development process. Furthermore, the methods typically require trained specialists. In addition to this, the methods must be applicable within a single sprint. These constraints have been applied to a range of widely used UX methods.

Not surprisingly, we only identified a limited number of suitable candidates. Furthermore, during the initial steps we observed that developers had difficulties with analysing the collected data. This finding limited the list even further [18]:

1. A modified focus group technique [22]. This is denoted Focused Workshop [17, 23].
2. Comparative usability testing, modified by [16]. This is denoted AB-testing [16, 23].
3. Contextual Inquiry as described by [24, 25] and modified and referred to as Contextual Interview [23].
4. Cognitive Walkthrough as first described by [26] and modified by [27, 28].
5. Instant Data Analysis (IDA) as described by [29].

This short list contains five methods, which cover the desired development phases. Furthermore, these methods were judged to be ideal as a starting point for the work, due to its level of complexity and time constraints. Since the time frame for the project was restricted, only three of the methods were included (Focused Workshop, AB-test and Contextual Interview). A more thorough description of the modified methods can be found in Sect. 3.5 and in [19, 23].

3.4 Research Method

The software developers at three companies (presented below) were trained in using the methods over a period of 2 years. The training approach and corresponding materials were updated and refined based on the experiences gathered in each iteration. Here we focus on the templates provided to the developers to design and plan the studies and report the results.

To introduce each of the methods, the developers participated in a 1-day hands-on teaching course for each method, for more details concerning the training see [16, 23]. The training session was based on principles and designs used by earlier studies, following a "presentations and exercises" approach [9, 12–14].

The notion of using guidelines and templates together with 1-day hands-on training sessions is the result of the experiences of previous studies reported in the literature coupled with the requests from the participating companies. Together these enable a quick, simple and efficient solution, which suits the pace of agile development.

During our initial observations at Radiometer (see description below), we found that the use of different artefacts in the development process was widely adopted. Particularly, the use of templates for documentation is widely used to efficiently track the progress and the validation process of the different products. It was therefore decided to develop guidelines and templates to guide the developers in how to plan, conduct, analyse and apply the different methods. In order to document the process and the findings, templates were developed as well. This approach is supported by Nielsen et al. [21], who point out that novice practitioners need structure, especially if conducting this type of work is not a main task.

During our work, it became apparent that templates acted as the pivotal instrument. Initially we hypothesized it would be the guidelines, but this was proved wrong. The templates were found to be the most useful instrument to steer the execution and documentation of the UX tasks. Therefore, the issue addressed in the remainder of the paper is how such templates should be designed to achieve the optimal acceptance and usefulness for the developers.

3.4.1 Study Sites

The empirical studies were carried out within the software development teams at three distinct companies: Radiometer Medical and TC Electronic in Denmark, and SenDx Medical in the US. All companies used the agile framework Scrum.

Radiometer Medical ApS is a global provider of solutions for acute care testing and develops medical devices. The company is headquartered in Denmark and has about 2400 employees worldwide with 250 in R&D. The company has used Scrum for 5 years as the primary development framework with 3-week sprints. Radiometer has focused on UX design for a number of years and due to increasingly strict regulatory demands from the U.S. Food and Drug Administration (FDA), to be in compliance with usability standards e.g. [30]. Consequently, Radiometer has a dedicated UX team in place, but intends the software developers to perform minor UX tasks on their own, thus minimizing potential UX bottlenecks and developing a shared language between the UX and development teams [31].

TC Electronic is a global company with headquarter and main R&D facility in Denmark. TC Electronic produces audio equipment primarily for the music industry, e.g. guitar and bass amplifiers, guitar pedals, sound and picture production systems, and broadcast systems. Worldwide TC Electronic has about 300 employees, with 30 in the R&D department. The company has 4 years of Scrum experience as the primary development framework using 3 weeks sprints. Each of three development teams has a mix of software, hardware, and mechanical engineers with a joint focus. TC Electronic has no dedicated UX team or employees and has no current plans in this direction, but expects the R&D teams to carry out UX tasks. [32]

SenDx Medical is an American based company located in California. SenDx is a subsidiary to Radiometer and develops medical devices. SenDx is under the same regulatory demands as Radiometer concerning the usability standards put forward by FDA. SenDx uses Scrum as the development framework and has 3-week sprints. The company has people working with usability, but relies on Radiometer's UX team for major UX tasks. By upgrading the developers' skills at SenDx they can perform minor usability and UX tasks on site instead of having to rely on the Radiometer UX team [33].

3.4.2   Research Approach

To record the effects of the training and the developers' attitudes towards the tasks, we carried out semi-structured interviews with the developers at three points: before and after the training, and a final interview after they had applied the methods on their own. For each interview, an interview guide was developed. Furthermore, observations and video recordings were performed throughout the sessions and transcribed and analysed together with the interviews.

The interviews and notes were transcribed and analysed by performing a meaning condensation of the data as described by Patton [34], followed by performing five steps in a cyclic manner: compiling, disassembling, reassembling, interpreting and concluding, as described by Yin [35]. This iterative process resulted in the identification of some overall themes, which led to further modification of the different usability and UX methods and corresponding materials. The themes related to the templates are described in Sect. 3.5.

3.4.3   Study Organization

In the final selection, three of the methods mentioned in Sect. 3.3, "Focused Workshop", "Contextual Inquiry" (later adapted to Contextual Interview) and "AB-testing" were chosen. These were applied at the three companies according to the overview shown below in Table 3.1. In the following, a study refers to training and evaluation of one usability/UX method within a company. This paper consists of six studies – three carried out at Radiometer, two carried out at SenDx and one carried out at TC Electronic.

As indicated in Table 3.1, not all methods were applied at all sites due to practical and logistical constraints. However, substantial empirical material was collected from the studies. This is presented in Sect. 3.5, where the iterative development of the templates also is described.

Table 3.1 Overview of the training and evaluation iterations

–	TC Electronic	Radiometer	SenDx
Focused workshop	–	Summer 2014	–
		Summer 2014	
AB-testing	–	Fall 2014	Spring 2015
		Winter 2015	Summer 2015
Contextual Interview	Fall 2013	Spring 2015	Summer 2015
	Winter 2014	Fall 2015	Summer 2015

3.5   Results of the Studies

This section presents the studies described in Table 3.1 above. The focus is on the development of the templates and materials, but the training approach is also discussed, however a more in-depth description of the training can be found in [17, 23]. The studies are described in chronological order, and each study may contain up to four iterations of the materials. The results quite broadly describe the initial studies and iterations to save space, but become more detailed as a detailed format emerges.

3.5.1   Contextual Inquiry at TC Electronic

We initiated the study cycles by training developers at TC Electronic. The method in this study was Rapid Contextual Inquiry (CI) including the tailored qualitative data analysis methods, as described in [24, 25] within the framework of Contextual Design (CD). The choice of introducing the CI method was based on a wish from TC Electronic to acquire a systematic and simple method for gathering insights of user behaviour. These insights would be used to support TC Electronic in determining the key features and the context of use of new product from an initial phase. It was further a request that the method should fit into their agile development process. The participants were introduced to the CI and the data analysis methods through a 1-day workshop (7 h) at the company facilities. At this point the training materials largely consisted of the materials described in [25] including samples of affinity diagrams, artefact models, etc., associated with CI. The training was well received and approximately 2 months later, the development team at TC Electronic planned and conducted out a CI. This was also successful, but at this point, we observed problems during the CI analysis phase and were called upon to assist. Interviews with developers confirmed that the teaching approach was well received, but revealed that the subsequent analysis was felt to be too hard and required external expertise. Additionally, it was experienced as too time consuming. Overall, the method was considered useful and a representative from the company later stated that several months had been cut from the product development time, as the CI demonstrated that many anticipated features would be superfluous and were omitted early in the process.

This study clearly showed that the structured approach imposed by the CI was a gain. However, we found that the analysis phase of CI seemingly required a stronger background within UX than we anticipated and the method needed to be adapted further. This was taken into account in the next iteration of the Contextual Inquiry method (see Sects. 3.5.8 and 3.5.9).

3.5.2 *Focused Workshop at Radiometer*

Radiometer requested a method that could facilitate a closer relationship between the developers and their end users. Therefore it was decided to go with a focus group approach, but customized to the agile, industrial setting. Pre-training interviews with Radiometer developers and the experiences from the training at TC Electronic including post-training interviews with TC Electronic developers formed the basis of the approach. The aim was to make the analysis part less prominent and we wanted to create some additional structure to this often less structured method. The resulting adaption is denoted a Focused Workshop. We developed a structured and rigorous guideline to support the developers, together with two templates – one for planning the session and one for reporting the findings. [17]

Instead of assigning a whole day to training, we decided to have two developers observe one of the authors conducting a Focused Workshop as trainees and act as note takers. From interviews with the developers it was clear that this approach resulted in high confidence about the results the method could provide as well as their ability to conduct a Focused Workshop session on their own. One of the developers subsequently planned, facilitated and analysed a Focused Workshop. Interviews made it clear that the practical training and the structure of the guideline were accepted. But when the developer facilitated a Focused Workshop independently, he did not use the templates at all and when going through his report, a number of important items and findings were left out. Such matters would had been emphasized in a more structured training session. [17, 23]

From this, it became clear that a strict *"observe and learn"* approach is not sufficient, even though it was well received and imparted the developers with a high level of confidence. A more directed and organized training supporting the information in the guideline and the templates was needed, and the templates must be easier to adopt.

---

1   Definitions, Acronyms, and Abbreviations

The subsections should provide the definitions of all terms, acronyms, and abbreviations required to properly understand this document. This information may be provided by reference to one or more appendixes in the document or by references to other documents.

2   Approach

2.1 Purpose and topic

A detailed description of the purpose of this experiment, including:

- *What is the question we would like to have answered?*
- *Why is this of importance?*
- *Define the independent variable (what you test) and the dependent variable (what you measure)*

2.2 Material

Consider:

- *Which type of material you have present to make the experiment – is it e.g. print out of screen shots, is it a click dummy or is it working code?*
- *For an AB-test you have to have two sets of the same material, where only one thing (variable) is different between the sets.*

2.3 Specify the experimental plan

Fig. 3.1 Initial version of the first page of the planning template for AB-testing

3.5.3   AB-Testing at Radiometer

AB-testing is a usability test, where the goal is to compare user performance and preferences for different design proposals and to help the decision process. In our approach, a variable can be anything from the colour of a button to the whole GUI design [16, 23].

We decided to use a structured training approach together with a guideline and two sets of templates (planning and reporting). An excerpt from the templates is shown in Fig. 3.1.

3.5.4   First Iteration of AB-Test at Radiometer

The training was conducted as a 1-day (7 h) training session with five developers. The training involved the participants planning, performing and analysing an AB-test for a real-life test case, taken from a current project. For more details concerning the actual training session, see [16, 23].

After the training, all felt confident about conducting an AB-test. The most important reason given was that they could rely on a structured and established process in combination with the provided materials. One participant pointed out: *"Just to know what making such a test involves, and what challenges there are – I think that is healthy"* [16].

The developers were very positive towards the materials. One stated: *"I think they (the guideline and templates) were very professional and thorough – and I liked the greyed out guiding texts"*.

However, it was clear that the templates were the central item, as one of the developers pointed out: *"We are not like the university; we have these tools because we are going to solve a specific problem. Therefore, I would turn it upside down. In my world the tool is the template."* The templates were used very closely: *"We used it [the template] a lot – step-by-step, and almost answered it."* This was supported by: *"They were really good. They were really, really good. We used them a lot. I think it would have taken us more than the double amount of time than it took us to do the task without them."*

From our observations during the training and the interviews, the importance of the guidelines and especially the templates were evident, as also noted above. However, some issues with the templates for scoping and reporting the findings were pointed out: *"It is just that the test script looks quite intimidating because there are so many entries, but you just need to understand that some of them are not applicable"*. And another participant had an idea of how he would like them to be: *"I think the report should just be a one-pager, where you have five lines to describe the purpose and some check boxes to check concerning if it is a within or between subject design, etc. It has to be as easy as possible"*.

Based on these findings, the templates were modified and made even more accessible and lightweight, and they were merged into one single template, thus including both a planning, and a report part, see Fig. 3.2.

Planning of the AB-testing of _____

Purpose and topic:

Question(s) answered:
- *What is the question we would like to have answered?*
- *Why is this of importance?*

Material:
- *Which type of material you have present to make the experiment – is it e.g. print out of screen shots, is it a click dummy or is it working code?*
- *Difference between the two designs*

Independent and dependent variable:
- *Define the independent variable (what you test) and the dependent variable (what you measure)*

Specify the experimental plan:

Experiment type: With-in subject: _____   Between subject: _____

Given task:
- *Describe the task the test participants is asked to perform? (E.g. enter a name and click "okay", conduct a whole maintenance workflow, etc.).*

Location:
- *State where the experiment should be performed (at your desk, in the canteen, at a hospital ward?)*

Fig. 3.2 The first page of the planning and report template for AB-testing after first iteration

3.5.5   Second Iteration of AB-Test at Radiometer

In the second iteration, four of the developers planned, implemented and analysed an AB-test on their own. We observed them during this work and interviewed them afterwards [16].

From the observations and the post-test interviews, it was clear that the participants were very appreciative of the templates. One said: *"We did not use the guideline when we organized the test – we only used the template"*, and he continued: *"When there is a template, we here at Radiometer are encouraged to follow it ... if there is a template we will follow it."* This is supported by: *"We followed it [the template] quite strictly – maybe we took out a little bit, because one part was not relevant"* and: *"We followed it [the template] very strictly, we tried to fill in as much as possible."* While these statements show a strong preference for the provided template they also show that any errors in these are likely to propagate directly into the studies. Thus, care must be taken when developing templates and a validation process must be in place.

An in-house UX specialist validated the developers' results from the AB-tests and found the obtained results valid.

3.5.6   Third Iteration of AB-Test at SenDx

To validate the results obtained at Radiometer a further training session was carried out at SenDx. Four developers participated. As previously, the template were well received and adopted. This was confirmed by statements like: *"We did not rely on the guideline, we followed the template"*, *"Lovely. It was like – okay, and then I have to go here and do this. It guided us quite well. All you have to do is sit and do the work and then you're done."* and *"I liked it cause it kind of summarized everything pretty well. It gave an entire overview of the entire process, that's why I liked it."* However, some of the appeal is probably due to convenience.

One participant suggested to: *"Have a real world example we can go through and just replace the text"*. We considered this idea, but discarded it, as our previous studies indicated it would be too risky. Participants would be tempted to follow templates too literally. Including a real world example in place of the instruction texts (see Figs. 3.1 and 3.2), would lead developers to adopt it directly without considering necessary adaptions.

3.5.7   Fourth Iteration of AB-Test at SenDx

Four developers subsequently planned, executed and analysed an AB-test on their own. We observed them and interviewed them afterwards. The same trends as found at Radiometer were found at SenDx. This is supported by statements like: *"Yeah, it [the template] helped us prepare the whole test, it helped us organize material – it makes everything a lot easier."* and: *"We basically followed the template directly. We followed it similar to how we did last time. So basically we answered all the questions presented there and ended up with a document."* Further: *"The document [template] is flexible enough that you basically fill in the blanks with as much detail as you can provide. So I think it works out fine that way."*

We conclude from this study that we have reached a stable version of the templates for the AB-testing case and consider the templates for AB-testing complete. The final version can be downloaded (and freely used) from [19].

3.5.8 First Iteration of Contextual Interview at Radiometer

The template-based approach has proved to work well for the AB-testing case, so we returned to Contextual Inquiry to investigate, if it was possible to adapt this method into a suitable form for our case. From the first trial with Contextual Inquiry at TC Electronic, it was clear that developers experienced some issues with the analysis phase. Furthermore, we propose that in an agile, industrial setting it is often not necessary to perform a full in-depth analysis as required by Contextual Inquiry.

We modified the method accordingly with a more shallow analysis phase and developed the materials for this. We denote the method Contextual Interview, to indicate the strong inspiration from Beyer and Holtzblatt's Contextual Inquiry [25]. As previously, we developed a guideline for the method, together with a lightweight planning and report template, see Fig. 3.3.

The training consisted of a 1-day training session, where five participants had the opportunity to obtain hands-on experience and to plan, execute and analyse a

---

Planning of the Contextual Interview(s) Concerning _____

Focus and participants:

Focus:
- *How do nurses interact with an ABL90 in a real work environment?*
- *How can this be handled in the design of the ABL900?*

Participants:
See Guidelines for Conducting a Contextual Interview, section: Find participants for the Contextual Interview for more details.

	Anesthesia Nurses	Surgical nurse	Service technician	Etc.
Riget (DK)				
Herlev (DK)				
John Hopkins (US)				
Heidelberg (DE)				
Etc.				

Table 1: Roles and context

Fig. 3.3 The first step of the planning and report template for Contextual Interview

---

Date of the Contextual Interview:

Location of the Contextual Interview:

Participants:

Names and initials of the interviewer and interpretation team:

Planning of the Contextual Interview(s) Concerning _____

Focus and participants:

Focus:
- *How do nurses interact with an ABL90 in a real work environment?*
- *How can this be handled in the design of the ABL900?*

Participants:
See Guidelines for Conducting a Contextual Interview, section: Find participants for the Contextual Interview for more details.

Interview style:
See Guidelines for Conducting a Contextual Interview, section: Interview style for more details.

Standard: ____;   Intermittent: ____;   Uninterruptible: ____;

Retrospective; ____;   Extremely focused: ____;   Environment centered interviews: ____;

Fig. 3.4 The first step of the planning and report template for Contextual Interview after first iteration

Contextual Interview of a real-world task. For more information about the training, see [23]. When interviewed after the training session the reactions were similar to what we observed from the AB-testing case. The template was used throughout the Contextual interview and the developers were satisfied, as one pointed out: *"There was what there should be and nothing more"* and another stated that: *"I really like that if I start from the top and run through it, then I have probably captured what was intended."* The participants expressed a desire to have a cheat sheet to support the work, since they found the guideline too text-heavy, but still liked the opportunity to look up details, as was pointed out: *"There has to be some sort of short guide – how to get started, do this and this."*

However, it was clear that the developers did not believe they would facilitate more than a single Contextual Interview at a given time. This led to the removal of the data consolidation phase (derived from Contextual Inquiry, see [25]) from the template, see Fig. 3.4.

3.5.9 Second Iteration of Contextual Interview at SenDx

The training was similar to that conducted at Radiometer. The four participating developers primarily used the template when planning, executing and analysing the Contextual Interview. They did not have many new comments for the templates, but observed: *"It was pretty similar to the AB-test."*

CONTEXTUAL INTERVIEW (CI)

– A BRIEF WALKTHROUGH

USE CI WHEN: You want to know how people really work.

TIME: 2 hours preparing + 2 hours per interviewee + 2 hours analysis.

NO OF PEOPLE: 2-3 conductors, from 1 interviewee.

1. PLANNING

- Find participants (page 5)
- Decide on an interview style (page 5)
- Set up the site visits (page 6 + 23)
- Confirm the interviews
  Remember things like: NDA, permission to record, they should not clean up, etc. (page 7 + 24 + 31)

2. CONDUCTING

Introductory group talk if you have more than two interviewees (page 8)

RUN EACH INTERVIEW:

- Introduce yourself, your project and the CI method, reinforce your focus, set expectations, set up the mentor/mentee role, the length of the interview, describe your confidentiality policy, get permission to record, etc. (page 9 + 24 + the Do's and Don'ts page 26 - 30)
- Remember: The transition – from questions to CI (page 10)

During interview be aware of: Observing and discussing, sticking to your focus, ask!, take notes, the different roles, collecting artifacts, share ideas, the surroundings etc. (page 10 - 11)

WRAPPING UP (PAGE 12)

3. ANALYZING

REMEMBER THE INTERPRETATION ROLES (PAGE 13 – 15)

CAPTURE THE USER AND ORGANIZATION PROFILES (PAGE 15 + 31)

WRITE NOTES (PAGE 16 - 17):

Capture: Interpretations of events, use of artifacts, problems, and opportunities, important characteristics of the work, breakdowns in the work, cultural influences, design ideas (flag with DI:), questions for future interviews (flag with a Q:), insightful user quotes.

(CONSOLIDATED) CAPTURE INSIGHTS (PAGE 17)

(CONSOLIDATED) SEQUENCE MODELS (PAGE 17 - 21)

Fig. 3.5 First example of a cheat sheet for Contextual Interview

As observed in the initial Contextual Inquiry case at TC Electronic, there were some problems with the analysis phase – especially how to analyses notes. We suggested using Contextual Design's Sequence Model for the notes [25]. This led to a proper analysis of the obtained data. Like the developers at Radiometer, several expressed a desire for some sort of cheat sheet, since the guideline is quite text-heavy and one developer actually made his own during the training session. See Fig. 3.5 for an example of a cheat sheet for Contextual Interview.

3.5.10 Third Iteration of Contextual Interview at SenDx

Similarly to the AB-test case, two of the developers planned, executed and analysed a Contextual Interview. We observed them during this work and interviewed them afterwards. Again it was clear that the template was the main focus in both planning and analysing. As one pointed out: *"We basically just filled out the sections to create the report. It is nice to have that kind overall structure already, it helps you to figure out – okay, I just have to put this in.".*

The cheat sheet was successful: *"I used the cheat sheet many times . . . I was able to quickly jump to the different areas."*

This concludes the results from the empirical studies carried out at the three sites. Stable versions of the training guides and templates for AB-test and Contextual Interview have been reached. These have been cross-validated by separately applying them at two participating companies, where feedback and observations are highly correlated.

3.6 Discussion

3.6.1 Selection of Methods

The three methods applied in the present paper were carefully screened and evaluated as feasible for integrating into an agile environment and teaching non-UX professionals [17]. Only a limited number of methods can be expected to fit these criteria. An important obstacle was observed during the training, as the developers experienced difficulties when analysing the collected data. This finding is supported by other studies; Eriksson et al. [13] found that developers find it difficult to interpret observations; Bruun and Stage [12] found that developers had problems with supporting observations with data; and Bruun et al. [4] found that developers have problems understanding how findings can be used for radical design changes. In our studies, we particularly observed problems with qualitative data analysis. This finding will limit the number of suitable methods, for our approach to those not requiring in-depth analysis of qualitative data.

3.6.2 Training Sessions

The training sessions and application of the methods provided new knowledge and skills to the developers as well as an accommodating attitude towards usability and UX work within the development teams. This shows that upgrading the developers' skills can facilitate a shared language in the development team.

Furthermore, our findings indicate that developers will be able to enter into a dialogue and provide useful input to UX specialists, when such are present in the organization. Furthermore, agile development requires quick and informal evaluation and by these studies, we have shown that developers can indeed acquire the skills and inclination to perform such tasks. We found it beneficial to conduct training sessions as hands-on and not just "observe and learn" and we found it highly successful to include real life tasks in the training sessions.

3.6.3 Training Materials

During the process, we found that a quite structured approach was required and guidelines, templates and cheat sheets were developed to support this. However, it was evident that the materials must be as lightweight as possible, while retaining the necessary amount of guidance and information.

The developed training materials can therefore be seen as addressing three different levels of guidance: The cheat sheets are the most lightweight, giving a quick overview of the method and the task sequence. The template is the next level, giving a bit more information and a bit more guidance. The templates ensure that, if followed from start to end, you have succeeded in applying the given method. The templates should therefore be easy accessible and self-explanatory. The final level is the guideline, where it is possible to look up more details concerning the method.

We do not claim the developed materials can stand alone. In our work, we have always provided training in their use.

3.6.4 Evaluation of the Training

The main evaluation criterion has been the subjective impressions of the participating developers. We have measured their confidence and trust in their abilities to carry out the tasks at three points: before and after the training sessions and later, when they have applied the method on their own. These are illustrated in Table 3.1. In all the studies we could detect a clear rise in developers' confidence and trust in their capabilities as reported throughout Sect. 3.5. In that sense the approach has clearly been successful.

In one study, AB-Testing at Radiometer, an external evaluator (a trained UX specialist with domain knowledge) was called upon to assess the usefulness and quality of the results produced by the developers. The assessment was positive and the results have indeed been included into the design process of the company's product. A more large-scale comparative evaluation scheme has not been possible, but could clearly be beneficial.

Concerning the training materials, we applied an iterative development strategy and used a saturation criterion to evaluate whether the materials needed more iteration. We judge that stable versions emerged through the iterations we performed and the quality and usefulness of the materials therefore are acceptable without further work.

3.7 Conclusion

Our goals with this work were to investigate how a company can perform UX tasks when no or little prior UX expertise exists in the organization, to see if it is possible to perform this work in line with the Scrum sprints, and to see how such work should be facilitated.

We chose to answer the questions by training software developers to perform certain selected UX tasks. We selected and modified three widely used UX methods and tailored them to be used in an agile, industrial development environment. We designed a training approach based on 1-day sessions with a group of developers and kept a focus on hands-on experiences and real-life cases rather than watch-and-learn and textbooks. Finally, we provided the developers with three different levels of materials – guidelines, templates and "cheat-sheets". The methods, training sessions and materials were then refined in up to six iterations in the organizations.

Through our observations and interviews, we found that especially the templates were highly valued by the developers. These templates gave the developers a quick overview of the present method, guided them in the work and gave them security in conducting this type of work independently. Using the templates boosted the developers' confidence in their own ability to conduct UX tasks.

We have contributed empirical knowledge on how to train software developers to perform minor UX tasks on their own. We conclude that the studies have successfully demonstrated the feasibility of training software developers to carry out certain usability and UX tasks within a sprint, when they are supported by the templates.

We have also identified the limitations of the approach. It became obvious that the participating developers had trouble analysing qualitative data and the approach should thus be limited to UX methods not relying heavily on qualitative data. This excludes more comprehensive explorative methods, such as ethnographic studies. However, a method might be modified to fit, as demonstrated with the Contextual Inquiry, where some steps of the analysis were omitted.

However, we do not see this as a stand-alone solution and it is important to note that we do not intend the results of our study as an argument towards removing UX specialists from the development process. Rather we have contributed to the limited research issue on how software developers can be a part of the on-going work with usability and UX design within companies. Finally, we have described a hands-on approach for working with usability and UX on a day-to-day basis, which has been missing in the existing literature [7].

3.8 Further Work

The goal is to develop a UX toolbox with a variety of UX and usability methods targeted for use by developers in an agile, industrial environment. The long-term plan is to collect the methods in a UX toolbox and develop an index making it possible for non-specialists to identify quickly the most applicable and cost efficient method for the given situation. The next steps are therefore to modify more usability and UX methods and work with a broader base of companies for further evaluation and validation. We therefore invite companies to make use of our material in order to refine the material further. The materials are freely available and can be downloaded from: http://UXToolbox.es.aau.dk and we invite researchers and practitioners to use the methods and templates and contribute with their own.

Acknowledgements We wish to thank all participating staff at TC Electronic, SenDx Medical and Radiometer Medical for participating in this work. Furthermore, we thank Aalborg University, Radiometer Medical and the Danish Ministry for Science and Education for funding the research presented here.

References

1. Bruun A (2010) Training software developers in usability engineering: a literature review. In: Proceedings of the 6th nordic conference on human-computer interaction: extending boundaries. ACM, New York, pp 82–91
2. Øvad T, Larsen LB (2015) The prevalence of UX design in agile development processes in industry. In: Proceedings of the 2015 Agile conference, pp 40–49
3. Lárusdóttir M, Bjarnadottir E, Gulliksen J (2010) The focus on usability in testing practices in industry. In: Forbrig P, Paternó F, Pejtersen AM (eds) Human-computer interaction, vol 332. Springer, Berlin, pp 98–109
4. Bruun A, Jensen JJ, Skov MB, Stage J (2014) Active collaborative learning: supporting software developers in creating redesign proposals. In: Saurer S, Bogdan C, Forbrig P, Bernhaupt R, Winckler M (eds) Human centered software engineering. Springer, Berlin, pp 1–18
5. Høegh RT (2006) The impact of usability reports and user test observations on developers' understanding of usability data: an exploratory study. Int J Hum Comput Interact 21(2):173–196
6. Salah D, Paige RF, Cairns P (2014) A systematic literature review for agile development processes and user centred design integration. In: Proceedings of the 18th international conference on evaluation and assessment in software engineering. ACM, New York, pp 5:1–5:10
7. Ferreira J, Sharp H, Robinson H (2012) Agile development and user experience design integration as an ongoing achievement in practice. In: Proceedings of the 2012 Agile conference, pp 11–20
8. da Silva T, Martin A, Maurer F, Silveira M (2011) User-centered design and agile methods: a systematic review. In: Proceedings of the 2011 Agile conference, pp 77–86
9. Bornoe N, Stage J (2014) Usability engineering in the wild: how do practitioners integrate usability engineering in software development? In: Saurer S, Bogdan C, Forbrig P, Bernhaupt R, Winckler M (eds) Human centered software engineering. Springer, Berlin, pp 199–216
10. Lee JC, McCrickard DS (2007) Towards extreme(ly) usable software: exploring tensions between usability and Agile software development. In: Proceedings of the 2007 Agile conference, pp 59–71
11. Lárusdóttir M, Cajander Å, Gulliksen J (2014) Informal feedback rather than performance measurements–user-centred evaluation in Scrum projects. Behav Inform Technol 33(11):1118–1135
12. Bruun A, Stage J (2014) Barefoot usability evaluations. Behav Inform Technol 33(11):1148–1167
13. Eriksson E, Cajander Å, Gulliksen J (2009) Hello world!–experiencing usability methods without usability expertise. In: Gross T, Gulliksen J, Kotze P, Oestreicher L, Palanque P, Prates RO, Winckler M (eds) Human-computer interaction, pp 550–565
14. Latzina M, Rummel B (2003) Soft(ware) skills in context: corporate usability training aiming at cross-disciplinary collaboration. In: Proceedings of the conference on software engineering education and training, pp 52–57
15. Agile User Experience (2014) In: Proceedings of the international conference on interfaces and human computer interaction. IADIS Press, pp 397–401
16. Øvad T, Bornoe N, Larsen LB, Stage J (2015) Teaching software developers to perform UX tasks. In: Proceedings of the annual meeting of the Australian special interest group for computer human interaction. ACM, New York, pp 397–406
17. Øvad T, Larsen LB (2014) Experiences from training agile software developers in focused workshops. In: Proceedings of the international conference on Interfaces and Human Computer Interaction, pp 397–401

18. Øvad T, Larsen LB (2014) Fast, faster, Agile UCD. In: Proceedings of NordiCHI
19. Øvad T, Larsen LB (2015) Radiometer UX templates http://uxtoolbox.es.aau.dk
20. Karat J, Dayton T (1995) Practical education for improving software usability. In: Proceedings of the SIGCHI conference on human factors in computing systems. ACM Press, New York, pp 162–169
21. Nielsen J, Bush RM, Dayton T, Mond NE, Muller MJ, Root RW (1992) Teaching experienced developers to design graphical user interfaces. In: Proceedings of the SIGCHI conference on human factors in computing systems. ACM Press, New York, pp 557–564
22. Krueger RA, Casey MA (2001) Designing and conducting focus group interviews. In: Social analysis selected tools and techniques. The World Bank, Washington, DC
23. Øvad T, Larsen LB (2016) How to reduce the UX Bottleneck by training your software developers. Behav Inform Technol. Taylor and Francis, http://www.tandfonline.com/doi/full/10.1080/0144929X.2016.1225818
24. Beyer H, Holtzblatt K (1997) Contextual design: defining customer-centered systems. Elsevier, Burlington
25. Holtzblatt K, Wendell JB, Wood S (2005) Rapid contextual design: a how-to guide to key techniques for user centered design. Elsevier, San Francisco
26. Wharton C, Rieman J, Lewis C, Poison P (1994) The cognitive walkthrough method: a practitioner's guide. In: Nielsen J, Mack RL (eds) Usability inspection methods. Wiley, New York, pp 105–140
27. Rowley DE, Rhoades DG (1992) The cognitive jogthrough: a fast-paced user interface evaluation procedure. In: Proceedings of CHI. ACM, New York, pp 389–395
28. Spencer R (2000) The streamlined cognitive walkthrough method, working around social constraints encountered in a software development company. In: Proceedings of the SIGCHI conference on human factors in computer systems. ACM, New York, pp 353–359
29. Kjeldskov J, Skov MB, Stage J (2004) Instant data analysis: conducting usability evaluations in a day. In: Proceedings of NordiCHI, Tampere
30. International Standards Organisation (2010) Ergonomics of human–system interaction – Part 210: human-centred design for interactive systems. ISO, Geneva
31. Radiometer Medical ApS (2015) Available: http://www.radiometer.com
32. TC Electronic (2015) Available: http://www.tcelectronic.com/
33. SenDx (2015) https://www.linkedin.com/company/sendx-medical-inc
34. Patton J (2002) Designing requirements: incorporating usage-centered design into an Agile SW development process. In: Wells D, Williams L (eds) Extreme programming and agile methods — XP/Agile universe LNCS 2418. Springer, Berlin, pp 1–12
35. Yin RK (2011) Qualitative research from start to Fnish. The Guilford Press, New York

Chapter 4
Integrating Scrum and UCD: Insights from Two Case Studies

Alvaro Aranda Muñoz, Karin Nilsson Helander, Thijmen de Gooijer, and Maria Ralph

Abstract This paper presents two case studies that suggest how to adapt Scrum for user-centered design (UCD) focused industrial projects and how to work with UCD in Scrum software development teams. The objective of the paper is to share insights gained from running such combined projects in industry in order to help others avoid some of the pitfalls associated with this way of working. There has been much published in this area within the research community. However, our work presents both perspectives: adapting a UCD way of working towards a Scrum way of working; and adapting Scrum for running projects from a UCD perspective. We explore the impact Scrum had on team members' work-practices during a project life-cycle and what lessons were learned from our experiences.

Keywords Agile Scrum • User-centered design (UCD) • Case study • Industrial application

4.1 Introduction

Agile methods have become very popular over the last several years with a number of published articles focusing not only on how to apply Agile methods for development projects, but also how these methods could be applied to user-centered design (UCD) focused projects as well [1, 2, 3, 4]. With its increased use, we were therefore interested in applying it to our current way of working in order to explore both the advantages and disadvantages of its use.

UCD is an approach which takes the perspective of having the user as the main focus at all times. It involves an iterative process of requirements gathering, concept design and testing with real end-users. Although it shares with Scrum the focus on iteration, it differs in the perspective it takes towards not only having a primary focus on the needs of the end-user as the main consideration for design decisions, but also

A. Aranda Muñoz (✉) • K. Nilsson Helander • T. de Gooijer • M. Ralph
ABB Corporate Research, Forskargränd 7, 721 78 Västerås, Sweden
e-mail: alvaro.aranda@se.abb.com; karin.nilsson-helander@se.abb.com;
thijmen.de-gooijer@se.abb.com; maria.ralph@se.abb.com

© Springer International Publishing Switzerland 2016   97
G. Cockton et al. (eds.), *Integrating User-Centred Design in Agile Development*,
Human–Computer Interaction Series, DOI 10.1007/978-3-319-32165-3_4

the need to collect and maintain a holistic perspective at all times. The core of this paper is therefore dedicated to presenting two case studies focused on; (1) how UCD fits into Scrum and how our project team used and adapted Scrum for a UCD focused project, and (2) insights from one of our team members who had the chance to work and observe the way Scrum was run in three different Scrum teams within the company, who were already using UCD in their product development process.

The insights from the first case study present our interpretation of the standard components associated with running a Scrum project, the challenges encountered when trying to integrate Scrum and UCD from the perspective of the project team and workarounds used to handle some of these challenges. The second case study presents insights into a Scrum software development team, which were made and observed by one of our co-authors who took part of their work process.

In this paper Sect. 4.2 outlines the Scrum framework used from three perspectives: details related to the Scrum team; details related to Scrum activities, most notably the sprint; and details relating to Scrum artifacts including the backlog and features/user stories or tasks. Section 4.3 describes two case studies, the first a project that introduces Scrum into a UCD way of working, and the second a case study which discusses how UCD was introduced into a Scrum way of working. Section 4.4 discusses possible adaptations that could be made to the Scrum process to support UCD focused projects and a proposed way of running these types of projects in the future.

4.2 Adapting Scrum in a UCD Project

4.2.1 Background

The team decided to use Scrum for a UCD focused project that ran over a period of 8 months. The team consisted of seven members with expertise in software development, software architecture, HCI, user experience (UX), and interaction design. All the members of the team were situated in the same building.

Given the project length of 8 months, there was no need to organise the sprints in increments (collections of sprints), which is something commonly used in larger projects to organise and keep control of progress.

The project employed a UCD approach to develop a Unity 3D prototype for improving information visualisation and situation awareness to support more effectively production processes in production factories. This type of project involves a large variety of roles and skills; such as user research (interviewing and observation skills), the creation of graphic art in 2D and 3D, user interfaces, animations, software architecture, programming and UX design to meet the needs of the users. These users consisted of production line managers responsible for different parts of the production process (e.g. assembling one part of a larger system) and other factory personnel who play a supporting role such as supply chain management.

Given the nature of working within a research environment and the futuristic focus of the project, it was difficult to estimate and plan in advance the length that the tasks would take and to break down the project into goals for each sprint with accurate information. This setup differs considerably from a consultancy project for example, in which experts in a particular field are continuously delivering the same type of product time after time, as this helps them to have a better understanding of the project to be delivered and how to estimate and plan accordingly.

Another consideration is that the outcome of the project was to deliver a prototype and not a real product. This implied that less than normal external resources or other roles were required for the team, e.g. no need for testers or integrators. However, there were external dependencies that are common in any UCD project, as for example the need to interact with users for field studies, and to test the different phases of the design and implementation.

4.2.2 Scrum Framework

In this section we outline: our interpretation of the key practices of Scrum, which generally follow the Scrum Guide [5]; and how we at first implemented these practices before making changes based on our experiences going through the project life-cycle. Since Scrum itself can have varying degrees of interpretation, it is important to outline our Scrum process in this way so that our approach is clear and leaves no room for misinterpretation or incorrect assumptions.

4.2.2.1 Team

In the beginning of our project we started to use Scrum without any team members having prior professional experience using Scrum, and with just one team member taking part in a Scrum training course. From this knowledge we began to develop the framework within which the project would be run.

According to Scrum practices each team is coached by a **Scrum Master** who is responsible for guiding the team in how to follow the Scrum process. We appointed one of our team members as Scrum Master and kept the same Scrum Master throughout the project. The Scrum Master was the same person that attended a Scrum course early on in the project and therefore it was felt by the project team that this person was best suited for this role.

In addition to the tasks associated with the Scrum Master (e.g. running morning meetings, review meetings and retrospective meetings, etc.), this person also needs to take on the responsibility of shielding the project team from outside work interruptions (e.g. outside people coming and asking for resources from the project), which often happens in larger organisations. The Scrum Master in our case tried to adhere to this as best as possible.

Scrum assumes the presence of a **product owner** who decides on the priority of features/user stories and whether a task can be considered as "done" at the end of each sprint. Our project had an internal receiver, someone within our organisation who is responsible for taking over the resulting prototype. For several sprints we did not get firm commitment from our receiver with regards to them taking over the product owner role. Therefore, the project leader – an internal project role responsible for managing deadlines and meeting project requirements – had to assume the product owner role for the remainder of the project. We therefore use the term proxy product owner to reflect this difference. However, the proxy product owner stayed in close contact with the real product owner (i.e. receiver), keeping them in the loop with constant project updates and arranging meetings when critical decisions had to be made. This proxy product owner also had some influence over the requirements in addition to the requirements collected during the interviewing phase with the real end-users. This was because the proxy product owner was also a type of end-user of the system (e.g. manager).

4.2.2.2 Activities

Scrum prescribes **fixed duration sprints** no longer than 1 month. At the very beginning of the project we decided on 2-week sprints as a starting point, because planning further ahead would remove the desired flexibility in a research project. After several sprints we decided to keep this sprint length since it was working well for the team but with the understanding that the sprint will involve 2 full weeks of work, that is 10 working days. Thus, those working days when the whole team was unavailable, e.g. public holidays, were added to the calendar time length of a sprint to make up the 10 full working days required. On some special occasions when some members of the team were not available, e.g. collaborating with other projects, the time length of the sprint was discussed and normally 1 extra week was added to compensate. Also some adjustments were made for project milestones, such as demonstrations of the software to the real product owner. These adjustments were made to ensure that availability of features required for demonstrations were always discussed one or two sprints in advance, as it was necessary to book and prepare the corresponding resources.

Scrum requires a **sprint planning meeting** which precedes each Scrum sprint. This meeting is time limited to 8 h for a 1-month sprint; thus we restricted ourselves to 4 h per 2-week sprint. The planning is done together with the entire team and results in a sprint goal and a selection of backlog items that support reaching the sprint goal. These items were estimated by the team using the Planning Poker method to ensure that a suitable number of items were selected for the sprint. In our case, the poker numbers on the cards represented the amount of work days (8 h) that the task was estimated to take for one team member. When several members of the team were involved in the task, the number of days was multiplied by the number of members involved, e.g. three members completing a task in 1 day would be estimated as a 3-day task. Time estimation within the group allows for everyone in the project to understand how long certain tasks will take to do, thus establishing a common ground within the group. Initially this planning process involved a lengthy time commitment, requiring approximately 4 h to complete.

Scrum typically involves having **timed stand-up meetings** every morning for no more than 15 min. During these meetings team members discuss past work (previous day) towards the sprint goal, challenges they faced or could face, and what will be done during the coming day. These discussions helped to increase transparency within the project. We held stand-up meetings every morning during the project unless a significant part of the team was out-of-office or could not attend, in which case those meetings were either held later during the day or cancelled altogether.

At the end of the sprint the team went through the deliverables for that sprint in a **sprint review meeting**. For each deliverable it was decided whether or not that deliverable could be declared as 'done' by the proxy product owner. In cases where the deliverable was partially done, the proxy product owner would readjust the deliverable requirements for the next sprint, so a new time estimate for that deliverable would be made during sprint planning. The Scrum Master was responsible for counting the number of deliverables that were completed during the sprint to have a better understanding of the burn-down for future reference in sprint planning.

The team also had a 30 min **sprint retrospective meeting** at the end of each sprint. During this meeting each team member spent 5 min reflecting on and writing about activities, one per post-it note, that they wanted to stop, start or continue doing based on their experience from the previous sprint. Each team member then placed their post-it notes one-by-one on a whiteboard under the appropriate heading for everyone to see, discuss around, and also vote on. We decided that a maximum of two actions per sprint were going to be added as rules for the next sprint. This was to ensure a progressive improvement in the workflow, and so that no major changes would occur from one sprint to the next. Therefore, the team voted on the post-its and the two with the most votes were implemented in the next sprint. We held retrospective meetings immediately after each review meeting throughout the project. It was during these retrospective meetings that we recorded most of our experiences with and changes to Scrum that will be presented in the remainder of this paper.

4.2.2.3 Artifacts

In Scrum all possible requirements and features that might be needed in the product are listed in the **product backlog**. It is the product owner's (or proxy product owner) responsibility to keep the backlog prioritised, with the backlog items having the highest priority at the top. In our case, some changes for handling the priorities were made after some sprints, which will be discussed later. During the planning meeting a suitable number of **backlog items** are chosen to be completed during the coming sprint, and are moved to the **sprint backlog**. The Scrum team estimate the complexity of the backlog items to make sure that the amount of work allocated

Fig. 4.1 Scrum board used for showing tasks and moving tasks from left to right for task started to tasks completed

for the sprint is reasonable to be completed during the fixed amount of time, for us 2 weeks. Often the Scrum team measures effort spent in order to construct forecasts, which use historical values to indicate how much work can be done per sprint. At the start of the project we attached time estimates to all backlog items for a sprint, but did not collect any statistics on our progress in for example a burn-down chart.

We chose to visualise the backlogs and track the progress of the sprint using a **Scrum board** (see Fig. 4.1). Each backlog item was described on a post-it note together with a time estimate and the name of the person responsible for that note. The post-it notes were placed either on the bottom of the board, in the product backlog, or in the column furthest to the left named 'not started' which represented the sprint backlog. The backlog items were broken down into tasks by the Scrum team and described on different colored post-it notes, one per task, together with its time estimate and person responsible for that task. By providing the name of the person responsible for each note, each team member could more easily find their individual notes, who was working on what, and also who to contact when further discussions were needed when one note had an effect on another note (i.e. task). During the sprint the post-its progressed across the columns on the Scrum board from 'not started' to 'started', and then passed on to 'test/review' to finally end up at 'completed'. This provided a transparency that other approaches, such as UCD, can sometimes lack since all team members can clearly see who is working on what during that sprint. This also opened up useful discussions about team members' tasks potentially having an impact on other team members, and suggestions for solving issues based on past experiences. The team members also felt more productive when they could see the progress of their work go from all post-its being on the left side of the board to in the end mostly on the right in the completed column.

4.2.3 Challenges of Using a Scrum Framework

Although there are benefits to using Scrum, the process itself is not without its fair share of challenges. The following sections address some of the challenges we faced trying to run our usual UCD process within a Scrum framework.

4.2.3.1 Team

The frequency of sprints and overhead for all events is high for part-time team members that are not allocated 100 % to the project. During the course of the project several team members were also assigned to other projects. The Scrum methodology promotes small, dedicated teams, with a diverse set of team members from each discipline needed (e g. graphic designers, programmers, user-experience researchers, testers, etc.). Our project team consisted of two senior researchers allocated for 50 % of their time, two junior researchers (50 and 100 % of their time) and three students (interaction design, software development and industrial design) working full-time on the project. Not having all team members allocated 100 % on the project proved challenging since team members who were only 50 % felt that: (1) meetings took away a lot of time from actual working time, (2) they were less productive than those working 100 % on the project especially on the morning meetings, (3) they had the additional stress of having to juggle more than one project at a time. This situation also impacted the amount of time team members who were not fully dedicated to the project had for meetings. This often resulted in meetings having to be missed or having to be rescheduled to accommodate all members involved in the project. In turn this had some impact on goal-completion rates. Ideally it would be better to involve team members who can commit all of their time to the project to make the process more effective.

In addition, the Scrum Master found it a challenge to be able to fully protect the team from outside influences. Often in industry there are a limited number of resources available that can be fully allocated to any one project for an extended period of time. Often team members are needed on several projects so trying to enforce a single project mandate is difficult in reality.

We also ran into some problems with those team members who finished their tasks for a sprint earlier than expected. We used as an initial test fixed sprints to focus on the tasks planned for the current sprint and this did not allow us to add new tasks from the backlog during the current sprint. Since each team member had different expertise it proved challenging for team members to jump-in and help with other members' on-going tasks. We needed to therefore find a workaround for this, which is discussed in a later section.

Even though this discussion might seem more focused on the Scrum processes related to the set up of the team, it does have a direct impact on UCD, as UCD focuses on understanding users and their needs. Providing the industrial context in which resources and project priorities might change during the process of the project, the allocation of resources such as time availability can affect the ability to connect fully to the needs of the end users. In our case, team members who were not 100 % allocated to the project felt that establishing and maintaining a connection with end-users' needs proved more challenging. This was due in part to these team members coming in and out of the project, thus disrupting their ability to stay focused on the user's problems at hand.

4.2.3.2 Activities

Running fixed sprints is a challenge. We found that it was difficult to predict in the beginning of the project what would happen during the coming 2-week sprint, and needed to be able to change the duration of the sprint accordingly once started. This was especially evident during user testing and user interviews. These events are tightly coupled to the availability of users who may or may not be available during the sprint. Also, users can cancel or need to rebook their sessions at the last minute due to work commitments, so the project team needs to be flexible.

Sticking to the tasks decided on for that sprint was also a challenge. Sometimes tasks needed to be re-prioritised during a sprint. In these cases, the team needs to be able to re-plan right away rather than having to wait 2 weeks until the end of the sprint to have the planning meeting.

Finding the time for team members to take part in the time/effort estimation during planning meetings for the upcoming sprint was also problematic. Planning meetings (i.e. engaging in the Planning Poker method) require a lot of time and proved difficult to schedule. For those working full-time on the project this was not an issue, however, for others with less time available these meetings were a challenge to schedule.

4.2.3.3 Artifacts

Developing concepts using a traditional Scrum sprint required some adjustment to the process, since concepts from a user-experience (UX) perspective are viewed from a more holistic viewpoint. That is, features impact each other and need to be thought of as a whole rather than broken up into separate parts, unless there are groups of features that are self-contained and can accommodate this. Concept development needs to always be approached from a UX perspective whereby the team is aware that changing one feature can have a significant impact on other features. So breaking down concepts and implementation into single features proved challenging for the team.

We also found it a challenge to move tasks on the whiteboard that were not considered completed but rather on-going throughout the project. These types of iterative tasks were continuously changing and proved problematic to track and record. For instance, coding modules that were modified needed to be kept track of to ensure completeness.

For some team members their role became more of a supporting one, whereby they gave feedback or reviewed material rather than producing their own work during a sprint. So showing tasks completed for those team members who are more involved in reviewing/supporting other people's work proved a challenge (because only the team member responsible for the task had their name on the note initially and they were responsible for moving that note during the stand-up timed morning meetings). Since the project team consisted of several different dedicated roles, when a sprint was more design intensive, those team members who were more focused on conducting user research (i.e. not designers) felt less productive. Although this may sound trivial it can affect the morale and in turn productivity of team members. It is therefore important to have all aspects of the work completed in the sprint recognised in order to highlight both hidden and visible aspects of the task completed.

Another issue we had was with the definition of "done" since the outcome of the user stories was quite different (e.g. implemented code versus concept sketches versus user evaluations). We struggled to find a clear definition of what "done" meant since it could mean different things for different types of tasks. We therefore relied on the proxy product owner's interpretation and experience to make this assessment during our review meetings at the end of each sprint.

4.2.4   Adaptations We Made to Scrum

We found that Scrum needed to be adapted to accommodate our way of working. As such we revised our approach to Scrum until we felt the process could support our needs and make the project team more effective rather than being a source of frustration. The following section outlines our experiences of changes needed to the Scrum process that worked well for our team. Our aim is to share these insights with other project teams so that they can learn and benefit from our experiences.

4.2.4.1   Team

One of the changes we made that worked well was to have each person in the project team write their own notes for their specific tasks, and make an initial effort estimate for those notes. This differed from the initial Planning Poker method, which required a lot of time since all team members voted on all tasks. It was felt that individual team members who were responsible for a task had a clearer perspective on time estimations for that task, and this new approach would reduce the amount of time needed to estimate task efforts. However, if needed, team members still had the flexibility to ask other team members for advice when doing their estimates. Although the Planning Poker method can be a useful exercise, we found it a challenge both from a time and expertise perspective. It requires additional project meeting time to engage in, which can be problematic for team members who are not full-time on the project. In addition, if the team consists of only one expert in each area (e.g. one interaction designer) it is often difficult for others in the team to give appropriate, if any, time estimates if they have no previous experience in that area. For instance, the software architect in the project found it difficult to give a time estimate for design-related activities. They felt that someone needed to be a designer or have had design experience to make such an estimate. Although we decided to no longer have the Planning Poker method for time estimation, establishing a common ground within the team was still achieved using post-it notes as a visualisation tool to convey how much effort different tasks required. By looking at the Scrum whiteboard, team members could still get a feeling for how much effort each task needed.

The proxy product owner in our case was a UX professional. Having a product owner (or proxy product owner) with knowledge about UX, who could drive the importance of good UX, made it easier for these types of related tasks to get higher priority and focus during sprints. Often a product owner does not have this insight, which can result in UX focused tasks being deprioritised or removed altogether since their importance may not be well understood. So having a product owner (or proxy product owner) with a good understanding of UCD and UX proved beneficial to achieving the best end-product. In addition, it was also helpful that our proxy product owner was also easily accessible, taking part in meetings and discussions within the team.

4.2.4.2 Activities

We also changed Scrum from having fixed tasks per sprint to "bottom-less" sprints where new tasks could be added from the backlog to the ongoing sprint backlog in cases where assigned tasks for that sprint had been completed. These bottom-less sprints were better at supporting UCD due to all the dependencies that UCD has associated with respect to the external factors that affect the planning of the sprint. These external factors can vary from collecting user input to iterating the current version of the prototype to fit new user insights recently collected. As an example, the team might have planned to develop and test a feature during a specific sprint, however, the user might not be available to test it, which means that the team must adapt to the new circumstances. This is even more relevant in industrial contexts, in which there is a heavy dependency on expert users who are not as available as other types of users, such as, for example, users for consumer market products. This can in turn impact whether a sprint goal can be achieved or not. It should be noted, however, that the planning meetings still aimed to assign an appropriate number of backlog items to the sprint backlog. This worked well since it ensured that everyone had control over what they worked on and could choose what to do next rather than having to do other tasks in a fixed task sprint. Discussions around what tasks were added to the sprint were made during the stand-up morning meetings to ensure all team members were informed of the new work being done and of any possible impact that task(s) may have. This was also beneficial when not all members of the team were available and there were some dependencies among tasks. In this case the team members could rely on the descriptions on the backlog and could continue with different tasks if they felt that they had come to a dead-end. This was also beneficial for the students who found that having a "bottom-less" sprint gave them a better perspective of the future sprints. They felt that they could take on different tasks when these tasks were grouped according to a related problem. This was especially useful for them when other team members were not available to support them so they could proceed with other work. The students however did have limitations in their work with respect to depending on junior and senior researchers. There were instances when students did not have the right access to information, which resulted in dependencies on other team members to help. The use of Scrum helped to highlight these issues sooner than perhaps other processes less transparent in nature.

Another change made was deciding to vary sprint lengths depending on the workload identified, or on the re-prioritisation of tasks required. This sometimes needed to happen either before the start of the next sprint, or during the current sprint being run.

Other considerations would include running field studies during the first sprint in the project or even before starting to use Scrum for the project, since pinning-down users for interviews proved problematic during sprints [6]. These studies provide not only the essential background knowledge needed to design a great UX but would also enable the product owner (or proxy product owner) and the team to prioritise the backlog to focus on those features/user stories that users value most. The product owner's views of the most important features for the product and users' needs are not always the same. It is important that the product owner gets this kind of knowledge about the end-user's needs since he/she has the main responsibility of prioritising the backlog. This kind of user knowledge can be presented at the review meeting(s)

4.2.4.3 Artifacts

Part of Scrum is to identify the amount of effort required for a task. This is to help team members learn how much effort will be required during future sprint planning for the sprint backlog. We initially used time in terms of days allocated per task. This however proved a challenge especially during concept development. Designing concepts is an inherently creative process that requires varying amounts of time, and

Fig. 4.2 Scrum details from Scrum board: how tasks were divided by area – goal task, software architecture (SWA) task, concept design task, implementation task, evaluation task

can involve heavy and lengthy discussions for the design team. So estimating time around these types of activities was a challenge for capturing effort estimations. We felt however that it was important to try and find a different way to capture the effort required for a task. In this case we tried using small, medium, and large post-it notes on our project whiteboard for showing effort required for a task. This can be reassessed at the end of the sprint to see how well expectations matched reality (e.g. was the task smaller than first thought, or larger).

We also added colour coded sticky notes to show differences between different types of tasks, i.e. goal tasks, software architecture focused tasks, implementation/coding, concept design, and evaluation/testing (see Fig. 4.2). We found this helpful especially during timed morning stand-up meetings since we could more easily and quickly find different types of tasks to discuss. As a side benefit, the color coding also helped identify where the project was in the bigger scheme of things, for instance if more implementation/coding was being done during that sprint than concept design or evaluation.

We also decided to add the names of all team members participating in a task to each note on the whiteboard instead of only including the name of main person responsible for completing the task. This worked well since it gave more visibility to those team members who played more of a supporting role during that sprint and made the team feel more productive.

4.3 Working with UCD in an Active Scrum Team (Second Case Study)

4.3.1 Background

One of our team members also worked on some different software projects run in another department of the same organisation, in which three other teams (team A, team B and team C) were running Scrum. This provided an opportunity to observe how other groups run Scrum, and to reflect and consider which things were done differently and if those differences could be proposed as an alternative to the way Scrum was run in our team as described earlier. Also it allowed us to observe the same type of problems as we experienced and to see how those problems were solved in a different way.

The teams were small; with groups of seven (team A), eight (team B) and two members (team C) respectively. Teams A and B were composed of different roles; programmers, testers and a software architect. In the case of team C, both members were UX designers and had tasks from both the other two teams and from other projects in the organisation.

In teams A and B a certified Scrum Master was responsible for the daily standup meetings. The Scrum Masters were also responsible for the retrospective meetings that were held every second week. The product owner was accountable for the sprint planning —in which other managers were involved— and for the Scrum reviews.

The sprints were run weekly. Each sprint would focus on a set of stories to be developed, and each story would be part of a feature that the system would have in the final release of the product. Due to the length of the project, the sprints were organised in increments, which consisted of eight sprints. Each increment would also have a goal or a set of goals defined according to the schedule to meet the important dates of the product such as releases, updates and upgrades.

There were also external collaborations with other teams, which took place on a daily basis, as an overseas team was also involved in the development of one of the projects. This was important for the scheduling and synchronisation of the different tasks.

4.3.2 Relevant Considerations for Improvements

This section highlights the main observations made from the two studies, taking into consideration the different backgrounds of the projects and teams.

4.3.2.1 UCD Requires More Planning and Better Communication in Scrum

An issue that was discussed by all teams during their retrospective meetings was the weekly planning of tasks, in which different stories or features were selected from the increment boards to be implemented during the week. Some UX work needs to be done in advance of a feature being implemented by the team. The UX work involved in a story can be quite difficult to pinpoint in advance in some cases, as most of the managers and lead programmers might not consider that any UX work is required until they see the need while the implementation is taking place. In these cases, the UX team would not have the necessary time to iterate and test different design options, and instead the design would be compromised by the need to finish a story before the end of the sprint or a deadline. This would result in not selecting the most optimal solution for the design, but the one that was fastest and easiest to implement. And in most cases the particular design would not be tested with users until a future demo or release, which would increase the risk of implementing something that the user does not need or understand, violating the principles of UCD.

This issue is mainly due to miscommunication during the increment planning, in which different roles might see the need for future features from different perspectives. For instance, lead programmers might communicate the need for features from a technical perspective in terms of functionality and time. From this perspective it may prove difficult for the rest of the team to see the impacts on UX related work until those features are under development.

This also happened more often in sprints that were close to a major release, as there were many tasks to plan, especially when user testing, bug fixing and other major issues needed to be prioritised in the sprint. The issue was discussed in different retrospective meetings and the solution suggested was to meet on a once per sprint basis with different members of the teams, mainly led by programmers and Scrum Masters, to spot which tasks could be marked in advanced as UX.

The problem of identifying possible issues for ensuring good UCD is a two-way issue since implementation and UX affect each other. Therefore, the UX team also had frequent synchronisation meetings with different members of other teams, normally involving a combination of roles, to discuss the latest information about UX. Normally these meetings took place after each iteration in the UCD process, for example after having feedback from users, new sketches, etc. This was a good way to guarantee communication and also planning for different tasks, as the lead programmers could quickly identify if the solutions proposed would challenge the framework that they currently had to develop for new features. This was also useful for spreading knowledge about UCD and its importance to the different parts of the development.

4.3.2.2 UCD Involves More External Dependencies

The dependencies UCD creates are mostly related to meeting users. These have an impact on the tasks that are in the backlog and tasks that are started, especially when the UX tasks have not been planned in advance. A natural consequence then is to reflect these dependencies on the Scrum board. In the case of the three groups, a space called "Waiting" was created for external dependencies and was used when tasks were started but were dependent on resources that were external to the Scrum team, e.g. feedback from users or renewing a license and waiting for approval from the organisation. This also helped to keep track of what actions still needed to be done in cases when a Post-it note was waiting for a long time. In some cases, the consequent action was to send a reminder, make a call, or contact a provider.

4.3.2.3 Synchronisation of Resources Is Key for Planning in Advance

In both the bigger teams a calendar for the next 3 months was printed. Each day contained a row for each member of the team representing the availability of the person, so the Scrum Master and the other members of the team could see the availability of the other members of the team ahead of time. This was especially important for roles that were involved in other projects and were working partially with other teams, as for example the architect, some programmers and the UX designers. But it was also important in terms of travel, meetings with other teams and private holidays. The Scrum Master and the product owner could use the calendar to adapt the different tasks based on the resources available.

Next to the calendar different notes could be found regarding the availability of other resources that were external to the team. For example, one could see when major testing was going to be performed and which time slots were allocated daily for that purpose (the testing was done in a different time zone and communication among teams was specifically important during testing).

Next to the printed calendar there was a sprint calendar in which the next five milestones of each sprint were listed. This was also done to support the planning and to provide a general overview of the implementation to the team. This is something that we also noticed helped our team, but we only included the goal of the current sprint and the goal for the next sprint, just to have a general overview and a background context of the status of the development.

4.3.2.4 Setting Up the Space for Collaboration Supports
the Synchronisation of Resources

As both teams were collaborating on the same project, a small part of each Scrum board was dedicated to a general description of what the other team was implementing. This supported collaboration and the sharing of knowledge between teams. It is also important to mention that the Scrum Masters of both teams were always in all the stand-up meetings, and in general when there were dependencies some members of the other team would attend the other team's meetings.

The time spent on meetings was optimised. During meetings, if the discussion was getting away from the original context any participant could raise their hand and the discussion would be postponed to another meeting. This was quite useful for standup meetings in which 12 participants had to report something in 15 min.

The Scrum boards were reversible, which allowed the inclusion of future stories. That was useful during daily planning, especially towards the end of a sprint when questions regarding the implementation of one feature could affect future stories. It meant that information was quickly available to see and modify.

A whiteboard (Discussion board) was entirely dedicated to daily planning and architect/UX reviewing. This allowed discussion notes to be kept in the same place, so team members who were not present could read them at any time. Different notes and screenshots could be added during the day, as team members involved in the stories could contribute from different perspectives, providing more examples or suggestions about the problem. When necessary, team members would call other members to discuss the problem. The next day the board would be prepared for continuing the discussion around the problem, and everyone could see the latest information about the story under development.

Two walls were dedicated to information about the project. One wall was always used to hang the latest sketches or wireframes for the feature that was currently under development. This would support discussions about necessary changes to the UI based on input from different team members during the sprint. When changes were required, the UX designer would be responsible for updating the sketches to the latest version. The other wall was dedicated to the general structure and architecture of the project. This wall was used mainly by the architect and the different lead programmers to organise and provide structure for the project. The advantage of these walls was the availability of information for part-time and external team members as they could quickly see what was currently under development and meet other members of the team to discuss dependencies.

4.4   Proposed Way of Running Scrum for UCD Focused Projects

This section outlines our suggestions for running a UCD focused project within a Scrum framework. Many of the steps proposed here also correlate with those proposed by Sy [6]. As shown in Fig. 4.3, our proposed approach advocates conducting field studies to collect user data early on in the project, i.e. during sprint 1 (also proposed by Sy [6]). This initial sprint involves conducting contextual inquiry to interview and observe end-users in their real working environments in order to capture as comprehensive a set of requirements as possible. Subsequent sprints (e.g. Sprint 2 to Sprint 4, etc.) involve an iterative process of design, evaluation and implementation. In these subsequent sprints, the project team engages in creating preliminary designs based on the requirements collected during sprint 1, which have been used to identify concept groups. Concept groups (as shown in Fig. 4.4), which Sy refers to as design chunking [6], refers to several features being grouped together and viewed as being inter-dependent/inter-related in the design. This grouping is done in order to maintain as much of a holistic perspective as possible and to minimise design changes on the overall user's experience.

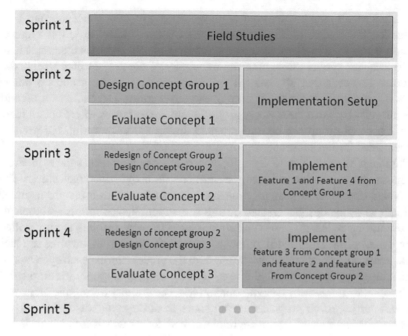

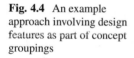

Fig. 4.3 Proposed process for incorporating Scrum into UCD focused projects

Fig. 4.4 An example approach involving design features as part of concept groupings

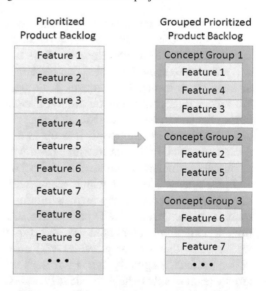

During sprint 2, designs for features from concept group 1 are not implemented but rather represented in low-fidelity prototypes/mockups, which are then evaluated with users. During sprint 2 the developers in the project team set up the development environment as preparation for starting their development work from sprint 3 onward. Sprint 3 then involves redesigning the designs from concept group 1 based on feedback collected during evaluation sessions with users. It is this redesigned version that is then implemented by the developers. This process then repeats itself for subsequent sprints throughout the remainder of the project lifecycle. It should be noted however that all features from any single concept group do not need to be implemented at the same time in the same sprint. Depending on secondary dependencies between the concept groups, there are instances where not all features from a concept group can be implemented during the same sprint, but need to be implemented during subsequent sprints.

Although very similar to Sy's [6] approach, our approach shown in Fig. 4.3 differs in that it involves collecting customer data using contextual inquiry (interviews and observation) primarily during cycle/sprint 1. End-users are involved in evaluations of the designs created during subsequent cycles/sprints and their input is used during redesign, however, requirements for new features are not collected after cycle/sprint 1. Sy's [6] proposed approach appears to involve conducting contextual inquiry and interviews throughout the process during each cycle/sprint, to collect input for designs created during subsequent cycles/sprints. Additionally, Sy [6] appears to implement design chunks (concept groups) during the same sprint, whereas our approach proposes having some flexibility towards organising which features within a concept group are implemented during which sprint. This is in part to accommodate any secondary dependencies which need to be resolved in earlier stages.

From our experience we also found that related design work and development can be done close together but not in parallel, with design work being done at least one sprint ahead of the development work to accommodate both design evaluation and redesign. It should be noted that implementation issues can also affect redesign in addition to evaluation feedback from users. Since some design work may be too labour intensive to pursue, trade-off decisions need to be made in the design during the sprint. Note also that all features within a concept group do not have to be implemented in one sprint. It is up to the team and their effort estimations to decide on which individual features from which concept groups can be completed during the sprint and which need to be held over for the next sprint.

For bigger projects in which teams with more members are involved, it is important to meet regularly to plan future sprints to spot which activities might require planning from a UCD perspective. These activities are time consuming and time dependent on other resources, and if they are not planned in advance the user testing and other similar activities will need to be postponed to future releases of the product. Regularly synchronising outcomes of the different UX activities among team members helps to identify and plan future activities and resources that otherwise would be missed or postponed. This again highlights the interdependency among tasks in a group, as design decisions affect the implementation and the implementation affects design decisions. From our perspective, we believe that our proposed approach will help other UCD project teams handle some of the pitfalls often associated with running UCD focused projects using Scrum.

Our proposed approach is similar to that of Sy [6] with the difference being the idea of grouping closely related features into groups to ensure that the dependencies between those features do not get lost during trade-off discussions innate to the UCD process, where iterative testing and redesign frequently occur.

4.5 Conclusion

What we found over the course of our project was that Scrum can be effective for running UCD focused projects, however, in our experience some changes to the Scrum process are needed. The changes from our perspective included: (1) involving team members who can dedicate 100 % of their time to the project, (2) being able to change the length of sprints and (3) the ability to add tasks from the backlog to the sprint backlog as needed. Scrum is also more effective if field studies (user interviews) have been completed early on in the project. Trying to run Scrum while this is still ongoing is problematic and requires considerable planning and synchronisation among team members. Another insight is to also provide those team members who are perhaps in a more supporting role during a sprint with a way in which to show their contributions on the Scrum board. Finally, it is important to maintain a holistic view of the project. This can be partially achieved by grouping related features and using those groupings during the design process to maintain a more holistic perspective. This can help to keep the team from getting lost in the sometimes narrowly-viewed incremental progression often associated with using Scrum.

Acknowledgements The authors would like to thank the team members who participated in the project for their valuable insights and feedback.

References

1. Budwig M, Jeong S, Kuldeep K (2009) When user experience met agile: a case study. In: Proceedings of CHI 2009. ACM Press, New York, pp 3075–3083
2. McInerney P, Maurer F (2005) UCD in agile projects: dream team or odd couple? Interactions 12(6):19–23
3. Sy D, Miller L (2008) Optimizing agile user-centred design. In: CHI '08 Extended abstracts on human factors in computing systems, CHI EA '08. ACM, New York, pp 3897–3900
4. Ungar J, White J (2008) Agile user centered design: enter the design studio – a case study. In: CHI '08 Extended abstracts on human factors in computing systems, CHI EA '08. ACM, New York, pp 2167–2178
5. Schwaber K, Sutherland J (2013) The Scrum guide. http://www.scrum.org/
6. Sy D (2007) Adapting usability investigations for agile user-centered design. J Usability Stud 2(3):112–132

Chapter 5
Integration of Human-Centred Design and Agile Software Development Practices: Experience Report from a SME

Carmelo Ardito, Maria Teresa Baldassarre, Danilo Caivano, and Rosa Lanzilotti

Abstract The integration of Human-Centred Design (HCD) and Agile software development approaches is gaining momentum in both the Human-Computer Interaction and Software Engineering communities. The common principles shared by the two approaches, i.e., iterative design, user involvement, continuous testing and prototyping, should facilitate their integration which, however, is not without problems. In this chapter we report a study conducted in a Small-Medium sized Enterprise (SME) that adopts a Scrum-based methodology. After identifying the integration points between HCD and Agile development activities, a tailored HCD-Scrum methodology has been applied to the development of a web application aimed at retrieving and comparing data related to public institutions.

Keywords Tailored HCD-Agile methodology • Case study

5.1 Introduction

Many research papers have suggested methodologies and techniques to be used in software development processes, in order to maximise the usability and user experience (UX) of the final product. Unfortunately, they are very seldom used in industrial settings, as our recent studies have also pointed out [1]. However, Ardito et al. [2] provide evidence that Human-Centered Design (HCD) techniques can successfully be integrated in the software engineering practices of a company adopting a waterfall model, provided that a depth analysis of company practices is performed by HCD researchers along with the practitioners, working together during the entire software development process from inside the company.

C. Ardito • M.T. Baldassarre • D. Caivano • R. Lanzilotti (✉)
Dipartimento di Informatica, Università degli Studi di Bari Aldo Moro,
Via Orabona 4, 70125 Bari, Italy
e-mail: carmelo.ardito@uniba.it; mariateresa.baldassarre@uniba.it;
danilo.caivano@uniba.it; rosa.lanzilotti@uniba.it

© Springer International Publishing Switzerland 2016   117
G. Cockton et al. (eds.), *Integrating User-Centred Design in Agile Development*,
Human–Computer Interaction Series, DOI 10.1007/978-3-319-32165-3_5

HCD was proposed in the 1980s and since then, Human-Computer Interaction (HCI) researchers have worked in order to define methods to design and evaluate usable interactive systems. Nevertheless, even recent literature provides many examples revealing that this research has had little impact on software development practices for different reasons, i.e. lack of knowledge about what usability is, practitioners' feeling that too many resources (e.g. time and costs) are necessary, the difficulty in recruiting trained usability/HCD experts [3–6].

In recent years, our research has focused on deeply analysing the reasons that prevent a fruitful integration of HCD principles in the practice of software development [1, 2]. Specifically, in this chapter we focus on Agile development and report a study conducted in a Small-Medium sized Enterprise (SME) that adopts a Scrum-based methodology. The first objective was to identify, in collaboration with experienced project managers of the company, the integration points between Scrum and HCD activities. Thus, a tailored HCD-Scrum methodology was defined. It was applied to a company project concerning the development of a web application for retrieving data related to public institutions and comparing them based on several economic indexes (e.g., number of employees, incomes, outcomes, taxes issued, etc.).

The main novelty of the defined methodology is related to the need of an initial step, longer than the following development sprints, for creating a software system skeleton (i.e., the basic architecture for enabling the core functionalities and the wireframe of the main user interfaces) according to the requirements identified during the initial meetings with the customer. Starting from the next sprints, such an evolutional prototype is discussed and evaluated with the customer, as is usually done in Scrum methodologies [7, 8].

Another significant result showed that both face-to-face and remote informal Verification & Validation sessions performed during a sprint proved to be very valuable for improving usability and UX. The customer is also involved and actively participates in the co-design of the prototype. This methodology has been generalised and further experimented in other projects and is currently used by the software company.

The rest of the chapter is organised as follows. Section 5.2 discusses related work on the topic of HCD in Agile software development. In Sect. 5.3 the Scrum methodology tailored to and adopted by an Italian SME is presented. Section 5.4 describes a case study that shows how the Agile technique has been adopted and how user experience has been involved during the development process. A final discussion concludes the chapter.

5.2 Related Work

Interest in the integration of HCD and Agile development approaches is growing, as demonstrated by the number of papers published in the last decade [9]. Although HCD and Agile are two different software development approaches, they share common principles, i.e., iterative design, user involvement, continuous testing and prototyping [10], that are analysed from different viewpoints by the two communities. The integration of these two approaches will result in complementing each other, in order to allow us to gain the advantages of both worlds and at the same time to minimise the deficiencies of both approaches: HCD can improve Agile development by providing a systematic way to analyse end-user needs, whereas Agile can improve HCD by providing more frequent iterations, which leads to more frequent usability evaluations [11].

However, there are studies indicating that the combination HCD-Agile presents two important problems. The first one is related to the communication between developers and designers [12]. HCD practitioners concentrate on issues such as ease of use, ease of learning, user performance, user satisfaction, aesthetics; Agile practitioners, on the other hand, mainly focus on implementing functional requirements into a running system [13]. The other important problem regards the distinction of the role of the two different actors, i.e. the customer and the user, participating in HCD-Agile development approaches [14]. Differently from the HCD, in the Agile development approach customer and user play the same role, not distinguishing between customers, who have required the system but could not use it, and users, who will actually use the system.

Several studies examine various aspects of the integration of HCD and Agile approaches and suggest ways for this integration. In many cases, researchers report about their experience and provide recommendations suggesting how HCD can effectively be integrated in Agile approaches. An interesting systematic review carried out by Silva da Silva et al. identified six main aspects concerning the integration of such two development approaches [15]: (1) Little Design Up Front (LDUF), (2) Prototyping, (3) User stories, (4) Inspection evaluation, (5) User testing, (6) One sprint ahead (see Table 5.1).

Concerning the first aspect, i.e. LDUF, many researchers agree that user research activities should be performed before the project kickoff meeting is held [16, 17] or in a Sprint 0 through a contextual inquiry and/or user interviews [12, 18, 19]. One of the HCD techniques suggested is Extreme Personas (as called by the authors in [20]), an extension of XP's user stories.

Table 5.1 The six main aspects concerning the integration of HCD and Agile approaches

Aspect	Strengths
Little Design Up Front	User research activities performed before the kickoff meeting or in Sprint 0
Prototyping	Prototypes throughout the whole project
User stories	User requirements are created in coordination with all the stakeholders
Inspection evaluation	Paper prototypes are evaluated for refining the user interface
User testing	Interactive prototypes are evaluated involving end users
One sprint ahead	HCD specialists work one sprint ahead or in Sprint 0

The importance of prototyping is recognised for reaching an effective integration of the two approaches. Researchers suggest the creation of prototypes throughout the whole project [2, 16, 18] also because they are a good communication tool between developers and HCD specialists [2]. Prototypes can be generated from personas and user stories previously defined and evaluated through inspection evaluations and usability testing [11].

The third aspect concerns the definition of user stories. User stories illustrate the user-required application features that are created by the customer in coordination with all the stakeholders. As previously mentioned, they are instrumental for creating system prototypes [11, 18]. Researchers recommend defining user stories that address the usability issues and acceptance testing criteria [21].

Evaluation takes into account both user testing and inspection. The common recommendation is to slim down the evaluation procedure. Such evaluations should be performed at different stages of the system development lifecycle. Specifically, some researchers suggest carrying out evaluation on paper prototypes, with the goal of refining the user interface for the next iteration [11, 17, 18, 22]. Others recommend performing user testing only on interactive prototypes [23], while others suggest integrating user testing into the acceptance tests to validate the user interface, e.g. [24].

Inspection is a cost-effective technique recommended to be performed on paper prototypes that should be carried out until the prototype is stable to serve as a basis for the user interface implementation [25]. Heuristic Evaluation is the most used inspection technique.

Finally, concerning One Sprint Ahead, it is suggested that HCD specialists work one sprint ahead of the development team and recommend that this practice should start in Sprint 0 or even two or three iterations ahead of the rest of the team [12, 26, 27].

In this paper we report our experience in integrating HCD activities in an Agile software development approach. In our work, we have taken into account the recommendations reported in literature.

5.3 Integrating HCD Activities in the Scrum Process of the SME

Software development trends are moving more and more towards Agile methods pushing, at the same time, for a constant integration of customer feedback and HCD within the Agile approach practices themselves. After describing in Sect. 5.3.1 a typical Scrum-Like process, in Sect. 5.3.2 we illustrate how the Action Research method was applied in order to identify the integration points between HCD and Agile development activities and, finally in Sect. 5.3.3 how the Scrum-Like process has been tailored to the needs of an Italian SME called SER&Practices (from here on SER&P) and how customer feedback and HCD have been integrated into their

Agile development approach. The concept underlying the process is its adherence to Scrum-based practices, which have been adapted to conform to the needs of the SME. Key points are: constant involvement of the customer; rapid development of code through iterative stepwise refinements; high frequency of releases due to the continuous iterations.

5.3.1 A Typical Scrum-Like Process

A typical Scrum-Like process is depicted in Fig. 5.1. It is made of three major steps – *Inception, Development, Deliver* – even if they are often not clearly identified and are referred to in several and diverse manners. There are clear key roles involved – *Product Owner, Scrum Master, Team, Customer* – there are also a set of time-box events – *Sprint Planning* meeting, *Daily Standup* meeting, *Sprint Review, Sprint*

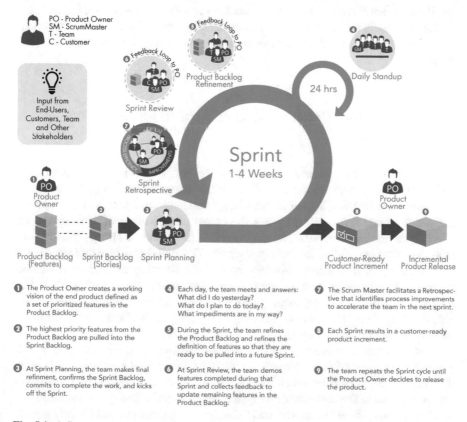

Fig. 5.1 A Scrum process representation rearranged from http://www.scruminc.com

Retrospective – and a couple of fundamental artifacts – *Product Backlog* and *Sprint Backlog*.

A key aspect of Scrum is the use of self-organised, cross-functional and empowered teams who organise their work into short development cycles, called Sprints.

A cycle begins with the input provided by stakeholders (End User, Customer, Team etc.). The Product Owner then develops a Prioritised Product Backlog, which contains a prioritised list of business and project requirements written in the form of user stories. Each Sprint begins with a Sprint Planning Meeting during which high priority user stories are considered for inclusion in the Sprint. A Sprint generally spans between 1 and 4 weeks and involves the Scrum Team working to create potentially shippable Customer-Ready Product Increments. During the Sprint, short, highly focused Daily Standup Meetings are conducted where team members discuss daily progresses. Toward the end of the Sprint, a Sprint Review Meeting is held during which the Product Owner and relevant stakeholders are provided a demonstration of the Product Increments. The Product Owner accepts the Product Increments only if they meet the predefined Acceptance Criteria. The Sprint cycle ends with a Retrospect Sprint Meeting where the team discusses ways to improve processes and performances as they move forward into the subsequent Sprint.

5.3.2   The Action Research Method Applied into a SME Process

Action research [28] is a social science methodology designed to help communities and organisations improve the way they address issues and solve problems and at the same time develop scientific knowledge about the problem and its solution. An action research process requires the active participation of individuals, i.e. researchers and practitioners, working together in a team to change the situation in an organisation, whilst conducting research. This collaboration results in a better understanding of the factors affecting the existing situation and the most suitable remedies. In past work with software companies aiming at integrating HCD in a company's software development practice [28], an action research approach was able to persuade practitioners and managers to incorporate UX activities into their software development life cycle.

In the current experience with SER&P, we performed action research in collaboration with experienced project managers of the company, in order to identify the integration points between HCD and Scrum activities. Thus, an HCI researcher was introduced to the software development team, in order to observe the team performing a Scrum-based approach, understand existing practices and identify aspects that were problematic from the involved practitioners' point of view. Data about current practices included notes of the practices reported in the researcher's diary, observations related to artifacts, and comments pertaining informal discussions with the other team members. Project managers and the HCI researcher met every 2 weeks. During these meetings, the researcher discussed with the project managers about significant episodes observed in the company and suggested possible HCI activities that could be integrated in the process.

At the end of the Action Research study, a methodology for integrating HCD and Scrum activities was defined, as shown in the next sub-section.

5.3.3   Tailored HCD-Scrum Methodology

In the current experience with SER&P, a methodology was defined which introduces in a Scrum-like process some fundamental improvements from both an HCI and an SE point of view. Its main characteristics are the following:

1. **Customer Committee**. One of the key roles in the process is the Product Owner. The Product Owner represents all the stakeholders and is the voice of the Customer. He or she is accountable for ensuring that the team delivers value to the business. The Product Owner writes customer-centric items (typically user stories), ranks and prioritises them, and adds them to the product backlog. "Typically" a Scrum team should have one product owner. This role is equivalent to the customer representative role in some other Agile approaches. SER&P has introduced the concept of Customer Committee that includes a Product Owner selected within the personnel of the Scrum Team and at least two people from the customer side, desirably an end user and a business domain expert. The Customer Committee is actively involved in the Product and Sprint Backlogs definition and Sprint Review.

2. **Inception**. In Scrum-based processes, at the beginning, the development of a software product or service usually starts with stakeholder inputs. In SER&P the inception phase consists of interviews to stakeholders, as well as a context and field study carried out jointly with the customer. The study provides the essential context background and knowledge necessary to design the application being developed and enable the Customer Committee and Team (the latter, typically, 4 persons or less) to evaluate and prioritise the issues/features to develop. It consists of market study, cost, portfolio and competitor analyses. In this way SER&P merges the needs and modus operandi usually adopted by HCI communities – that typically and almost exclusively refer to end users, lead users and customers during requirement definition – and software engineers – who refer prevalently to field studies, competitor legacy systems in use, market studies etc., with limited contact with end users or customers. This fundamental step allows the Customer Committee to pin down priorities, backlogs, user stories and features that customers consider most relevant. In each case, during the process itself, given its iterative characteristic of gradually adding features to the

final product, customers are continuously involved in designing and approving developed features and versions before they are released.

3. **Sprint n.0.** In a Scrum-like process, during this step a preliminary architecture of the application is conceived and main modules and sub-systems are identified. Nevertheless, the software development and the software source code usually take place in the Development phase during the Sprint execution. The SER&P process explicitly identifies a *Sprint n.0* in which a high level prototype is built. The basic architecture and infrastructure of the system are developed with the aim of having the foundations where the bricks produced in the next Sprints can be easily added. The goal is to obtain a highly modularised software system skeleton with basic software services such as data, communication, reporting, computation services etc., that enable effective software modules and functions development during the next Sprints. Another important objective is to reduce as much as possible the time needed for having a first version of working software. Only after having obtained this result, the Development phase can be executed effectively. Otherwise, the system development proceeds in a risky way due to the impossibility to have a constructive and effective feedback from customers.

4. **Scrum Islands**. SER&P typically uses teams of 4 persons or less. One of them is the Product Owner included in the Customer Committee that also covers the role of team member (involved in the software design and development) when not engaged in any committee activity. Another team member is usually a graphic designer with a basic knowledge of HCI techniques. The others are software engineers. When a project begins, the selected team members are transferred in a "Scrum Island" (see Fig. 5.2). A Scrum Island is a 4-seat working desk. This solution allows maximising the information flow, avoiding management gap and improving communication and collaboration between team members. For this reason in SER&P, the Daily Standup Meeting is not formally adopted. If a member is included in different islands or involved in more than one project, he/she physically moves between islands. Obviously, the company tries to minimise the sharing of persons across ongoing projects.

5. **1 Week Time Boxed Sprint.** SER&P adopts sprints with a fixed duration of 1 week. Every week the sprint outputs are reviewed and the next sprint backlog is defined by including the new tasks to be executed together with the still open and not closed ones. So the sprint duration is not the result of an ex-ante estimation but it is predefined. Estimations concerning the whole project are done by the Customer Committee at the end of every sprint, during the Product Backlog Refinement. This is possible thanks to the active involvement of the customer in the process. Thus, estimations about project termination and release deliver are carried out at the start of the project and updated weekly. A first draft of issues and their priority is made during the so-called *Inception* phase in order to have a general idea of the roadmap to follow and a first estimate of the effort required.

6. **(IN)Sprint Review.** The SER&P process includes a continuous Verification & Validation (V&V) activity. This activity temporally spans along the entire sprint. When a first/draft working software is available (after Sprint n.0 or few sprints

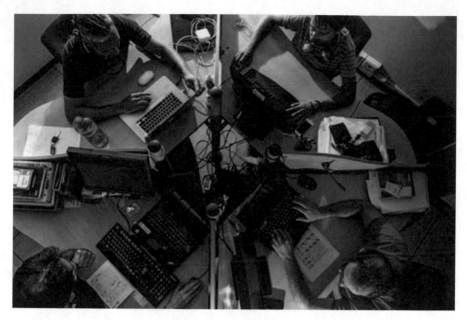

Fig. 5.2 A Scrum Island

later), the end users of the *Customer Committee* are asked to use the system and make a sort of user test or functional system test. This allows stressing and assessing the functionalities developed during a sprint and verifying their proper integration with what already exists. The results of the V&V activities are then discussed and analysed within the Sprint Review at the end of the Sprint. Here the Customer Committee is involved in the analysis of the results, from both functional and technical point of view, passing throughout the operating and business issues.

7. **Project Retrospective.** A Scrum process typically includes the *Sprint Retrospective* that is an official event in the Scrum methodology where all the parties (Product Owner, Scrum Master, Team) involved in the product development try to improve the process by sharing its strength and weaknesses. SER&P's process does not include it. Scrum means self-organised, cross-functional and empowered teams who organise their work autonomously. Thanks to the adoption of the Customer Committee, (IN)Sprint Review and Scrum Island an excellent information flow, a good communication level, a good coordination and prompt feedbacks from both team members and customer are assured. Thus, the Team can share, analyse and improve the process continuously without the need of a formal Sprint Retrospective event. Instead, what SER&P does is a *Project Retrospective*. Here all the available project data are analysed, strengths and weaknesses are highlighted and improvement opportunities and initiatives are defined and executed. In doing so SER&P refers to well known best practices and approaches in the Software Engineering community inspired to the Learning

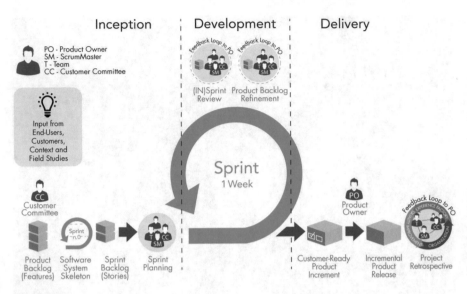

Fig. 5.3 Scrum process tailored by SER&P

Organisation and Experience Factory Models [29, 30]. This allows having a feedback loop within the entire SER&P organisation that enables and stimulates the company's growth. Another key point of this event is the active involvement of the customers in the retrospective analysis by means of a thematic focus group. During the focus group the customers are informally interviewed (to establish a friendly and relaxed atmosphere), in order to explore improvement opportunities and better address customer satisfaction and product quality improvements. The feedback collected is then used by SER&P to globally improve its strategies, management organisation and process.

An overview of the SER&P tailored HCD-Scrum process is showed in Fig. 5.3.

SER&P uses an *Application Lifecycle Management* (ALM) tool to manage its Scrum-based process called Redmine (www.redmine.org). In accordance to the tool characteristics, requirements are classified into the following possible categories: TO DO (new feature to develop), BUG (a corrective maintenance intervention to fix a bug related to a functionality that has already been developed), FEATURE (an evolutionary maintenance, i.e. a change in terms of modification or evolution of a functionality to add to the system). All issues are then prioritised into one of the following: low, normal, high, urgent, and immediate. The ALM therefore becomes the Product Owner's central channel towards the development team. The Product Owner uses the tool to formalise backlogs, classify issues and assign them to development team members, who in turn use their accounts to track the issues to develop during each sprint. It allows following progress of the project through an interactive Scrum board interface and tracking information such as tasks by category, statuses, workload of developers, issue tracker and so on.

Another tool used by SER&P during development to address software product quality is Kiuwan (www.kiuwan.com). It allows measuring, assessing and tracking software product quality and also improves it by means of a focused improvement plan. The Product Owner and Team use it during each Sprint Review where a quality report is produced for each sprint.

Data automatically collected through Redmine and Kiuwan are also used in the Project Retrospective for deciding on possible improvements.

5.4 Case Study

This section presents a case study that explores how the Scrum methodology, tailored to SER&P's production processes, has been used to carry out an industrial project called "PublicAccounts". The basic research question of this case study was: "How has SER&P integrated stakeholder input and feedback into their Agile software practices related to the PublicAccounts project?"

The project consists of creating a web portal able to integrate and elaborate several different data sources, in order to obtain precious information pertaining to the performance of public administrations and public bodies. The portal draws data in the form of open data from official sources on the web, such as for example www.soldipubblici.it, and from other databases provided by the Central Bank of Italy as well as the Ministry of Economy and Finance. It elaborates and classifies the data according to specific criteria and produces reports showing economical values of public institutions such as expenses, revenue, how public money is spent and invested, and so on. The application currently integrates data from 8000 Italian cities and will be extended to include all provinces, regions, and healthcare institutions. It provides a general overview of each single administration (Fig. 5.4) and also allows comparing public administrations, producing reports, elaborating statistics and rank virtuous cities compared to non-virtuous ones. The perspective users of the web portal are citizens, journalists, and public administration employees.

From a technological point of view, two critical issues for the project are the difficulty of contemporarily integrating and elaborating several heterogeneous data sources in terms of contents and structure on one hand, and on the other maximising the portal's usability assuring it is easy, immediate and intuitive to use.

At the time of writing the project has been running for 10 months and is expected to last a total of 18 months employing five staff each with at least 5 years of experience. Overall up to now a total of 1000 person days (including management effort) have been spent on the project.

SER&P adopted the Scrum-based process, illustrated in the previous section, to develop the portal. In accordance to the process, the work was carried out in incremental iterations. The work performed in the current Sprint and the next activities were planned.

The Customer Committee was defined. It included one person from SER&P and two from the customer side: an end user, i.e. a technician of the customer company

Fig. 5.4 Overview of revenues and expenses for the city of Firenze in the last 5 years

who uses the portal for his every day job, and a top manager with experience of the business role and business domain the portal refers to. Three development team members, two of which full time and one part time, were dedicated to the project. Daily Standup meetings were not conducted, given the characteristic of the Scrum Islands in SER&P, but instead weekly Sprint Reviews and Product Backlogs were scheduled.

Weekly meetings with the Customer Committee were scheduled. In particular, in the Sprint n.0 they were systematic and feedback was continuous, in order to define a general picture of the project, customer needs and the software system skeleton. Sprint n.0 was indeed the longest (40 days). The longer duration allowed to define a more detailed picture of requirements, architecture and front-end design, and to produce a first working prototype. In this sprint, more than in others, a greater portion of time and effort was arranged for planning and gathering customer data to produce upfront design and a starting-point prototype. Meetings were arranged in both SER&P sites and in the customer offices and took place mainly face to face. Communication channels such as video conferencing, email and teleconference were also used, but more during the later project sprints and especially during the (IN)Sprint Review in order to jointly analyse between the end user included in the

Product Backlog Items	New	In progress	Resolved	Closed		Rejected
#861: USER INTERFACE V3		#857: SHOW IDENTIFIERS		#856: SHOW ERROR		#858: MODULE FOR CONTACTS
#862: REPORT V2				#859: SHOW GRAPHICS AND HISTOGRAMS	#860: REPRODUCE YEAR INFORMATION	

Fig. 5.5 Project sprint board

Customer Committee and Product Owner from SER&P, the defects, bugs or non conformities discovered by the end user during the continuous V&V activities.

Overall 17 sprints were carried out, the first lasting 40 working days (in about 3 months) and 1 week each for the other ones. The ALM tool, Redmine, was used to conduct and manage the project in term of sprints, tasks assigned to the development teams, prioritisation of user stories, features and tasks, customer feedback and suggestions. Figure 5.5 illustrates an example of a snapshot of the Scrum board used for showing tasks related to specific product backlog items and moving them from one column to another depending on their status. A backlog item can either be *new*, if it is a new feature assigned to the sprint; *in progress* if it is being developed during the current spring, *resolved* if it is a bug that has been fixed; *closed* once the task has been completed during the sprint or *rejected* when a task (either todo, bug or feature) suggested by the Customer Committee is not accepted by the Product Owner to be taken into consideration for the product being developed. The colors of the post-its are also meaningful in indicating the type of task category. In this case red means TODO (new feature to develop) and orange indicates a BUG (corrective maintenance).

So for example, a backlog item related to the user interface (#861) has some tasks, belonging to both TODO and BUGS categories, that are InProgress (#857: show identifiers), Closed (#856: show error) and Rejected (#858: module for contacts). The interface also specifies the name of the developer the task has been assigned to. For sake of space, only a small portion of the board has been reported.

Figure 5.6 provides a snapshot of monitoring and controlling activities. Moreover, thanks to the features of the process, the Product Owner is able to have an overview of the entire project. In particular tasks are grouped by status, category and management. This helps summarising the information of the project sprint board related to all of the Sprints, identifying for example which tasks are new, in progress, resolved, closed or rejected; which categories they belong to, i.e. how many are bugs, features or todo and what their delivery status is.

As the project went on, at the end of each (IN)Sprint Review features were verified by the Customer Committee and Product Owner. In particular, product quality was verified in terms of usability features and also from a perspective of internal product quality through the Kiuwan platform. Figure 5.7 shows an example of the indicators generated for the report produced following to a Sprint.

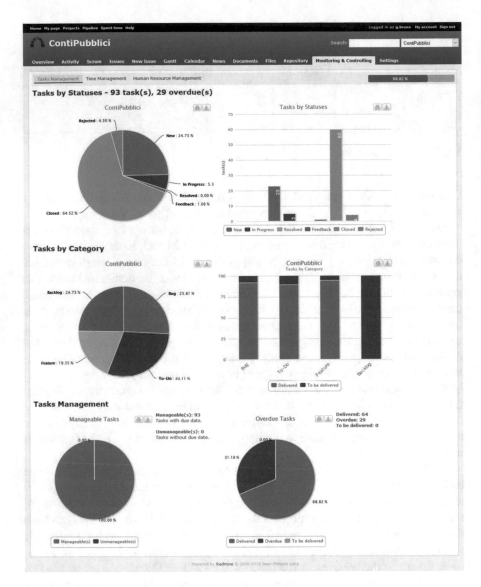

Fig. 5.6 Use of Redmine for managing the Scrum-based process

More specifically, the report summarises the general characteristics of the software being analysed providing structural information such as lines of code, number of files, level of complexity and amount of duplicated source code. In terms of internal quality, Kiuwan analyses source code with respect to quality characteristics such as: maintainability, reliability, portability, efficiency and security. It compares the current values of these quality characteristics to the baseline target threshold

Fig. 5.7 Use of Kiuwan for product quality control

values, which can be set on a scale from 0 to 100 for the analysis. In this case, the target values were all set to 70 and the graph shows that the thresholds are fulfilled except for maintainability and portability. Improving these characteristics to target values will require an effort of 102 person hours, to be planned in the following sprints. Indeed, the report is used as discussion point for the (IN)Sprint Review. It is also used in the Project Retrospective phase of the Delivery step, before a version of the product is released to the customer. This activity enforces interaction between Customer Committee, Product Owner, and Team in the light of a continuous improvement cycle towards the development and release of the final product.

5.5 Discussion and Conclusions

The successful development of the web application in the case study has shown the possibility of effectively integrating HCD techniques in the SME's Scrum practices. This has certainly required some tailoring of the Scrum practices. Changes have involved including staff who are totally dedicated to the project, the possibility of considering a flexible sprint length based on the workload and priority of features to be developed, use of an iterative-incremental progression of the Scrum development practices and most of all, customer interviews/field studies concentrated especially early on in the project.

The Project Owner with this iterative-incremental Scrum-based approach tries to combine her/his ideas of the final product with customers' input, and prioritises and sorts out feedback to make issues feasible for development. Customer feedback is crucial for the entire process. It has to be systematically gathered and appropriately filtered during each step of the process starting from end user and customer input collected during the Inception step; verified and validated during the (IN)Sprint review of the Development step; and feedback has to be provided by the Customer Committee in the Project Retrospective of the Delivery step before releasing the final product. On the other hand, it often happens that in the early stages of the process communication with the customer is difficult due to the different background of people involved. However, this difficulty is quickly and naturally overcome after the short period needed for participants to become accustomed to each other's habits and practices. We have also found that use of an Application Lifecycle Management (ALM) tool is crucial as it provides an important infrastructure for the entire team.

Strategically speaking, positive lessons learnt from integrating HCD into Scrum-based practices that have made SER&P successful in project execution include:

- carrying out an initial sprint, longer than the other development sprints, for creating a software system skeleton according to the requirements identified during the initial meetings with the customer;
- considering customer feedback early in the project sprints (especially in the first one) for upfront design and as a guideline for developing a prototype used as a communication means in the rest of the process in addition to face to face communication;
- working iteratively and incrementally during each sprint;
- planning for testing during the sprint and iterating in the next sprint based on the results, allowing customers to actively interact in the acceptance test of individual issues as well as of the entire release;

– using a project management tool, i.e. an ALM tool, which includes Scrum-based practices, to support the entire process and simplify organisation for Product Owners and development team members.

The experience described in this chapter has shown that customer feedback is valuable for HCD and in turn Agile practices seem well suited to be mapped to customer involvement. It is important that feedback and customer involvement are set at multiple points throughout the development process. To this end, the Scrum-based process adopted by SER&P indeed includes several points in all steps (Inception, Development, Delivery) that take into account such aspects. We have found that it is important that interviews/meetings/field studies are carried out in the first part of the project, during the first sprint, in order to have a clear picture of what is going to be developed. This is because the first sprint is most likely to be longer than the subsequent ones, which focus more on development, evaluation, implementation and integration aspects.

Customer feedback should be filtered, i.e., not everything a customer wants can be carried out or is actually a good idea. In this sense, SER&P practices involve decision points where suggestions can either lead to a new issue/change request or be rejected. As implementation issues can be affected by customer feedback it is important to closely evaluate the requests and discuss them, in order to reach trade-offs during project sprints.

All the status and evolution points should be tracked as the project proceeds. For this reason, decision making and project status monitoring on behalf of the Project Owner with respect to the development team members is simplified by using an ALM tool to support organisation of sprints, daily meetings, issue assignments and so on.

The Scrum process described in this chapter has been generalised and further experimented on in other projects and is currently used by SER&P. We are confident that the community is slowly moving in the right direction as user needs are becoming systematically ingrained into the production processes, especially Agile ones.

Acknowledgments This work is partially supported by the Italian Ministry of University and Research (MIUR) under grants PON02_00563_3470993 "VINCENTE", PON04a2_B "EDOC@WORK3.0", and PON03PE_00136_1 "DSE" and by the Italian Ministry of Economic Development (MISE) under grant PON Industria 2015 MI01_00294 "LOGIN". We are also immensely grateful to Prof. Maria Francesca Costabile and Prof. Giuseppe Visaggio for their valuable and constant support.

References

1. Ardito C, Buono P, Caivano D, Costabile MF, Lanzilotti R, Bruun A, Stage J (2011) Usability evaluation: a survey of software development organisations. In: International conference on software engineering and knowledge engineering (SEKE'11). Knowledge Systems Institute, Skokie, pp 282–287

2. Ardito C, Buono P, Caivano D, Costabile MF, Lanzilotti R (2014) Investigating and promoting UX practice in industry: an experimental study. Int J Hum Comput Stud 72(6):542–551
3. Rosenbaum S, Rohn JA, Humburg J (2000) A toolkit for strategic usability: results from workshops, panels, and surveys. In: SIGCHI conference on human factors in computing systems (CHI'00). ACM, New York, pp 337–344
4. Boivie I, Aaborg C, Persson J, Lofberg M (2003) Why usability gets lost or usability in In-house software development. Interact Comput 15(4):623–639
5. Cajander A, Gulliksen J, Boivie I (2006) Management perspectives on usability in a public authority: a case study. In: Nordic conference on human-computer interaction (NordiCHI'06). ACM, New York, pp 38–47
6. Seffah A, Donyaee M, Kline RB, Padda HK (2006) Usability measurement and metrics: a consolidated model. Softw Qual Control 14(2):159–178
7. Schwaber K, Beedle M (2001) Agile software development with Scrum. Prentice Hall PTR, Upper Saddle River
8. Dybå T, Dingsøyr T (2008) Empirical studies of agile software development: a systematic review. Inf Softw Technol 50(9–10):833–859
9. Jurca G, Hellmann TD, Maurer F (2014) Integrating Agile and user-centered design: a systematic mapping and review of evaluation and validation studies of Agile-UX. In: Agile conference (AGILE'14). IEEE Computer Society, pp 24–32
10. Blomkvist S (2005) Towards a model for bridging agile development and user-centered design. In: Seffah A, Gulliksen J, Desmarais M (eds) Human-centered software engineering – integrating usability in the software development lifecycle, vol 8. Springer, Dordrecht, pp 219–244
11. Hussain Z, Milchrahm H, Shahzad S, Slany W, Tscheligi M, Wolkerstorfer P (2009) Integration of extreme programming and user-centered design: lessons learned. In: Abrahamsson P, Marchesi M, Maurer F (eds) Agile processes in software engineering and extreme programming, vol 31. Springer, Berlin/Heidelberg, pp 174–179
12. Chamberlain S, Sharp H, Maiden N (2006) Towards a framework for integrating agile development and user-centred design. In: Abrahamsson P, Marchesi M, Succi G (eds) Extreme programming and agile processes in software engineering – XP'06, vol LNCS 4044. Springer, Berlin/Heidelberg, pp 143–153
13. Memmel T, Gundelsweiler F, Reiterer H (2007) Agile human-centered software engineering. In: British HCI group annual conference on people and computers: HCI . . . but not as we know it, vol 1 (BCS-HCI'07). British Computer Society, Swinton, pp 167–175
14. Highsmith J (2002) Agile software development ecosystems. Addison-Wesley Longman Publishing Co., Inc., Boston
15. Silva da Silva T, Martin A, Maurer F, Silveira M (2011) User-centered design and agile methods: a systematic review. In: Agile conference (AGILE'11). IEEE Computer Society, pp 77–86
16. Detweiler M (2007) Managing UCD within agile projects. Interactions 14(3):40–42
17. Williams H, Ferguson A (2007) The UCD perspective: before and after agile. In: Agile conference (AGILE'07). pp 285–290
18. Fox D, Sillito J, Maurer F (2008) Agile methods and user-centered design: how these two methodologies are being successfully integrated in industry. In: Agile conference (AGILE'08). IEEE Computer Society, pp 63–72
19. Kollmann J, Sharp H, Blandford A (2009) The importance of identity and vision to user experience designers on agile projects. In: Agile conference (AGILE'09). IEEE Computer Society, pp 11–18
20. Wolkerstorfer P, Tscheligi M, Sefelin R, Milchrahm H, Hussain Z, Lechner M, Shahzad S (2008) Probing an agile usability process. In: Extended abstracts of SIGCHI conference on human factors human factors in computing systems (CHI EA'08). ACM, New York, pp 2151–2158

21. Beyer H, Holtzblatt K, Baker L (2004) An agile customer-centered method: rapid contextual design. In: Zannier C, Erdogmus H, Lindstrom L (eds) Extreme programming and agile methods – XP/Agile Universe 2004, vol LNCS 3134. Springer, Berlin/Heidelberg, pp 50–59
22. Larusdottir MK (2012) User centred evaluation in experimental and practical settings. Media Technology and Interaction Design, KTH Royal Institute of Technology, Stockholm
23. Federoff M, Villamor C, Miller L, Patton J, Rosenstein A, Baxter K, Kelkar K (2008) Extreme usability: adapting research approaches for agile development. In: Extended abstracts of SIGCHI conference on human factors human factors in computing systems (CHI EA'08). ACM, New York, pp 2269–2272
24. Benigni G, Gervasi O, Passeri F, Kim, TH (2010) USABAGILE_Web: a web agile usability approach for web site design. In: Taniar D, Gervasi O, Murgante B, Pardede E, Apduhan B (eds) computational science and its applications – ICCSA 2010, vol LNCS 6017. Springer, Berlin/Heidelberg, pp 422–431
25. Hellmann TD, Hosseini-Khayat A, Maurer F (2010) Supporting test-driven development of graphical user interfaces using agile interaction design. In: International conference on software testing, verification, and validation workshops (ICSTW'10). IEEE Computer Society, pp 444–447
26. Sy D, Miller L (2008) Optimizing agile user-centred design. In: Extended abstracts of SIGCHI conference on human factors human factors in computing systems (CHI EA'08). ACM, New York, pp 3897–3900
27. Illmensee T, Muff A (2009) 5 Users every friday: a case study in applied research. In: Agile conference (AGILE'09). IEEE Computer Society, pp 404–409
28. Checkland P, Holwell S (1998) Action research: its nature and validity. Syst Pract Action Res 11(1):9–21
29. Basili VR, Caldiera G, Rombach HD (2002) Experience factory. In: Encyclopedia of software engineering. Wiley, New York
30. Schneider K, Von Hunnius J-P, Basili V (2002) Experience in implementing a learning software organization. IEEE Softw 19(3):46–49

Chapter 6
Communication Breakdowns in the Integration of User-Centred Design and Agile Development

Silvia Bordin and Antonella De Angeli

Abstract Despite several calls for a more systematic integration of User-Centred Design and Agile development methodologies, no satisfactory agreement has been found yet. We articulate three breakdowns that may occur when integrating these two software engineering approaches, namely a variable interpretation of user involvement, a mismatch in the value of documentation, and a misalignment in iterations. These themes emerged from theoretical grounding as part of action research in a case study where UCD and Agile were integrated to develop mobile applications for a user community. We discuss attempted strategies for improving community involvement alongside the evolution of the project team, composed of developers, designers, users, and customers. We finally suggest ways to promote a receptive organisational culture for the integration of UCD and Agile, drawing inspiration from participatory design and design thinking, retaining the richness of community voice, and effectively timing the combination of the two methodologies.

Keywords Working practices • Organisational culture • Research into design

6.1 Introduction

In recent years there has been a growing interest in understanding the combination of the user-centred design (UCD) and Agile development approaches, both in the human-computer interaction community and in the software engineering one. This convergence would lead to a more holistic software engineering approach relative to the application of one of the individual methodologies alone [1]. The advantage is twofold: on the one hand, Agile methodologies do not explicitly address usability or user experience (UX) aspects in their understanding of the development process, although valuing customer satisfaction [2, 3]. Yet, these aspects cannot be overlooked anymore, since a carefully designed UX can provide an advantage over competing products [4]. In fact, despite its problematic nature

S. Bordin (✉) • A. De Angeli
Department of Information Engineering and Computer Science, University of Trento,
Trento, Italy
e-mail: bordin@disi.unitn.it; antonella.deangeli@disi.unitn.it

© Springer International Publishing Switzerland 2016   137
G. Cockton et al. (eds.), *Integrating User-Centred Design in Agile Development*,
Human–Computer Interaction Series, DOI 10.1007/978-3-319-32165-3_6

and high costs [5], effective user involvement results in high reward and several expected benefits including improved quality, understanding, and acceptance of the product [5], and generally overall "positive effects on both system success and user satisfaction" [6].

On the other hand, UCD does not explicitly address how the implementation of the design should be performed, despite needing to ensure that no "design drift" [1] occurs by maintaining a tight connection with the development. Agile methodologies appear to fill this gap because of their capability to flexibly respond to change in requirements, priorities and context, benefitting from a constant involvement of the customer in the process. These features have facilitated their widespread adoption in companies [7]. Furthermore, the intrinsically iterative nature of Agile implies continuous testing and incremental improvement of stable versions of a software product, fostering an overall higher quality of the final outcome, and aligning in principle with the iterative nature of UCD.

Despite these benefits, no satisfactory way to integrate UCD and Agile has become established yet, if one exists. We contribute to filling this gap by reflecting on our own experience as researchers and designers in a project where the integration of UCD and Agile was used in mobile application development, not for a single business customer, but for a whole community of users. By intertwining research into design [8] and a literature review, we identified three communication breakdowns that are likely to occur because of a mismatch in the formalisation of key themes in the two approaches, namely the interpretation of user involvement, the value of documentation, and the synchronisation of iterations. We believe that the analysis of such communication breakdowns can provide a distinctive analytical tool to facilitate a shared understanding of the respective assumptions of UCD and Agile and of the potential conflicts between them, thus supporting new kinds of collaborative work arrangements.

Consistently with [9], we observed that all breakdowns are manifested at the work process level, but that their solution requires changes in the organisational structure. As a result, we propose some reflections on the need to foster the establishment of a suitable and receptive organisational culture in order for an effective integration of UCD and Agile to occur; these considerations are inspired by the participatory design and design thinking approaches. We also reflect on how to retain the articulation of the needs and positions expressed by a whole user community and, in a more process-oriented perspective, on which is the most suitable timing to integrate UCD and Agile, taking into account the peculiarities of the two methodologies.

6.2   State of the Art

User-centred design is an umbrella term used to denote a set of techniques, methods, procedures and processes that places the user at the centre of an iterative design process [10]. As stated by Norman already 30 years ago, when UCD was struggling to establish itself in a predominantly technology-pushed environment, "the purpose of the system is to serve the user, not to use a specific technology, not to be an elegant piece of programming" [11]. Agile also presents a variety of methods advocating a lightweight approach to software development where rapid and flexible adaptation to change is the key to maximising customer satisfaction. Such adaptation is achieved through a process of continuously improving, evolutionary development carried out by a self-organising, cross-functional team that communicates through face-to-face and often informal meetings rather than through formal documentation. Agile methodologies are grounded on the principles and values listed in the Agile Manifesto [12], which, among other things, highlights the concept of customer collaboration: the customer is in fact expected to be actively involved in the development process, although to a variable extent depending on the specific form of the methodology in practice, and to have the power to steer the direction of the project by intervening on the requirements according to his/her possibly changing needs [13].

We highlight that both UCD and Agile can be instantiated in a large variety of practices: this makes it difficult to present a definitive position on the integration of the two approaches. However, in the next sections we will discuss three themes in particular that may have diverging interpretations in the two methodologies, namely user involvement, documentation, and synchronisation of iterations. These themes, which emerged from a case study and were then corroborated through a literature review, are most likely to cause communication breakdowns, i.e. examples of "disruption that occurs when previously successful work practices fail, or changes in the work situation (new work-group, new technology, policy, etc.) nullify specific work practices or routines of the organizational actors and there are no ready-at-hand recovery strategies" [9]. Communication breakdowns occur in the absence of a shared meaning among team members and can be counteracted by designing for translucence (i.e. the combination of visibility, awareness and accountability); shared meaning is nurtured by grounding (the communication process aimed at the creation of mutual knowledge, assumptions, and beliefs [14]) and consolidated by knowledge sharing.

6.2.1 Integration

A growing interest in understanding the combination of UCD and Agile is emerging, as witnessed for instance in the literature reviews performed by Jurca [4] and Salah [1], which consider 76 and 71 papers respectively. The papers were selected based on their focus on methodologies for integrating UCD and usability engineering with Agile approaches, with an accent on the software engineering community, to which the authors belong. Results suggest that much literature on the topic consists of "experience reports", with "few rigorously conducted studies in Agile-UX" [4] or systematic guidelines. Moreover, that research is dispersed over a large number of venues and is likely to not fully reach its intended target community. Both studies conclude that there is a need for design and development methodologies that can "draw on the best practices and tools of the two disciplines" [3].

Attempts at integrating the practices of UCD and Agile development have been made over time [e.g. 15], leveraging the similarities of the two methods while mitigating their differences. An approach called *Agile usability* is proposed in [16], enriching the Extreme Programming methodology with several artefacts drawn from HCI each used in different moments. Similarly, some experts suggest applying discount usability methods by involving a very small number of users (one to three), with frequent testing and with constant updates to the team and the clients [17]. Others propose to lighten UCD approaches in order to keep the pace of Agile iterations [18]: for example, the presence of an onsite customer is reported as a common practice in Agile projects to facilitate the communication of requirements to developers [3]. Ungar and White [19] describe a case study in which the application of the design studio approach might effectively bridge UCD methods and Agile ones, such as Scrum: this approach envisages a rapid, iterative process of ideas generation, discussion, and reconciliation into a unique design concept to be implemented. Lean UX [20] is a practitioners' proposal for the integration of UCD practices into Agile; yet, as argued in [21], the organisation applying this methodology has to be ready for it, developing an appropriate internal culture, which is often a non-trivial condition to achieve.

While acknowledging the large and robust common ground [14] that the two approaches anyway share, in the next paragraphs we will introduce three communication breakdowns [9] that are likely to affect their integration.

6.2.2 User Involvement

The concept of user-centredness is complex and covers a broad range of perspectives, which according to [22] are articulated around four dimensions: user focus, work-centredness, involvement or participation, and system personalisation. Different and at time conflicting interpretations of processes, practices, and goals exist within these macro-areas. The dimension of involvement is particularly interesting for our work as it describes different approaches related to the user role in design, ranging from an *informative* role (users act as providers of information and as objects of observation) to a *consultative* role (users comment on predefined design solutions) to a *participative* role (users actively take part in the design process and have decision-making power regarding solutions) [5]. User involvement in the informative/consultative role stresses a functional empowerment of users in its focus on designing usable and satisfying systems; this differs from the participatory design perspective, which aims at a democratic empowerment [23] by allowing people to shape the tools which will affect their work or personal life.

In UCD, user-centredness is typically described in this continuum between involvement and participation [22]: user needs and activities are thoroughly researched and understood by the design team upfront or in direct collaboration with a small sample of selected users. Agile techniques also encourage the customer's collaboration throughout the development process; however, in the Agile terminology, the notion of customer is often blended with that of a user [24], with contrasting interpretations of the distinction between these two concepts and of whom is supposed to take this role. Most Agile methods in fact define the customer as a representative of the end users who has direct and regular contact with them [e.g., 2, 25, 26]. However, some authors report that it is infrequent for a real end-user to act as a customer [15, 27], subsequently questioning the extent to which the customer can actually represent the real user and his/her needs [3, 28]. Others [15] recommend that the customer's engagement should also be supported by a number of other roles within the team, such as a proxy user, or that the customer role should be filled by one or more members of the product team [29], since customers are part of the release planning and iterative development process [28]. The duties of the customer, in their fuzzy definitions, include acting as the voice of the end user, evaluating performance and helping to prioritise and plan cycles and releases [30]. This responsibility can turn out to be overwhelming [25] and some authors argue that there is no guidance on how the customer should be able to articulate his/her needs in order to communicate the requirements to developers [28, 31].

Indeed, the very same capability of users to articulate their own working practices or to design a system can be questioned [28]; furthermore, because of a mutual learning effect, some authors claim that the more the "representative" customer becomes part of the development team, the less useful he/she is as a user surrogate [28, 32]. The same authors also propose a distinction between the user and the customer: the user interacts with the system being designed directly and uses it to accomplish his/her job, while the notion of customer is broader: understanding the users is needed to achieve a good design, understanding the customer is needed for its acceptance.

In general, given all these considerations, it seems that the integration of user needs within the feature-oriented Agile development process has not been fully achieved yet; as concluded in [3], one of the reasons is "a lack of tactics and practices" within organisations.

6.2.3   Documentation

Independently of the key issue about who is expected to be a team member (developers, designers, usability experts, users and/or customers) in an integrated UCD/Agile project, both methodologies place an emphasis on frequent communication among team members to support project awareness. However, while UCD has produced a number of design tools to support communication with developers, such as scenarios or personas, Agile tends to emphasise face-to-face informal communication. In a UCD process, formal documentation may record design rationales, list user and interface requirements, and provide the ground truth about the overall design vision, becoming "crucial for estimation and implementation efforts" [10]. Therefore, the experts will devote an important amount of time to analysing users and their tasks and then iteratively collecting feedback; these activities need to be performed and documented before the implementation phase begins.

Conversely, in Agile development the use of documentation is diminished [33], to the point that one of the principles of the Agile manifesto [12] states that "the most efficient and effective method of conveying information to and within a development team is face-to-face conversation". In [34], three types of collaborative work to realign designers and developers are identified: all of them are oral and the use of documentation is not even mentioned. Because of this, rather than having requirement documents, the Agile approach incorporates the user (or his/her representative) directly in the development team. There is anyway an on-going discussion within the Agile community concerning the fact that documentation should not be discarded altogether, especially given the complexity of modern systems, and that it just needs to be adapted to more dynamic processes [35]: the argument is hence about what is to be documented [35], how, and for what purposes (e.g. supporting organisational memory and communicating with stakeholders [36]). Nonetheless, often usability goals are documented in a very general way, relying on an oral common understanding instead [7]: this may however make a quantitative evaluation of such goals problematic and make the fulfilment of the "big picture of UX" more difficult [37].

6.2.4   Synchronisation of Iterations

One of the generally accepted principles of UCD defines it as iterative [38]; Agile development is instead intended as being not only iterative, but also incremental [30]. A further challenge is about how to synchronise the periods of UCD and Agile [1, 4], and in particular whether the two methodologies should proceed in parallel or not. Several proposals envision designers and developers working closely together in a synchronised manner. For example, in [39] a daily interaction between them is defined as "essential" for a successful outcome of the project; in [34], their collaboration is defined as informal, oral and ad-hoc. Schwartz [31] found that the development pace was better maintained in a project with a usability expert than without one: in addition, the former situation gave rise to *pair designing*, in which the developer and the usability expert worked together and learned from each other, thus improving HCI practices and knowledge in the whole team and in general resulting in a better project dynamic.

Other researchers propose to keep UCD and Agile separate instead, while just synchronising their periods of iteration [15] so that design stays ahead of development. This is the interpretation of Agile usability given by Nodder and Nielsen [40], who describe a process where design and development belong to two parallel tracks and the former feeds the latter with progressively refined user requirements, prototypes and tests. Similarly, in [29] the author recommends that the lengths of the iteration of the design and development tracks have to be carefully balanced so as to allow some advance for the design activities. Another successful example of dual-track approach is described in [39]: the author reports that, in order to accommodate the different paces of UCD and Agile, the timing and frequency of data collection, rather than the methods, changed considerably.

A distinct issue concerns the amount of work, and specifically design, to be performed before the implementation phase begins [41]. UCD encourages the team to understand their users as much as possible before writing code [15]: experts will devote an important amount of time to analyse users and their tasks in order to create the interface specification document and then to iteratively collect feedback from users through various usability techniques. Despite being time-consuming activities, data collection and analysis are nevertheless considered to be necessary to inform implementation. Conversely, given its feature-oriented nature and the emphasis put on early software delivery, Agile methods are largely against an up-front period of investigation at the expense of writing code [15]: they capture "user stories" [24] instead, that is high-level requirements to be addressed at the beginning of each iteration, therefore reducing upfront work to a minimum. Still, several authors advocate a solid understanding of the user [28] also in terms of time and effectiveness and suggest the relevance of an "Iteration 0" (e.g. [1, 29]) in which upfront design and requirement elicitation are carried out, with some degree of compromise about the duration of such activities, in order to ensure the establishment of a holistic design vision that can be shared within the team [37].

Related to this, we underline that Agile approaches are prone to focusing on the details at the expenses of the overall project vision [1]. In order to mitigate this, the responsibility for carrying the UX vision forward should be explicitly shouldered by the management and the organisational context [7, 37].

6.3   The Smart Campus Project

A large set of observations on the potential and challenges of the integration of UCD and Agile development derives from our experience in the Smart Campus project, where the two methodologies were applied to mobile application development for a community of users. Smart Campus started in 2012 in the context of establishing a living lab in the Province of Trento and lasted 3 years. The University campus was selected as the playground to experiment with a vision emphasising the role of the community as builder of services. The project aimed at creating an ecosystem that could foster students' active participation in the design and development of services for their own campus [42]. A service infrastructure was the main technological outcome of the project [42–44]; on top of that, a set of eight mobile applications (Fig. 6.1) was developed to help students with a variety of professional (tracking university achievements; managing email), social (creating and managing groups; getting information about events in the city), and private tasks (travelling through the city; keeping a multimedia diary; receiving information about the university cafeterias) [45].

UCD and Agile were chosen as useful methodologies for a project that needed a fast delivery of the product while ensuring a focus on user needs [46]: the former was applied to interface design, the latter was used to build the service architecture. The project team consisted of approximately 25 members, including interaction designers and software engineers. Furthermore, several groups of students were

Fig. 6.1 The Smart Campus
mobile applications set

involved, reaching over 500 people in total; they played the role of users or
customers at different points of the project. Approaches for community engagement
changed as the socio-technical infrastructure was evolving, as discussed in [42].
Some of these students were directly included in the living lab as interns, in a
participatory development effort, while others played a consultative role commenting on the applications as they were developed. The dialogue between developers,
designers and users was mediated by a set of communication channels including a
forum (based on *phpbb*, a simple open source bulletin board system, a beta testing
community in Google Play, and social networks (i.e. Twitter, Google+, Facebook,
LinkedIn). In an effort to promote the sustainability of the project [47], the code was
released as open source on GitHub, a platform for collaborative development.

6.3.1   Project Methodology

During the first year of the project, design and development proceeded on two
parallel tracks: design focused on conceptual work and community engagement,
while development focused on the service infrastructure. Several design activities
such as focus groups, diaries, online ethnography and workshops were put in
place, engaging 60 bachelor and master students overall; these activities aimed
to investigate the life of the student population and understand the design space

Fig. 6.2 Different examples of low-fidelity prototypes for the Smart Campus applications

of the project. At the same time, we also performed a benchmarking of mobile apps offered by other universities and studies of online student communities. This information was used to build personas, scenarios, and later storyboards and sketches that informed the vision of Smart Campus as a toolbox containing separated but interrelated services for students' use (Fig. 6.2).

In parallel, the backend functionalities of the service platform began to be developed following a rather traditional, incremental, and non-Agile approach. The apps were then released to a growing community of campus students, starting from 90 students on the Human-Computer Interaction course for bachelor students within the local Department of Computer Science. This first group of users was also provided with a smartphone and a paid data plan in order to ease the testing, as few of them had a suitable device and we aimed to seed a user community [42].

These initial UCD and development techniques required both time and documentation. However, as the technological infrastructure became more mature and demands for more frequent app releases became more urgent, the management realised that a much faster development pace was needed: therefore, almost a year into the project, the development team quickly transitioned to an Agile development methodology, namely Scrum. Since the team had little experience with this approach, the CTO read manuals about how to implement it, involving the management in this training as well, and then briefly introduced the Agile practices to the team during a sample sprint planning meeting. Scrum was not applied by the book, but it required accommodating the peculiarities of the existing team: for instance, the CTO also took the role of the Scrum master, while the rest of the project management kept prerogatives such as maintaining relationships with the University and administrating personnel and funds; appointed "champions" of the apps, i.e. members of the development or management who were responsible for a specific app and in charge of tracking its progress, became different product owners; interns were incorporated as on-site user representatives (at least in principle, as we will see later).

The transition to Agile disrupted the alignment between the design and the development team: even though they were both following iterative approaches, it soon became clear that the iterations required by UCD were longer than those envisaged by the Scrum sprints, which were set to last 1 or 2 weeks. In fact, the design team was supposed to be ahead of the development team by at least one cycle [48], in order to be able to transfer prototypes and requirements to the development team in a timely manner. At the same time, however, designers had to face a large amount of qualitative feedback continuously coming from the user community, analyse it, and prioritise extracted requirements. A ticket was created in an internal system for most relevant user suggestions; designers would prepare design solutions and then pass them on to the developers for the implementation.

Overall, the project needed to find a suitable collaboration protocol between the design and the development team that could effectively accommodate the feedback coming from the community while not impeding the development pace. To this end, we tried several approaches to maximise team communication, which for our convenience will be classified based on their methodological structure as *formal*, *semi-formal*, and *informal* approaches.

The Formal Approach The formal approach was encouraged by the management and consisted of passing on any design issues and decisions in a written manner: this conflicted with the prescriptions of the Agile methodology. The first attempt was to use an internal wiki for collaborators, where a table of issues to be solved was maintained: this method was good for keeping track of all the problems encountered, but was not a self-explanatory procedure, as it often required additional information to be provided through different media as shared documents. The wiki was eventually abandoned in favour of maintaining a presence on GitHub, in order to promote open source contributions to the project and encourage the interventions of the community directly related to the code. This approach proved somewhat restrictive for designers as GitHub is used mostly to report bugs or issues with software behaviour, but it is not meant to support the tracking of progress about the overall UX design or the usage by people without technical expertise.

The Semi-Formal Approach In the semi-formal approach, we include different kinds of meetings. Notably, none of them directly involved any user representatives with the exception of the students involved in the Smart Campus development lab, who were actively contributing to a participatory development approach. *HCI meetings* usually gathered the whole design team and the champions of the apps. *Matchmaking meetings* were usually held once every 2 weeks and involved all of the Smart Campus staff (managers, developers, interns and designers): during these meetings, project landmarks and dates were discussed, problems brought up, and work divided. *Scrum meetings* basically replaced matchmaking ones when the team adopted an Agile approach. They were quick daily meetings, usually held early in the morning, aimed at checking the status of the project and estimating how a specific task was progressing. In turns, the members of the group involved in the Scrum reported about any problems they encountered, tasks performed and plans for the day. The Scrum Master coordinated the activity by annotating this information on a progress chart to check the status of the work and the feasibility of set goals.

The Informal Approach The informal approach consisted of face-to-face meetings between a developer and a designer, often resulting in pair designing, i.e. in the two working together in close collaboration to modify and improve the user interface during the sprints. In line with the Agile development spirit, these meetings produced no documentation. Similarly, at times developers engaged in quick chats over instant messaging systems such as Google Hangouts or Skype. In general, this approach was applied to solve specific user interface issues, not to address overarching UX themes such as for instance transitioning to the most recent look and feel suggested by the Android design principles.

The Mixed Approach Mixed approaches, between semi-formal and informal, were used in specific situations like the so-called *crazy weeks*, i.e. accelerated sprints where the whole team concentrated its efforts in order to reach a mutually agreed goal. This method was used two or three times in a year, usually to enhance aesthetics and functionalities when envisioning an immediate release of the apps. At the beginning, developers, managers and designers met to discuss on "show-stoppers", i.e. issues that would seriously compromise the usability of the app and would not allow its release; each issue could include different tasks, such as prototyping and development, and was usually assigned both to a designer and a developer, in a *pair designing* effort.

Despite this wealth of attempted collaboration strategies, the project team felt that none of them was actually fully satisfactory in integrating design and development activities. As problematic situations emerged in the project, we referred to literature in order to understand whether the issues were specific to the project or whether they had also been encountered elsewhere. We therefore combined two complementary approaches to research into design [8]: a bottom-up one, aimed at extracting themes from the analysis of project data, and a top-down one, aimed at consolidating such themes through a substantial literature review.

6.3.2   Data Analysis

The data reported in this work were collected through a number of different sources, including formal interview studies involving team members and the student community, and personal observations of the authors, who participated in the project respectively as an interaction designer and the principal investigator. In claiming the value of the findings derived from personal observations, we refer to the concept of "autobiographical design" [49]: while its authors define it as "design research drawing on extensive, genuine usage by those creating or building the system", we intend autobiographical data as drawing on the same kind of usage, but this time by those creating or building *practices* rather than a system.

A first interview study was performed in summer 2013 after an intense period of Agile development to investigate the perception of user involvement in the project, also focusing on issues of team coordination and awareness. It engaged 20 people: 7 staff members (developers and HCI researchers) and 13 students with different levels of involvement with the project. A second study was carried out in spring 2014, focusing on the project documentation and the practices to create and use it. Among the 12 interviewees, 7 were developers in the Smart Campus lab, while 5 were students involved in the participatory development activities.

To decrease possible social bias, all interviews were conducted by a researcher external to the project. Audiotapes were transcribed and iteratively coded by the authors through thematic analysis [50]; double coding was performed on 25 % of the transcripts yielding an inter-rater reliability of 93 %. Interview analysis was conducted after the end of the project, in parallel to the literature review previously presented. Citations in the next paragraphs will be attributed to interviewees as follows: *Dev* for developers; *Des* for designers; *Int* for interns; *Stud* for students in the community.

6.4 Results

This section is composed of three parts focusing on the communication breakdowns previously introduced. For each of them we articulate the strategies employed in the project and discuss their perception according to the team.

6.4.1 User Involvement

The user and the customer were clearly differentiated in Smart Campus; we fully embrace the vision outlined for instance in [15, 27], according to which these figures denote different targets of design interventions. The customer of the project was the local University: in line with the funding scheme of the project, they contributed the case study and some personnel time. Most of the allocated personnel were appointed either from high-level administrative managers in charge of Education and IT, who participated in formal meetings with the project team, or from academic staff, who supported the research work leveraging on a richer variance of communication contexts by keeping in close contact with the Smart Campus team. The relationship with the customer was always complex and led to a partial dismissal of the project result after the ending of the financial support from the funding body. The fact that the University is no longer sponsoring the Smart Campus apps as we write is a clear sign that the communication with the customer failed during the project, reinforcing Bjørn and Ngwenyama's considerations [9] about the organisational structure being the main responsible for the failure or success of working practices. However, the discussion of this topic is outside the scope of this chapter.

User involvement in the Smart Campus project ranged along the continuum between involvement and participation [22] and evolved over a period of 3 years, where we attempted to transform our users (the students in the campus) into a community of service developers [42]. Students were in fact involved in the project initially with an informative role, for example through questionnaire and diary studies, then with a consultative role when they acted as beta testers of the apps developed by the lab, and finally as participants in the development of their own apps when integrated as interns in the project team. This process was successful in that it delivered a set of eight mobile apps, two of which entirely designed and developed by the student community, which were adopted in everyday life often with positive evaluations. Despite the convenience of our user target, especially as both authors fulfil educational duties in the local University campus, the relationship with the students often led to difficulties and to the need of reconciling the meaning of user involvement between the designers and the developers. The communication with the students therefore spanned through the continuum of our interventions, from a formal approach (when students were required to evaluate the apps as part of a coursework) to a very informal one, as in frequent corridor conversations or short text messages.

During the project we highlighted a variable and at times contrasting perception of user involvement between designers and developers. In particular, the typical breakdowns occurring in the integration of UCD and Agile were exacerbated by what the community role actually entailed: this became evident at a management meeting in April 2013. The discussion regarded the case of a student who was particularly active in the forum and willing to contribute to the development, but was perceived as patronising by the developers, who reported discomfort during interaction; the discussion was then extended to the overall communication between developers and users, which, especially over the forum, was not always smooth, sometimes leading to communication breakdowns in a literal sense:

Dev2: "There are different kinds of users: on the one hand some are really careful or even shy, but on the other hand some are kind of arrogant [. . .] I prefer not to answer myself, but wait for someone that replies in a better way than I would."

This opened a reflection on the role of students in the project and the perception of participation within the Smart Campus community. To further explore this kind of issues, the first interview study was organised. All members of the Smart Campus team reported being aware of the project aiming towards participatory development [42] and having a positive attitude towards the active participation of the users' community in the project. However, when probed at a deeper level, it became evident that the concept of involvement was intended more as informative, rather than participative [22]: instead of becoming true partners in the design process, students were expected to just express their opinions, which had to be taken into account by the lab. Especially in the case of developers, therefore, users were perceived as being requirement providers and application testers (i.e. informants), without any active role during the design and development stages:

Dev2: *"External persons can suggest ideas, report bugs and the team has to listen to them and consider them for the next steps."*

Dev2: *"They are free to suggest ideas and even concrete improvements and we do take the information seriously, because they will use the application and that's why their opinion is important."*

A designer indeed explicitly raised a concern about the lab understanding of participation:

Des4: *"Sometimes I think that we don't listen very much to the students. We need feedback, we have to make more effort to understand and to listen to their opinions [. . .]. Sometimes we take decisions without a real participatory design approach. We take the decisions from the top of the hierarchical organization. This is only for making it easier and faster. We cannot listen to every little thing from the students."*

We can see from these quotations that the perception of the community role retained some UCD/PD elements in designers and some Agile elements in developers: for instance, developers maintained an understanding of the customer as the funding agent whose requirements, although changing, were binding; on the other hand, designers expressed unease at their limited possibility to fully take into account the needs coming from the community. Yet, the compromise resulting from the integration of the two methodologies was unclear. In fact, the community was not understood as a proper customer, as it was not expected to actively participate in the management of the development process (for instance, it was not part of the community's duties to prioritise needs) and it appeared unable to adequately articulate its requirements for developers. On the other hand, the community lost part of its prerogatives as a user, since the management ultimately decided how to steer the direction of the project.

Indeed, students themselves were aware of the importance of their involvement, but they still confined it to a role of informants and consultants rather than of active participants who could effectively modify the outcome of the project:

Stud2: *"The impact is strong: most of the participants are checking [Smart Campus] out and using at least one app frequently."*

Stud10: *"As a tester, you give me the smartphone and I can give you feedback. I can do something in exchange".*

This attitude was evident also in the forum, which counted approximately 500 users who wrote about 2000 posts: over 67 % of threads reported problems and issues with the applications or the smartphone, and only 27 % reported suggestions for the evolution of the project. This in turn raised different expectations about what kind of contribution users could provide and what kind of feedback needed to be returned to them, in a vicious circle: being users' posts seldom focused on proposals for improvement, developers increasingly consolidated a perception of the community as a group of testers, therefore not entirely committing to acknowledging the actual suggestions for functionality enhancement; as a result, such kind of contributions seemed to appear less over time.

6.4.2   Documentation

As exemplified by the question asked by *Dev1: "What do you mean by document-ing?"*, documentation did not appear to have an intrinsic value as a communication tool, neither for developers nor for interns; the first ones wrote it when explicitly required, the second ones mainly because they had to report to supervisors.

Dev3: "I document some piece of code [...] only if somebody asks me to because it is needed by others. Otherwise it's rare that a developer comments his code."
Dev4: "I document my development process sometimes, because it depends on the time that I have ... If I have time, I spend some time to write a document"

To further investigate this aspect, the second interview study was organised. Since the development team was collocated and consisted of a limited number of members, writing documentation became just overhead in practice, as developers found it arguably quicker and easier to just meet and discuss in person within the office:

Dev7: "For the discussion between developers with different points of view, it's quicker to go to the office with the other developer and discuss it."

One of the interns however explicitly realised that this tended to create a closed, connected, fast-paced group:

Int3: "In my opinion, developers should participate in the forum, that is talk to the users without staying in a closed group. This would be counter-productive, as we [developers] meet every day."

The limited actual documentation was typically written and located within the code in the form of comments; developers shared more extensive online documents in case they needed to describe a complex process or provide more detailed information on what they did to a colleague who was meant to take over their work. Graphical documentation (wireframes and quick hand-drawn sketches) was used to discuss interface design, to align work between designers and developers and to supplement the written one in illustrating complex processes; it was usually transient and kept for personal use.

Dev5: "Well, the code is open source, so ... they read my code and in the middle of my code there is some comment"

Dev5: "If it's a UI feature, I try to draw it ... But I do not share this kind of sketches with anyone. It's just for me ... when I complete the feature, I throw them away."

The attitude with regards to documentation instead changed in the case of designers or of interns who did not typically share the same space and time in the lab anymore due to academic commitments or end of their internship: they tended to habitually use documentation to organise and manage their progress. Designers regularly shared reports and reflections through Dropbox and online documents; interns reported first using everyday objects such as post-its and then moving to shared online documents as well as their collocation became less frequent.

Int5: "At first we used a lot of post-its that we would stick on the whiteboard and we work there as a group ... we wrote all the points to develop, what one would do, what the other would do ... when I basically remained the only one working there, I started to use shared online documents to communicate with other developers ... and then that became the main communication method ... The same things that we would write on post-its, we would then write on these shared documents."

The introduction in the team of several members (typically students) who worked during different shifts, remotely, or from different locations however reduced the chances of non-mediated communication while increasing the need for a shared, accessible knowledge base: yet, how to effectively support such need while leveraging on existing working practices remained an open point.

In general, the interviews showed how a series of attempts at effectively supporting documentation yielded contrasting results. In the following paragraphs we summarise what happened with reference to different articulation platforms used to facilitate the communication within the project team (developers, designers, and interns) and between the team and the user community.

Developers' Wiki This platform mainly hosted technical documentation for internal use. Developers reported checking it almost exclusively to read information; active contributions had been generally limited to the first steps of the project, as the lack of guidelines on how to structure the wiki rapidly led to a very confusing articulation which finally resulted in the CTO of the project being the only one "legitimated" to write content in it. Developers stated that they seldom edited minor points, typically to update sections concerning the tasks they were working on:

Dev1: "I know that on the Smart Campus Developers' wiki every library has documentation ... these are done by G. and R. [CTO]"

GitHub Both interns and developers recognised in principle the relevance of documentation for involving external developers from the community and promoting the project, and some acknowledged that it should be placed in GitHub along with the code; in practice, however, developers did not use GitHub for documentation beyond the comments attached to code commits.

Dev4: "If I use open software, it's more important to publish the code and the documentation because if a developer needs to use my code he can learn where it is, how it works and so."

In fact, GitHub was considered to be quite cumbersome to search and likely to be too "geeky" to be widely used by the users' community.

Dev3: "I find [GitHub] quite hard to navigate, because there is development, tips, hints . . . there should be some guidelines"

Forum While the wiki and GitHub were more oriented to facilitating communication within the Smart Campus team, this bulletin board was aimed to open a dialogue between the project team and the community of users and was perceived as more suitable for this purpose.

Int1: "If [the forum] is for documentation purposes within the developers and the community, it can make sense. If it is just between me and the other people of the group, I don't think so."

One of the students claimed that the forum could indeed be a good tool for supporting the open source project and discussions related to code:

Stud1: "It would be important [to have a dedicated section for developers] to help each other and exchange information and opinions about code and development."

Yet, while students perceived the forum as a place for discussion, developers saw it just as a unidirectional informative tool from the users to the lab and did not perceive it as a suitable support for shared project documentation. Because of this, and despite the forum being acknowledged as a rich source of information, it was not seen as a suitable support for documentation, but at most as a supplement.

Dev1: "[The forum] It's not an instrument designed for that . . . the documentation should be more structured documents where I can navigate like in a tree and search . . . It's something that is missing in the forum, but it's not designed for that"

Int4: "If there is the official documentation and you want to go deeper into a topic, then you can visit that section of the forum . . . "

Moreover, developers interpreted engaging in conversations on the forum as extra work that got a relevant priority only if it was related to their current tasks:

Dev2: "[I use the forum] only to receive feedback on the application situation."
Dev2: "[The forum] It's a good way to interact with people and understand . . . but to document the development of the topic, it's not good."

Interestingly, however, while interns generally acknowledged the relevance of the forum to interact with the community, they tended to check it less and less often as their role in the project became more similar to that of a proper developer.

Int3: "The forum is an additional thing, I do not get any notifications, I have to go check it myself."

6.4.3   Synchronisation of Iterations

In Smart Campus, where the customer was actually a whole community, and as it also happens in mobile app development more in general (let us think of the wealth of apps published on Apple's App Store or on Google Play), the amount of user feedback escalated quickly: in our opinion, this has been one of the most disruptive elements in an effective synchronisation of the periods of UCD and Agile. As a side note, we report that feedback management and prioritisation is often mentioned in the software engineering community (e.g. [51, 52]) as a major issue in Agile projects.

At least in the first stages of Smart Campus, some members of the management team were appointed to review user feedback and prioritise it before passing it on to designers; this contributed to complicating the attempt of designers to find a suitable balance with the development pace. As a result, the development team sometimes took design decisions on their own, proactively checking the forum and looking for suggestions to implement or bugs to fix without waiting for the designers or the management to filter the information for them, but rather relying on the users' community contribution; the design team then resorted to many ad-hoc design interventions performed through a face-to-face interaction with one of the developers requesting it.

D2: "To read the situation [. . .] of some application that I am developing in part [. . .] I read the application topic to understand if there are some problems"

Despite developers being generally sensitive to HCI themes, this situation often caused parts of the apps to be modified in subsequent iterations in order to better fit the holistic UX design, thus requiring the same piece of interface to be implemented over and over again, each time differently. Different studies prove that the synchronisation of UCD and Agile can indeed be complex: for instance, in [15], the length of iterations in the two approaches and their "different timescales" are identified as factors contributing to the difficulties in aligning designers and developers; however, the authors report development being significantly slower at prototyping than design, while we experienced the opposite situation.

In fact, what was discussed earlier about the perception of community involve-ment also influenced the struggle for effective feedback management, especially affecting how feedback was returned to users. Students in fact often asked for more transparency on the project organisation and for greater feedback about their suggestions; the developers however claimed that these aspects were ensured in the forum. Actually, suggestions provided on the forum were either addressed directly by developers or mediated by designers; in both cases, a ticket was created in an internal system and was then closed upon solution of the issue. However, users had no way to access these tickets or to know whether their proposals were being taken into account unless someone from the lab explicitly notified this again on the forum, which was infrequent. The situation was expected to improve with the introduction of GitHub, as the ticketing system became public, yet this approach remained quite obscure for users, as if the project team did not perceive the need to keep them informed about the outcome of their suggestions.

6.5 Discussion

The present work has discussed a project adopting both UCD and Agile in the context of mobile application development for a user community: reflecting on such experience has allowed identifying three main communication breakdowns that may hamper the fruitful integration of the two approaches if the user/customer is no longer uniquely identified, namely a variable interpretation of user involvement, a mismatch in the value of documentation, and a misalignment in iteration phases. We acknowledge that the data we presented are to be conceived within the specific context of our case study: yet, the three themes are also discussed in literature from different points of view, even though not systematically. Therefore, given the data collected from the project and the literature review that reinforced them, we propose some considerations on how to favour the convergence of UCD and Agile in a setting oriented towards a user community and to leverage on its benefits.

6.5.1 User Involvement

We have seen the difficulties in defining the role of the Smart Campus user community and how these affected several aspects of the project. Misunderstandings in user involvement have been echoed also in the literature: for instance, authors debate on the extent of user/customer involvement both in the UCD [5, 22] and in the Agile perspectives [15]. In the case of the integration of UCD and Agile for a user community, we propose to draw inspiration from participatory design [32] because of its intrinsic familiarity with the involvement of a variety of users, each representing its own needs and values, and with the resulting complexity. This was attempted also in Smart Campus by seeding a user community that could communicate directly with the developers through the forum and the beta testing experimentation. We believe that the availability of a platform such as the forum, supporting the dialogue not only between the community and the project team, but also within the members of the community, has been beneficial for the maturation of a sense of ownership of the users with respect to the applications and for a livelier discussion about the needs of the community itself.

We have also referred to our instantiation of participatory development [42], i.e. integrating users in the development team by having interns in the lab. This peculiar context has in our opinion given some advantages to the development process: by providing a direct, explicit link between the project team and the community, interns allowed mutual learning to take place and contributed a domain knowledge that resulted in a more informed feedback management; on the other hand, however, as found in [28, 32], such bond with the community became less and less meaningful as the time spent by students in the lab passed and they transformed into developers.

We acknowledge that the nature of Smart Campus as a funded R&D project put it in a privileged position that could afford having interns from a largely technically skilled user community as part of team. Yet, despite Smart Campus being a very specific case, we argue that, particularly when addressing a user community as it is often the case in mobile app development, informing the design and development process with participatory elements is still a valid suggestion and, retaining the richness and articulation of the voices of the community, is likely to be a sustainable approach in the long term.

This also provides a possible answer to the concerns appearing in literature about the customer's role in Agile: this figure is entitled to steer the direction of the project by redefining and re-prioritising his/her own requirements even while development is on-going [12], but at the same time he/she is overwhelmed by responsibility [25], his/her actual representativeness is questioned [3, 28, 31] and he/she is likely not to have the competence to exert such decision-making power, to the point that some authors have suggested that a member of the development team is most suited to play this role [29] instead. We believe that the context of mobile application development might open further possibilities if the community is composed of technically skilled people, as it was partly the case in Smart Campus: in this case, in fact, the decision-making power of users can be extended to cover choices that concern not only design, as it happens in participatory design, but also development.

6.5.2 Documentation

In our experience documentation can be kept to a minimum, as encouraged by the Agile principles [12, 33], and intended only for internal use as long as the development process is confined within a lab, as it was in our case. Yet, if we envision a scenario in which users are active participants engaged in participatory development, documentation becomes a means to ensure greater transparency over the development process, especially for coordinating the evolution of an open piece of software; the theme of geographical distribution is by the way also presented in [53] as one of the main differences between the open source and the Agile approaches. Furthermore, in [54] authors highlight that shifting to a distributed team, and thus having to create high-quality documentation and specifications, "requires different types of competences than simply expertise in programming and concomitant tacit knowledge": professional identities and work practices change, as the "articulation work" required to coordinate becomes a larger share of regular work.

6.5.3 Synchronisation of Iterations

We have also seen how the amount of user feedback coming from a community can quickly escalate and how handling it can affect the smoothness of the development process. Despite information loss in feedback management being unavoidable [52], we believe that an organisational culture informed by participatory design is likely to appropriately recognise the value in this continuous feedback and effectively handle it, integrating the users' voice while retaining as much as possible of its articulation. This context may also ensure greater transparency over the development process, showing in an organic way what the outcome of the feedback and suggestions provided by the community was and therefore establishing a dialogue with users, rather than having communication flowing just unidirectionally as it happened in the Smart Campus forum.

Indeed, how to effectively achieve this remained an open point in Smart Campus, as the project team was not able to envision a lightweight process for feedback implementation that did not interfere with the speed of the development pace; as a result, design lagged behind development, differently from what reported in [15] and suggested in [29, 40]. Yet, we believe that, as also shown by several suggestions in literature [e.g. 55], the management of user input can be facilitated if the integration of UCD and Agile fully occurs only after the conceptual design has been finalised, i.e. after the so-called "Iteration 0" [41], which can even be regarded as exceeding the scope of Agile methods [55]. In Smart Campus, for instance, while the user research was being performed, the backend functionalities of the platform were being developed as well. Once the conceptual design is ready, UCD can address the interface design, while Agile can proceed with the implementation of the business logic. In our opinion, it is likely that the feature-oriented framing of Agile is somehow too constraining in respect of the creativity and flexibility that characterise the early stages of UCD. A critical point is however still present in the handover of the conceptual design from this stage, where UCD and Agile proceed in parallel, to the subsequent iterations, where the two approaches merge.

6.5.4 Fostering Integration

We finally remark that as the integration between the UCD and Agile methodologies occurs, a compromise seems to be needed between their respective understandings of the user and the customer, both in terms of working practices [37] and in terms of organisational vision, especially in the case where the user/customer is no longer uniquely defined and is rather replaced by a community like in Smart Campus. In fact, some authors advocate the establishment of a suitable managerial and organisational context as one of the conditions for the integration of UCD and Agile to effectively happen [7, 37]. Clearly, an organisational culture that values participation and recognises the relevance of user input throughout the whole design and development process is likely to endorse a conceptual design that takes the users' voice into account, acknowledging and actively addressing the issues related to the responsibility towards users' needs and to the risk of losing track of the holistic UX design over time [7, 37].

In order to foster such a receptive organisational culture, we propose the adoption of design thinking [56], a methodology grounded on a "human-centred design ethos" that pervades all stages of a product lifecycle, from inspiration to ideation to implementation. This discipline leverages on "the designer's sensibility and methods to match people's needs with what is technologically feasible" and marketable, acknowledging the "value of a holistic design approach". In his work, Brown emphasises that design thinking is not just a prerogative of people in design schools, but is rather an attitude that can be assimilated also by other professionals. For what concerns specifically the integration of UCD and Agile, we believe that this perspective can foster an organisational culture which values and achieves empathy with users and endorses, both in the project management and its team, a common awareness of elements such as the relevance of user needs, a holistic UX vision, and a shared acceptance and ownership of the conceptual design and ultimately of the product.

6.6 Conclusions

In this paper we have proposed three themes that can be used as an analytical tool in the management and facilitation of projects involving UCD and Agile. Such themes, or communication breakdowns, concern potential mismatches in the formalisation of key concepts in the two approaches, namely the interpretation of user involvement, the value of documentation, and the synchronisation of iterations; they emerged from a case study in mobile application development for a user community and were reinforced with a literature review. We believe that reconciling them by promoting a receptive organisational culture that draws inspiration from participatory design and design thinking can be a fruitful way to effectively integrate UCD and Agile.

Acknowledgements Smart Campus was funded by TrentoRISE. The analytical work presented in this chapter has been possible thanks to the funding granted by the Italian Ministry of Education, University and Research (MIUR) through the project "Città Educante", project code CTN01_00034_393801. We wish to thank the Smart Campus team and all the students who contributed to the project.

References

1. Salah D, Paige RF, Cairns P (2014) A systematic literature review for agile development processes and user centred design integration. In: Proceedings of the 18th international conference on evaluation and assessment in software engineering. ACM, New York, p 5
2. Kane D (2003) Finding a place for discount usability engineering in agile development: throwing down the gauntlet. In: Agile development conference, 2003. ADC 2003. Proceedings of the IEEE, pp 40–46
3. Sohaib O, Khan K (2010) Integrating usability engineering and agile software development: a literature review. In: Computer design and applications (ICCDA), 2010 International conference on, vol 2. IEEE, pp V2–V32)
4. Jurca G, Hellmann TD, Maurer F (2014) Integrating Agile and user-centered design: a systematic mapping and review of evaluation and validation studies of Agile-UX. In: Agile conference (AGILE), 2014. IEEE. pp 24–32
5. Damodaran L (1996) User involvement in the systems design process-a practical guide for users. Behav Inform Technol 15(6):363–377
6. Kujala S (2003) User involvement: a review of the benefits and challenges. Behav Inform Technol 22(1):1–16
7. Cajander Å, Larusdottir M, Gulliksen J (2013) Existing but not explicit-the user perspective in Scrum projects in practice. In: Human-computer interaction–INTERACT 2013. Springer, Berlin/Heidelberg, pp 762–779
8. Frayling C (1993) Research in art and design. Royal College of Art, London
9. Bjørn P, Ngwenyama O (2009) Virtual team collaboration: building shared meaning, resolving breakdowns and creating translucence. Inf Syst J 19(3):227–253
10. Rogers Y, Sharp H, Preece J (2011) Interaction design: beyond human-computer interaction. Wiley, Chichester
11. Norman DA (1986) Cognitive engineering. In: User centered system design. L. Erlbaum Associates, Hillsdale, pp 31 61
12. Beck K, et al. Manifesto for Agile software development. http://www.Agilemanifesto.org
13. Verdiesen B (2014) Agile user experience. MSc dissertation, Radboud University Nijmegen, Nijmegen
14. Clark HH, Brennan SE (1991) Grounding in communication. In: Perspectives on socially shared cognition, vol 13. American Psychological Association, Washington, DC, pp 127–149
15. Chamberlain S, Sharp H, Maiden N (2006) Towards a framework for integrating Agile development and user-centred design. In: Extreme programming and Agile processes in software engineering. Springer, Berlin/Heidelberg, pp 143–153
16. Wolkerstorfer P et al (2008) Probing an Agile usability process. In: Proceedings of CHI 2008. ACM Press, New York, pp 2151–2157
17. McGinn J, Chang AR (2013) RITE+Krug: a combination of usability test methods for Agile design. J Usability Stud 8(3):61–68
18. Memmel T, Gundelsweiler F, Reiterer H (2007) Agile human-centered software engineering. In: Proceedings of the 21st British HCI group annual conference on people and computers: HCI . . . but not as we know it-Volume 1. British Computer Society, Swinton, pp 167–175
19. Ungar JM, White JA (2008) Agile user centered design: enter the design studio – a case study. In: Proceedings of CHI 2008. ACM Press, New York, pp 2167–2177
20. Gothelf J (2013) Lean UX: applying Lean principles to improve user experience. O'Reilly Media, Inc., Beijing
21. Liikkanen LA, Kilpiö H, Svan L, Hiltunen M (2014) Lean UX: the next generation of user-centered agile development? In: Proceedings of the 8th Nordic conference on human-computer interaction: fun, fast, foundational. ACM, New York, pp 1095–1100
22. Iivari J, Iivari N (2011) Varieties of user-centredness: an analysis of four systems development methods. Inf Syst J 21(2):125–153

23. Bjerknes G, Bratteteig T (1995) User participation and democracy: a discussion of Scandinavian research on system development. Scand J Inf Syst 7(1):1
24. Ambler SW. Introduction to user stories. http://www.agilemodeling.com/artifacts/userStory. htm. Accessed 11 Dec 2015
25. Martin A, Biddle R, Noble J (2004) The XP customer role in practice: three studies. In: Proceedings of the ADC 2004. IEEE. pp 42–54
26. Schwartz L (2014) Agile-user experience design: does the involvement of usability experts improve the software quality? Int J Adv Softw 7(3&4):456–468
27. Sharp H, Robinson H (2004) Integrating user-centred design and software engineering: a role for extreme programming? http://citeseerx.ist.psu.edu/viewdoc/download?doi=10.1.1.99. 4554&rep=rep1&type=pdf
28. Beyer H, Holtzblatt K, Baker L (2004) An Agile customer-centered method: rapid contextual design. In: Extreme programming and Agile methods-XP/Agile universe 2004. Springer, Berlin/Heidelberg, pp 50–59
29. Sy D (2007) Adapting usability investigations for Agile user-centered design. J Usability Stud 2(3):112–132
30. Schwaber K, Sutherland J (2011) The Scrum guide. Scrum.org
31. Schwartz L (2013) Agile-user experience design: with or without a usability expert in the team? In Proceedings of the ICSEA 2013. IARIA, pp 359–363
32. Gregory J (2003) Scandinavian approaches to participatory design. Int J Eng Educ 19(1): 62–74
33. McInerney P, Maurer F (2005) UCD in Agile projects: dream team or odd couple? Interactions 12:19–23
34. Brown JM, Lindgaard G, Biddle R (2011) Collaborative events and shared artefacts: Agile interaction designers and developers working toward common aims. In: Agile conference (AGILE), 2011. IEEE, pp 87–96
35. Selic B (2009) Agile documentation, anyone? Softw, IEEE 26(6):11–12
36. Ambler SW. Agile/Lean documentation: strategies for agile software development. http://www. agilemodeling.com/essays/agileDocumentation.htm. Accessed 6 Nov 2015
37. Lárusdóttir MK, Cajander Å, Gulliksen J (2012) The big picture of UX is missing in Scrum projects. In: Proceedings of the 2nd international workshop on the interplay between user experience evaluation and software development, in conjunction with the 7th Nordic conference on human-computer interaction. http://ceur-ws.org/Vol-922/I-UxSED-2012-Proceedings.pdf# page=49. Accessed on 11 Dec 2015
38. Gould JD, Lewis C (1985) Designing for usability: key principles and what designers think. Commun ACM 28(3):300–311
39. Miller L (2005) Case study of customer input for a successful product. In: Proceedings of Agile. pp 225–234
40. Nodder C, Nielsen J (2010) Agile usability: best practices for user experience on Agile development projects. Nielsen Norman Group, Fremont
41. Fox D, Sillito J, Maurer F (2008) Agile methods and user-centered design: how these two methodologies are being successfully integrated in industry. In: Agile, 2008. AGILE'08. Conference. IEEE, pp 63–72
42. De Angeli A, Bordin S, Menéndez Blanco M (2014) Infrastructuring participatory development in information technology. In: Proceedings of the 13th participatory design conference: research papers, vol 1. ACM, pp 11–20
43. De Angeli A, Bordin S, Menéndez Blanco M (2014) Reflections over a socio-technical infrastructuring effort. In: Proceedings of 2nd Workshop on Cultures of Participation in the Digital Age, CoPDA'14, Como, Italy, May 27, 2014, CEUR-WS.org, online CEUR-WS.org/ Vol-640/paper1.pdf
44. Menéndez Blanco M, Bordin S, De Angeli A (2014) Sociotechnical infrastructuring for participation. Workshop on cooperative technologies in democratic processes – Beyond e-Voting, COOP. http://www.iisi.de/fileadmin/IISI/upload/IRSI/2014Vol11Iss1/IRSI_Vol11_ Iss1_Menendez_Bordin_De_Angeli_Socio-technical_infrastructuring_for_participation.pdf. Accessed on 11 Dec 2015

45. Bordin S, Menéndez Blanco M, De Angeli A (2014) ViaggiaTrento: an application for collaborative sustainable mobility. EAI Endorsed Trans Ambient Sys 14:4
46. Bordin S, Menéndez Blanco M, De Angeli A (2014) Catch me if you can: reconciling Agile and UCD. https://ucdandagile.files.wordpress.com/2014/10/nr2-nordichi2014-agile-ucd-workshop-bordin.pdf, Workshop on the Integration of UCD and Agile Development, NordiCHI 2014
47. Teli M, Bordin S, Blanco MM, Orabona G, De Angeli A (2015) Public design of digital commons in urban places: a case study. Int J Hum Comput Stud 81:17–30
48. Sy D, Mille L (2008) Optimizing Agile user-centred design. In: CHI'08 extended abstracts on Human factors in computing systems. ACM, pp 3897–3900
49. Neustaedter C, Sengers P (2012) Autobiographical design in HCI research: designing and learning through use-it-yourself. In: Proceedings of the designing interactive systems conference. ACM, pp 514–523
50. Smith CP (1992) Motivation and personality: handbook of thematic content analysis. Cambridge University Press, Cambridge, MA
51. Gartner S, Schneider K (2012) A method for prioritizing end-user feedback for requirements engineering. In: Cooperative and Human Aspects of Software Engineering (CHASE), 2012 5th international workshop on, IEEE. pp 47–49
52. Lee MJ, Ko AJ (2012) Representations of user feedback in an Agile, collocated software team. In: Cooperative and Human Aspects of Software Engineering (CHASE), 2012 5th international workshop on, IEEE. pp 76–82
53. Goldman R, Gabriel RP (2005) Innovation happens elsewhere: open source as business strategy. Morgan Kaufmann, Amsterdam
54. Matthiesen S, Bjørn P, Petersen LM (2014) Figure out how to code with the hands of others: recognizing cultural blind spots in global software development. In: Proceedings of the CSCW 2014. ACM press, pp 1107–1119
55. Schwartz L (2013) Agile-user experience design: an Agile and user-centered process?. In: ICSEA 2013, The Eighth International Conference on Software Engineering Advances. IARIA XPS Press
56. Brown T (2008) Design thinking. Harv Bus Rev 86(6):84

Chapter 7
Towards Understanding How Agile Teams Predict User Experience

Kati Kuusinen, Heli Väätäjä, Tommi Mikkonen, and Kaisa Väänänen

Abstract In this chapter, we compare UX assessments of users and agile team members to learn to what extent developers can predict how users experience (UX) the product the developers are working on, and where user involvement is truly required. We compared UX assessments of agile team members (N = 26) and users (N = 29) of six enterprise applications with statistical tests. Moreover, we analyzed the data with principal component analysis to reveal the main dimensions of UX for enterprise software. Our results confirm prior research findings that agile team members can put themselves in the users' position when evaluating instrumental aspects of UX of the software they are working on. However, it seems that developers cannot evaluate non-instrumental quality. Therefore, direct user involvement from participation to evaluation or other means to support user empathy in development process is needed. We recommend additional means, such as personas to help agile team members empathize with the users and their needs for non-instrumental qualities of the enterprise software.

Keywords UX evaluation • Agile software development • Enterprise software

7.1 Introduction

Building on advances in software technology, rapid and continuous development approaches have become a viable option for numerous end-user applications. With such infrastructure, developers can expose new features to randomized experiments in real-life context, where data regarding actual users' preferences can be collected and analyzed with statistical hypothesis testing. However, executing such tests requires a substantial number of real users, which can be a problem in enterprise

K. Kuusinen (✉) • H. Väätäjä • T. Mikkonen • K. Väänänen
Tampere University of Technology, Tampere, Finland
e-mail: kati.kuusinen@alumni.aalto.fi; heli.vaataja@tut.fi; tommi.mikkonen@tut.fi; kaisa.vaananen@tut.fi

© Springer International Publishing Switzerland 2016
G. Cockton et al. (eds.), *Integrating User-Centred Design in Agile Development*, Human–Computer Interaction Series, DOI 10.1007/978-3-319-32165-3_7

163

software development, which is targeted for work-related use. Moreover, such tests reveal only user behavior with the system, leaving the developers unaware of users' subjective experiences.

The interest in gathering real-life user data reflects the differences between users, who perceive the software via user interfaces, and developers, who know the software from inside out. Gathering data from real-life use can be regarded as a way to address claims that developers do not truly understand users, and that users do not really understand what they eventually want [1]. These problems have been partially solved with rapid iteration cycles promoted by agile software development approaches. Still, while at best, such approaches advocate a paradigm shift from front-heavy planning and design to short development cycles, where user feedback is constantly collected, delay is introduced when getting feedback from end users as well as when analyzing the feedback.

UX work has traditionally followed the user-centered design process defined in [2], and mechanisms for integrating UX work in agile development frameworks remain largely unestablished. The most widely used approaches include a design upfront phase and (often unsuccessful) attempts to maintain the pace of development iterations with user testing [3, 4]. To truly include UX work in agile development, lightweight methods are needed to evaluate UX as a part of iterative development.

Given an improved understanding regarding how agile teams and users assess UX, developers themselves may handle some aspects of UX, at least to a certain degree, thus lightening the workload of UX specialists (UXS). To address developers' ability to predict UX, quantitative measurements are needed to measure and compare UX as assessed by development team members and users. Moreover, to allow frequent evaluation of UX in agile projects, simple evaluation frameworks that minimize work are needed.

We aim to make UX work more rapid in enterprise software development. By enterprise software we refer to applications that are intended for work purposes and are primarily developed to meet organizational rather than user needs; by UX work we mean activities, such as research, design, development, and evaluation that aim at developing software that is usable, fulfills user needs, and provides desired interaction qualities. Our research has three practically oriented goals:

1. To enable collecting rapid user feedback to support iterations that synchronize UX and software development work.
2. To place the focus of limited UXS resources on issues that software developers are not able to handle by themselves.
3. To enable setting clear, meaningful UX goals to focus on big picture and to unify design effort based on real user preferences.

To meet these goals, we study to what extent developers are able to understand UX so that some of the validation steps with real end users could be eliminated. The goal is to understand if some of the UX validation could be performed as a part of the software creation, and, if so, what are the things that truly need experimentation with actual end users.

To this end, we compare assessments of UX between users and team members (developers, product owners (PO), and UXSs). We asked team members to assess the software from two perspectives: as themselves and when trying to put themselves in the users' place. We conducted a survey in six agile development projects from five companies working on enterprise software. We surveyed 26 team members—including developers, UXSs, and POs—and 29 end users considering their perception of UX in the software that was produced in each project. We measured UX using a scale with 16 items from UX dimensions identified in [5, 6]. Our results suggest that developers are able to understand the practical quality (such as usefulness) of the developed system, but understanding hedonic qualities (such as pleasure) seems to need support to help agile team members empathize with the users. In addition, our results contribute towards understanding the main UX dimensions for enterprise software.

The rest of this Chapter is structured as follows. Section 7.2 introduces work related to mechanisms of measuring UX and studies regarding the differences in how users and development teams perceive UX. Section 7.3 describes our research methods. Section 7.4 presents results of the principal component analysis and related varying assessments of UX. Section 7.5 discusses the validity and limitations of this research. Section 7.6 discusses the main contributions and the implications of our results, and finally, Sect. 7.7 draws some final conclusions.

7.2 Background and Related Work

The study presented in this Chapter is based on an earlier study [7] of the same projects with the same participants from agile teams, in which we studied how the participants contributed towards UX work. In that study, we found that UXSs (UX specialists) collaborated the most with developers during demo sessions, when discussing the UI design and when determining how to implement design details. Developers did not participate in user studies or tests, or in clarifying end user definitions or target user groups. Thus, developers' understanding of users remained shallow and many of them wished to be more involved in user communication. Those findings motivated us to continue our research with these projects with a further study, reported in this Chapter.

7.2.1 Concept of UX

UX is subjective, context-dependent, and dynamic [8]. It is affected by *users'* expectations, needs, and motivation, *systems'* characteristics, such as purpose and functionality, and the *context of use* including physical, organizational, and psychological aspects [9]. The standard definition of user experience (UX) is as follows: a *"person's perceptions and responses resulting from the use and/or anticipated use of a product, system or service"* [2].

According to Law et al. [10], in academic research, the most commonly utilized frameworks for UX are the *hedonic-pragmatic model* [11] and *sense-making experience* [12]. The hedonic-pragmatic model divides user experience into *hedonic* or the non-utilitarian dimension and *pragmatic* or the instrumental dimension [11]. Hassenzahl [11] further divides the hedonic into two subdimensions of identification and stimulation, while the instrumental contains mostly items related to usability and usefulness. Usability is often seen as a necessary precondition for good UX [13, 14].

Väänänen-Vainio-Mattila et al. [15] discuss the differences in the conception of UX between academic UX research and industrial UX development. They conclude that while the research concentrates mostly on hedonic aspects and emotions, companies concentrate more on functionality and usability issues [15]. Moreover, although early HCI studies concentrated almost exclusively on task- and work-related usability issues and achievement of behavioral goals [9], UX research has mainly concentrated on consumers and leisure systems (see e.g., [16]) for categorization of publications applying the hedonic). Thus, it is unclear what shapes UX of enterprise software or work-related tools: what are its dimensions and is it different from UX of leisure systems?

7.2.2   UX Evaluation in Agile Development

Vermeeren et al. [17] identified 96 different UX evaluation methods originating both from academia and industry. The methods included lab, field, and online data gathering activities, such as surveys, focus groups, expert-based methods, controlled observations, and contextual inquiries. Most of the methods were intended to be used with functional prototypes or with working products. Regarding online evaluation methods, Vermeeren et al. [17] conclude that whilst they can be lightweight, cheap, and fast, some of them are problematic because they require laborious analysis, which can decrease their practical feasibility.

In industrial agile development, ensuring the desired UX of implemented features is often addressed with user tests [18]. According to Da Silva et al. [18], user testing is one of the most commonly used practices in agile UCD work, and it is equally conducted on low-fidelity prototypes and on working software. In the most traditional form, user tests are conducted by recruiting users to arranged test sessions where users perform planned use cases or scenarios while a researcher observes them [19]. Arranging and interpreting these sessions require time and resources [19–21]. Ardito et al. [22] found in their survey conducted in Danish software development organizations that the most common obstacles regarding usability evaluation was the lack of resources and suitable methods. Lárusdóttir et al. [23] state that integrating traditional user testing into agile context is challenging, and thus companies tend to perform evaluations informally with only few users, gathering qualitative data during unplanned sessions.

In contrast to the traditional model discussed above, user tests can also be conducted remotely either synchronously (with a human moderator) or asynchronously (with a software moderator) [20]. Asynchronous user tests can save considerable time compared to traditional laboratory tests [24] and help to find a number of usability issues, especially when predefined tasks are given for users to conduct [25]. However, according to a recent literature review, automated user tests still seem to be rarely used in agile software development: utilizing "some kind of automated tool" was reported in 10 % of the included papers [26] (it should be noted that [26] included also studies conducted in academic context in their review). Also, despite the perceived popularity of the user testing method, remote testing was mentioned in only one of the publications included in the systematic review of [18]. Another remote evaluation method is to publish the feature in a beta group or on the market and collect data of real users' actual use with methods, such as application performance management (APM) and real user monitoring (RUM) [27]. These methods can provide more realistic usage data from a larger amount of users but are mainly aimed for aftermarket evaluation [27].

Finally, randomized experiments with control and treatment groups consisting of real users (e.g., A/B testing) can be utilized for evaluating new features. This, however, requires a large user base. In addition, remote methods lack many qualitative aspects that can be perceived while observing the user, such as user's emotional state, level of satisfaction, or the reasoning behind user's choices [21, 28]. Thus, remote evaluation should be accompanied with subjective UX surveying.

7.2.3   Measuring Dimensions of UX

A systematic review of UX measurements in HCI [29] categorized the measured dimensions of UX. Generic UX was found to be the most commonly measured UX dimension (41 %). Other commonly measured dimensions were affect or emotion (24 %), enjoyment or fun (17 %), aesthetics or appeal (15 %), and engagement or flow (12 %). Motivation (8 %), enchantment (6 %), and frustration (5 %) were also reported. Only 14 % of the analyzed papers in this review measured hedonic quality [29]; they used Hassenzahl's [10] AttrakDiff or AttrakDiff2 scale or a self-modified version of it [29]. In addition, 20 % of studies that used questionnaires to assess UX used AttrakDiff or AttrakDiff2, whereas 51 % used self-developed questionnaires.

A more recent review of UX measurement reporting scale use found that AttrakDiff was the most used scale [16]. Of the reviewed papers, 58 % used it or its adaptations, while the second most used group of scales, namely scales from consumer research, was utilized only in 8 % of the included papers. Despite the wide usage of AttrakDiff, Diefenbach et al. [16] claim that it has issues with inter-correlations between the subscales; it does not separate between the UX dimensions clearly enough. Thus, they also conclude that the hedonic itself requires a clearer concept [16].

Other well-known scales include SAM (Self-Assessment Manikin) by Bradley et al. [30] for measuring emotion, a scale by Lavie and Tractinsky [31] for measuring visual aesthetics, the HED/UT scale [32], Pleasures of Play Scale [33], the Subjective Mental Effort Questionnaire (SMEQ) [34], the Flow State Scale (FSS) [35], Attrak-Work [36], Emocards [37], Pleasure-Arousal-Dominance (PAD) [38], and Subjective Usability Measurement Inventory (SUMI) [39].

UX-related measure scales that are utilized for evaluation of enterprise software mainly measure usefulness, productivity, performance, and ease of use. The Technology Acceptance Model (TAM) by Davis [40] predicts users' intention to use through perceived usefulness and perceived ease of use. Technology Satisfaction Model (TSM) is an alteration of TAM, where the intention of use is replaced with user satisfaction, since the use of enterprise software often is mandatory for the user [41]. In addition to perceived usefulness and perceived ease of use, [41] included perceived loss of control and perceived market performance in their scale. Finally, Task-Technology Fit [42] measures the impact of individual performance via effectiveness, productivity, and the system's ability to increase the productivity of the user. Thus, to the best of our knowledge, there are no validated scales available for specifically assessing hedonic quality of work-related software.

As Lindgaard and Kirakowski [43] point out, creating rating scales is tricky. Still, a considerable amount of UX researchers decide to utilize none of the validated scales but create their own scale: authors of 51 % of analyzed papers in [29] and 27 % in [16] utilized self-developed scales or single items of established scales. Based on our own experiences with rating scales, we assume that current validated scales do not properly assess researchers' needs. While research on dimensions of UX and measuring those has been conducted, it is still unclear how (and with which items) the dimensions actually are (and should be) measured. In addition, most of the validated scales are originally intended for consumer products. Consequently, there is a lack of evidence regarding how well existing scales fit to work-related contexts.

7.2.4 Different Roles' Perceptions of UX

Few studies have investigated how different stakeholder groups construe UX, i.e., what kind of personal constructs or perceptions they have about UX. Hertzum et al. [44] conducted a study with 48 participants from China, Denmark and India to study the effects of both the nationality and the stakeholder group. The study looked at the constructs of developers and users with the repertory grid interview technique. Concerning the nationality, no significant differences were found. For the two stakeholder groups, there were differences of the UX constructs. While users associate ease of use with leisure time systems and difficulty of use with work-related systems, developers do not have this distinction in their constructs. Furthermore, users conceive usefulness as related to frustration but separate from ease of use, whereas developers perceive ease of use, usefulness, and fun as related. Both users and developers have several constructs that are not visible in the dominant usability definitions at the time of this study, e.g., [2], such as fun and security.

In a study of 24 Chinese, Danish, and Indian usability professionals, Hertzum and Clemmensen [45] used repertory grid interviews to study usability professionals' constructs of usability. In this study, it was found out that goal-oriented performance is central for usability professionals, whereas their perceptions have less emphasis in experiential aspects of UX. Also in this study, the definition of usability [2] was found to be more limited than the constructs of the usability professionals, whose perceptions were broader especially in the experiential aspects of UX. In line with Hertzum et al. [44], usability was found to be construed similarly across the three nationalities of usability professionals studied.

Clemmensen et al. [46] studied the personal constructs of 72 usability professionals, developers, and end users with the repertory grid technique. Their finding was that usability professionals focus more on emotional aspects of UX, whereas users' perceptions of system use is more focused around the utility. Furthermore, usability professionals focus more on subjective aspects of UX than developers. This is in line with the usability professionals attempt to have empathy with the end users and to understand their viewpoint [47].

Sundberg [5, 6] carried out research on the importance of UX factors in metals and engineering industry to support new product development. She compared the views of developers and users of industrial products on the most important UX related factors in three supplier cases. The three cases were three supplier companies, each with two of their customer companies. Both developers and users assessed pragmatic aspects more important than experiential (hedonic) aspects. Differing from this work, our research looks into how agile team members and users assess UX of enterprise systems in selected cases, how UX is construed by different groups, and the capability of agile team members to assess user experience in the role of users in order to assess when user involvement is needed in agile development activities.

7.3 Method

We conducted a survey study to examine how users and agile team members assess UX of enterprise systems created by the agile teams. The aim was to gain understanding regarding how users and team members assess UX and to reveal the main constructs through which they construe the UX of enterprise systems. In the survey, we asked the team members to give evaluation first as themselves (team measurement TO, *team* member evaluating in *own* role) and then as they think a member of a particular user group would answer (team measurement TU, *team* member evaluating in role of *user*). Users answered in a separate survey regarding their experience with the system (*user* measurement US).

Table 7.1 Items (word-pairs) selected for the scale and associated UX dimensions [5, 6]

	Category	Item left	Item right
1	Overall system quality	Bad	Good
2	Overall system quality	Useless	Useful
3	Productivity	Hard to learn	Easy to learn
4	Productivity	Slow to use	Fast to use
5	Interaction quality	Difficult to use	Easy to use
6	System reliability	Unreliable	Reliable
7	Appeal	Undesirable	Desirable
8	Appeal	Not recommendable	Recommendable
9	Identification	Unconvincing	Convincing
10	Stimulation	Suppresses creativity	Promotes creativity
11	Affective quality	Discouraging	Motivating
12	Affective quality	Dull	Fun
13	Aesthetic quality	Unaesthetic	Aesthetic
14	Aesthetic quality	Amateurish	Professional
15	Aesthetic quality	Unpresentable	Presentable
16	Aesthetic quality	Conservative	Innovative

7.3.1 Forming the Survey

We selected the UX measurement items based on a data-driven analysis (of a systematic review) of items utilized in previous UX measurement scales, which was used to create a measurement tool for UX in work contexts in the metals and engineering industry [5, 6]. We utilized data from a preliminary analysis of Sundberg's [5] study to form our scale by selecting such UX items that cover all the main UX dimensions identified by Sundberg [5] and are relevant in the context of enterprise software. The items we used in the survey are presented in Table 7.1. The selection process in more detail was as follows. We selected items from both instrumental and non-instrumental quality categories. We aimed at covering all the main dimensions of UX identified by Sundberg [5, 6]; we selected items from all categories containing more than one group of items. We selected items based on their frequency of occurrence found in [5, 6]. When possible, we selected at least two items per group for internal validity and to increase measurement accuracy. Altogether, we selected eight items from both instrumental and non-instrumental categories.

We adopted the phrasing of question from AttrakDiff [10] as follows:

- In measurements TO (team member evaluating in own role) and US (evaluation by user): "*With the help of the word-pairs, please enter what YOU PERSONALLY consider the most appropriate description for the software.*" The measurement scale was a seven-point semantic differential.

- In measurement TU (team member evaluating in role of user): "*With the help of the word-pairs, please enter what you think USERS consider the most appropriate description for the software.*" The measurement scale was a seven-point semantic differential.

We specified user roles for the measurement TU to ensure that teams were responding with the particular user group that participated in the user survey in mind (i.e., not the customer). Additionally, we asked in separate questions the overall UX and the ability of the software to fulfill user needs as follows:

- Overall UX: In measurements TO and US: "*How would **you** rate the overall user experience of the software?*" and in measurement TU: "*How do you think **users** would rate the overall user experience of the software?*", both on a seven-point scale from" bad" to" good."
- Need fulfillment: In measurement US: "*How well does the software respond to **your** needs?*" and in measurement TU: "*How well does the software respond to **users'** needs?*". Both were on a seven-point scale from "*not at all*" to "*completely.*"

The question addressing overall UX was used as a reference question for the scale, and the word-pair scores were compared to it in the analysis. We also asked team members to *list one to three most important and least important UX goals for the developed software* from a predefined list of UX items measured in the survey. In addition, we asked the respondents to report their role as users or team members and the version of the system being evaluated. Users also reported their length of experience in using the system.

7.3.2 Description of Participants, Participating Projects, and Evaluated Software

Participants included both team members of projects developing enterprise software and users of the software under development. We selected development projects with following constraints:

- The project utilizes agile methods. The basic criterion was that the PO considers the project agile.
- The project has a release cycle of 6 months or less. For each new release in each project, UX was measured with no existing UX data made available for the team.
- The outcome of the project is enterprise software that will be used by several people.
- The outcome has a graphical user interface that requires design work.
- UX design work is ongoing or starting soon.
- Team members are willing to participate (not only the contact person).

Table 7.2 Participating companies, project teams and their development practices

P	Company description	Team size	Team practices
P1	An engineering and technology company with around 20 000 employees worldwide. Utilized both waterfall and Scrum practices. Several small distributed UX teams and UXSs	11, of which 8 developers located in Russia, 1 PO and 1 part-time UXS co-located in Finland	Scrum project. PO communicated with users, UXS drafted high-level design. PO selected the design that was communicated to developers. Developers decided about UX design details.
P2	An IT service company with 100–500 employees in Finland. UXSs working in project teams	6, of which 4 developers, 1 PO, 1 UXS, all co-located in Finland	Kanban project. UXS worked closely with developers. UXS's tasks were chunked and presented on the Kanban board. The UXS had partially also the PO role.
P3	An IT-service company with 100–500 employees in Europe. Utilized Scrum. A centralized UX team in one site and distributed UXSs in others	5, of which 2 developers, 1 PO, 1 UXS, all co-located in Finland	Scrum project. UXS tried to work one sprint ahead. Most of the UX budget was spent already during (heavy) design upfront, and there was less change for iteration during development.
P4	An IT service company with around 20 000 employees worldwide The company mainly utilized customer-defined processes. It had a centralized UX team on one site and numerous distributed UXSs on several sites.	P4: 7 of which 2 developers in China, 2 developers and 1 UXS in Finland in location A, 1 developer and 1 PO in Finland in location B, the whole team working part-time for the project.	Both projects applied methods from agile frameworks and were moving towards continuous development. Projects had prioritized backlog, Kanban board and continuous integration in use. Demo sessions were arranged on demand. PO was responsible of communicating with users. In P4 the UXS made UX design whereas in P5 a developer made the majority of UX design work and the UXS was more a graphic designer.
P5		P5: 4 of which 2 developers in Finland in location A, 1 PO in Finland in location B, and 1 UXS in Latvia	
P6	A mobile technology company with 100–500 employees worldwide. Utilized agile practices and customer processes. A centralized UX team	2, of which 1 developer and 1 PO co-located in Finland. Possibility to consult a UXS in another location in Finland	Free-form agile development. PO communicated with the UXS who made the UX design.

Legend: Scrum is an agile methodology presented in Ref. [48]. Kanban board is a tool for lean development introduced in Ref. [49]. Continuous development is discussed in Ref. [50]

We recruited the participant projects (Table 7.2) by participating in company events (e.g., fairs), from our previous business contacts and by snowball sampling. Participants in a user role were recruited by our contact persons in the projects.

Table 7.3 Participants from agile teams

Role	Developers (N = 17)	Product owners (N = 6)	UX specialists (N = 3)
Mean age (years)	M = 31.	M = 35	M = 40
	(SD 5.)	(SD 3)	(SD 8)
Educational background	Information technology	Information technology	Information technology, society and culture, or industrial design
Education in HCI	None to major subject. The majority had some either self-learning or some courses.	Some self-learning or some courses	Some courses or major subject
Development experience (years)	R: 0–20,	R: 2–9,	R: 0–20
	M:8,	M: 7,	M: 9
	SD: 5	SD: 2	SD: 10
UX design work experience (years)	R: 0–10,	R: 0–1,	R: 5–20,
	M: 2,	M: 0,	M: 11,
	SD: 4	SD: 0	SD: 7
Project management experience (years)	R: 0–5,	R: 0–6,	R: 0–5,
	M: 1,	M: 4,	M: 2,
	SD: 1	SD: 2	SD = 2
Agile work experience (years)	R: 0–8,	R: 0–7,	R: 5–9,
	M: 4,	M:5,	M: 6,
	SD: 2	SD: 2	SD: 2

R range, *M* mean, *SD* standard deviation, *HCI* human-computer interaction

Participants Survey participants were agile team members from six software development projects from five companies and users of each system being developed. Our sample consisted of users (N = 29) and team members (N = 26) including software developers, UXSs, and POs (Table 7.3). User participants and project details are described in 3. Education in HCI was self-rated as: none, some self-learning or training, some studies (a compulsory course or similar), more than a couple of courses but less than a minor subject, minor subject, major subject.

The majority (N = 19, 73 %) of the participants in agile teams were from Finland. Five participants were from Russia, one was from Latvia, and one from China. In total, there were 40 team members working for the projects, of which 26 responded to our survey, resulting in a response rate of 65 %.

As for the users, we did not ask where they were from in the survey. They were aged between 28 and 58 years (M = 42, SD = 9 years), and their roles are listed in Table 7.4. User response rate is unknown, since in some projects, invitation links to participate were put on an intranet or mailed to user organizations to be further distributed. However, we attached the survey with instructions on qualifications to participate and asked the users to report their role as users and the length of experience in using the system to evaluate participants' eligibility.

Table 7.4 Studied projects (P1–P6), description of the system each project developed and surveyed user roles of the systems

P	Developed system	User role	N of team members (26)	N of users (29)	Users' length of experience of using the developed system
P1	License generator	Sales engineers	6	3	'Tried it once or twice' to 'Used it several times'
P2	Communal online service for officers and citizens	Communal inspectors	4	4	'Tried it once or twice' to 'Used it a few times'
P3	Information system for nursery schools	Nursery school teachers	3	3	'Used it regularly for over a month but less than a year'
P4	Customer process monitoring feature	Service managers	6	2	'Used it regularly for over a month but less than a year'
P5	Launchpad and single sign-on for web applications	Employees of a IT services company	5	14	'Tried it once or twice' to 'Used it regularly for over a month but less than a year'
P6	Tool for software testing	Testers and developers	2	3	'Watched somebody using or demonstrating the system' to 'Tried it once or twice'

Number of participants per role and the time respondents had been using the system prior to the evaluation

7.3.3 *Analysis*

We utilized the following quantitative analysis methods for the data:

Normality Test We utilized Shapiro-Wilk test for normality of the distribution; the data was non-normal.

Item Counts We counted occurrences of mentioned items to assess projects' most and least important UX goals.

Descriptive Statistics We calculated means and standard deviations to summarize the sample. As the number of participants and the evaluated software varied case by case, we utilized means when analyzing equality between responses of users and team members.

Tests for Equity and Difference We chose to use nonparametric tests in our analysis. Our data consisted of both related and independent samples. We collected paired samples from team members in measurements TO (team member evaluating in own role) and TU (team member evaluating in role of user). For this data, we ran Wilcoxon signed rank test. Our null hypothesis was "*the median difference between* *measurements TO and TU is zero*", or, in practice, "*there is no difference between measurements TO and TU*". The test was run separately for each UX item. We utilized a Mann-Whitney U test for equality of means to compare responses of agile teams and users. We analyzed the difference between the following:

1. Users' responses (measurement US) and team members responding as themselves (team measurement TO) and
2. Users' responses and team members responding as they think users would respond (team measurement TU).

Our null hypothesis was "*the distribution of [UX item] is the same across categories of respondent type (user or team member)*."

We determined correlations pairwise for each UX item variable in all the measurements between the UX item and (1) overall UX score and (2) the need fulfillment score using Pearson product-moment correlation. We calculated similarity matrices and included values with significance level $p < .01$. We utilized a critical value table and included cases as follows: measurements TO and TU ($N = 26$, $df = 24$): $r > .496$, and in measurement US ($N = 29$, $df = 27$): $r > .471$.

Principal Component Analysis (PCA) PCA is a multivariate statistical method that is used for extracting the important information from data and compressing the data set size by discarding other information, thus analyzing the structure of the data [51]. Principal components are obtained as linear combinations of the original variables and each component has the largest possible variance under the constraint that it must be orthogonal to the preceding components [51]. We conducted PCA with SPSS to detect structure in the data and to reduce the correlated observed variables to a smaller set of UX items. We used Varimax with Kaiser normalization as the rotation method. The amount of extracted principal components was selected based on eigenvalue (>1) and coefficients with absolute value less than 0.5 were suppressed in the analysis.

Scale Reliability/Internal Consistency We calculated Cronbach's Alpha coefficients for created principal components to measure internal consistency of the items loaded to the component. We interpret the alpha according to Nunnally [52] and use 0.70 as the threshold of acceptable consistency. Generally, a correlation coefficient of 0.7–0.9 indicates *high correlation*, whereas 0.5–0.7 indicates *moderate correlation*.

7.4 Results

We begin by presenting results of the principal component analysis and continue by presenting results of the assessments of agile team members and users.

7.4.1 Principal Component Analysis (PCA)

The 16 measured items loaded into four components in PCA (Table 7.5). Item scores in Table 7.5 indicate the strength of correlation between the item and the component. The first four principal components account for 69 % of the variation (Fig. 7.1). Table 7.6 presents the internal consistency of each component, indicating the extent to which items in the component measure the same dimension of UX.

Based on the strongest correlations of each component, we named the generated components as follows: 1. *Motivation*, 2. *Usability and willingness to use*, 3. *Usefulness*, 4. *Professionalism*. Items in each component vary accordingly.

The first component (motivation) explains the system's ability to motivate user via positive affect. It consisted of the following components: *motivating, fun, promotes creativity, presentable, aesthetic,* and *innovative*. It contains items from categories of affective and aesthetic quality and stimulation defined during the review. This component holds many items related to traditional hedonic quality, and it is also in line with *stimulation* defined by Hassenzahl [53].

The second principal component (usability and willingness to use) measures usability. It is thus connected with the user's willingness to use the system. The following items loaded to the second component: *easy to use, easy to learn, fast to use,* and *desirable*. In addition, item *good* partially loaded to this component. Based on the presence of components *desirable* and *good* with traditional usability metrics,

Table 7.5 Rotated component matrix presents significant component loadings of PCA

Item	Component			
	1	2	3	4
Motivating – Discouraging	.81			
Fun – Dull	.79			
Promotes creativity – Suppresses creativity	.77			
Presentable – Unpresentable	.61			
Aesthetic – Unaesthetic	.57			
Innovative – Conservative	.56			
Easy to use – Difficult to use		.80		
Easy to learn – Hard to learn		.77		
Fast to use – Slow to use		.74		
Desirable – Undesirable		.53		
Good – Bad		.64	.52	
Useful – Useless			.71	
Recommendable – Not Recommendable			.58	
Professional – Amateurish				.85
Convincing – Unconvincing				.67
Reliable – Unreliable				.53

Rotation was converged in 9 iterations using Varimax with Kaiser Normalization using SPSS. The data consists of measurements TO and US, N = 55

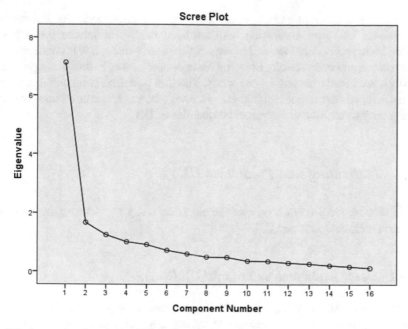

Fig. 7.1 Scree plot for the variables. Cumulative percentage of variance for the first four components is 69. The first principal component explains 45 % of the variance, the second 10 %, third 8 %, and fourth 6 % of the variance

Table 7.6 Internal consistency of principal components

Component name	Cronbach's Alpha	N of items in component
Motivation	.87 (good)	6
Productivity	.81 (good)	5
Usefulness	.75 (acceptable)	3
Professionalism	.69 (questionable)	3

this component can be interpreted that if the perceived usability of the system is low, users in general are not willing to use the system. The second component contains items from productivity, interaction quality, appeal, and overall system quality categories defined in [5].

The third component (usefulness) measures the scope of the system; how well does it fit to its purpose and is it useful? It is correlated with overall satisfaction and recommendability.

The fourth component (professionalism) seems to relate to work-related use itself and to the system's appropriateness to professional use. It contains items of *professional*, *convincing*, and *reliable*. The component can also be associated with the plausibility of the system's ability to complete required tasks.

These results from our work-related sample indicate that in work contexts, the dimensions of UX might not be the same as in leisure systems, and UX items might measure different aspects in work-related and leisure systems. For instance *professional* has been connected with aesthetic quality in leisure systems—the system *looks* professional instead of amateurish. In our study, it was connected with items *convincing* and *reliable*. Still, the basic dimensions of hedonic and pragmatic quality were clearly present in our study. The first principal component explained the majority of traditional hedonic UX aspects, whereas the second one explained the majority of traditional instrumental qualities of UX.

7.4.2 Estimating and Predicting UX

In this section, we present results of the empirical study considering the way users and team members assessed UX.

7.4.2.1 Users' Evaluation on Projects' UX Goals

We asked team members to list one to three of their most and least important UX goals for the project and then compared those goals with users' assessments. In all projects, team members emphasized the importance of pragmatic aspects of UX. The three most often mentioned UX goals were the following: *easy to use* (of the 26 participants, 18 mentioned this), *easy to learn* (13 mentions) and *fast to use* (13 mentions). Each of these three goals was mentioned in all six projects by at least one team member. *Fun* (16 mentions) and *promoting creativity* (13 mentions) were named as the least important UX goals in every project. This result was expected since pragmatic aspects, productivity in particular, are often emphasized in enterprise system development [54]. Similarly, importance of pragmatic aspects was emphasized in a study carried out in metals and engineering industry [5, 6].

With this data from developers, we then analyzed how users evaluated those items that teams considered the most and least important UX goals compared to other UX items. Users did not give higher assessments for these dimensions compared to other dimensions; *fast to use* was in fact among the lowest scored items. Users gave the highest evaluations for the following dimensions: *good* (6.1), *useful* (6.1), and *recommendable* (6.1) while the lowest were the following: *fun* (4.5), *promotes creativity* (5.0), aesthetic (5.1), and *fast to use* (5.1). The mean of users' overall UX evaluation was 5.7, while the mean over all the UX dimensions was 5.6.

7.4.2.2 Differences Between Measurements

When evaluating the UX of the outcome, team members were more critical when they were asked to evaluate as they think a member of a particular user group would evaluate (measurement TU) compared to when the team members responded as

Table 7.7 Distribution of differences between users' (measurement US) and team members' (measurements TO and TU) mean evaluations grouped by the direction of the difference. The mean difference between measurement US and measurement TO or TU is presented in brackets

	Measurement TO	Measurement TU
US is higher (mean difference)	47 % (0.6)	65 % (0.7)
US is lower (mean difference)	43 % (0.6)	28 % (0.6)
US and TO or TU are equal	10 %	7 %

themselves (measurement TO). The mean evaluations were systematically lower in measurement TU compared to measurement TO. We compared mean values of each item separately per project and found that in 60 % of the cases, the mean value in measurement TO was higher than in measurement TU, while the value of measurement TU was higher in only 14 % of the cases. All the roles (developers, POs, and UXS) systematically gave lower assessments in measurement TU compared to measurement TO. However, when comparing team members' assessments (TO and TU) to users' assessments (US), only for UXSs and POs did putting themselves in the users' role improve their UX assessments compared to users (measurement TU was closer to measurement US for UXSs). We consider this finding interesting and worth further studies.

There was a statistically significant difference between team members' and users' responses on six UX items when team members were asked to respond as they thought users would respond (comparison of measurements TU and US) (Table 7.7). The equity of distribution across users' (US) and team members' responses was greater when team members were asked to respond as themselves (measurement TO). In the latter case (comparison of measurements TO and US), the null hypothesis remained for all items.

The distribution of cases where user evaluation was higher than team evaluation and vice versa was relatively even when comparing measurement US with measurement TO (US is higher in 47 % and lower in 43 % of the cases, Table 7.8). However, when comparing measurement US with measurement TU, cases where user evaluation was higher than team evaluation were overly represented. User evaluation was higher in 65 % of the cases and lower in 28 % of the cases.

Based on the above, developers were overly critical with their responses in measurement TU, whereas developers' evaluations corresponded with users' evaluations better when they were not trying to predict the user assessment. In contrast, both POs' and UXSs' assessments were closer to users' assessments when they put themselves in the users' place. On average, developers assessed UX items 0.3 points lower than users when assessing as themselves (measurement TO) and 0.5 points lower than users when they tried to predict users' assessment (measurement TU) (on a seven-point scale). POs' assessments in measurement TO were 0.2 points higher than users' (US) and in measurement TU 0.1 lower than users' (US), on average. UXSs assessments were on average 0.2 points higher than users' in measurement TO and 0.1 points lower than users' in measurement TU. We consider POs' and UXSs' assessments quite accurate with users' assessments while developers'

Table 7.8 Results of tests of equity between user and team responses when team members were asked to respond as they think users would

UX item	Mann-Whitney U	Z	Asymp. Sig. (2-tailed)
Easy to learn – Hard to learn	229.0	−2.67	**<.01**
Fast to use – Slow to use	362.5	−.260	.80
Easy to use – Difficult to use	271.0	−1.87	.06
Reliable – Unreliable	328.5	−.856	.39
Desirable – Undesirable	255.5	−2.136	**<.05**
Recommendable – Not Recommendable	258.5	−2.17	**<.05**
Good – Bad	217.5	−2.88	**<.005**
Useful – Useless	330.5	−.855	.39
Motivating – Discouraging	231.5	−2.60	**<.01**
Fun – Dull	332.5	−.77	**<.05**
Aesthetic – Unaesthetic	321.0	−.98	.46
Professional – Amateurish	334.0	−.779	.44
Convincing – Unconvincing	277.5	−1.80	.07
Presentable – Unpresentable	316.0	−1.08	.28
Promotes creativity – Suppresses creativity	307.5	−1.21	.23
Innovative – Conservative	287.5	−1.56	.12

Test statistics grouping variable is respondent type (user or team member). Rejection of the null hypothesis (p < .05) is indicated by emboldening the value.

assessments differed from those of users'. Given that in the participating projects UXSs and POs handled communication with users while developers' understanding of users and their needs remained shallow (Kuusinen 2015), we conclude that trying to empathize with users seems to be unsuccessful with lacking understanding of the user. This finding is in line with [55]. However, our sample included responses only from three UXSs and six POs, and thus we want to be cautious with our conclusions.

In general, team members' evaluations varied more between measurements TO and TU for items measuring non-instrumental quality. We compared team members' responses between measurement TO and TU with Wilcoxon test using the following null hypothesis: "the median of differences between measurement TO and TU for each UX item separately is zero"; that is there is no difference between measurement TO and TU item-wise. The null hypothesis was rejected for the following items:

- good (Z = −2.83, p < .005)
- motivating, (Z = −2.94, p < .005)
- fun (Z = −2.50, p < .05), and
- innovative (Z = −2.18, p < .05).

Thus, team members changed their evaluation more for abovementioned items.

Table 7.9 Significant correlations (Pearson's r, p < .1) between overall UX evaluation scores and measured UX items per measurement

Measurement TO		Measurement TU		Measurement US	
Item	R	Item	R	Item	R
Good	.73	Easy to use	.60	*Presentable*	.71
Desirable	.66	Useful	.59	Innovative	.71
Innovative	.61	Easy to learn	.56	Convincing	.68
Recommendable	.51	Convincing	.55	Easy to use	.68
		Good	.537	Good	.63
		Professional	.52	*Aesthetic*	.62
		Innovative	.50	*Reliable*	.61
				Desirable	.60

N = 26 in measurements TO and TU and N = 29 in measurement US. Item name is in italics when correlation was found only in measurement US

7.4.2.3   Assessments of Overall UX and Need Fulfillment

The survey asked two questions about overall UX and the scope of software (as responding to needs). To assess overall UX and need fulfillment, we compared evaluations of measured UX dimensions to the evaluation of overall UX with Pearson's product-moment correlation. These results are presented in Table 7.9.

The following correlations were found only in measurement US: *presentable, aesthetic,* and *reliable. Desirable* was found in measurement US but not in measurement TU, and *convincing* was found in measurement US but not in measurement TO. Of the correlated items in measurement US, only *"easy to use"* measures instrumental quality. Thus, non-instrumental aspects correlated with the overall UX assessment clearly more than pragmatic ones. None of the items measuring instrumental quality correlated with the overall UX assessment in measurement TO (team members as themselves). In general, Pearson's r value grew smaller in measurement TU compared to measurement TO, which might indicate that the team members were less confident with their responses in measurement TU.

The following items (Table 7.10) had a strong and statistically significant correlation with the users' assessment of how well the system fulfills their needs: *Recommendable, useful, motivating, aesthetic, convincing, presentable,* and *innovative.* They all belong to hedonic UX dimensions except *useful,* which is considered to measure the overall quality of the system.

7.5   Limitations

Threats to External Validity   We have only studied a restricted set of companies all operating in Finland, which threatens population validity. The number of studied companies was limited to five, and as the data was collected from development

Table 7.10 Strong and significant correlations of measured items with the user assessment of the system's ability to fulfill user needs

Item pair	Pearson's r value	2-tailed significance (p)
Presentable – Unpresentable	.78	<.001
Innovative – Conservative	.72	<.001
Useful – Useless	.61	<.001
Recommendable – Not recommendable	.60	<.001
Motivating – Discouraging	.59	<.001
Aesthetic – Unaesthetic	.58	<.001
Convincing – Unconvincing	.54	<.01

projects, the sample is clustered; projects, their outcomes, and users are unique and thus not directly comparable. We utilized the same team population in another study before, which subjects the study to multiple-treatment interference. As the sequence of measurements TO and TU was fixed, the study is prone to order bias.

The data was small (55 participants) for PCA; it would be beneficial to double the number of participants. We based our sampling on [56], where the writers argue for smaller sample sizes, even for samples of 20. Therefore, we consider our sample size sufficient, but also admit that a larger size would have been beneficial. For instance, Gorsuch [57] argues there should always be at least one hundred participants even for a small number of variables. Comrey and Lee [58] consider that having 100 participants is sufficient but poor and a good sample size would be 500 participants.

Threats to Internal Validity Selection bias always exists when comparing groups. In this particular setting, utilizing randomized groups was impossible. Measurements TO and TU might be affected by learning effect, as participants answered the same questions twice (as themselves and as they think users would answer). We did not select the user participants by ourselves, and thus we are unaware of the possible level of implementation bias. Although we guided the contact persons in selecting user participants, some of them might have selected, for instance, users that they knew who were positive towards the software. Moreover, we did not control for a user answering the survey twice.

Using semantic differentials is prone to several types of evaluation bias. Those include the following: Central tendency bias occurs when respondents tend to favor the middle levels of a scale [59]. This was also observed in our study. Position bias concerns the order of evaluated items; users tend to treat the middle items differently than those in the beginning and in the end [60]. We did not utilize counterbalancing, which can lead to position bias. PCA is prone to this bias since it can have an impact on the correlations between variables.

7.6 Discussion

7.6.1 UX Scale

The scale we utilized showed strong internal consistency in measuring 1 (hedonic qualities of UX) and 2 (instrumental qualities of UX). Internal consistency was acceptable for measuring 3 (scope or overall quality of the system) and questionable for measuring 4 (fitness for professional use). However, internal consistency can be improved by increasing the number of items in the category [62]. It is possible in this case since there were only three items in components 3 and 4. Thus, confirmatory studies should be conducted for further validation of the dimensions of enterprise software UX. Also, different phrasing of items could be tested for improved fitness, and the determined dimensions and their interpretation should be further analyzed.

It seems that some items behave differently when measuring enterprise and leisure software. In leisure software such items as presentable, professional, and innovative (design) have been used for measuring aesthetic quality. For instance, Lavie et al. [31] understand aesthetic in a broad sense, and they divide it to dimensions of *classical* and *expressive aesthetics*. They describe the latter as follows: *"The expressive aesthetics dimension is reflected by the designers' creativity and originality and by the ability to break design conventions"*. Especially in enterprise software the UX design often concentrates on user interaction or UI design. Thus, "breaking design conventions" most probably indicates bad design decisions since design conventions, in style guides for instance, have been created to instruct on developing fluent user interaction [62]. In addition, the phrasing of questions in our study asked the participants to evaluate the system (as a whole) and not just its design or appeal. Thus, the results cannot be directly compared to studies where the appeal of UI designs alone have been evaluated.

7.6.2 UX as Assessed by Team Members and Users

Based on our findings, it seems likely that developers are able to understand the pros and cons of the developed enterprise software quite well. However, they tend to focus on pragmatic aspects of the system neglecting the non-instrumental ones that in fact seem to be more important to users in terms of their UX. As enterprise software typically provides tools that are used to perform practical tasks, instrumental quality naturally should be sufficient. However, non-instrumental quality contributes to user satisfaction and thus to human productivity, which might be an important organizational goal.

The first principal component (motivation), revealed in our analysis, measured mainly the system's ability to motivate the user while the second one measured usability and is correlated with the user's willingness to use the system. Both these qualities of enterprise software are important for productivity and job satisfaction

[63, 64]. Developers seemed to think that users would appreciate especially qualities related to efficiency and productivity. They emphasized instrumental qualities even more when they were asked to assess the system as they think users would. This finding is in line with [45] who found that usability professionals have a tendency towards utilitarian dimensions of usability. Also, Innes [54] argued that developers of ERP systems tend to neglect the hedonic. In our study, in comparing measurements TO and TU (team members assessing UX (TO) in individual roles vs. team members (TU) placing themselves in users' role), it seems that the tendency towards the instrumental was increased when developers were to think how users would assess the UX. However, in users' assessments, the hedonic correlated most with their overall UX evaluation, and in PCA, it was the first component.

Clemmensen et al. [46] did not find many differences between users' and developers' perception on usability. On the other hand, usability professionals construed usability differently from developers and users. Given that only three UXSs participated in our study, we want to be cautious to make generalizations about differences between developers' and UXSs' assessments. However, in our study, UXSs and POs were the best to predict user evaluation of both the pragmatic and the hedonic. Developers tended to be overly negative in their evaluations. Such finding might be explained by the fact that UXSs and POs were the most involved with users and that they thus have the best understanding of user needs and capabilities. However, the frequency of user communication [7] seemed not to improve the ability of POs to predict the UX as assessed by users. Altogether, the small number of POs and UXSs make this finding questionable, and it definitely requires more research.

Developers were more critical towards the UX when they were asked to evaluate the software from the users' point of view compared to their own evaluation and users' evaluation. This finding is interesting considering the common practice among developers to try to think as they believe users would. The result might indicate that if developers do not have a proper understanding of the user, putting oneself in an imaginary user's place seems to lower the ability to predict the actual user evaluation. Again, the small number of UXSs and POs in our study allows only cautious conclusions. However, in our population, putting oneself in the user's place seemed to improve the accuracy of UXSs' and POs' evaluation. This finding provides an interesting opportunity for future work: does, for instance, utilizing personas or exposing developers to users improve the developers' ability to put themselves in the users' place and thus improve developers' ability to predict UX? Another question is if it has an impact whether the UI is designed by the developers themselves or by a UXS. Also, it can have an impact how closely the developers work with the UXS.

Neither users nor teams gave better evaluations to those UX dimensions that the teams considered the most important ones. Teams focused on usability and productivity, whereas affective and aesthetic qualities seemed to better predict the overall UX of the users. Thus, we hypothesize that setting clearer UX goals informed by user preference and shared among the whole project team might improve both the overall UX and the rating of the most important aspects.

7.6.3 Using the Scale to Focus UX Goals

When designing work related systems, such as enterprise systems, selecting and setting UX goals to support design and development activities is equally important as when designing consumer products [65–67]. Setting a limited and carefully selected set of high-level UX goals enables focusing the design effort on the most important experiential aspects. A plain list of UX dimensions can be useful when considering the UX goals and setting measurable UX targets for a project. The list itself can act as a constant reminder for developers of the multidimensionality of UX in a similar way the *personas* method is often used. In the personas method, archetypes of users are created based on user data. Descriptions of personas are often hung on walls to remind developers for whom they are developing. In our study, agile teams considered productivity items as the most important UX goals. This finding is in line with Innes [54]. To be able to guide the UX implementation during development, the team needs information on how users perceive the software being developed. In our study, we found that teams considered *fast to use* as one of the most important UX goals, while users considered it as one of the poorest performing dimensions. The team can use this information to focus their improvement work on the experienced speed of use.

It would be interesting to measure if improving a quality with a low evaluation score would improve the overall UX score. On the other hand, another hypothesis could be that improving performance on dimensions with the strongest correlation to the overall UX score would increase the overall UX score. Users might also expect that items related to productivity and efficiency need to be on a sufficient level not to lower the UX. However, after that, other qualities become more important predictors of the perceived UX. Thus, a third hypothesis is that concentrating on items belonging to the first principal component (motivation) would increase the overall UX assessment of users.

7.7 Conclusions

We compared UX assessments of members of agile teams and users of the software systems under development. Our results indicate that developers concentrate on instrumental aspects of UX, whereas for users, non-instrumental aspects might be a more important predictor of their perception of overall UX. Moreover, it seems to be difficult for developers to place themselves in the user's position, and thus trying to do so can even be harmful when the team member does not have sufficient understanding of the user. These findings contribute towards understanding development team members' ability to understand UX in order to enable allocating UX tasks between team members and thus focusing the limited UXS resource to those tasks that developers cannot handle by themselves.

Acknowledgments We thank Timo Partala for us on the data analysis methods. We are grateful to all the study participants. Our research has been supported by TEKES as part of the Cloud Software and Need for Speed research programs of DIGILE (Finnish Strategic Centre for Science, Technology and Innovation in the field of ICT and digital business) and by TEKES as part of the User Experience and Usability of Complex Systems (UXUS) research program of FIMECC (Finnish Metals and Engineering Competence Cluster).

References

1. Saiedian H, Dale R (2000) Requirements engineering: making the connection between the software developer and customer. Inf Softw Technol 42(6):419–428
2. ISO 9241 (1998) Ergonomic requirements for office work with visual display terminals (VDTs) – part 11: guidance on usability. International Organization for Standardisation, Genève
3. Salah D, Paige R, Cairns P (2014) A systematic literature review on agile development processes and user centred design integration. In: Proceedings of the 18th international conference on Evaluation and Assessment in Software Engineering (EASE'14). ACM. Article 5, 10 p
4. Sy D (2007) Adapting usability investigations for Agile user-centered design. J Usability Stud 2(3):112–132
5. Sundberg HR (2015) The importance of user experience related factors in new product development—Comparing the views of designers and users of industrial products. In: 23rd Nordic academy of management conference, Copenhagen, Denmark, 12–14 August 2015
6. Sundberg HR (2015) The role of user experience in a business-to-business context. Doctoral dissertation. Tampere University of Technology. Publication, 1278. http://URN.fi/URN:ISBN:978-952-15-3450-8
7. Kuusinen K (2015) Task allocation between UX specialists and developers in agile software development projects. In: Proceedings human-computer interaction – INTERACT 2015, LNCS 9298, Springer International Publishing, pp 27–44
8. Law E, Roto V, Hassenzahl M, Vermeeren A, Kort J (2009) Understanding, scoping and defining user experience: a survey approach. In: Proceedings CHI'09, ACM, pp 719–728
9. Hassenzahl M, Tractinsky N (2006) User experience – a research agenda. Behav Inform Technol 25(2):91–97
10. Law ELC, Hassenzahl M, Karapanos E, Obrist M, Roto V (2015) Tracing links between UX frameworks and design practices: dual carriageway. In: Proceedings HCI Korea. Hanbit Media, Inc., pp 188–195
11. Hassenzahl M (2004) The interplay of beauty, goodness and usability in interactive products. In: Proceedings HCI. Lawrence Erlbaum Associates, 19, 4, pp 319–349
12. McCarthy J, Wright P (2004) Technology as experience. Interactions 11(5):42–43
13. Hassenzahl M (2008) User experience (UX): towards an experiential perspective on product quality. In: Proceedings 20th international conference of the Association Francophone d'Interaction Homme-Machine. ACM, pp 11–15
14. Lallemand C, Gronier G, Koenig V (2015) User experience: a concept without consensus? Exploring practitioners' perspectives through an international survey. Comput Hum Behav 43:35–48
15. Väänänen-Vainio-Mattila K, Roto V, Hassenzahl M (2008) Towards practical user experience evaluation methods. In: Law ELC, Bevan N, Christou G, Springett M, Lárusdóttir M (eds) Meaningful measures: Valid Useful User Experience Measurement (VUUM) (2008), pp 19–22

16. Diefenbach S, Kolb N, Hassenzahl M (2014) The 'Hedonic' in human-computer interaction. In: Proceedings of the 2014 conference on designing interactive systems (DIS), ACM, pp 305–314
17. Vermeeren AP, Law ELC, Roto V, Obrist M, Hoonhout J, Väänänen-Vainio-Mattila K (2010) User experience evaluation methods: current state and development needs. In: Proceedings of the 6th Nordic conference on human-computer interaction: extending boundaries. ACM, pp 521–530
18. da Silva TS, Martin A, Maurer F, Silveira M (2011) User-centered design and Agile methods: a systematic review. In: Proceedings of the international conference on agile methods in software development, AGILE 2011, IEEE
19. Holzinger A (2005) Usability engineering for software developers. Commun ACM 48(1):71–74
20. Dray S, Siegel D (2004) Remote possibilities? International usability testing at a distance. Interactions 11(2):10–17. ACM
21. Ivory MY, Hearst MA (2001) The state of the art in automating usability evaluation of user interfaces. Comput Surv 33(4):470–516. ACM
22. Ardito C, Buono P, Caivano D, Costabile MF, Lanzilotti R, Bruun A, Stage J (2011) Usability evaluation: a survey of software development organizations. In: Proceedings of the international conference on Software Engineering and Knowledge Engineering, SEKE 11. Knowledge Systems Institute, Skokie, pp 282–287
23. Lárusdóttir MK, Cajander A, Gulliksen J (2013) Informal feedback rather than performance measurements – user centred evaluation in Scrum projects. Behav Inform Technol 33(11):1118–1135
24. Bruun A, Gull P, Hofmeister L, Stage J (2009) Let your users do the testing: a comparison of three remote asynchronous usability testing methods. In: Proceedings of the SIGCHI Conference on Human Factors in Computing Systems (CHI), ACM, pp 1619–1628
25. Bruun A, Stage J (2012) The effect of task assignments and instruction types on remote asynchronous usability testing. In: Proceedings of the SIGCHI Conference on Human Factors in Computing Systems (CHI), pp 2117–2126
26. Salvador C, Nakasone A, Pow-Sang JA (2014) A systematic review of usability techniques in agile methodologies. In: Proceedings of the 7th Euro American Conference on Telematics and Information Systems (EATIS'14). Article 17, ACM, 6 p
27. Panwar M (2013) Application performance management emerging trends. In: Proceedings of the Cloud & Ubiquitous Computing & Emerging Technologies (CUBE), pp 178–182
28. Bastien JMC (2010) Usability testing: a review of some methodological and technical aspects of the method. Int J Med Inform 79(4):e18–e23. Elsevier
29. Bargas-Avila J, Hornbæk K (2011) Old wine in new bottles or novel challenges? a critical analysis of empirical studies of user experience. In: Proceedings of the annual conference on human factors in computing systems. ACM, pp 2689–2698
30. Bradley MM, Lang PJ (1994) Measuring emotion: the self-assessment manikin and the semantic differential. J Behav Ther Exp Psychiat 25:49–59
31. Lavie T, Tractinsky N (2004) Assessing dimensions of perceived visual aesthetics of web sites. Int J Hum Comput Stud 60(3):269–298
32. Voss KE, Spangenberg ER, Grohmann B (2003) Measuring the hedonic and utilitarian dimensions of consumer attitude. J Mark Res 40(3):310–320
33. Costello B, Edmonds E (2007) A study in play, pleasure and interaction design. In: Proceedings of the 2007 conference on designing pleasurable products and interfaces (DPPI'07). ACM, pp 76–91
34. Zijlstra R (1993) Efficiency in work behaviour. A design approach for modern tools. Delft University Press, Delft
35. Jackson S, Marsh H (1996) Development and validation of a scale to measure optimal experience: the flow state scale. J Sport Exercise Psychol 18:17–35

36. Väätäjä H, Koponen T, Roto V (2009) Developing practical tools for user experience evaluation: a case from mobile news journalism. European Conference on Cognitive Ergonomics (ECCE'09). VTT Technical Research Centre of Finland, VTT, Finland, pp 240–247
37. Desmet P, Overbeeke C, Tax S (2001) Designing products with added emotional value; development and application of an approach for research through design. Des J 4(1):32–47
38. Mehrabian A (1996) Pleasure-arousal-dominance: a general framework for describing and measuring individual differences in temperament. Curr Psychol 14(4):261–292
39. Kirakowski J (1996) The software usability measurement inventory: background and usage. In: Jordan PW et al (eds) Usability evaluation in industry. Taylor & Francis, London, pp 169–178
40. Davis FD (1989) A technology acceptance model for empirically testing new end-user information systems: theory and results. MIS Q 13(3):319–340
41. Lee TM, Park C (2008) Mobile technology usage and B2B market performance under mandatory adoption. Ind Mark Manag 37(7):833–840
42. Goodhue DL, Thompson RL (1995) Task-technology fit and individual performance. MIS Q 19(2):213–236
43. Lindgaard G, Kirakowski J (2013) Introduction to the special issue: the tricky landscape of developing rating scales in HCI. Interact Comput 25(4):271–277
44. Hertzum M, Clemmensen T, Hornbaek K, Kumar J, Shi Q, Yammiyavar P (2011) Personal usability constructs: how people construe usability across nationalities and stakeholder groups. Int J Hum Comput Interact 27(8):729–761
45. Hertzum M, Clemmensen T (2012) How do usability professionals construe usability? Int J Hum Comput Stud 70:26–42
46. Clemmensen T, Hertzum M, Yang J, Chen Y (2013) Do usability professionals think about user experience in the same way as users and developers do? Interact 2013, Part II, LNCS 8118, pp 461–478
47. Shackel B (2009) Usability-context, framework, definition, design and evaluation. Interact Comput 21(5–6):339–346
48. Schwaber K (2004) Agile project management with Scrum, 1st edn, Microsoft professional. Microsoft Press, Redmond
49. Poppendieck M, Poppendieck T (2003) Lean software development: an agile toolkit. Addison-Wesley Professional, Boston, 203 p
50. Fitzgerald, B. & Stol, K.-J. (2014) Continuous software engineering and beyond: trends and challenges. In: Proceedings of the 1st international workshop on Rapid Continuous Software Engineering (RCoSE 2014). ACM, New York, NY, USA, pp 1–9
51. Abdi H, Williams LJ (2010) Principal component analysis. Wiley interdisciplinary reviews: computational statistics, 2(4), pp 433–459. Wiley, Hoboken
52. Nunnally J (1978) Psychometric theory, 2nd edn. McGraw-Hill, New York
53. Hassenzahl M (2005) The thing and I: understanding the relationship between user and product. In: Blythe M, Overbeeke K, Monk A, Wright P (eds) Funology: from usability to enjoyment. Kluwer Academic Publishers, Dordrecht, pp 31–42
54. Innes J (2011) Why enterprises can't innovate: helping companies learn design thinking. In: HCII 2011, LNCS 6769:442–448. Springer, Berlin/Heidelberg
55. Cockton G, Woolrych A (2001) Understanding inspection methods: lessons from an assessment of heuristic evaluation. In: People and computers XV – interaction without Frontiers. Springer, London, pp 171–191
56. Preacher KJ, MacCallum RC (2002) Exploratory factor analysis in behavior genetics research: factor recovery with small sample sizes. Behav Genet 32:153–161
57. Gorsuch RL (1983) Factor analysis, 2nd edn. Erlbaum, Hillsdale
58. Comrey AL, Lee HB. A first course in factor analysis. Erlbaum, Hillsdale
59. Yu JH, Albaum G, Swenson M (2003) Is a central tendency error inherent in the use of semantic differential scales in different cultures? Int J Mark Res 45(2):213–228
60. Blunch NJ (1984) Position bias in multiple-choice questions. J Mark Res 21(2):216–220
61. Cronbach LJ (1951) Coefficient alpha and the internal structure of tests. Psychometrika 16(3):297–334. Springer

62. Kuusinen K, Mikkonen T (2014) On designing UX for mobile enterprise apps. In: Proceedings of the Software Engineering and Advanced Applications (SEAA 2014), pp 221–228
63. Calisir F, Calisir F (2004) The relation of interface usability characteristics, perceived usefulness, and perceived ease of use to end-user satisfaction with enterprise resource planning (ERP) systems. Comput Hum Behav 20(4):505–515. Elsevier
64. Hafeez-Baig A, Gururajan R (2013) Expectations, usability, and job satisfaction as determinants for the perceived benefits for the use of wireless technology in healthcare. In: Pervasive health knowledge management. Springer, New York, pp 305–316
65. Kaasinen E, Roto V, Hakulinen J, Heimonen T, Jokinen JPP, Karvonen H, Keskinen T, Koskinen H, Lu Y, Saariluoma P, Tokkonen H, Turunen M (2015) Defining user experience goals to guide the design of industrial systems. Behaviour & Information Technology Journal, Taylor & Francis. doi:10.1080/0144929X.2015.1035335
66. Varsaluoma J, Väätäjä H, Kaasinen E, Karvonen H, Lu Y (2015) The fuzzy front end of experience design: eliciting and communicating experience goals. In: Proceedings of the OZCHI 2015, Brisbane, Australia
67. Väätäjä H, Savioja P, Roto V, Olsson T, Varsaluoma J (2015) User experience goals as a guiding light in design and development—early findings. In: INTERACT 2015 Adjunct Proceedings. University of Bamberg Press (2015), 521–527

Part II
Future Directions

Chapter 8
Workshop on the Integration of User-Centred Design and Agile Development: Approach, Findings and Themes

Peggy Gregory, Marta Lárusdóttir, Åsa Cajander, and Gilbert Cockton

Abstract This chapter reports on a workshop held at NordiCHI 2014 on the integration of user-centred design (UCD) and Agile Software Development (Agile). The workshop brought together academic researchers and industrial practitioners to discuss challenges, success stories and future trends when working with UCD and Agile. Eight papers were accepted, of which seven reported the results of empirical studies and one presented a theoretical comparison. The workshop day was inspired by Agile methods. It was time-boxed, incremental, interactive, collaborative, used a visual workspace and a team-based approach. Post-it notes capturing features from paper presentations and discussions were written and displayed on the walls throughout the day. These were divided into two groups, one for 'interesting points' and the other for 'challenges and obstacles'. At the end of the day the two groups of post-it notes were themed using an affinity diagram approach. Eight higher-level themes were identified by the authors during a post-workshop analysis. These were: People and roles, Teams and communication, Culture, Methods and practices, Time and synchronisation, Artefacts and tools, Research and problems, and Miscellaneous. Six themes were applicable to both affinity diagrams, the 'Culture' theme was only found in the 'challenges and obstacles' set and the 'Research and problems' theme was only found in the 'interesting points' set. Key elements of the themes were about practices, people, culture and time. The workshop illustrates the importance of industry-based empirical research to investigate challenges and innovate solutions for the ever-changing landscape of software development.

P. Gregory (✉)
School of Physical Sciences and Computing, University of Central Lancashire, Preston, UK
e-mail: AJGregory@uclan.ac.uk

M. Lárusdóttir
School of Computer Science, Reykjavik University, Reykjavik, Iceland

Å. Cajander
Department of Information Technology, Uppsala University, Uppsala, Sweden

G. Cockton
School of Design, Northumbria University, Newcastle upon Tyne NE1 8ST, UK

© Springer International Publishing Switzerland 2016
G. Cockton et al. (eds.), *Integrating User-Centred Design in Agile Development*,
Human–Computer Interaction Series, DOI 10.1007/978-3-319-32165-3_8

Keywords User-centered design • User experience • Agile software development

8.1 Introduction

User-Centred Design (UCD) and Agile Software Development (Agile) come from strong but distinct disciplines that have their own cultures, histories and practices. Although they share common links, each discipline has developed in different ways and has grown out of very distinct communities. Agile approaches do not specifically mention UCD, and industry practitioners often face difficulties in integrating UCD processes into the very short development iterations that are commonly used by Agile teams. The integration of the two approaches presents practitioners and researchers with many opportunities for innovation, research and discussion.

In this chapter we present a summary of the outcome of the Workshop on Integrating User-Centred Design and Agile Development: Approaches and Challenges, held at NordiCHI in 2014. The workshop addressed a range of issues around the integration including: challenges and success stories from practice; values and perspectives underpinning UCD and Agile in theory; theories and methods relevant for doing research on Agile and UCD; and also future research trends.

8.2 Background

Agile approaches such as Scrum, Extreme Programming (XP) and Dynamic Systems Development Method (DSDM), are increasingly widely used in industry [1, 2]. Agile approaches focus on individuals and interactions, delivering working software, customer collaboration and responding to change [3]. UCD enables designers and developers to consider user perspectives when developing software. UCD is reflected in a number of approaches such as the ISO standard 9241–210:2010 for Human-Centred Design [4], contextual inquiry [5], participatory design [6], value sensitive design [7, 8], rapid contextual design [9], and human-centred design [10, 11]. Examples of UCD activities include creating personas to communicate user research, doing field studies to observe users, and usability evaluations for gathering user feedback.

An implicit assumption for many who have adopted Agile has been that it addresses user perspectives better than traditional approaches [12]. However, research has shown that this is not always the case and that the context in which Agile approaches are adopted impacts user involvement [13, 14]. There are a number of challenges for integrating UCD and Agile, including culture, resource allocation, work dynamics, modularisation, documentation, testing and time allocation [15, 16]. A number of research studies have tried to uncover and analyse the conditions under which Agile and UCD work together in order to find solutions to some of these challenges. Much of this work is based on empirical studies [13, 17–19], but some is based on reasoning and model-building [20]. Four systematic reviews have provided overviews of the literature in this area: in 2010 Sohaib and Kahn [21] included 35 papers in their rather unstructured literature review; in 2011 da Silva et al. [16] reviewed 58 papers, in 2014 Salah et al. [15] reviewed 71 papers, and in 2015 Bhrel et al. [22] reviewed 83 papers. These show that there has been a considerable body of research in this area.

However, challenges remain for practitioners. The rate of Agile adoption has quickened over recent years [1], and it is now considered a mainstream approach. This has resulted in Agile being used in a variety of software development application areas such as embedded systems, large enterprise systems and open source software projects, amongst others. This expansion has resulted in practitioners facing a wide set of challenges such as issues to do with organisation, culture, team management, sustainability and scaling [23].

8.3   Workshop Approach

The two goals of the workshop were (1) to identify challenges and success stories when working with UCD and Agile and (2) to identify future trends for research into Agile and UCD. With these goals in mind, the workshop was designed in order to maximise opportunities for engagement, discussion and learning. We gave it an agile flavour by making it time-boxed, incremental, interactive, collaborative, using a visual workspace and a team-based approach. We therefore spent the bulk of the day considering each paper in turn and integrated presentations and discussions.

Eight papers were accepted and presented at the workshop and 14 participants took part (Table 8.1). Paper 1 described open source development for social innovation, paper 2 was about Agile being used by an SME (Small and Medium-sized Enterprise) in the finance domain, paper 3 was about medical device development, paper 4 discussed Agile in medium to large companies, paper 5 was an empirical study completed in the domain of enterprise systems development, paper 6 was based on work done by an industrial research and development lab, paper 7 discussed a one-off development project, and paper 8 compared Agile and Lean in terms of their compatibility with UX design principles.

The day started with introductions. Following this we ran a series of time-boxed half hour sessions during which each paper was presented for 15 min and then discussed for 15 min. The presentations consisted of a 10-min talk followed by 5 min for questions. We set up the room so that participants were grouped around three tables. After the presentation the groups sitting at each table discussed the paper for 10 min, following which each group gave feedback to the whole room and we had a short whole group discussion. During the presentation and discussion participants wrote down any interesting elements on pink post-it notes, and any challenges or obstacles on yellow post-it notes. These were posted onto the back

Table 8.1 Workshop papers

	Title	Authors and affiliations	Topic
1	Catch Me If You Can: Reconciling Agile and UCD	Silvia Bordin, Maria Menendez, Antonella De Angeli	The integration of UCD and Agile within an open source social innovation project
		University of Trento, Italy	
2	Customer Feedback and UCD in Agile Software Development	Oliver Stickel, Sebastian Draxler, Gunnar Stevens	Integrating customer feedback and UCD into Agile in a German SME
		University of Siegen, Germany	
3	Fast, Faster Agile	Tina Øvad, Lars Bo Larsen,	Development of a UCD toolbox to support software developers doing UCD work themselves, in a medical devices domain
		Aalborg Uiversity, Denmark	
4	Integration of UCD and Agile Development: Action Research Can Help	Carmelo Ardito, Paolo Buono, Danilo Caivano, Maria F. Costabile, Rosa Lanzilotti	An Action Research approach to identifying and removing obstacles Agile and UCD integration
		University of Bari, Italy	
5	Beyond the "One Sprint Ahead" Approach: Organizing User Experience Work in Agile Software Development Adapting Scrum for UCD	Kati Kuusinen,	Problems in Agile UX integration and guidance on rearranging the upfront design phase for UX specialists using a collaborative approach.
		Tampere University of Technology, Finland	
6	Adapting Scrum for UCD focused projects: An industry experience perspective	Karin Nilsson Helander, Thijmen de Gooijer, Maria Ralph	Insights into adapting Scrum for UCD focused projects in industry.
		ABB Corporate Research	
7	Attending Experiential Qualities in System Development	Rikard Lindell	Interaction design and programming as craft, and the merging of design and development processes
		Mälardalen University, Sweden	
8	User Experience (UX) Design: Agile or Lean?	Effie Law, Marta Lárusdóttir	A comparison of Agile and Lean to ascertain which is more compatible with UX principles
		Leicester University and Reykjavik University	

wall of the workshop room before the start of the next discussion (Fig. 8.1). Before the next presentation two members of each group moved to different tables so that over the course of the day the discussion groups gradually changed. After all the papers had been discussed the workshop participants divided into two groups. One group analysed the yellow post-it notes and the other analysed the pink post-it notes (Fig. 8.2), using an affinity diagram approach [5, 24]. At the end of the day the affinity diagrams were removed from the wall and typed up.

Several months after the workshop we (the workshop organisers) added three new groups to the 'interesting points' affinity diagram due to the large number of

Fig. 8.1 'Challenges and obstacles' (*pink*) and 'Interesting points' (*yellow*) collected during the workshop

Fig. 8.2 Affinity theming the 'interesting points' post-its during the final session

'miscellaneous' items. We also moved some items to different groups. We discussed and grouped the affinity categories into higher-level themes for the purposes of drawing out broader topics from the workshop.

8.4   Results

We collected 120 'challenges and obstacles' on pink post-it notes and 125 'interesting points' on yellow post-it notes during the workshop discussions. Although one of the workshop aims was to collect challenges and success stories on the pink post-it notes, on the day everyone focused on challenges and not success stories. During affinity grouping the 'challenges and obstacles' were divided into 17 groups (Table 8.2) and the 'interesting points' were divided into 16 groups (Table 8.3).

We identified eight higher-level themes from the affinity groups during the post-workshop analysis: People and roles (34 post-its); Teams and communication (49); Culture (8); Methods and practice (91); Time and synchronisation (23); Artefacts and tools (16); Research and problems (11); and Miscellaneous (13). Six higher-level themes were applicable to both affinity diagrams. The 'challenges and obstacles' set had a 'Culture' theme, which was not shared with the other set; the 'interesting points' set had a 'Research and problems' theme that was not shared.

8.5   Discussion

The papers presented at the workshop show the diversity of Agile UCD research, with notable similarities and differences in elements of the work. Of the eight papers, six reported empirical studies (papers 1, 2, 3, 4, 6, 7), one reported findings from empirical work as well as a theoretical model (paper 5), and one was purely theoretical, exploring the differences between Agile UX and Lean UX (paper 8). One of the notable commonalities between the papers was the predominance of Scrum. Out of the eight papers, five were about Scrum (papers 1, 2, 3, 4, 6). Of the three papers that did not focus on Scrum, paper 4 discussed Agile in general, paper 7 discussed Kanban, and paper 8 compared Agile and Lean. The prevalence of Scrum in the papers reflects its popularity as the Agile approach of choice in industry [1].

The papers presented at the workshop highlighted how many challenges remain in this field. Although many familiar issues were discussed – synchronising UCD with software development activities, big-design-upfront, cultural differences between designers and developers, getting the right people on teams – the day focussed on how these challenges are evolving as Agile matures and becomes more mainstream. A notable feature of the work presented was how Agile is now being used in a wide variety of domains.

The workshop approach was inspired by Agile methods. Hence it was time-boxed, incremental, interactive, collaborative, used a visual workspace and a team-based approach. The 30-min time-boxes or sprints helped to shape the working day by giving an equal amount of time to each paper. The approach was incremental in that for each time-box we completed all the elements required for that paper – presentation, questions, discussion and data collection – before moving on to the next session. The equal amount of time given to each sprint gave the day a certain

Table 8.2 'Challenges and obstacles' affinity groups and themes

Themes (No. of post-its collected)	Affinity Groups (No. of post-its collected)	Example post-it (Paper no., see Table 1)
Challenges and Obstacles		
People and roles (16)	Product owner (8)	*Getting access to POs is a challenge (6)*
	Roles (8)	*User roles: client, end-user (1)*
Teams and Communication (33)	Team (7)	*Inexperienced team (1)*
	Power and relationships (6)	*Who's got the power? Software developer or UX designer? (1,3)*
	Communication (5)	*Lots of electronic communication rather than f2f (2)*
	Feedback (8)	*Micro design cycles might require constant access to users (for testing etc.) which might be difficult to achieve (or impossible) (5)*
	Teaching and learning (7)	*How to get 'call for tenders' to understand UCD/UX (4)*
Culture (8)	Culture/awareness (8)	*Agile comes from software developer culture not UCD culture – less ownership of Agile amongst the UX community (5)*
Methods and practices (32)	Methods (10)	*Do more prescriptive methods help practitioners (by suggesting good practice) or stifle them (by giving too much detail)? (8)*
	Theory and Practice (12)	*Adopting a methodology requires adapting it to the peculiarities of the company (3)*
	Filtering (10)	*Filtering the users perspective to get the 'right' product (2)*
Time and synchronisation (15)	Time/tempo (10)	*Figuring out when to do user research/testing in order to be able to prioritise and estimate time properly (6)*
	Synchronising (5)	*Synchronisation of implementation, design and test (5)*
Artefacts and Tools (12)	Documentation (5)	*Documentation practice vs. open source ethics (1)*
	Design artefacts (4)	*Chunking big idea into manageable and meaningful small units (7)*
	Tools/toolboxes (3)	*IT that supports the process did not work properly (2)*
Miscellaneous (4)	Miscellaneous (4)	*The intrinsic difficulty of programming effectively and beautifully (and of designing something beautiful and effective) (7)*

Table 8.3 'Interesting points' affinity groups and themes

Themes (No. of post-its collected)	Affinity Groups (No. of post-its collected)	Example post-it (Paper no., see Table 1)
Interesting points		
People and roles (18)	User involvement (7)	*Users: Informant v customer (1)*
	Roles (11)	*Programmers are creative as well as designers (7)*
Teams and communication (16)	Team (5)	*Change from beneath (4)*
	UX team (2)	*UX team using Scrum for themselves (6)*
	Pairwise work (5)	*Informal approaches worked well – Pair designing; no documentation; ad-hoc intervention (1)*
	Internal communication (4)	*Communication in open-source project – different needs (1)*
Methods and practices (59)	Methods (17)	*Clashes in viewpoint are ok (2)*
	Organising UCD (10)	*Making a working UX design or software in every sprint (5)*
	User feedback (12)	*Different media to collect user feedback (2)*
	Developers doing UCD (20)	*Teaching developers about UCD techniques (3)*
Time and synchronisation (8)	Time (8)	*UX changes over time – temporal aspects (8)*
Artefacts and tools (4)	Tools (2)	*Git Hub seen as restrictive? (1)*
	Documentation (2)	*Different sized post-it notes (6)*
Research and problems (11)	Research (3)	*Agile research for Agile practice (4)*
	Problems with agility (8)	*Is programming supported as a craft in Scrum/Kanban (8)*
Miscellaneous (9)	Miscellaneous (9)	*Philosophical reflections on creative products, combining technical, art and design perspective (7)*

sense of rhythm – similar to the flow encouraged by Kanban. Work in progress was limited by the focus on one paper at a time, but there was still some multi-tasking. Participants had to write 'challenges and obstacles' and 'interesting points' on post-it notes throughout each session, take part in the group discussion and pull out salient points for the whole group session – so every participant was actively involved in each part of the process. The whole day was interactive in a variety of ways. We had presentations, small group discussions, whole group discussions, one-to-one introductions and group-based activities. Participants were grouped around three tables for small group discussions after each presentation, but before the next sprint two people moved from each group to different tables. Changing the groups between each session meant that the groups always had a different dynamic and over the course of the day each participant had a chance to talk to everyone else in the workshop. A visual workspace was maintained throughout the day by sticking post-it note comments onto the back wall at the end of each sprint (Fig. 8.1). The final affinity theming session was completed using the front and back the walls of the room, challenges and obstacles were themed on the front wall by half of the group, interesting points on the back wall by the other half of the group (Fig. 8.2). Standing up to do the theming also introduced some welcome activity at the end of the day.

During affinity theming 17 themes were identified for 'challenges and obstacles' and 16 for 'interesting points'. The affinity group with the most post-its in 'challenges and obstacles' was the 'theory and practice' group with 12 post-its. This grouping identified a range of obstacles for integrating Agile and UX ranging from broad comments such as *'Perhaps different Scrum/UX models work in different contexts'* to very specific comments about specific practices *'Biased views of the developer; to evaluate their own creation is not impartial'*. Other large groups, with 10 post-its, were 'methods', 'filtering', and 'time/tempo'. The smallest groups, with 3 post-its, were 'tools/toolboxes' and 'synchronising'. This indicates that much of the focus of the challenges was on fitting the big picture of theory and methods into the lower level detail of day-to-day practices, and innovating new practices that ameliorate the challenges while maintaining an Agile ethos. Some of the challenge areas were familiar such as 'culture/awareness'; 'roles'; 'time/tempo'; 'synchronising', 'design artefacts'. Others indicated that new areas are opening up such as 'filtering', 'feedback', 'teaching and learning', 'power and relationships'. There was discussion about practices such as collecting continuous customer feedback and the need to filter that feedback in order to make a meaningful contribution to UCD. Other discussions opened up interesting challenges around Agile teams learning UCD techniques, and addressing and understanding power dynamics.

The largest affinity group in 'interesting points' was the 'developers doing UCD' group with 20 post-its. This grouping identified points from papers 1, 3, 4, 5 and 7, and it included points about individuals *'Developers want to do UX work'*; team working *'Pair designing as a phenomenon is interesting; UX person plus programmer'* and organisational set-ups *'Two types of companies; central group for UCD – large corporations; small corporations with no resources to have a UCD team'*. The second largest group was 'methods' with 17 post-its. The 'methods' group was also one of the largest groups in 'challenges and obstacles'. The smallest groups, with 2 post-its, were 'UX team', 'tools' and 'documentation'. However, compared to the 'challenges and obstacles' more of the affinity groups for the 'interesting points' focussed on particular elements of practice such as 'user involvement, 'pairwise work', 'internal communication' and 'user feedback'. There were many similarities between the themes identified for the two groups of post-its: 'roles', 'team', 'methods', were identical and 'internal communication', 'user feedback', 'time' and 'tools' had similar corresponding groups. There was more variation in the 'interesting points' post-its than the 'challenges and obstacles'. In the former group some of the post-its presented challenges, i.e. *'How do (UX) issues relate to a Scrum backlog?'*, others were philosophical musings, i.e. *'Is Scrum orthodoxi important?'*, and yet others were expressions of approval, i.e. *'Involving developers is a very good idea!!'*. The 'miscellaneous' grouping was quite large. This was to be expected, as we wanted to elicit diverse thoughts on the presentations.

We identified eight broad themes (column one in Tables 8.2 and 8.3) after the workshop. These were, in size order: Methods and practice (91 post-its), Teams and communication (49), People and roles (34), Time and synchronisation (23), Artefacts and tools (16), Miscellaneous (13), Research and problems (11), and Culture (8). Interestingly the themes cross both sets of post-it notes, and hence provide a higher-level view of the discussion topics during the day. The largest theme was 'Methods and practice'; this reflects the broad focus of the studies presented on the day, which was about integrating UCD into the structure of Agile approaches, and the practices that make that possible. Second came the two people-centred themes, 'Teams and communication' and 'People and roles'. The position of these themes near the top of the agenda shows that the people-focus of Agile is also essential for UCD and a key element to solving the problems of integration. The other themes identify important aspects of the topic, from 'Culture' and 'Time and synchronisation', both core elements of the design/develop conundrum; to 'Artefacts and tools', the focus of some novel solutions; to Miscellaneous and 'Research and problems', indications of the need for further work.

8.6   Conclusions

The workshop provided an excellent opportunity for researchers and practitioners from a wide variety of backgrounds to meet and discuss the issue of integrating Agile and UCD. The presentations, discussions and identification of issues and themes helped participants to successfully achieve the two workshop aims (1) to identify challenges and success stories when working with UCD and Agile and (2) to identify future trends for research into Agile and UCD. Using an Agile-inspired approach made the workshop engaging and fun, as well as enabling participants to identify key findings through the collection of data and the creation of an affinity diagram. The research papers presented at the workshop showed both depth and breadth, and were firmly grounded in empirical studies. Although familiar themes were raised, the findings from this workshop show that the ever-changing landscape of software development work provides new challenges and innovative solutions for designers and developers alike.

References

1. Papatheocharous E, Andreou AS (2014) Empirical evidence and state of practice of software agile teams. J Softw Evol Process 26(9):855–866
2. Version One, State of Agile Survey (2014)

3. The Agile Manifesto (2001) [cited November 2015]. Available from: http://www.agilemanifesto.org
4. International Standards Organisation (2010) Ergonomics of human–system interaction – Part 210: Human-centred design for interactive systems. ISO, Geneva
5. Holtzblatt K, Jones S (1993) Contextual inquiry: a participatory technique for system design. In: Schuler D, Nomioka A (eds) Participatory design: principles and practices. L. Erlbaum Associates, Hillsdale, pp 177–210
6. Schuler D, Namioka A (1993) Participatory design: principles and practices. CRC Press, Boca Raton
7. Friedman B (1996) Value-sensitive design. Interactions 3(6):16–23
8. Friedman B, Kahn PH Jr, Borning A, Huldtgren A (2013) Value sensitive design and information systems. In: Doorn N, Schuurbiers D, van de Poel I, Gorman ME (eds) Early engagement and new technologies: opening up the laboratory. Springer, Dordrecht, pp 55–95
9. Holtzblatt K, Wendell JB, Wood S (2004) Rapid contextual design: a how-to guide to key techniques for user-centered design. Elsevier, San Francisco
10. Maguire M (2001) Methods to support human-centred design. Int J Hum Comput Stud 55(4):587–634
11. Gulliksen J, Göransson B, Boivie I, Blomkvist S, Persson J, Cajander Å (2003) Key principles for user-centred systems design. Behav Inform Technol 22(6):397–409
12. Baxter G, Sommerville I (2011) Socio-technical systems: from design methods to systems engineering. Interact Comput 23(1):4–17
13. Cajander Å, Lárusdóttir M, Gulliksen J (2013) Existing but not explicit: the user perspective in scrum projects in practice. In: Human-computer interaction, INTERACT 2013. Springer, Heidelberg, pp 762–779
14. Lárusdóttir M, Cajander Å, Gulliksen J (2014) Informal feedback rather than performance measurements: user-centred evaluation in scrum projects. Behav Inform Technol 33(11):1118–1135
15. Salah D, Paige R, Cairns P (2014) A systematic literature review on agile development processes and user centred design integration. In: Proceedings of the 18th international conference on evaluation and assessment in software engineering. ACM, London, p 5
16. da Silva TS, Martin A, Maurer F, Silveira MS (2011) User-centered design and agile methods: a systematic review. In: Proceedings of AGILE, pp 77–86
17. Ferreira J (2011) User experience design and agile development: integration as an on-going achievement in practice. PhD thesis, Open University
18. Plonka L, Sharp H, Gregory P, Taylor K (2014) UX design in agile: a DSDM case study. In: Cantone G, Marchesi M (eds) Agile processes in software engineering and extreme programming. Springer, Berlin, pp 1–15
19. Chamberlain S, Sharp H, Maiden N (2006) Towards a framework for integrating agile development and user-centred design. In: Abrahamsson P, Marchesi M, Succi G (eds) Extreme programming and agile processes in software engineering. Springer, Berlin, pp 143–153
20. Blomkvist S (2005) Towards a model for bridging agile development and user-centered design. In: Seffah A, Gulliksen J, Desmarais MC (eds) Human-centered software engineering — integrating usability in the software development lifecycle. Springer, Dordrecht, pp 219–244
21. Sohaib O, Khan K (2010) Integrating usability engineering and agile software development: a literature review. In: International conference on computer design and applications. IEEE (2010)
22. Brhel M, Meth H, Maedcher A (2015) Exploring principles of user-centered agile software development: a literature review. Inf Softw Technol 61:163–181
23. Gregory P, Barroca L, Taylor K, Salah D, Sharp H (2015) Agile challenges in practice: a thematic analysis. In: Lassenius C, Dingsøyr T, Paasivaara M (eds) Proceedings of the 16th international conference XP 2015, LNBIP 212. Springer, pp 64–80
24. Scupin R (1997) The KJ method: a technique for analyzing data derived from Japanese ethnology. Hum Organ 56(2):233–237

Chapter 9
BoB: A Framework for Organizing Within-Iteration UX Work in Agile Development

Kati Kuusinen

Abstract Most research on Agile UCD recommends scheduling of UX work one iteration ahead of development. There is, however, some evidence arguing for an approach where software developers and UX specialists work in cross-functional teams conducting design and implementation tasks during the present iteration. This within-iteration approach can, for instance, improve communication between UX designers and software developers and thus help the team to better concentrate on value-adding work. This chapter discusses problems related to the iteration-ahead approach and introduces a framework called BoB (Best of Both Worlds) that utilizes the within-iteration approach to integrate UX work in agile development. Furthermore, we present guidelines related to factors that support the within-iteration approach and the cross-functional team.

Keywords User experience (UX) • Agile development • User-centered design (UCD) • UX design work • Agile UX • Human-computer interaction (HCI)

9.1 Introduction

Good user experience (UX) can be a significant competitive advantage in the market for a software product e.g. [1, 2]. However, good UX should not be a game of chance, but it requires deliberate work. By the phrase *UX work*, we refer to activities that aim at developing software that is usable, fulfills user needs, and provides desired UX. Furthermore, *UX design* defines how users interact with, and react to, software In many cases, designing for user interaction and UX requires special skills that are beyond the skills that software developers are expected to possess. Thus, a role of a UX specialist (UXS) is often needed to ensure fluent user flow and desired UX from use of the software under development. However, current agile development methodologies provide no guidance on how to include a UX specialist

K. Kuusinen (✉)
Tampere University of Technology, Tampere, Finland
e-mail: kati.kuusinen@alumni.aalto.fi

© Springer International Publishing Switzerland 2016
G. Cockton et al. (eds.), *Integrating User-Centred Design in Agile Development*,
Human–Computer Interaction Series, DOI 10.1007/978-3-319-32165-3_9

role in a project, nor do they guide organizing collaboration between UX specialists and software developers.

UX work has traditionally relied on heavy upfront studies and careful design before starting the implementation. Although the UCD process produces design solutions in repeated phases of design and evaluation with users, such iterations are not compatible with agile development iterations. Researchers and practitioners have been developing more compatible practices since agile methodologies started becoming popular. According to recent systematic literature reviews [3, 4], academic research most frequently recommends utilizing the *iteration-ahead* approach originated by Miller [5] and Sy [6]. Here, UX work is conducted one to two iterations ahead of development according to the time requirement of, for instance, user research or UX design activities. Thus, there are distinct sequential phases for user studies, design work, and implementation. In addition, most of the related research recommends conducting an upfront design phase before starting implementation [3, 4]. Furthermore, most UX work is conducted by UX specialists [3]. These practices are against the most popular agile principles (e.g, Scrum) in that they necessitate pre-planning before each development iteration and divide design and development activities among distinct persons.

In this chapter, we introduce BoB framework as an alternative to the commonly recommended iteration-ahead approach for integrating UX work in agile development. In our framework, UX design and even some lightweight user studies are conducted together with development activities in the same iteration, i.e. it utilizes the within-iteration approach. We have named the framework BoB. The name comes from *Best of Both worlds*, as it combines such advantages from UCD and agile development that normally are considered to be mutually exclusive, i.e. it is expected that one cannot have both at the same time. The naming was influenced by the television series *Star Trek: The Next Generation* episode with the same name [7]. Our approach aims to tackle several challenges connected to the iteration-ahead approach, for instance, related to communication and timing of the work. BoB builds on the practices of conducting development work iteratively, and having a cross-functional team including both software development and UX specialist competences.

We have developed BoB based on empirical research on agile UX work in nine software companies based in Finland over the years 2011–2015. Most of the research has been conducted on organizations and projects developing enterprise software and work-related tools. The contributing research is presented in [8–16]. Although features of BoB have been used in the studied companies, the framework as such has not been fully used in none of them.

The rest of this chapter is structured as follows: Section 9.2 introduces the iteration-ahead approach and describes problems related to it. Section 9.3 discusses the concept of a cross-functional team. In Sect. 9.4, we introduce factors that we find supporting the within-iteration approach, and in Sect. 9.5, we present the BoB framework for organizing UX work when using a cross-functional team and the within-iteration approach. Section 9.6 discusses the introduced framework. Finally, Sect. 9.7 presents closing remarks for the chapter.

9.2 Iteration-Ahead Approach

9.2.1 Overview

Sy [6] introduced the "*one sprint ahead*" approach (Fig. 9.1) in 2007. Since then, it has become a popular means to integrate UX work in agile development [3]. When following the approach, development starts with *iteration 0,* during which upfront planning and studies are conducted. Most research in agile UCD suggests doing some upfront planning but also keeping it to a minimum since heavy design upfront is against agile principles [3]. After iteration 0, development is divided to two separate tracks, one of them concentrating on technical implementation (the upper track in Fig. 9.1) and the other concentrating on UX work. Developers start by building features that have less impact on the UX, such as certain backend solutions in the first actual iteration. At the same time, UX specialists design for features that will be implemented in iteration 2 and study for features that will be implemented in iteration 3. Following iterations are conducted similarly; UX specialists design one and study two iterations ahead of development. They also conduct user tests on the functionality implemented during the preceding iteration.

The approach was developed at the Autodesk company to adopt agile practices within UX work after utilizing waterfall development for years. The company had a functional and proficient UX team with established practices before agile adoption [6]. Thus, the company culture was presumably already supporting UX work. In contrast, agile development was new to the company. Sy [6] reported that the "one sprint ahead" approach was introduced to tackle problems, such as excessive design inventory, outdated design, and lack of common vision in the project. Design inventory is produced when UX is designed ahead of development, such as in waterfall development, and ready-made design has to wait to be implemented. If,

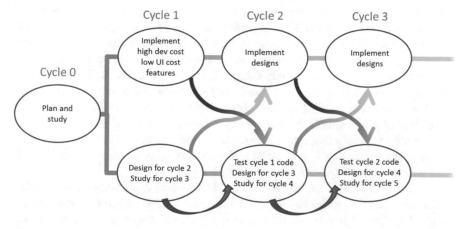

Fig. 9.1 The "one sprint ahead" approach [6]

for instance, requirements change during the waiting time, the design may become outdated and require revision. Indeed, compared to waterfall development, the one sprint ahead approach surely reduces the size of design inventory since only a small amount of design is waiting to be developed at a time. Moreover, as the design is produced just in time, it should be up to date. There are, however, some challenging issues in the iteration-ahead approach that we will discuss next.

9.2.2   Challenges in the Iteration-Ahead Approach

Utilizing the one iteration-ahead approach has its drawbacks. As it consists of successive design and development phases, it easily becomes a mini-waterfall where development proceeds in small phases of studying, designing, implementing, and testing. The iteration-ahead approach practically divides development work into two separate tracks yielding that technical implementation is conducted on one track and user studies, UX design, and user testing are conducted on another track that is scheduled to serve the implementation pace.

Most of the challenges in using the iteration-ahead approach are related to the fact that utilizing the model necessitates pre-planning before and testing after each development iteration. For instance, in 2-week implementation cycles, developers need to know 2–4 weeks in advance what they will be implementing whereas test results will be available 2 weeks after the development. Thus, the iteration-ahead approach makes the feedback loop grow from 2 to 6 or 8 weeks which makes responding to change slower and more difficult. Although the idea of the iteration-ahead approach is to get continuous user feedback, the actual developed artefacts, i.e. the working software, can be tested with users only after three to four iterations instead of one.

A major issue that agile methodologies were developed for is that in software engineering, one cannot know in advance what the system under development should be like and how it should be implemented [17]. Thus, a fundamental principle of agile methodologies is to welcome late change [18, 19]. When there is a change in the development order, UX design work cannot adapt to that if UX specialists need, for instance, 2 weeks to study and another 2 weeks to design. The situation is illustrated in Fig. 9.2, where in the fourth iteration, priorities on the backlog change and developers start building functionality C instead of functionality B, which they were originally planning to implement next. Therefore, there is no UX design for functionality C available. In such situations, UX designers start to hurry the design and developers need to improvise [8]. We have observed that although the UX suffers in this case, it will rarely be improved later [8, 9].

Another drawback in the approach is that UX specialists test the implementation in the next iteration while developers are already writing new code based on the current implementation. In practice, this usually means that implementation cannot be iterated based on the findings—it would be too costly and require rework [8, 9]. This is illustrated in Fig. 9.2 where functionality A fails the usability test conducted

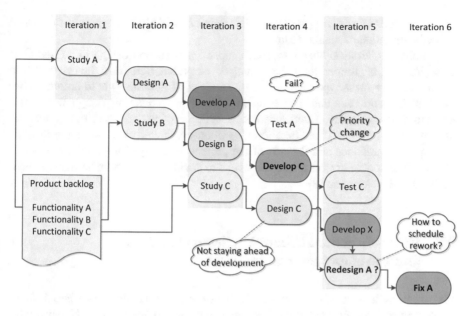

Fig. 9.2 Waterfall characteristics of the iteration-ahead approach. Changes in backlog priority order or failing a user study are problematic when utilizing the approach

in Iteration 4. If one fixes Functionality A, it will be redesigned in Iteration 5 and re-implemented in Iteration 6. To avoid building on erroneous code, developers need to be working with something that is not influenced by Functionality A. In practice, this necessitates UX design inventory, or that the developers can focus on something that does not require UX design work.

Both aforementioned issues make it more difficult to keep the UX design work iteration ahead of development. Moreover, both scenarios are common in agile development. For instance, in Scrum, the task list is re-prioritized before each iteration [20], and user testing would be unnecessary if it did not reveal defects. One of the biggest challenges in agile UX work is to synchronize the UX specialists' and developers' work [21]. In addition, although Sy [6] emphasized continuous communication between developers and UX specialists, communication problems in utilizing the approach are common [21, 22]. Communication between disciplines is generally more challenging than within a discipline [23]. Also, within-team communication is more efficient than communication with people outside the team [22]. The third issue we have noticed that makes the communication more difficult is the temporal difference between the mindsets of developers and UX designers [15]. When a UX designer asks developers to evaluate certain decisions, the designer is planning to consider a feature the developers will be implementing in the next iteration; however, the developers cannot really relate to it. They have not been thinking about that particular feature yet, and thus it is hard for them to make good decisions considering it. Thus, their opinion is likely to change as they start implementing that particular feature.

Finally, the iteration-ahead approach separates front-end design to an iteration 0, which can be longer than the actual development iterations; however, "*they occur in weeks rather than months*" [6]. The idea of iteration 0 is to arrange time for planning and user data gathering [6]. However, separating design work into an upfront design phase often means that agile practices are used only after the upfront design [6, 8]. Thus, iteration 0 is often conducted with non-agile project management practices and the rest of the project is managed with agile practices. This leads to double project management and to having an avoidable barrier between design and development [8].

9.3 Cross-Functional Team Vs. Separate UX and Development Teams

Ideally, an agile team should include all the expertise necessary to define, design, build, and test running software that satisfies customer needs [19]. A team with all the required expertise is cross-functional. However, agile UCD practices rarely include a UX specialist in the development team [3]. Instead, the UX specialist often works outside of the team, which easily hinders collaboration [8, 22] and thus does not make the best use of UX expertise. Attempts to improve the situation have been made. For example, "*dual track Scrum*" [24, 25] is an approach similar to the one sprint ahead approach in that it divides product discovery and implementation into separate tracks. In dual track Scrum, however, a cross-functional team instead of UX specialists only is responsible for the second track. The team–typically consisting of a product owner, UX specialist and a developer–works towards refining and validating product backlog items for the forthcoming development iterations [26]. Unfortunately, we could identify no research articles on dual track Scrum and thus cannot build on any formal studies of its advantages and disadvantages.

Ferreira et al. [22] found that organizational values have an impact on how it is beneficial to integrate UX work with agile development: some organizations value separate UX and development work, while others value togetherness. Cross-functional team approaches for integrating UCD with agile development practices can thus be especially beneficial for organizations valuing togetherness. Ferreira et al. [22] studied two projects, one of them utilizing a separatist approach in which a UX specialist directed developers' work—basically utilizing the iteration-ahead approach—and the other working in a cross-functional team within the iteration sharing the power of decision. They [22] observed that communication was more efficient in the cross-functional team and the team did not need such activities as interpreting the design as it did in the separatist approach.

Including people from different disciplines makes communication generally more challenging [23], but separating UX specialists into their own teams, instead of including them in agile development teams, may easily lead to degraded communication. In such situations, developers tend not to take ownership of UX issues and UX specialists become seen as outsiders. When UX specialists and developers are separated, teams encounter problems with timing and the implementability of the design [8, 27]. Moreover, in those settings where a separate UX team delivers the UX design, the development team needs additional coordination activities to interpret the design, to identify mismatches between the new design and existing code, and to determine what is already implemented [22]. Several authors discuss the role of UX specialists compared to development teams. Isomursu et al. [28] concluded that UX specialists' responsibilities should be in line with the expectations of development teams. Hodgetts [29] considered it vitally important for UX practitioners to see themselves as part of a project team and to conduct their tasks according to that perception. Lee [30] stated that UX specialists need to be active participants in order to be embedded in agile teams. Finally, Kuusinen et al. [8] found that including UX specialists in development teams was the preferred approach amongst practitioners for integrating UX work with agile development practices.

Thus, while much related research argues for separation of UX design and development activities [3], it is not an approach that is suitable in all cases. Moreover, to our knowledge, there are no earlier frameworks in related research for organizing agile UX work in cross-functional teams working within-iteration.

9.4 Method

Our research goal was to develop a construct for integrating UX work with agile practices in the context of enterprise software development. Our research question was as follows: *Which activities support the integration of agile development and UX work?* To support answering the main research question, we studied also tasks and goals that comprise agile UX work, and the challenges that companies encounter while integrating UX work with agile development.

We selected a 'building theories from case studies' research strategy [31] for developing the construct (Table 9.1). It is a *"research strategy that involves using one or more cases to create theoretical constructs, propositions, and/or midrange theory from case-based, empirical evidence"* [32].

A case study is *"an empirical inquiry that investigates a contemporary phenomenon within its real-life context, especially when the boundaries between phenomenon and context are not clearly evident."* Previous research guides data collection and analysis in case studies, and both multiple sources of evidence and research methods are utilized ([33], p. 13).

We selected the research strategy for the following reasons: Firstly, case studies are a common research methodology when studying software engineering [34]. We had very limited ability to control or affect the studied phenomenon, and the phenomenon was not well-known before. Secondly, our aim was at building

Table 9.1 Process of building theory from case study research [31]

Step	Activity
Getting started	Definition of research question
Selecting cases	Theoretical, not random sampling
Crafting instruments and protocols	Multiple data collection methods, qualitative and quantitative
Entering the field	Overlap data collection and analysis
Analyzing data	Within-case analysis, Cross-case pattern search using divergent techniques
Shaping hypotheses	Iterative tabulation of evidence, Replication, Search evidence for "why" behind relationships
Enfolding literature	Comparison with literature
Reaching closure	Theoretical saturation when possible

a construct for explaining and supporting the phenomenon. Thus, we consider Eisenhardt's [31] strategy appropriate for our research.

9.4.1 Research Process

Our research consisted of four rounds of empirical research and of activities that aimed to build a construct (BoB) based on the research (Fig. 9.3). First, we conducted explorative case studies with surveys and interviews in three companies concentrating on challenges organizations encounter in their agile UX work and practices they find beneficial for the work [8, 9, 13]. Having developed an initial understanding here, we next conducted a literature review. Based on the first round research results and the literature review, we planned a second round of more structured studies concentrating on the actual contributing tasks and roles present in UX work in agile projects [10, 12]. We based the study on six development projects in five companies with repeated surveys and interviews. In the third round of research, we included the user perspective in our studies by surveying the perceptions that development teams and users have towards the UX of the software systems the teams have been developing [16]. The third round of research was conducted in the same six projects as the second round. Most of the framework was built after the third round. Finally, we conducted a fourth round of research by interviewing practitioners to evaluate the built framework.

We started to build the BoB framework after the first round of research. We presented the first version of the framework draft in [11]. Most of the framework shaping was conducted after the three first rounds of research in 2014 and 2015. Thus, shaping BoB was based on the three first rounds of research. During year 2015 we compared the framework to practices described in related research as following guidance from Eisenhardt [31] (phase: literature contextualization (called "enfolding literature" in [31])). Finally, in the fourth round of research, we discussed

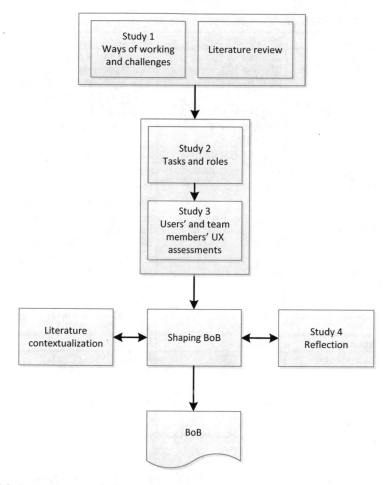

Fig. 9.3 Research process for building the BoB model

the framework and its viability with UX specialists and a developer from three companies in an interview study to evaluate BoB's practical validity. The research was conducted between years 2011 and 2015. We discuss research methods and limitations in more detail in the original publications.

9.4.2 Participants

Participants and studied companies are introduced in the original publications; we give here only an overview of them. Altogether, we conducted 75 interviews and received 282 survey responses from nine companies (Table 9.2).

Table 9.2 Summary of methods and participants per study

Study	Method	Participant roles	Countries	N
S I	Survey 1	Dev, PO, UXS, Arc, Manager, SM,, other (e.g. tester, user support)	Finland 58.0 %, Other 25.87 % (mainly France, Sweden, Czech Republic and Malaysia), Unknown 16.1 %	143
	Interviews 1	Dev, PO, SM, UXS,, Arc, Manager, Tester, Customer	Finland 95.2 %, Sweden 2.4 % and China 2.4 %	50
	Survey 2	Dev, PO, UXS, Arc	Finland 100 %	8
	Interviews 2	Dev, PO, UXS, Arc	Finland 100 %	7
S II	Pilot interviews	Dev, UXS, Arc	Finland 50.0 %, China 25.0 %, Belarus 12.5 %, India 12.5 %	8
	Pilot survey	Dev, PO, UXS, SM, Tester	Finland 36.8 %, China 26.3 %, Belarus 26.3 %, India 10.5 %	19
	Long-term survey	Dev, PO, UXS	Finland 45.2 %, Russia 25.8 %, China 22.6 %, Latvia 3.2 %, Estonia 3.2 %	31
	Retrospect survey	Dev, PO, UXS	Finland 53.8 %, Russia 30.8 %, China 26.9 %	26
	Interviews	PO, UXS	Finland 100 %	6
S III	Team survey	Dev, PO, UXS	Finland 73.1 %, Russia 19.2 %, Latvia 3.8 %, China 3.8 %	26
	User survey	User	Majority from Finland	29
S IV	Interviews	Dev, UXS	Finland 100 %	4

Legend: *Arc* Architect, *Dev* Developer, *PO* Product Owner, *SM* Scrum Master, *UXS* UX specialist

Some participants were interviewed or surveyed more than once. Since we did not identify the respondents of the first round surveys, and one of the companies participated in three first rounds of research, we do not know the number of individual participants. Moreover, we did not ask in which country the user participants of the third round of research were based. However, the whole user base of two participating projects was in Finland.

All nine participating companies were developing enterprise software or work-related tools. Five were IT service companies, three were engineering and technology companies, and one was developing its own specialized systems for several platforms. Three companies focused on developing mobile enterprise applications, one developed wireless industrial systems, one developed large industrial safety-critical software-hardware systems, one developed embedded systems for specialist users, one developed tools for both business and consumer users, and two companies developed basically whatever software customers order. Two of the companies were large with around 20,000 employees, two employed 1000–2000 persons, four had 100–500 persons, and one was small with 10–30 employees. Six of the companies were operating globally while three had sites only in Finland. All but one company employed UX specialists. All the companies utilized agile practices at least in some of their organizations.

9.5 BoB Framework for Organizing Within-Iteration Agile UX Work

In the resulting BoB framework, developers and UX specialist(s) form a cross-functional team. Work towards certain functionalities is conducted in a cross-functional team within a single iteration. Work can be chunked in several iterations when necessary; however, an iteration should always include both analysis and building activities. In the case of UCD, it means that each iteration should contain activities for understanding the user's needs, designing and developing towards them, and evaluating the appropriateness of the result [35]. Thus, we consider the approach more compatible with agile development.

9.5.1 Guidelines to Support the Cross-Functional Team

We organize our guidelines to support the cross-functional team and the within-iteration approach into factors related to *people, process, tasks, tools,* and the *developed artefact* (Table 9.3). We base the taxonomy on the categorization of [3, 36]. Brhel et al. [3] classify agile UCD integration types into *process, people, practices,* and *technology.* Chow et al. [36] classified critical success factors of agile software development as *organizational, people, process, technical,* and *project* factors. Instead of UCD *practices* and supporting *technologies,* we concentrate on *tasks* related to UX work and supporting *tools* in general, respectively. Finally, we consider factors related to the *artefact* developed in a project context. This fifth group of *artefact* factors are omitted from Table 9.3, but are only discussed in the text as we do not want to give actual guidelines on the software under development. Instead, we discuss the impact on the type and characteristics of the software for the within-iteration approach.

Furthermore, agile principles require a motivated cooperative team to deliver, from early on and continuously, software that satisfies the customer [18]. We build our guidelines both on agile principles and a user-focused mindset.

People Factors First of all, the team must value togetherness as defined in [22]; team members need to be willing to work together. They should have a positive and curious attitude towards the disciplines of other team members. Cooperation gets easier if team members understand the work of other team members to some extent. For instance, Gulliksen et al. [37] suggest that UX specialists should have some knowledge of software development to improve the communication. Working in a

Table 9.3 Supporting guidelines for the within-iteration approach

People	Process	Tasks	Tools
Learn from others: Broaden your competence areas.	Work within one iteration.	Integrate UX work via tasks not via roles.	Communicate UX tasks via backlog.
Be willing to cooperate.	Produce working design.	Minimize user studies.	Establish feedback channels.
Respect people from other disciplines.	Allow trial and error: accept design debt.	Treat UX-related tasks similarly to other development tasks.	Utilize technologies that allow rapid design and development.
Involve the whole team in user communication.	Hurry to markets to enable actual user feedback.	Appreciate professionalism when allocating tasks.	Allow maturity difference in visual and functional readiness.

cross-functional team becomes a virtuous circle as team members learn from each other [10]. Learning eases task allocation as competence areas of team members become partially overlapping [10].

Like in agile development in general, the team benefits from close collaboration, the emphasis being on face-to-face communication. At the minimum, either the PO or developers should be co-located with the UX specialist [10]. Regarding the big picture of the project and being able to satisfy the user need, the whole team should be involved in communication with users [12]. This is also in line with the principles of UCD. Continuous communication with the user and the customer is especially important in rapid development where all the required information should be at hand whenever needed.

Task Factors When a UX specialist is working with the development team and the team expects that she/he will do almost all the UX related work, the UX specialist will become a bottleneck [8]. When a single person is responsible for a bunch of work, the work naturally is conducted serially, which will mean waiting time. Thus, we suggest involving several persons of the team in the UX work. We have studied which tasks can be performed by developers and the PO and which tasks require special professionalism in UX [10, 12, 16]. Figure 9.4 presents a summary of our findings. To conclude, POs have learned to successfully conduct workshops with users to understand the user need and to gather user feedback to improve the software [10, 12]. Developers have been able to lead the UI design work in mobile development where the platform style is prominent and the user need is well understood [11]. Moreover, developers are able to understand the instrumental quality of the software under development [16]. Instrumental quality refers to perceived utilitarian or functional quality such as usefulness in contrast to hedonic quality that provides pleasure and experiences to the user [38, 39]. Thus, we suggest integrating UX work with agile development via UX tasks instead of trying to integrate a distinct UX specialist role as such. Moreover, UX tasks should

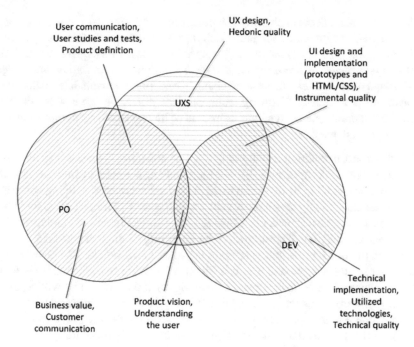

User communication,
User studies and tests,
Product definition

UX design,
Hedonic quality

UI design and
implementation
(prototypes and
HTML/CSS),
Instrumental quality

UXS

PO

DEV

Business value,
Customer
communication

Product vision,
Understanding
the user

Technical
implementation,
Utilized
technologies,
Technical quality

Fig. 9.4 General task allocation between roles (Legend: *PO* product owner, *UXS* user experience specialist, *DEV* developer)

be treated similarly to other development tasks and tasks should be allocated based on professionalism and interest.

There is one fundamental difference compared to the iteration-ahead approach in the nature of UX tasks. Where UX specialists in the iteration-ahead approach seem to often produce rather ready-made UX design that the developers implement as is [6, 8, 22], the within-iteration approach emphasizes the active role of the developer in participating in UX work. This collaboration is essential for being able to design and develop during the same iteration. Without it, the UX specialist would indeed need time to produce the design ahead of development.

Process Factors An obvious process factor is to work within one iteration at a time; the whole team should concentrate on the same tasks at hand. Thus, the mindset should be changed from holistic UX design (big design upfront) to completing only one or a few functionalities at a time and then changing the design and related code later as needed. This does not mean that one should have no holistic idea of the system and that nothing should be thought about beforehand. It simply means that full designs are not deliberately produced, but instead, building the software can be started as soon as the team has some idea of it. To enable such a way of working, the team must allow trial and error and thus to be ready to refactor, iterate, and even discard the already built design whenever reasonable. Thus, the team should welcome technical debt considering UX design in that design decisions can be made on incomplete information. Technical debt has been defined as follows: "*not quite right code which we postpone making it right*" [40, 41]. Consequently, UX design debt can be defined as *not quite right design which we postpone making it right;* it is design that is likely to require changes and improvement later when more information is available. Allowing technical debt in UX design enables the team to work on incremental design chunks instead of having to have a complete holistic UX design available early.

Furthermore, in addition to delivering working software, the process should allow the delivery of working design. By working design, we refer to functionality that is "working enough" to be tested by users. Thus, we encourage building something that the user can actually test in the first place. In the early phase, it can be something that the user can, for instance, click through. Later it can be, for example, an added feature that has only the user interface with no or only simulated backend.

Finally, the quicker the software is on the market, the quicker the team will get actual user feedback from real use. It is difficult for a user to evaluate if they would really use some feature, if they need something, or if they would be willing to pay for a service before it is actually available [42, 43]. In addition, we have learned that users are more prone to give feedback when the system is already in use compared to when they just are asked to test something without actually benefitting from its use. Testing on actual users and developed artefacts can also save time from arranging user tests and therefore help to avoid wasteful activities.

Tool Factors Several factors related to tools and technologies have an impact on how effortless it is to work with the cross-functional team. UX-related tasks should be communicated via the same tool than other development tasks, for instance, via a backlog management tool [12]. Moreover, UX tasks should be chunked to pieces with similar size and level of detail compared to other development tasks [12]. Depending on utilized technologies and platforms, UX design can be designed and communicated as working software, for instance, in HTML and CSS code. If UX designers use such tools, they are able to produce the design as working software in the same time or even quicker than by drawing the design [15]. Furthermore, modern UX design tools allow varying the design fidelity [15]. Thus, the high-fidelity production design can be produced whenever feasible offering more flexibility to the timing of the work instead of fixing its delivery to a certain iteration. Finally, mechanisms and channels for collecting user feedback should be established to allow rapid feedback gathering.

Factors Related to the Developed Artefact and the Context The cost of building something needs to be kept in mind. The idea of the approach is to decrease the cost of unneeded and thus wasteful planning and to increase the revenue from reaching the market early. However, in some contexts, for example, when hardware is present, the cost of iteration can be higher than the cost of wasteful planning. Thus, if, for instance, a new costly piece of hardware needs to be built for each iteration, the one iteration-ahead approach might be more suitable to increase the likelihood of getting the overall system right with a smaller number of iterations. The same applies for highly regulated contexts in which heavy testing is needed before entering the markets. Thus, the within-iteration approach might be less suitable for situations where cost of error is high. However, we have no empirical data to support that planning and designing ahead of development actually would be less prone to error.

9.5.2 Ways of Working in BoB Framework

Most of the related research suggests separating product discovery and development phases [3]. We agree that there should be a high-level idea or an early vision of the product before starting to implement it. However, early product definition can be very small, and the understanding can be fostered throughout the project.

The BoB framework includes a process that consists of analysis and build tasks that are conducted continuously during the development cycle (Fig. 9.5). The process is intended for within-iteration UX work conducted in cross-functional teams. In principle, the same cycle is utilized throughout the project; thus, the process mitigates the concept of separate upfront design phases. Instead of having a particular upfront design phase, we suggest including the design and planning work into several "normal" iterations that can contain both UX design and development tasks. A UX specialist once described such an approach as follows: "*One time we started a project and we could not reach the user in the beginning. All we knew was that the user needed to be able to fill in forms. So we implemented a fillable form.*" Thus, implementation can be started with a minimal understanding of the

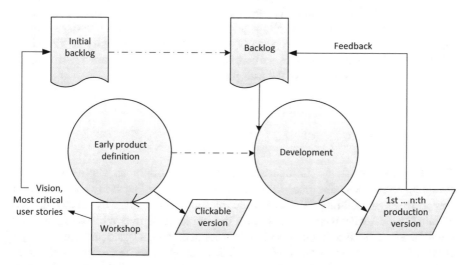

Fig. 9.5 BoB process model for the within-iteration approach. *Dashed* lines indicate the transfer from early product definition to development

user's need and possible design. However, the early phase (design upfront or the fuzzy front end) differs from the rest of the development in that there might be nothing tangible available yet. The understanding of the project vision is minimal and communication with the user and customer might be more abstract. We suggest starting with a few short user workshops in which the product vision and most critical user stories are evolved. In between those workshops, the team works towards something tangible for the users to make it easier for all the stakeholders to understand the early product vision similarly enough. An initial backlog is formed based on the early vision and most critical user stories that have been created during the early iterations. The deliverable from this early phase can be, for instance, a partially functional prototype or a click-through template that realizes the most important user story (or stories).

After the clickable version has been evaluated with users, the team starts to work towards the first production version of the system (transfer from Early product definition cycle to Development cycle in Fig. 9.5). The UX specialist either implements the user interaction or pairs up with a front-end developer. The user interaction is built based on continuous communication within the team and together with users when needed. When a UX-related issue cannot be solved within the team, developers start to build the next task on the priority list, and the UX specialist investigates the problem until a solution is found, or until it is decided to postpone the task. The team hurries a production version to the market to start getting actual user feedback and then continues increasing the product incrementally. The team works similarly during forthcoming iterations. Thus, the approach is similar both in the early product definition phase and during the actual development phase. In addition to working software, we recommend allowing the delivery of working prototypes and partially functioning features to gain user feedback. Thus, the system can contain both fully working features and forthcoming features that are delivered for some user groups in order to allow getting early user feedback before launching the feature. This approach is especially beneficial for the majority of situations where a randomized experiment with control and treatment groups (A/B testing) is not feasible due to the size of the user population

9.6   Discussion

The BoB framework we introduce in this chapter offers an alternative to the commonly recommended one iteration-ahead approach. Our aim is to provide a way to focus on building the user interaction modularly feature by feature instead of running excessive user studies before the implementation. Whereas in the one iteration-ahead approach implementation is conducted on studied and tested design chunks [6], in our framework UX specialists conduct as few user inquiries as possible and small functionalities are designed and implemented possibly in hours or days after which the functionality is exposed to actual usage or usage that is close to actual (for instance, partially functional features or clickable prototypes). The functionality or some larger part of the system is then iterated based on the user feedback and new functionalities are designed based on what was learned.

The framework as such has not been in use in none of the studied companies. Although cross-functional team approach was the most preferred way to organize UX work among the participants, it was rarely utilized in the companies [8, 9, 13]. Companies preferred separate UX and development teams. However, this started to change during the research process [11], and some of the companies have utilized similar practices in their projects [12]. Those practices have included working in cross-functional teams and having UX specialists and developers working in the same iteration. In addition, Fig. 9.4 is fully based on what we have witnessed in the studied companies. We built BoB to support this within-iteration work as there has not been guidance on how to organize agile UX work in such setting.

Utilizing BoB framework requires that the UX specialist works from inside the cooperative development team. Furthermore, it benefits from a mindset that allows trial and error: when the UX design needs to be modified, the user interface will be iterated and refactored. Compared to the one iteration-ahead approach, we expect collaboration within the BoB framework to offer better visibility to the common vision, the big picture, of the project as the team including a UX specialist works in closer collaboration and makes design decisions together. We expect that the close collaboration improves the team's communication and increases developers' commitment towards UX tasks as they are more involved in UX work. Finally, we expect to get feedback from actual usage faster than in the one iteration-ahead approach as getting to the market may require only one design-development iteration instead of conducting design work first and then implementation work in the following iteration. While user studies are valuable, it is the actual usage that really validates the viability of the system.

Although we expect BoB framework to tackle several challenges in agile UX work, it does not come without its limitations. BoB works best with small, co-located teams—as agile methods do in general. Scaling up the framework is an interesting possibility for future research. Based on what we have seen in our research; such an approach has only been in use in co-located teams. Thus, as developers are in a central role in the within-iteration UX work, it might be that the approach only works when a UX specialist is co-located with the rest of the team. Therefore, it might be needed that in larger projects with several teams, there should be a UX specialist working in each team, or at least those teams that concentrate on user interaction should include a UX specialist.

9.7   Summary and Conclusions

In this chapter, we presented BoB framework for integrating UX work into agile development. The idea of our framework is to organize UX work in such a way that designing ahead of development during the development iterations would not be necessary. We presented both supporting factors and a process model that enables the within-iteration approach.

BoB increases possibilities to react to change, and it is to improve communication and common understanding on a team. In addition, it brings UX matters closer to developers and welcomes them to participate to the UX work as well. Thus, it is expected to mitigate the workload of the often overburdened UX specialist. The fundamental goal of BoB is to minimize the amount of upfront design and study activities and instead encourage trial and error in designing and developing for UX.

Acknowledgment Our research has been supported by TEKES (Finnish funding agency for technology and innovation) as part of the Cloud Software and Need for Speed research programs of DIGILE (Finnish Strategic Centre for Science, Technology and Innovation in the field of ICT and digital business).

References

1. Cyr D, Head M, Ivanov A (2006) Design aesthetics leading to m-loyalty in mobile commerce. Inf Manag 43(8):950–963
2. Mahmood MA, Burn JM, Gemoets LA, Jacquez C (2000) Variables affecting information technology end-user satisfaction: a meta-analysis of the empirical literature. Int J Hum Comput Stud 52(4):751–771
3. Brhel M, Meth H, Maedche A, Werder C (2015) Exploring principles of user-centered agile software development: a literature review. Inf Softw Technol 61:163–181
4. da Silva T, Martin A, Maurer F, Silveira M (2011) User-centered design and Agile methods: a systematic review. In: Proceedings of the Agile methods in software development (Agile 2011)
5. Miller L (2005) Case study of customer input for a successful product. In: Proceedings of the Agile Conference '05. IEEE Computer Society, pp 225–234
6. Sy D (2007) Adapting usability investigations for Agile user-centered design. J Usability Stud 2(3):112–132
7. Roddenberry G (writer), Piller M (writer), Bole C (director) (1990) The best of both worlds: part 1 [Television series episode]. In: Berman R (executive producer), Star Trek: the next generation, USA
8. Kuusinen K, Mikkonen T, Pakarinen S (2012) Agile user experience development in a large software organization: good expertise but limited impact. In: Proceedings of the Human-Centered Software Engineering (HCSE'12). Springer, Berlin/Heidelberg, pp 94–111
9. Kuusinen K, Väänänen-Vainio-Mattila K (2012) How to make agile UX work more efficient: management and sales perspectives. In: Proceedings of the 7th Nordic Conference on Human-Computer Interaction: making sense through design (NordiCHI '12). ACM, pp 139–148
10. Kuusinen K, Mikkonen T (2013) Designing user experience for mobile apps: long-term product owner perspective. In: Proceedings of the 20th Asia-Pacific Software Engineering Conference (APSEC'13), IEEE Computer Society Order Number E5158, pp 535–540
11. Kuusinen K, Mikkonen T (2014) On designing UX for mobile enterprise apps. In: Proceedings of the software engineering and advanced applications, IEEE Computer Society, pp 221–228
12. Kuusinen K (2015) Task allocation between UX specialists and developers in agile software development projects. In: Proceedings of the Human-Computer Interaction – INTERACT 2015, LNCS 9298. Springer International Publishing, pp 27–44
13. Kuusinen K (2015) Overcoming challenges in agile user experience work: cross-case analysis of two large software organizations. In: Proceedings of the 41st Euromicro conference series on Software Engineering and Advanced Applications (SEAA'15). IEEE Computer Society (2015), doi:10.1109/SEAA.2015.38

14. Kuusinen K (2015) Continuous user experience development. In: INTERACT 2015 adjunct proceedings: 15th IFIP TC. 13 International conference on human-computer interaction 2015, vol 22. University of Bamberg Press, p 233
15. Kuusinen K (2015) Integrating UX work in agile enterprise software development. Doctoral thesis, Publication 1339, Tampere University of Technology
16. Kuusinen K, Väätäjä H, Mikkonen T, Väänänen K (2016) Towards understanding how agile teams predict user experience. In: Integrating user-centred design in agile development. Springer, Cham
17. Cockburn A, Highsmith J (2001) Agile software development: the people factor. IEEE Comput 34(11):131–133
18. Beck K et al (2001) Agile alliance. Principles behind the Agile Manifesto. Available at: http://agilemanifesto.org/principles.html
19. Highsmith J, Cockburn A (2001) Agile software development: the business of innovation. Computer 34(9):120–127
20. Schwaber K (2004) Agile project management with Scrum, 1st edn, Microsoft professional. Microsoft Press, Redmond
21. Salah D, Paige R, Cairns P (2014) A systematic literature review on agile development processes and user centred design integration. In: Proceedings of the 18th international conference on Evaluation and Assessment in Software Engineering (EASE'14). ACM, Article 5, 10 p
22. Ferreira J, Sharp H, Robinson H (2010) Values and assumptions shaping agile development and user experience design in practice. In: Proceedings of the XP 2010, LNBIP 48:178–183
23. Gulliksen J (1999) Bringing the social perspective: user centred design. In: HCI (1) 1999, pp 1327–1331
24. Cagan M (2012) Dual-Track Scrum. Blog post 17 September 2012. Available at: http://www.svproduct.com/dual-track-scrum/. Accessed 9 Mar 2016
25. Zaman K (2014) Dual track Scrum. Scrum alliance member article 18 December 2014. Available at: https://www.scrumalliance.org/community/articles/2014/december/dual-track-scrum. Accessed 9 Mar 2016
26. Patton J (2014). User story mapping. discover the whole story, build the right product. O'Reilly Media, 324 pp
27. Ferreira J, Sharp H, Robinson H (2011) User experience design and agile development: managing cooperation through articulation work. Softw Pract Exp 41(9):963–974, (Wiley)
28. Isomursu M, Sirotkin A, Voltti P, Halonen M (2012) User experience design goes agile in lean transformation—a case study. In: Proceedings of the Agile Conference (AGILE 2012), pp 1–10.
29. Hodgetts P (2005) Experiences integrating sophisticated UX design into agile process. In: Proceedings of the Agile Conference 2005, IEEE, Denver, CO, pp 235–242
30. Lee JC (2006) Embracing agile development of usable software systems. In: Proceedings of the Conference on Human Factors in Computing Systems CHI 2006. ACM, pp 1767–1770
31. Eisenhardt KM (1989) Building theories from case study research. Acad Manag Rev 14(4):532–550
32. Eisenhardt KM, Graebner ME (2007) Theory building from cases: opportunities and challenges. Acad Manag J 50(1):25–32
33. Yin RK (2003) Case study research: design and methods, 3rd edn. Sage, Thousand Oaks, 181p
34. Runeson P, Höst M (2009) Guidelines for conducting and reporting case study research in software engineering. Empir Softw Eng 14:131–164
35. Gulliksen J, Göransson B, Boivie I, Blomkvist S, Persson J, Cajander Å (2003) Key principles for user-centred systems design. BIT 22(6):397–409
36. Chow T, Cao DB (2008) A survey study of critical success factors in agile software projects. J Syst Softw 81(6):961–971
37. Gulliksen J, Göransson B, Lif M (2001) A user-centered approach to object-oriented user interface design. In: van Harmelen (21), chapter 8

38. Holbrook MB, Hirschman EC (1982) The experiential aspects of consumption: consumer fantasies, feelings, and fun. J Consum Res 9:132–140
39. Lantos GP (2015) Consumer behavior in action: real-life applications for marketing managers. Routledge, New York
40. Kruchten P, Nord RL, Ozkaya I (2012) Technical debt: from metaphor to theory and practice. IEEE Softw 6:18–21
41. Cunningham W (1992) The WyCash portfolio management system. OOPSLA' 92 Experience report
42. Anastassova M, Mégard C, Burkhardt JM (2007) Prototype evaluation and user-needs analysis in the early design of emerging technologies. In: Human-computer interaction, Interaction design and usability. Springer, Berlin/Heidelberg, pp 383–392
43. Van Kleef E, van Trijp HC, Luning P (2005) Consumer research in the early stages of new product development: a critical review of methods and techniques. Food Qual Prefer 16(3):181–201

Chapter 10
Challenges from Integrating Usability Activities in Scrum: Why Is Scrum so Fashionable?

Marta Lárusdóttir, Åsa Cajander, Gudbjörg Erlingsdottir, Thomas Lind, and Jan Gulliksen

Abstract Scrum is currently a widely used process in most areas of software development. Conversely, usability activities as prescribed in the area of HCI are not widely used in the software industry, especially not in agile software development projects. Through an analysis of interview and survey data from five studies we scrutinize the reasons for choosing Scrum, consequences of using Scrum, and study the challenges of integrating usability activities in Scrum projects are scrutinized. Our results show that the IT professionals appreciate the inherent values in Scrum, which are speed and communication internal to the Scrum team. Also, working in teams and focusing on a small number of tasks at a time is valued. The main challenges are that including specialists in the teams is hard and Scrum does not always match with external requirements for the organizations. Usability activities in Scrum are found to be informal and implicit, even sometimes hidden behind more fashionable concepts such as security and accessibility to increase priority. In addition, usability activities are often seen as not fitting in the pace of the project. Two of the underlying questions in the paper are: Why is Scrum so fashionable? How can usability activities be better integrated in agile projects? Answers to these questions are discussed in the chapter.

M. Lárusdóttir (✉)
School of Computer Science, Reykjavik University, Reykjavik, Iceland
e-mail: marta@ru.is

Å. Cajander • T. Lind
Department of Information Technology, Uppsala University, Uppsala, Sweden
e-mail: asa.cajander@it.uu.se; thomas.lind@it.uu.se

G. Erlingsdottir
Lund University, Lund, Sweden
e-mail: gudbjorg.erlingsdottir@design.lth.se

J. Gulliksen
KTH Royal Institute of Technology, Stockholm, Sweden
e-mail: gulliksen@kth.se

© Springer International Publishing Switzerland 2016
G. Cockton et al. (eds.), *Integrating User-Centred Design in Agile Development*,
Human–Computer Interaction Series, DOI 10.1007/978-3-319-32165-3_10

Keywords Agile software development • Scrum • Usability • User experience • User centred design • Fashion management

10.1 Introduction

Software development methods and processes have changed over the years, and one management idea adapted to software development has been followed by the other. Some of these processes focus on project management, whereas others include everything from business modelling to code structuring as for example the previously popular process the Rational Unified Process [1]. Some of the software development methods that have been popular are based on explicit core values such as communication or customer satisfaction that are emphasised in agile software development processes [2]. Since the launch of the Agile Manifesto in 2001 [3], agile methods such as Extreme Programming, Dynamic Systems Development Method and Kanban have gained popularity with Scrum as being the most popular process [4]. Scrum has indeed become so popular that it has expanded the domain of software development and moved into other areas. The ideas and core values of Scrum are hence integrated areas far beyond software engineering and computer science. Recently we have observed it being used as the silver bullet of supervision for PhD students, as well as in the instructional enterprise of teaching computer science. Here the ideas used are continuous feedback as well as planning ahead in sprints. One of our underlying questions in the paper is hence: Why is Scrum so fashionable?

From the survey that Version One launched in 2014 [4] one can see that the reasons given for using Scrum are: "Accelerate product delivery" (59 %), "Enhance ability to manage changing requirements" (56 %), "Increase productivity" (53 %) and "Enhance software quality" (46 %). When asked about how they measure the success of their agile initiatives, the most frequent measurements are: "On-time delivery" (58 %), "Product quality" (48 %) and "Customer/user satisfaction" (44 %). It is interesting to note that when asked about the benefits of using agile, extended customer/user satisfaction is not on the list. Moreover, when explicitly asking companies about why they use Scrum, we often also get the answer that this development process works better than the previous processes used, but also that Scrum has both advantages and disadvantages [5–7]. Still, there is truly a collective belief that using Scrum is a better way of working. It has been an implicit assumption about Scrum is that it addresses user perspectives better than traditional software processes [8], and that by simply applying an agile development process, systems could become usable for end-users. However, previous research has shown that this is not always the case, and that the context of Scrum impacts user involvement as described in, for example [5, 7]. Another underlying question in the paper is: How can usability activities be better integrated within agile projects?

There is still much to explore when it comes to the reasons for some methods to become popular, whereas others remain unknown. Hence, based on five empirical studies of Scrum and usability activities, we scrutinize the reasons for using Scrum, what the consequences of the choice were and what challenges were met when integrating usability activities in Scrum. Hence the main contribution of this paper is answering the following questions:

- What are the companies' reasons for using Scrum?
- What are the experienced consequences of using Scrum?
- What are the challenges of integrating usability activities in Scrum?

Finally, we also discuss the two underlying questions above. We discuss if one of the reasons for Scrum being so popular could be that it has become a management fashion, as defined by Abrahamson [9]:

"a relatively transitory collective belief, disseminated by management fashion setters, that a management technique leads rational management progress" (p. 257). Moreover, we discuss and relate the popularity of Scrum to the Diffusion of Innovation model by Rogers [10]. Additionally, we discuss how usability activities could be better integrated in Scrum projects.

The main contribution of the paper is a deeper understanding of the work environment that IT professionals working in Scrum projects have and the challenges they have when integrating usability activities in their software development.

10.2   Background

In this section we present the definition of the Scrum development process in the literature, how usability activities are explained in the literature and how these are practiced in the industry, the background of the integration of usability activities in Scrum in practice and finally the theories on fashion and diffusion of innovation.

10.2.1   Defining the Scrum Development Process

Scrum is currently a popular process used in most areas of software development [4]. In this subsection we will describe how the originators of Scrum define the process.

Jeff Sutherland and Ken Schwaber described the Scrum process in 1995 [2, 11]. They are the official pioneers of the process. In that document, Scrum is called a process. Today the process is owned by the Scrum Alliance, which certifies consultants and provides courses in Scrum. The paper that inspired Scrum had the title "The new new product development game" [12]. The authors explain "the rules of the game in new product development are changing. It takes more than high quality, low cost, and differentiation to excel in today's competitive market. It also takes speed and flexibility".

Some discussions have been whether Scrum is a framework or a process. Among the information that IT professionals ordinarily want to extract from descriptions of software development processes are information on: what is going to be done, when and where it will be done, how and why it will be done, who is going to do it, and who is dependent on it being done [13]. This is provided by Scrum, so we therefore call it a *process* in this paper.

Various types of software development processes have been suggested for the last 30 years. The main types are sequential software development, iterative development and incremental software development. The sequential software process is often named the Waterfall process [14]. The fundamental thought in this process is that it is sequential, so that each stage should be more or less finished before the next begins. In the 1990s more emphasis in software development was on delivering parts of the software to customers iteratively and incrementally, so time to market would be shorter [14]. In incremental software development the software requirements are divided into parts, which are implemented and a deliverable version of that part of the software is made [15]. The basic idea is that the IT professionals use the knowledge they gained in previous increments, both from developing the software and from users, to iterate the current version of the software during the development of current and future increments. The implementation starts with a simple set of requirements, and iteratively evolves until a full version of the software is implemented in a plan-driven way. This is also the fundamental idea behind Scrum.

In Scrum, the projects should be split up into 2–4 week long iterations called *sprints*, each aiming to end up with a potentially shippable product. In Scrum, self-organizing and strongly united teams are heavily emphasized, typically with six to eight interdisciplinary team members. One of the benefits of using agile development processes was claimed to be that customers' needs are taken more into account than when developing software using sequential processes [2]. Scrum is a simple process with a few ceremonies, roles and artefacts. The roles are called Product Owner, Scrum Master and Team Member [16]. The Scrum team is self-organising and works independently during the sprints. Daily Scrum meetings are prescribed where the Scrum team meets and plans the work during the day, and where the tasks are distributed in the group. The work in the Scrum team should be guided by collaboration and communication. Demos of the outcome are made at the end of every sprint.

The Product Owner has the responsibility to represent the needs and ideas of the customer, being responsible for writing the so called user stories and for managing these in a document called the Product Backlog. User stories are described in a standardised way to express the users' needs and the business value in sentences with a specific structure. The Product Backlog contains the requirements for the software to be built, often described as user stories. Parts of the Product Backlog may be technical and parts may be more human oriented. The project is often analysed to some extent and a vision of the product is made before the actual iterations start. That period is often referred to as Sprint Zero or pre-study phase.

The sprints are planned in sprint planning meetings, and the requirements to be addressed in each sprint are defined in the Sprint Backlog. By the end of each sprint, the Scrum team should release a potentially shippable product. At this point it is recommended in Scrum that the team collect feedback from the stakeholders to adapt the software to the users' needs in subsequent sprints. The team and the Product Owner define an exit-criterion of the items in the Sprint Backlog called "the definition of done". It describes when the items are completed and can be delivered to the customer. The definition might include descriptions of tests to be done. The Scrum board is a physical or electronic task board used by the team members to manage the different tasks and what to do during each sprint. The Scrum Master is often considered as a coach for the Scrum team. The Scrum Master is responsible for the process used during the software development and can, for example, decide how long the sprints should be.

10.2.2 Usability Activities

When computer development grew from being systems developed by operators for the operators themselves, to developing computer systems to be used by non-computer science users for the purpose of supporting their work tasks, the need to focus on usability became evident. The multidisciplinary research field of human computer interaction grew out of human factors and cognitive psychology, providing a theoretical framework for the study of humans interacting with systems [17].

The ISO 9241-210 standard [18] called: "Human-centred design for interactive systems", is a common framework for defining how to include the users' needs in software development in theory. Four major usability activities are described in the ISO 9241-210 [18] standard that shall take place during the development of software. First the usability activities should be planned. Then the four major four activities are explained: (a) Understand and specify the context of use, (b) Specify the user requirements, (c) Produce design solutions to meet these requirements, and (d) Evaluate the designs against requirements. It is stated in the standard that these four usability activities are interdependent and each activity uses outputs from the other activities. This means that it is recommended in the standard that when a specification of the context of use has been made, the user requirements could be described based on this understanding. Additionally, design solutions could be made based on these user requirement specifications. The outcomes of each of the three human-centred design activities should be evaluated and iterated according to the evaluation results, where appropriate. The ISO 9241-210 standard [18] defines the human-centred design as: "An approach to system design and development that aims to make interactive systems more usable by focusing on the use of the system, applying human factors/ergonomics and usability knowledge and techniques (p. 2)" It is also stated in the standard that: "Human-centred design activities can be incorporated in design approaches as diverse as object-oriented, waterfall, HFI (human factors integration), agile and rapid development (p. 10)." The usability activities should therefore have the capability to fit into the agile development process of Scrum as well as in any other development processes.

In the late twentieth century discussions of user experience (UX) broadened consideration of usage qualities beyond usability, and sought a concept to include more satisfaction-related qualities that were already associated with games and entertainment technologies [19]. UX considerations extended usability activities beyond quality-increasing testing and improvement to focus more on attractiveness (with the intention of increasing sales), and relating more to design than to testing [20]. UX has become a concept that people relate to outside of the immediate sector, meaning that marketing and project managers need to address these issues on a more strategic level [21]. Thus we now see interaction designers and UX lead roles at a managerial level [22]. All of a sudden there is money to be earned through proactive UX/usability work, instead of this only being a reactive quality-increasing activity.

The establishment of the field as a profession was accompanied by the standardization efforts conducted by ISO [18, 23]. Even though the role developed and an increasing number of people could claim this role from education and work [24, 25] usability professionals have always struggled with the justification of the role [26] and the call for a need to cost-justify its activities [27]. One approach of making the field more attractive was tighter integration with software engineering models [28, 29], but still integrating usability activities into agile development has challenges. In studies in practical settings, the main challenges found for the integration of usability activities were availability of IT professionals and time [30, 31]. The profession gained further popularity with the growth of accessibility [32] since legal binding obligations to adhere to accessibility requirements made it necessary to incorporate accessibility professionals. It did however not reach the level of being popular and one reason for this may be the view that the profession's work is too research focused, and does not include the demanded levels of agility.

10.2.3   The Integration of Usability Activities into Scrum in Practice

In Scrum the customer's needs and thereby the user needs are meant to be taken more into account than in older development processes, like Waterfall and RUP [2]. Through the product owner role, the priorities of the customer are considered. That does not necessarily mean that the users' needs are taken into account, because the customer representatives are not always the ones who will use the software. The Product Owner does not always state the needs for usability of the software in practice either [33]. One of the main conclusions in an extensive literature survey from 2010 on the integration of the usability needs into agile processes in the software industry is that the users´ needs were not sufficiently included in the agile development processes [34]. A recent literature study from 2015, states that usability methods are often used too late in the development of software in the industry and managing the product vision and time boxing the user-centred design work are well known continuous challenges [35].

Recent results show that many IT professionals frequently use some kind of usability techniques in Scrum projects, to support the four usability activities, and that they generally rate the techniques as being useful [5]. The highest rated usability techniques according to this study were workshops, informal usability evaluation with users and meetings with users. It is noticeable that all of these techniques are rather informal. Similar results have been presented in a study showing that all kinds of prototypes are used more frequently in Scrum projects than when using software development process made by the corresponding software company [36]. An extensive literature study shows that the most common usability techniques in agile development are low fidelity prototypes, user testing aimed at refining the prototypes in the next iteration and inspections [37].

Organisational and contextual settings for successfully integrating usability activities into agile software development have been explored in several research studies. Close collaboration between the development team and the usability professionals has been considered as one of the biggest success factors for integrating usability activities in Scrum projects [37, 38]. The usability professionals' understanding of their job role and the need to establish and communicate an overall team vision were pointed out as the two major themes highly important for the success of integrating user activities in agile development [39]. Often user experience issues are considered important both on strategic and operational level, but the current work processes and management styles can limit the impact of the usability professionals' work [40].

10.2.4 Diffusion and Fashion

Rogers [10] has shown that modelling diffusion processes typically result in a characteristic S-shaped curve. The curve traces the accumulated adoption of an innovation over time as it initially accelerates, reaches a peak rate of diffusion, and then decelerates as the level of saturation approach its maximum. Early on, when diffusion is slow, only those categorised as "innovators" and "early adopters" are interested in the innovation. The rate of diffusion increase as the interest of the majority of potential users peaks, influenced by factors such as the perceived maturity of the innovation, financial incentives provided by investors promoting the innovation, proximity and relationship to other innovation adopters, etc. Upon approaching saturation, the rate of diffusion decrease as the group categorised as "laggards" is the only group left in the population of agents that will eventually adopt the innovation.

The fashion metaphor has been widely used to describe and explain the popularity and rapid diffusion of certain "new" management ideas in the form of concepts, models, methods and techniques [41]. The metaphor draws on aesthetic fashions, notably the clothing industry, but according to Abrahamson [9] there are two important differences between management fashions and aesthetic fashions: "First, whereas aesthetic fashions need only appear beautiful and modern, fashionable management techniques must appear both rational (efficient means to important ends) and progressive (new as well as improved relative to older management techniques)" (p. 255).

Much research on the use of the fashion metaphor in management research builds on the perspective of new institutionalism [42–45] and describe how management ideas are chosen based on an organization's wish to be more "fashionable" rather than actual needs. Czarniawska and Joerges [44] describe how organizations adapt to new ideas and how these ideas get their velocity, i.e. ability to spread widely, mainly from being in vogue in the sense that many people/organisations in different places and over time will "catch on" to fashionable ideas and use them. Fashion can thus explain "many puzzling developments in and between organizations" (p. 24). In other words the metaphor of fashion can be helpful in understanding changes that occur across an organisational field and even how institutions are altered or changed.

Clark [46] points out that organizational conformity to the latest fashion may result in disappointment and frustration as the models and techniques do not always live up to the expectations set for them. This in turn may result in the lack of institutionalization and organizations abandoning the ideas in favour of others in the process of becoming fashionable.

10.3   Method

The results and discussions in this chapter builds upon several qualitative interview studies with usability and user experience professionals and quantitative survey studies in agile projects. It is a synthesis chapter that integrates results on how IT professionals working with software development in agile projects conduct user-centred activities. An overview of the studies described as study 1–5 is given in Table 10.1. In total 37 IT professionals were interviewed and 74 took part in surveys.

Table 10.1 An overview of our studies that are integrated in this paper

Study no. (id)	Research method (year of study)	Information on the studies
Study 1 (S1)	Survey and interviews (2009)	25 IT professionals from 18 software companies in Iceland responded to the survey, 6 of the same respondents took part in interviews
Study 2 (S2)	Survey (2011)	49 IT professionals mainly in Sweden responded
Study 3 (S3)	Interviews (2010)	21 IT professionals from 14 companies in Sweden interested in usability and UX
Study 4 (S4)	Interviews (2013)	6 IT professionals in Sweden working at a software company developing a system for health care
Study 5 (S5)	Interviews (2013)	10 IT professionals in Iceland working at 10 companies with systems development

Hence, data was gathered from 111 professionals mainly in two countries. All the participants used agile processes and conducted some usability activities in their software development.

The motivation for Study 1 was to compare usability evaluation to other types of testing in Scrum projects. The participants were also asked about how they use Scrum in their projects and what the positive and negative aspects arise from using Scrum. The informants were mainly working at software companies developing various types of software, but some were working at banks and telecommunication companies developing software for that company. Around half of the companies had more than 40 employees.

The objective of Study 2 was to get an overview of what user-centred techniques were used by IT professionals working in Scrum projects mainly in Sweden. In this study the informants were also asked how they use Scrum and what the drawbacks and advantages are. One third of the respondents were working at companies having more than 250 employees, and one third had between 50 and 250 employees. Almost half of the respondents were working in Internet and e-commerce systems, and 20 % were working in the computer industry. The remaining respondents were working on telecommunication, in the financial sector, e-health or in other areas.

In Study 3 we interviewed IT professionals in four different roles: Team members, Scrum managers, business analysts and usability experts. The informants came from 14 companies in various organisational contexts. The main types of organisations were product development and consulting companies, or a combination of those. Some of the companies were international, having employees worldwide. The number of employees reached from 8 to 12,500. The purpose of the study was to understand the challenges that IT professionals interested in usability activities face when integrating usability activities in agile software development.

Study 4 was an interview study related to the introduction of a controversial eHealth system where Scrum was used by the vendor company. The purpose of the study was to evaluate the development process from a usability perspective. The interviewees were members of the Scrum team or managers. The vendor company had approximately 10,000 employees.

Lastly, study 5 was an interview study focusing on the strengths and weaknesses of using agile processes such as Scrum and Kanban. The interviewees were all managers or project managers are software companies in Iceland, developing various types of software. The sizes of the companies varied from 4 employees to over 500.

We have published seven papers describing and discussing the results of each of the studies [5–7, 47–50] and three theses have been written by HCI students [51–53]. Some material gathered in these studies has not been published in these scientific papers, but is used in this chapter.

We use a mixed methods approach in the synthesis research for this chapter. Data from five previously conducted surveys and interview studies are analysed again using the fashion metaphor described in Sect. 10.2.4, so all the material from these studies was analysed again for gathering new perspectives. The main themes that we analysed now were: reasons for using Scrum, consequences of using Scrum and usability activities in relation to Scrum.

The analysis used a mix of predefined categories as well as categories that emerged during the analysis. Two of the researchers analysed and coded the data together and discussed the results with the other authors. The quotes in the paper are from our informants. In some cases, we have adjusted the words used to make them more readable. We refer to the source of the particular result using study numbers in Table 10.1 (e.g., S1, S5).

10.4 Results

In the results section, we start by presenting results that indicate why Scrum can be seen as a fashion. We will elaborate on the reasons mentioned in S1–S5 for choosing Scrum as a systems development method. We will start by presenting results in relation to why companies choose Scrum, where the inspiration comes from and motivations behind the choice. We will also present results in relation to the consequences of choosing Scrum. We will also elaborate on perspectives found in S1–S5 on why conducting usability activities in Scrum have not become fashionable.

10.4.1 Reasons for Using Scrum

There are many reasons behind choosing Scrum as a development process. These reasons are often presented in a rational and objective manner, as if the choice was based on an objective and rational decision-making process. In our studies many say that the inspiration of using Scrum comes from the ideas inherent in the method, and these are very appealing to the system developers (S1, S2, S3, S4, S5). One of the inherent values that are appreciated in Scrum is the focus on "speed" and the "agile" way of working or as one of the informants describes it: "get the f***ing work done as fast as possible" (S4). One of the benefits of using Scrum, according to the interviewees, is that the team is to work independently, and this made the systems development model appealing to use (S3). By working independently, the team can focus on their task and does not have to use time on synchronizing with many others. The process leaves the decisions to the team, and this is inspiring for the system developers. Another appealing feature in Scrum is the focus on communication within the team, for example in the stand-up meetings (S3, S5). One can notice that these stand-up meetings are the most valued part of Scrum, and the most popular Scrum activity when implementing the process (S1).

Another advantage is the short sprints used, where a potentially shippable product is delivered to the customers after each sprint, which gives the developers a good pace to work in (S3, S4). One informant explains: "I guess for a programmer it's perfect to get a small piece of work that you can develop and deliver" (S3).

Additionally the team members mention that focusing on only several tasks during the sprint and not being interrupted all the time by requests from the customer is one of the advantages of Scrum. One informant explains that the team members are protected from interruptions from customers (S5). These sprints imply that the visions of the customers are considered through the whole development process. When following this process with short sprints one avoids discovering failure at the end of the whole systems development project when it is too late to do anything about the problems, as one of the informants described: "When we start to work and showing the end-users the product as often as we do using Scrum, we always get the feedback that now I understand what you were talking about. And then you can continue that discussion: Is this what we are showing you what you were expecting to get? And then you have this discussion all the way from the beginning instead of the ordinary way when you have 2 weeks to deliver when you are showing them: This is what you get and they go: Wooooaaaaa! We don't want this. So we get all that very early in the project which means that when we have the final delivery we know that this is the product that the customer actually can use because it is well suited in their way of working and the kind of process that they need" (S3). The short sprints provided a suitable framework for managing the direction of the software being developed as the project's vision could be described as a moving target depending significantly on external factors such as necessary integrations with third party systems, a precarious political situation regarding this kind of (nationally) unprecedented service, and rulings from national regulating authorities (S4).

The choice of Scrum as a development process is also based on previous development processes used and many informants position their choice of Scrum in relation to the waterfall model (see the citation above where the informant refers to "the ordinary way"). However, it seems to be easier to say what did not work in previous systems development processes (or waterfall), and why they did NOT work. It is more difficult to say what DID work with them, as this informant exemplifies: "I think the waterfall model is really bad." (S3) Another informant describes the differences between Scrum and waterfall by saying: "But I think that maybe the most important thing with Scrum is the knowledge that it's a fluid world. The requirements will change. And that's in your mind set, so you're more liable to cope with that. In a more traditional waterfall development you believe that these are the requirements and they're going to remain fixed, which is never the case. So that's probably the most important thing about agile methods that you realise that things are going to change as we go along" (S3). Moreover, as can be seen in the citation the choice of Scrum is motivated by the values inherent in Scrum regarding the inevitability of changing requirements. Many organisations tend to use their experience from their previous methods, choosing a development process that is different from the old process used. One informant describes the situation in Iceland by saying: "So my experience in Iceland is that usually companies have no strict processes. In many companies there is no process defined. A little bit of chaos or some kind of process but no formal process" (S5). Introducing Scrum to those companies gave the developers structure to the previous less organised way of working the informant explained (S5).

10.4.2   Consequences of Using Scrum

In our studies we have seen that most companies have adapted Scrum or introduced a few inspirations from Scrum, and they describe that they are using a "Scrumish method" (S3, S5). This can be seen as an indication that Scrum does not actually fit as a development process and one of the consequences of choosing Scrum was that it needed to be adapted.

Possibly some of the core values of Scrum are currently fashionable, such as speed and agility, and these are the ones organisations choose to implement. Most companies do however use the majority of the roles, activities and artefacts recommended in Scrum (S1, S2, S4, S5). Most Scrum projects have a Product owner, and a Scrum master but in some cases their roles have been omitted, replaced by a project manager or by members of the teams. Like one of our informants described: "We are not terribly concerned with the Scrum Master role. We have one (rotating) pair working outside the sprint to take care of technical support, disturbances and general application health not directly related to customer needs" (S2). The most popular activities used are sprint planning used for planning the scope of the starting sprint and stand-up meetings for checking the status of the sprint on daily basis. When looking at the artefacts, the least used artefact is the burndown chart (S1, S2).

Some informants find it problematic that the Scrum team is supposed to consist of team members that share the workload according to oral agreements made in the team. There is not really a good way to include specialist roles focusing on one of the quality aspects of systems development. Either the specialists are team members, or they are working outside the teams. None of these work situations are without problems, and organisations have tried out different solutions to solve this. Being outside can make the specialist feel like an "add on" to the project, and not a core member (S3), or as another expert explained it: "I worked in a small parenthesis outside of the team" (S4). In the interviews it became obvious that members of the development organisation were described and presented according to their background and education, as well as their speciality in systems development rather than as being team members. The specialist roles do not have an obvious place in the Scrum structure, and this is a problem for many projects (S4). The Scrum development process does not handle this need for specialists in the development projects. One of the usability specialists says: "I interfere in their process to help" (S3). Some of the specialists think that Scrum does not fit their needs, and that they would have liked a development process that supported their work in a better way.

Sometimes Scrum does not match with external requirements in the organisation (S3). Scrum does not fit since there are numerous other requirements due to adherence to standards, and the requirement of a specific area of application. Some projects need to dissolve the Scrum structure in order to comply with external circumstances, and the Scrum process does not really fit the circumstances of the organisation, as in this quote: "Right now we have mixed the teams up, because we have to do so at the end of our development cycle" (S3). One problem that was mentioned is that it is not possible to add functionality within a sprint, even though the customer really needs that functionality (S3). This makes Scrum somewhat inflexible despite the fact that it is presented as very flexible. Several organisations using Scrum feel that it is a problem that the sprints are fixed, and in some cases the Product owner has the rights to add emergency work during the sprint (i.e. even though this was not planned in the sprint planning). "Some requirements are urgent, cannot wait 2 weeks. We have created exceptions to the sprint process for specific tasks" (S5).

One disadvantage mentioned with Scrum is that there is no clear vision of the product, which can be problematic in several ways. One informant describes: "There is no clear description of what the system is going to be when the project starts, and Scrum requires that the procurer or customer is much more active all through the project. It is problematic for the procurer or customer not to have a clear vision of the product. They pay for something without having a clear idea of what they will receive." (S3). Another informant describes the problems with the vision in this way: "But the problem is, that there is now no one that actually is responsible for putting this piece of functionality into the big picture. So there is no one responsible for the full user experience. That's the problem. After a while you have added so many pieces that you don't know where to put them anymore. And if you don't have the vision clear in your head or on paper it's starting to get quite difficult to know what to do with this piece of functionality and then you do something, just to squeeze it in. And that's the reason for that I think it's so important to do a thorough pre-study before prototyping and testing. Because if you have that it's so much easier to prioritize and say okay say that from this vision we have decided to do this piece now and that piece then. At least we know where it all fits in. And then of course this vision will change all the time, because the market changes or whatever. But still you can work on the vision then and know where to put the pieces" (S3). Several other informants share this concern, that the holistic view for the system is missing, since the sprints slice the development project in small groups of functionality that become potentially shippable product after each sprint.

10.4.3 Usability Activities in Scrum Projects

Usability activities are mostly not an obvious part of Scrum projects, and usability experts face problems when integrating their work (S3, S4, S5). Activities such as usability evaluations, as for example defined by Benyon [54] are rarely used in the way described in such standard literature, despite the fact that the organisations had well educated usability experts in the teams [7].

Some organisations see usability activities as something completely different and less prioritized than the rest of the system development tasks and other user stories (S3). User stories connected to usability are placed on a separate Scrum board. The two Scrum boards live in parallel in the projects, and they had one Scrum board that was the "ordinary Scrum board" and one Scrum board that was the "usability

Scrum board". However, the most important thing in the project was to work with the ordinary Scrum board, and the user stories on the usability board were only dealt with if the system developers in the team had time. This was explained by one informant: "we had kind of a second Scrum board. Whenever there was time over, because often we could do it in half an hour to an hour. So then we could take one of these notes and fix it and just check, this is done, put it back and then he evaluated it. All this was kind of informal" (S3).

It is noticeable from the studies that some usability experts wrap usability problems in more fashionable concepts. One example is the usability expert who rephrases the usability problems as security problems, and makes them more interesting for the organisation in this way: "We are working on really enhancing the benefits of usability in the area of IT security" (S3). Another usability expert explains that the only way to make usability problems interesting in the organisation is to present them as new user stories that needs to be solved, not improvements to the old system from the usability perspective, or re-launching old user stories (S3).

Usability work is sometimes carried out as a completely separate activity from the work in the team (S3, S4), and sometimes due to the fact that the level of usability and the design needs attention (S4). The usability experts are not a part of the Scrum team, but merely give written input from a distance and are invited to sprint demos and project meetings, but otherwise they do not work closely with the development team. One informant explains her position in this way: "I have only been working with some kind of test of the system, and then given small comments on the user interface" (S4). The same informant also says that she was a part of the team during the most intense period of the development, as is described in this quote: "During the period that I worked full time with testing and evaluation, then I was participating in the stand-up meetings, but I did not really participate in the meetings" (S4). So, even though the informant was working actively on the project and technically included in its activities, she was not an active part of the team. Another usability expert who had been working at the company for 6 months, explains that he, when trying to find out what the team is doing, asks the Scrum team: "Can I be at your meetings?" (S3), i.e. from his perspective he is not included in the team. He explains that he is carefully taking small steps to change this culture.

One of the reasons frequently mentioned for why usability activities are not emphasised is that it is too time consuming (S1, S3, S4). When comparing why developers use some testing techniques less often than other techniques while developing their software, lack of time is the most frequent reason for not conducting usability testing (S1). This is also true, for security and performance testing. An interesting outcome from the comparison in the study (S1) is that the four core testing types, unit, integration, system and acceptance testing [55], are always budgeted for, but for the quality aspects like usability, performance and security are not in the budget by default and sometimes that is the reason for not conducting those (S1). Many informants mention the vagueness of the concept usability. It is often seen as something fuzzy, hard to measure and usability requirements are always changing (S1, S2, S3). This perspective could be one of the reasons for why the IT professionals see usability activities as time consuming.

One respondent explained that if the project is really agile, the changes are not that extensive each time and the importance of being quick to market is strong, so usability testing is really not needed, because a shippable product has been delivered and the customers can complain (S1, S3, S4). Furthermore, because the changes are small, extensive usability testing is not needed and is too expensive. "The main thing is to confess your fault and change quickly according to the customers' complaints so you can be very quick in adjusting to their needs" (S1) one of the respondents remarked. This respondent explained that asking for usability testing was really the customer's responsibility. We have also heard the opinion that IT professionals really want to gather feedback from users, but users were not always willing to take part because they were busy doing their own work and did not want to be involved in software development.

Some informants describe that they launch the system, and expect the users to tell if the system doesn't work while using the system (S1, S3, S5). One informant describes her experiences by saying: "As soon as the user gets the possibility to start clicking himself then it feels like their brain is finally working – they say: Oh now I understand even though you can simulate it on the whiteboard as well. But I think that is a big difference that we actually have a product in the end of every sprint." However, users seldom complain due to numerous reasons related to not having the vocabulary, power, and blaming problems with the system on themselves (S5). The system developers hence get very little feedback, and they interpret this silence as if the users are satisfied with the system.

10.1.4 Summary of Results

In our studies we have seen that Scrum has become popular for a number of reasons. In the following, we summarise the reasons and the consequences of using Scrum. Furthermore, we summarise the challenges of integrating usability activities in Scrum projects.

The main reasons we have seen of using Scrum are:

1. Many of our informants mention that the emphasis on speed, reflected in the short sprints and frequent deliveries, is very positive in Scrum.
2. The team members can focus on a few issues at a time and get the feeling of achievement every other week.
3. The team works independently and communication is encouraged within the team. This is described as beneficial for the work environment and group culture of the team.
4. The acceptance for requirements changing over time is seen as positive.

However, there's also a negative side of what is described as primarily positive. In our cases we have detected a number of aspects where Scrum falls short of being the ultimate process for all purposes for all actors involved. Below is a summary of the consequences of using Scrum:

1. Scrum does not seem to fit everyone, the respondents in our cases referred to themselves as using a "Scrumish method", indicating that they do not do Scrum by the book.
2. The consequence of the frequent deliveries in Scrum is that often there is no time for usability activities. We have seen that often the team members do not find time to gather feedback from users. This may be because of the emphasis on speed in Scrum and the changes of requirements from the users are not always welcomed by the team members. We have also seen that the developers rely on users to provide feedback after using the latest delivery for some time, but that is not often the case.
3. The team is supposed to provide expert knowledge but Scrum makes it hard for experts to fit into the team structure. The experts feel like outsiders in the process.
4. Due to the fragmented nature of the Scrum process it is hard for both the team and the customer to have a clear vision of the result of the process early on.

Additionally, we analysed the challenges for integrating usability activities in Scrum projects in practice. Our main results are summarised below:

1. The fragmented nature of Scrum, mentioned above, is fundamentally at odds with the methods of experts working with usability, as they want to grasp the whole picture from the beginning. Also this lack of a holistic approach leads to that none has the full responsibility of the whole user experience.
2. The usability experts do not become members of the teams, but give written feedback from a distance.
3. The usability aspects do not fit into the "quick" processes of Scrum and are thus perceived as too time consuming and costly and are often not even a part of the budget.

10.5 Discussion

In this section we discuss the two underlying questions in the paper: Why is Scrum so fashionable? and: How can usability activities be better integrated in agile projects?

10.5.1 Why Is Scrum so fashionable?

According to Abrahamsson [9] management fashion differs from aesthetic fashion in two ways. Firstly, fashionable management techniques need to come through as both rational and progressive and not only as beautiful and modern. Secondly, whereas aesthetic fashion is shaped by socio-psychological forces alone, management fashion is shaped by economical and technical forces ([9], p. 255). Many of the people we interviewed in our studies said that they were using a Scrumish method, only using bits and pieces from the Scrum process. One indicator of Scrum being a fashion, is the fact that it seems more important for many companies using Scrum to be able to say that Scrum is used, than it is to actually use the whole process and incorporate its ideas extensively. It is also obvious that many different actions are performed under the Scrum label. Scrum has become one of the most used methods for software development and this homogenization can be interpreted as an urge amongst organizations operating in the same field to show that they have knowledge of the latest management models [56]. This might thus indicate that the organizations using Scrum are interested in retaining legitimacy amongst their "peers" [42]. Scrum might thus be used as a tool in the employer branding of the companies so the employers are proud to be able to say they are using the fashionable Scrum process and use that as a sign of being one of the leading companies. However, it should be noted that few management models used for software development are fully incorporated without adaptations in an organisation. Also a model like Scrum can be seen as fashionable when it is chosen for its legitimizing effect rather than for practical reasons.

This does not mean that Scrum does not fit the purposes of these organizations. On the contrary, the process is put forth as a rational way to develop software as it allows for an iterative and swift development process, where the development team is able to focus on a few requirements at the time. Also, delivery through sprints provide continuous results which is seen as beneficial for the customer since they have control of the progression of the development. There are thus many rational reasons for using Scrum present in our data, which according to Abrahamsson [9] is necessary for a management technique to become fashionable. The question is rather if Scrum is always the best alternative, in every case where it is used. As listed above, in the summary of results section, there are several aspects of the Scrum process that are criticised by the IT professionals in the studied cases, indicating that other development processes might have been more useful but Scrum was chosen because it was fashionable. In a recent study, one of the conclusions is that IT professionals are leaning towards Kanban, since Scrum does not fit their needs [57].

From a diffusion perspective [10], the Scrum principles can be seen as a factor facilitating its diffusion. As mentioned above, the Scrum principles are few and flexible enough for organizations to be able to claim having adopted Scrum with minimal need for adapting their earlier way of working. In Rogers' terminology, Scrum offered a high *relative advantage* through its increasing legitimacy and fashionability while enjoying a high level of *compatibility* with previous processes, coupled with low *complexity* thanks to the comparatively lightweight principles. With Scrum being an intellectual innovation, not requiring any hardware or other specific artefacts to diffuse, its low complexity could also be seen as contributing to a higher level of *trialability* and *observability*. Thus, once considered fashionable enough, Scrum could diffuse rapidly as it did not require a significant investment in time or resources for an organization to climb aboard the Scrum bandwagon. Scrum could also reach a large portion of the software development community as the principles allowed for the process to be adopted, whether by name or in earnest, by a wide range of organizations. However, as there are other processes belonging to the agile family based on even fewer and more flexible principles that have not been widely adopted like the Kanban process, this could suggest that the perceived relative advantage of Scrum was the deciding factor. The successful diffusion of Scrum could then be attributed to an initial advantage over other Agile processes, such as XP, DSDM and Kanban, through serendipitous events, its popularity and legitimacy (*relative advantage*) then gaining faster than that of its competitors through a process of increasing returns as more and more organizations adopt Scrum.

10.5.2 How Can Usability Activities Be Better Integrated in Agile Projects?

One of the aspects that comes through in the accounts of the IT professionals in our cases is that Scrum is a development process that foremost suits the developers themselves. Usability experts and other experts find difficulties in becoming included in the development process as it is fragmented and the sprints provide only a short-term perspective. We have also seen that the responsibility for usability activities is not clearly defined. This is also enhanced by the lack of documentation in the Scrum process. Also it seems like the usability experts, at least in some cases, will refer to usability problems as for instance security problems to "sneak" the usability aspect into the process. This may also indicate that the usability aspects are out of fashion in the software development business and rebranding it is a way to make it more up to date and attractive [58]. There are of course many ways to better integrate usability activities in the different cases, adding a responsible person in some of the projects and better define the documentation in other projects, but there seems to be a lack of a holistic view on how the vision is for integrating user centred design in agile processes.

Management processes like Scrum may thus endure and be used successfully in the sense that they are perceived as useful by those using them, whilst they may fail in the sense that they do not create an adequate development process in terms of the final product or service from the end users' point of view. Important factors may be overlooked in the process. This can be seen for example in one of our studies where the developers did not know how the customers use the developed product and the communication between developers and customers was not frequent. Even when the Scrum process is performed in business to business, the Scrum team may perceive it as problematic to involve the customer in the process and as illustrated in one of our studies, where we have seen that team-members are almost protected from customers. This shows that the urge to involve the user is low in that case. When the end user is not the same as the customer paying for the system the risk of the end users' needs to be overseen in the development process is even greater. Agile processes strongly encourage customer participation, but what Scrum does not address is the user's involvement. Often the difference between the customer and the user is not clear for agile software developers [57], so they think that by including the customer's perspective they have included the users' needs, which is not always the case in practice. Providing IT professionals with tools or techniques to plan user involvement, by defining who would be preferred participants, when it should preferably happen, where it should preferably happen and what should be the main goal of the user involvement could be one way of better integrating usability activities in agile projects.

Some software development companies market themselves as producing software with good user experience, e.g. Google. However, surprisingly few have adopted usability methods and successfully incorporated these into development practices. This can for example be seen in the results in one of our interview studies, where only very few interviewees named particular usability methods such as heuristic evaluation and user testing. In the same study, the interviewees contacted users informally and usability activities were not explicitly integrated into the development process. However, developers in general believe that they already develop highly usable software. Even if it leads to (even) better software from the user's perspective, it is not obvious to a software development company why they should extend usability practices beyond what they are already doing. This is a significant difference from the greening trend [41] where many consultants relied on rhetoric and associating environmental responsibility with established traits and values, e.g. by calling it a challenge that only the flexible and far-sighted companies would prosper from. Fineman [41] describes how the greening trend of incorporating environmental responsibility into management methodologies in the 1980s and 1990s was hard to sell on its altruistic values alone, they also had to satisfy more salient management issues such as profitability, efficiency, and performance. Growing public concern and environmentalist movements were not enough. Though it has become fashionable to appear green, Fineman [41] concludes that actually embracing all of the diverse environmental issues applicable to a corporation remains a quite complex and confusing task for managers.

There are many similarities in these two trends, the greening trend and the user experience trend. It has been hard to sell to managers that usability is important at least in the 1980s and 1990s and the reasons were similar, the managers emphasise profitability, efficiency, and performance that are hard to associate with usability work. Nowadays, UX has become more fashionable in the software industry and it is commonly respected by IT professionals that UX activities are important.

Still, integrating usability and user experience activities in Scrum projects remains quite a complex and confusing task and it remains a challenge for HCI researchers to help them to solve that task. Since usability professionals want to grasp the whole picture of the user experience from the beginning of the software development, the fragmented nature of Scrum is fundamentally at odds with their vision of how to approach their work. The usability aspects do not fit into the "quick" processes of Scrum and are thus perceived as too time consuming and costly and are often not even a part of the budget nor are the usability professionals a part of the teams, and end up being outsiders. Also this lack of a holistic approach means that none has the full responsibility for the entire user experience. The understanding of the reasons for choosing Scrum, the challenges for using the process and the challenges for integrating usability activities into Scrum explained in this paper, gives a good basis for both describing new ways for supporting usability professionals and for planning research on this topic.

10.6 Conclusion

The forces behind the development of the Scrum process were probably the rapidly increasing demand for new IT systems in the late 1990s, creating a need for new methods and techniques for managing the software development process. One of the approaches is the iterative way of developing software, which is illustrated by the sprints in Scrum. However, the downside can be that the holistic view is missing in the development process and that it may be difficult for the customers to continuously receive and implement new features of the system and learn how to use those.

In some cases, a certain development process, selected for being fashionable, may be used to produce a solution aimed at improving the work environment for a particular group. Management models that are chosen for the wrong reasons may endure and be used successfully in the sense that they are perceived as useful processes by those using them, in the case of this paper by IT professionals, whilst they may fail in the sense that they do not enable other stakeholders to improve their users' work environment or create an adequate IT system from the users´ point of view. The consequence of Scrum being fashionable is that important factors may be overlooked in the development process of the IT system. The bottom line is that management processes that seem to work for IT professionals may not give a final result that works for those who will actually use the IT system. It remains a challenge for us HCI researchers to help IT professionals to integrate the users' perspectives in their agile software development.

Acknowledgement We would like to thank COST Action IC0904 Twintide for the financial support that they have provided for completing study 3. Also, we would like to thank Professor Emeritus Liam Bannon for his valuable feedback on a draft of this paper.

References

1. Kruchten P (2004) The rational unified process: an introduction. Addison-Wesley Professional, Boston
2. Schwaber K (1995) Scrum development process. In: Business object design and implementation. Springer, London, pp 117–134
3. Beck K, Beedle M, Van Bennekum A, Cockburn A, Cunningham W, Fowler M, Thomas D (2001) Agile manifesto

4. VersionOne (2014) State of Agile Survey. Online at: http://www.versionone.com/pdf/stateof-agile-development-survey-ninth.pdf
5. Jia Y, Larusdottir MK, Cajander Å (2012) The usage of usability techniques in Scrum projects. In: Proceedings of the HCSE conference, Toulouse
6. Cajander Å, Larusdottir MK, Gulliksen J (2013) Existing but not explicit – the user perspective in Scrum projects in practice. In: proceedings of INTERACT conference
7. Larusdottir M, Cajander Å, Gulliksen J (2014) Informal feedback rather than performance measurements–user-centred evaluation in Scrum projects. Behav Inform Technol 33(11):1118–1135
8. Baxter G, Sommerville I (2011) Socio-technical systems: from design methods to systems engineering. Interact Comput 23(1):4–17
9. Abrahamsson E (1996) Management fashion. Acad Manag Rev 21(1):254–285
10. Rogers EM (2003) Diffusion of innovations, 5th edn. Free Press, New York
11. Sutherland J (1995) Business object design and implementation workshop. In: Addendum to the proceedings of the OOPSLA 1995 on object oriented programing system, languages and applications. Austin, Texas, USA
12. Takeuchi H, Nonaka I (1986) The new new product development game. Harv Bus Rev 64(1):137–146
13. Curtis B, Kellner MI, Over J (1992) Process modeling. Commun ACM 35(9):75–90
14. Boehm B (2006) A view of 20th and 21st century software engineering. In: Proceedings of the 28th international conference on software engineering. ACM Press, Shanghai, China
15. Basili VR, Turner AJ (1975) Iterative enhancement: a practical technique for software development. IEEE Trans Softw Eng SE-1(4):390–396
16. Schwaber K, Beedle M (2002) Software development with Scrum. Prentice Hall, Upper Saddle River
17. Card SK, Newell A, Moran TP (1983) The psychology of human-computer interaction. L. Erlbaum Associates, Hillsdale
18. International organisation for standardisation: ISO 9241-210:2010 (2010) Ergonomics of human-system interaction – Part 210: Human-centred design process for interactive systems. International Organisation for Standardization, Geneva
19. Hassenzahl M, Law ELC, Hvannberg ET (2006) User experience-towards a unified view. UX WS NordiCHI 6:1–3
20. Law ELC, Roto V, Hassenzahl M, Vermeeren AP, Kort J (2009) Understanding, scoping and defining user experience: a survey approach. In: Proceedings of the SIGCHI conference on human factors in computing systems. ACM, New York, pp 719–728
21. Wale-Kolade AY (2014) Integrating usability work into a large inter-organisational agile development project: tactics developed by usability designers. J Syst Softw 100:54–66
22. Plonka L, Sharp H, Gregory P, Taylor K (2014) UX design in agile: a DSDM case study. In: Agile processes in software engineering and extreme programming. Springer, Cham, pp 1–15
23. International organisation for standardisation: ISO 9241-11: 1998 (1998) Ergonomic requirements for office work with visual display terminals. International Organisation for Standardization, Geneva
24. Gulliksen J, Boivie I, Göransson B (2006) Usability professionals—current practices and future development. Interact Comput 18(4):568–600
25. Boivie I, Gulliksen J, Göransson B (2006) The lonesome cowboy: a study of the usability designer role in systems development. Interact Comput 18(4):601–634
26. Gulliksen J, Lantz A, Boivie I (1999) User centered design in practice-problems and possibilities. Royal Institute of Technology, Sweden
27. Mayhew DJ, Bias RG (eds) (1994) Cost-justifying usability. Academic, Boston
28. Seffah A, Gulliksen J, Desmarais MC (2005) An introduction to human-centered software engineering. In: Human-centered software engineering—integrating usability in the software development lifecycle. Springer, Dordrecht, pp 3–14

29. Göransson B, Lif M, Gulliksen J (2003) Usability Design-extending rational unified process with a new discipline. In: Interactive systems. Design, specification, and verification. Springer, Berlin/Heidelberg, pp 316–330

30. Bruno V, Dick M (2007) Making usability work in industry: an Australian practitioner perspective. In: Proceedings of the 19th Australasian conference on computer human interaction: entertaining user interfaces. ACM, New York, pp 261–264

31. Cajander Å, Nauwerck G, Lind T (2014) Things take time: establishing usability work in a university context. In: Proceedings of the EUNIS 2014: higher education in the digital era. ICT Services and System Development, Umeå University

32. Persson H, Åhman H, Yngling AA, Gulliksen J (2014) Universal design, inclusive design, accessible design, design for all: different concepts—one goal? On the concept of accessibility—historical, methodological and philosophical aspects. Universal Access in the Information Society, May 2014, Springer, pp 1–22

33. Singh M (2008) U-SCRUM: an agile methodology for promoting usability. In: Agile, 2008. AGILE'08. Conference. IEEE, pp 555–560

34. Sohaib O, Khan K (2010) Integrating usability engineering and agile software development: A literature review. In: International Conference on Computer Design and Applications (ICCDA), 2010, vol 2. IEEE, pp V2–V32

35. Brhel M, Meth H, Maedche A, Werder K (2015) Exploring principles of user-centered agile software development: a literature review. Inf Softw Technol 61:163–181

36. Larusdottir MK, Haraldsdottir O, Mikkelsen B (2009) User involvement in Icelandic Software Industry. In: Proceedings for the 2nd international workshop on the interplay between usability evaluation and software development – I-Used at the INTERACT conference 2009. Uppsala, Sweden, pp 51–52

37. Silva da Silva TS, Martin A, Maurer F, Silveira MS (2011) User-centered design and agile methods: a systematic review. In: AGILE, pp 77–86

38. Kuusinen K, Mikkonen T, Pakarinen S (2012) Agile user experience development in large software organization: good expertise but limited impact. Human-Centred Software Engineering, Toulouse

39. Kollmann J, Sharp Hl, Blandford A (2009) The importance of identity and vision to user experience designers on agile projects. In: Proceedings of the Agile 2009 conference, pp 11–18

40. Kuusinen K, Väänänen-Vainio-Mattila K (2012) How to make agile UX work more efficient: management and sales perspectives. In: Proceedings of NordiCHI 2012 coference. ACMPress, Copenhagen, Denmark, pp 139–148

41. Fineman S (2001) Fashioning the environment. Organization 8(1):17–31

42. Mayer JW, Rowan B (1977) Institutionalized organizations – formal structure as myth and ceremony. Am J Sociol 83(2):340–363

43. DiMaggio PJ, Powell WW (1991) Introduction. In: Powell WW, DiMaggio PJ (eds) The new institutionalism in organizational analysis. The University of Chicago Press, Chicago

44. Czarniawska B, Joerges B (1996) Travels and ideas. In: Czarniawska B, Sevón G (eds) Translating organisational change. de Gruyter, Berlin

45. Czarniawska B, Sevón G (2005) Global Ideas: how ideas, objects and practices travel in the global economy. Liber, Malmö

46. Clark T (2004) The fashion of management fashion: a surge too far? Organization 11(2):297–306. doi:10.1177/1350508404030659

47. Larusdottir MK, Bjarnadottir E, Gulliksen J (2010) The focus on usability in testing practices in industry. Paper in the human computer interaction symposium at the World Computer Congress

48. Larusdottir MK, Cajander A, Gulliksen J (2012) The big picture of UX is missing in Scrum projects. In: Proceedings of the International Workshop on the Interplay between User Experience and Software Development – at NordiCHI

49. Scandurra I, Holgersson J, Lind T, Myreteg G (2013) Development of novel eHealth services for citizen use: current system engineering vs. best practice in HCI. In: Proceedings of INTERACT conference

50. Larusdottir MK, Cajander A, Simader M (2014) Continuous improvement in agile develop-ment practice – the case of value and non-value adding activities. In: Proceedings of the HCSE conference 2014
51. Bjarnadóttir E (2009) Analysis of software testing in Icelandic Scrum projects. BS thesis, Reykjavik University
52. Jia Y (2012) Survey on Scrum and UCD. Master thesis, Uppsala University
53. Simader M (2013) Insights into waste in agile software development. Master thesis, Reykjavik University
54. Benyon D (2013) Designing interactive systems: a comprehensive guide to HCI, UX and interaction design. Pearson Education, London
55. Graham D, Veenedaal EV, Evans I, Black R (2007) Foundation of software testing: ISTQB certification. Thomson, Belmont
56. Sahlin-Andersson K, Engwall L (2002) Carriers, flows and sources of management knowledge. In: Sahlin-Andersson K, Engwall L (eds) The expansion of management knowledge – carriers, flows and sources. Stanford University Press, Redwood City
57. Law ELC, Lárusdóttir MK (2015) Whose experience do we care about? Analysis of the fitness of Scrum and Kanban to User Experience (UX). Int J Hum Comput Interact 31(9):584–602. doi:10.1080/10447318.2015.1065693
58. Erlingsdóttir G, Lindberg K (2005) Isomorphism, isopraxism and isonymism: complementary or competing processes? In: Czarniawska B, Sevón G (eds) Global Ideas: how ideas, objects and practices travel in the global economy. Liber, Malmö, pp 47–70

Chapter 11
Integrating Both User-Centered Design and Creative Practices into Agile Development

Gilbert Cockton

Abstract Tensions between software development methodologies and user-centered design (UCD) have always existed, but waterfall methodologies do provide a process context within which UCD methods can be clearly integrated whenever this is required. Popular agile methodologies such as Scrum create different challenges to integrating UCD. However, fitting UCD into agile methodologies will not necessarily result in high software quality. The combined approaches can still have significant design gaps that must be addressed by additional creative design practices. This chapter relates selected historical methodological trends to tensions between software and creative design. To resolve these tensions, innovative software development needs to draw on creative design practices in addition to UCD and agile methods. Specifically, innovative software development needs to draw on three key insights from design research: creative design work co-evolves problem and solution spaces; design materials talk back; and, the best design work is generous in scope and intent. These three insights are used firstly to structure a critique of the Agile Manifesto and secondly to provide the basis for proposing a balanced approach to software development that can appropriately integrate engineering, user-centered and creative design practices.

Keywords User-centered design • Agile software development • Worth-focused design • Creative design • Balanced integrated generous design

11.1 Agile, UCD and Rational Engineering Design

In the late 1960s, engineering practices became advocated as the solution to difficulties with software development, where software was delivered late, over budget and with inadequate functions and/or performance. A software development process was advocated and adopted, with linear development based on rigid separation of problem analysis, requirements specification, design and implementation [1].

G. Cockton (✉)
School of Design, Northumbria University, Newcastle upon Tyne NE1 8ST, UK
e-mail: gilbert.cockton@northumbria.ac.uk

© Springer International Publishing Switzerland 2016
G. Cockton et al. (eds.), *Integrating User-Centred Design in Agile Development*,
Human–Computer Interaction Series, DOI 10.1007/978-3-319-32165-3_11

Table 11.1 The scientific method and the engineering design process [4]

The scientific method	The engineering design process
State a question or problem	Define a problem or need
Gather background information	Gather background information
Formulate hypothesis; identify variables	Establish design statement or criteria
Design experiment, establish procedure(s)	Prepare preliminary designs
Test hypothesis by doing an experiment	Build and test a prototype(s)
Analyse results & draw conclusions	Verify, test & redesign as necessary
Present results	Present results

This linear process has well recognized origins in management models [2, 3] for military and space projects at both programme (e.g., NASA's PPBS: planning-programming-budgeting system) and project level (NASA PPP's: Phased Project Planning). This process was assumed to transfer well from large military and space projects to less well-resourced and faster moving contexts than defence and space programmes and projects that last several years.

Half a century later, NASA's 1960s idealized engineering practice remains attractive. It can be aligned with 'the' scientific method, as in Table 11.1's acceptability criteria for a Science and Engineering Expo for 6th–12th grade students [4].

The choice of the High School Science and Engineering Expo example in Table 11.1 is not unfair, because similar comparisons of idealized method and process can be readily found in undergraduate text books on engineering design [5, 6]. Vocabularies sometimes differ slightly from the simple language in Table 11.1, but not markedly so. A linear process of problem definition, problem analysis, requirements specification, design, implementation, verification and validation is common to most accounts of rational engineering design.

The phase order for rational engineering remains linear even when its underlying 'waterfall' structure is bent into a V or curled into an iterative spiral [1]. It is idealized and normative, as it states what *should* happen rather than reflecting what *does* happen. After three decades of attempts to live up to rational engineering ideals, agile software methodologies, "undeniably one of the most important recent developments in software engineering" [7], emerged across the 1990s as realist responses to the failed appearance of rational engineering, which turned out to be more mythical than actual, like a unicorn (extensively known, immediately recognizable, but absolutely imaginary).

Requirements are the essential wall between problem analysis and solution synthesis in rational engineering. Ideally these requirements will be complete, correct and unambiguous. When they are not, documentation associated with information gathering and requirements specification can be very wasteful, since as development progresses, new information and client feedback can invalidate much carefully prepared requirements documentation. Agile software development methodologies ('Agile' for short) are in part a reaction to the inevitable waste here, with differing degrees of response to minimising 'upfront tasks' of problem analysis and requirements specification.

There are over a dozen agile methodologies, and most have one or more 'upfront' phases of analysis and specification (e.g., Crystal Clear, DSDM, FDD [8]). However, the agile methodologies that are currently in extensive use do not have significant upfront phases. The most popular agile methodologies are currently Scrum and related variants, as used by 72–80 % of 2014 respondents to the State of Agile™ Survey [9]. These come close to eliminating what they see as wasteful bureaucratic 'upfront tasks' [7]. As a result, their iterations cannot span a complete waterfall process of problem definition, problem analysis, requirements specification, design, implementation, verification and validation. Problem definition and analysis become folded into iterative requirements identification. Also, verification and validation largely happen through customer use of released software versions.

UCD [10] as standardized as ISO's *Human-Centered Design Process for Interactive Systems* [11], has not made this break from rational engineering design. One small relaxation of a waterfall sequence in [11] was the addition of more flexibility in iteration (originally all phases had to be iterated through, but now any phase can be jumped back to after evaluation). Apart from this ability to jump back to any previous development phase following evaluation, 'Standard' UCD (SUCD [11]) is essentially an extension of rational engineering with human science practices. Investigative human science methods are used for problem definition and analysis (early focus on users and tasks [10]). Experimental human science methods have been adapted for verification and validation (empirical measurement [10]). SUCD is thus not well placed to integrate with popular agile practices, because it depends on a rational engineering design process to provide stable contexts for user-centered analysis and evaluation. Popular agile methodologies remove both these contexts as separate homogeneous development phases, by reducing or removing problem definition and analysis as distinct phases, and by releasing versions of software to clients without prior empirical evaluation.

Most attempts to (re-)integrate UCD within Agile follow the majority of methodologies (i.e., the less popular ones) and require considerable upfront activity before development sprints. Such a 'Sprint 0' recreates the ISO 9241-210 [11] context for problem definition and analysis. Adding empirical evaluation is less straightforward, and has to either occur within the current or a subsequent sprint. The tactic here is to reimpose as much of SUCD as possible. However, this ignores how Agile has been motivated by early delivery of business benefit and the ability to respond promptly to change. To ensure these benefits, the most popular agile methodologies restrict most development work to sprints combining design and implementation [7]. We should not underestimate what is being asked when UCD advocates expect advocates for the most popular agile methodologies to move back towards a waterfall structure, even when it is incremental, iterative or both.

The apparent impasse here is only a problem if we expect the integration of unmodified SUCD with revised popular agile practices to be sufficient to support the design of high quality software. However, it is not clear within popular agile practices or SUCD where design work actually gets done. The former subsume design under implementation, whereas the latter focuses on problem analysis and evaluation of user experiences. Neither have strong distinct approaches to software design.

11.1.1   Add Creative Design Too?

An alternative to simply combining UCD with popular agile practices is a broader flexible balanced integration of engineering, creative and user-focused practices that can be adapted to the specific needs of a software project. Agile and UCD already cover much of the required engineering and user-focused practices. However, creative design practices are not well represented, and the gap between creative and engineering design has widened since the 1960s.

In the 1960s, creative and engineering design appeared to be alignable, and where they were not, the belief was that they could be. This position barely outlasted that decade: design research largely abandoned normative methods for studies of how designers actually worked (method research remained popular in engineering). Over four decades of design research on actual work practices provide insights that should be considered as a basis for effectively integrating UCD and agile practices into a broader high quality development process.

This chapter identifies and reviews three key design insights in the next section, relating them to UCD and agile:

- Creative design work co-evolves problem and solution spaces
- Design materials talk back
- The best design work is generous in scope and intent

These three key insights are primarily based on four decades of published design research. The origins of these insights, which were distilled by the author, are explained in Sect. 11.2. Selected key references (e.g., [2, 3, 10–13]) are related to their historical context. Section 11.3 next revisits the Agile Manifesto's principles [14] from the perspective of these three key insights into creative design practice.

The argument developed below is primarily based on the author's experience as a researcher in an academic design department since 2009, but is also informed by the author's experience of design-lead software development (1981–1996, e.g., [1], a collaborative IFIP Working Group report which is referenced several times below), Critical UCD practice (1995–2011, e.g., [15, 16]) and creative design practice (e.g., [17, 18]). Having worked in software engineering, UCD and creative design contexts, it has been clear that all three contexts bring strengths and weaknesses. These contexts can however be combined to maximize their strengths and minimize their differences. Section 11.4 proposes that this can be explored in the context of an integration of creative, engineering and user-centred design paradigms proposed by this chapter's author, known as BIG Design [18].

11.2   Creative Design Practices

Most people with experience in software development and UCD genuinely and appropriately believe that they know about design. The author was among them for the first quarter century of his software career. On moving into creative design contexts a decade ago, I learned that I didn't know everything about design, and I also learned that much of what I believed about engineering design practices (i.e., the ideals) had little basis in fact (e.g., [12, 13]). Belief in rational engineering design practices remains very widespread and well intentioned. However, it does stand in the way of understanding creative design practices that have served humans well for most of history: creative design practices span millennia, whereas engineering design only spans centuries and UCD only decades. In this chapter, I argue that some difficulties with agile development and UCD, both separately and in combinations, can be overcome by embracing three key creative design practices. I begin with the historical context of design methods research.

The NATO Science Committee conferences on Software Engineering in 1968 and 1969 made software development a focus for rational engineering methods [19]. However, creative design research was several years ahead. A major conference on Systematic and Intuitive Methods in Engineering, Industrial Design, Architecture and Communications had been held in 1962 [20]. From the outset, design methods research had sought to be cross domain, and thus both engineering ('systematic') and creative ('intuitive') design were within scope. However, disillusion and suspicion about systematic methods quickly set in within creative design research. Idealized normative methods were never widely adopted in creative design practice. The NATO Science Committee conferences on Software Engineering were thus going in the opposite direction from creative design research, i.e., aiming to be more systematic and less intuitive.

Design research studies quickly refocused on how designers actually *did* go about their work, rather than on how they *should* do their work. Following Herbert Read's distinction between education into and through art, for Frayling [21] these studies would be research *into* design, i.e., they have design work practices as an object of study. In contrast, earlier design methods research had been research *for* design [21] that aimed to create novel practical knowledge that would be applicable across design work.

In the three decades after the demise of the 1960s Design Methods movement (research *for* design), research *into* design predominated in design research, but with a continued broad range of domains from creative craft practices to technical practices in engineering, with the aim of producing domain independent knowledge (e.g., with engineering, industrial design, architecture and communication design being four specific domains of design practice). Studies of actual engineering design across diverse practices, such as electronics [12] and software [13] revealed that engineering designers move opportunistically between supposedly linear homogeneous phases:

the sudden discovery of new requirements and partial solutions … the immediate development of solutions for newly discovered requirements, and drifting through partial solutions are shown to be important causes of opportunistic design … top-down appears to be a special case for well-structured problems when the designer already knows the correct decomposition [13]

A range of *designerly ways of knowing* [22] were identified as a result of many such case studies. For example, the "immediate development of solutions for newly discovered requirements" and "drifting through partial solutions" in [13] are examples of *co-evolving problem and solution spaces*. However, experiences from decades of research into design have not been fully exploited yet in software engineering research ([13] is largely overlooked). Research *into* design here is part of an area known as *empirical software engineering*, but that "objective study of software processes, … [is] still a science in progress" [7]. The lack of progress here makes software development methodology prone to extremism and dogmatism a half century after design research lost its appetite for normative methodologies, and focused instead on evidence-based understandings of design work, where, for example, Cross identified five strongly evidenced designerly ways of knowing [23]:

1. Designers tackle 'ill-defined' problems.
2. Their mode of problem-solving is 'solution-focused'.
3. Their mode of thinking is 'constructive'.
4. They use 'codes' that translate abstract requirements into concrete objects.
5. They use these codes to both 'read' and 'write' in 'object languages'.

These five aspects can be distilled into two key insights, one related to the design process and the other to design products, i.e.:

• Creative design work co-evolves problem and solution spaces
• Design materials talk back

This reduction of these five aspects into two key insights simplifies the translation of design research into practical applications. Cross first two aspects relate to the co-evolution of problem and solution spaces, as covered in Sect. 11.2.1 below. The ill-defined ('wicked' [2]) nature of design problems is largely addressed by 'solution-focused' practices, which improve designers' understandings of problems through the exploration of possible solutions. This solution focus is constructive (third aspect), i.e., designers "build to think" [24] and is guided by 'codes' that should be understood as being largely tacit, being used generatively to form and realize design ideas (fourth aspect). However, codes also support critique of the outputs of design work, through which design materials 'talk back' (second key insight, Sect. 11.2.2 below).

A third insight is clear in Cross' synthesis on Design Thinking [25], where he provides examples of designers going beyond what was asked for or thought possible.

• The best design work is generous in scope and intent.

This insight is covered in Sect. 11.2.3 below. The three-decade span across Cross' research here [23, 25] emphasizes the extent of design research that underpins our current understandings of creative design practice.

Within creative design research, research *for* design is expected to be compatible with research *into* design across a broad range of design domains. In other words, research for design must be compatible with the results of research into creative design practices. This does not mean that new proposed knowledge and practices in support of creative design should leave it unchanged (there would be no point in that), but it does mean that it should be feasible to incorporate new proposed knowledge and practices. The best way to demonstrate feasibility is through use, which involves Frayling's third mode of research in art and design: research *through* design [21]. Here, practice-based or (practice-led) research applies new proposed knowledge and practices in the context of realistic projects, keeps adequate records, and applies reflection to assess the effectiveness of design practice innovations.

There is thus a longstanding opportunity to integrate not only UCD, but also creative design practices into software development. Furthermore, creative design research brings with it a range of mature knowledge and practices that can accelerate effective innovation in software design practices. The relevance of the three key insights above (co-evolving problems and solutions, talk back, generosity) for the integration of agile development and UCD is now discussed within the broader context of designers' knowledge of artefacts, use and production, including the tacit knowledge implicit in design work, openness to change, reflection in and on action and dealing with uncertainty, instability, uniqueness and value conflicts [23].

11.2.1 Creative Design Work Co-evolves Problem and Solution Spaces

In design research, 1960s 'first generation' design methods were quickly seen as overly simplistic and rigid, and only able to deal with 'tame problems' which can be defined clearly, completely and uncontroversially, in contrast to 'wicked problems' [2], which are much harder to address systematically and rationally.

> The classical systems-approach of the military and the space programs is based on the assumption that a planning project can be organized into distinct phases. Every textbook of systems engineering starts with an enumeration of these phases: "understand the problems or the mission," "gather information," "analyze information," "synthesize information and wait for the creative leap," "work out solution," or the like. For wicked problems, however, this type of scheme does not work. One cannot understand the problem without knowing about its context; one cannot meaningfully search for information without the orientation of a solution concept; one cannot first understand, then solve ([2], p. 162)

Note the last clause: "one cannot first understand then solve". Studies of creative design work have consistently shown that it is not organized sequentially into two rigidly separated high level phases of problem framing and then solution framing (e.g., [26]). Instead, problem and solution spaces co-evolve during creative design work (i.e., all design work that does not address a 'tame problem', which includes much engineering design). This understanding however has not yet become common place in Software Engineering, and thus Meyer scolded popular agile practices for abandoning "normal engineering practice – the practice, in fact, of any rational endeavor – of studying a problem before attempting to solve it" [7]. This assumes that all engineering design is a rational practice, when the evidence is overwhelmingly that this is not so (e.g., [12, 13]). While much engineering design addresses tame problems [2], this does not mean that it does so rationally, i.e., without recourse to creative design practices.

In their analysis of Wicked Problems, Rittel and Webber [2] noted the limitations of rational engineering design, which could handle 'tame problems', but not the complex problems that NASA's PPP (Phased Project Planning) aimed to address. This critique of NASA's influential approaches was repeated over a decade later in the paper that inspired Scrum [3]. However, as idealized engineering design, SUCD aligns with Meyer's assumptions, i.e., that one can first understand then solve [7]. SUCD requires users and tasks to be thoroughly understood before any design work starts [10, 11]. The belief here is that one can "meaningfully search for information without the orientation of a solution concept" [2]. However, the resulting understanding of the problem may have no implications for any solution, since with no orienting solution concept, relevant information is unlikely to be acquired and considered. Put another way, understandings of users and tasks may not be translated into requirements, nor may requirements include criteria for success from a user experience perspective. SUCD has thus found places for itself in rational engineering design, but it has not always been able to do so in ways that systematically, consistently or effectively influence core design and evaluation activities.

Rational engineering exerts a powerful hold over human scientists, who pioneered UCD practices, as well as those who continue to advocate them. Analogies with 'the' scientific method (as in Table 11.1 above) marginalize other conceptualizations of design, especially opportunistic design. Nevertheless, Gould and colleagues [10], who established SUCD's three key principles of usability, eventually reported that they had come to work opportunistically [16]. Although their first principle (early focus on users and tasks) insisted on upfront user studies ahead of any design work, after a decade of applying their principles, they reported that up to 75 % of their user-centred activities had become focused on usage of the current version of working software in the field [16]. This is exactly what would happen in agile practice. Even so, Gould and colleagues continued to insist that their three key principles for usability had stood the test of time over almost two decades.

SUCD is philosophically opposed to opportunistic co-evolution of problems and solutions, even though the latter is the reality confirmed by studies of design work [12, 13]. In contrast, rational engineering design remains an ideal (apart from when dealing with tractable 'tame problems' [2]). Given this, agile development is potentially more open to creative design practices than SUCD, but not totally open. Agile has simply increased the pace of iteration, largely by reducing development work to agreeing a task list for the next sprint, implementing the agreed features on this list, and then delivering what Scrum calls a 'potentially shippable product' to the client [7]. Requirements under consideration are thus phased and frozen (the closed-window rule, [7]). The difference between agile iterations and those within previous structured methods is largely down to the length of the sprint. While this is a conceptually small difference, it brings considerable benefits, especially the ability to evolve requirements and to receive rapid verification and validation feedback from software in actual use. However, the closed window rule (no changes to requirements during sprints) will limit co-evolution of problem and solution spaces. Requirements discovered during design and implementation [13] cannot be acted on during the particular sprint or iteration where they were discovered without breaking the closed window rule.

While agile methodologies have distanced themselves from the impossible norms of rational engineering, they have not completely cut themselves free. Lean has a preference for making decisions as late as possible when all necessary information is available [7], mirroring the UCD belief that one must first understand before any attempt is made to solve. Similarly, Scrum's co-creator Jeff Sutherland has written that not until "the customer need is clear" do "you write the minimal lines of code to meet the defined need" [27]. How this can happen in the absence of upfront tasks is unclear: perhaps clarity on 'the customer need' is left to the product owner role in Scrum (if so, this will only work for 'tame problems' within the product owner's experience, since by definition only tame problems can be correctly specified in advance of design and implementation [2]).

The first problem for the most popular agile processes as regards problem-solution co-evolution is that they continue to separate problem focused activities from solution focused implementation. Each iteration can become a truncated waterfall sequence (especially where Kanban boards are used [7]). Thus neither SUCD nor agile methodologies are compatible with creative design practices that impose no constraints on co-evolution of problem and solution spaces. A flexible balanced integration of engineering, creative and user-focused design and evaluation practices requires minimal constraints on co-evolution of problem and solution spaces [25]. If co-evolution of problem and solution spaces is constrained, then so are creative design practices, since these have been identified to be the only ones that are capable of handling the complexity inherent in 'wicked problems' [2]. The appropriate balance of foci on problem and solution framing is project specific. Methodologies should not impose specific balances of activities, either by focusing overly on problem analysis or on solution synthesis. Agile methodologies tend to be biased towards the latter as a result of adverse experiences with overemphasis on problem analysis. What has not been considered is that both problem and solution spaces can be developed in parallel.

A second problem specific to popular agile practices arises from the truncation of the waterfall phase sequence (due to the near removal of upfront activities [7, 8]), which largely discards problem focused activities, which are seen as sources of 'waste' in popular agile methods (lean approaches avoid waste [7]). Solutions (as working software) are preferred over understandings to drive the development process forward. However, understandings are still important, but there are few representations of these in popular agile methods, where only solutions are visible, not problems. The resulting ad hoc solutions are "no substitute for serious requirements and design" [7].

Even when an agile activity represents some aspects of a problem space, these can disappear. For example, an early explicit form for *User Stories* (developed at Connextra, one of the earliest adopters of Extreme Programming [28]) – "As a *<role>*, I want *<goal/desire>* so that *<benefit>*" – covers benefits, beneficiaries (roles) and work goals/desires related to these. However, "so that *<benefit>*" can be dropped and goals/desires are expressed as system capabilities, and not the actual goals or desires of an appropriate role. Also, roles can be reduced to 'user' [29] and thus lose contextual specificity. User stories can thus be reduced to "user wants *<feature>*", which ignores the problem space. It is simply *<feature>*.

Similarly, if both test-driven development and Scrum's "definition of done" [7] remain narrowly technical within the solution space, then opportunities to integrate problem space insights will be missed. Software may thus pass internal quality checks, but not deliver value for the customer or user. Here the lack of a high level holistic overview will direct attention away from anticipating the consequences of design decisions.

This raises issues with the Agile manifesto [14], which values 'working software over comprehensive documentation'. As with all four clauses of the manifesto, value in the latter is recognised, but the former is valued more ('over'). This begs the question of how valuing is demonstrated, which must be either through people, places or things. That aside, it is not clear how popular agile practices and roles value documentation, comprehensive or otherwise. Popular agile methods are overly focused on the solution space as working code. The same applies to the Agile manifesto's valuing of 'responding to change over following a plan' [14]. While the manifesto's authors may well have rigid waterfall methodologies in mind here, and the plans that came with them, a backlog of user stories is still a plan of sorts. It is of course expected to change, but with limited, if any, evidence of the value that these user stories address, responding to changes is likely to be inevitable, rather than valued. Furthermore, the idea of 'changing requirements' introduces the danger of blaming inadequate problem framing on some mythical change to a world that has not changed. Related to this, valuing 'customer collaboration over contract negotiation' [14] can constrain the customer's role to agreement on solutions without prior agreement on problems.

In contrast, creative design practices can support an appropriate balance of co-evolving problem and solution focused activities, tracked through a 'brief' in project contexts with minimal contractual detail or constraints. Creative design has always valued customer collaboration over contract negotiation, to the extent that potential customers who are overly focused on contractual details are unlikely to become customers. Partnership with clients is fundamental to successful creative design practice. In the UK, IT, software and computer services [30] are:

> The largest constituent part of the Creative Industries, accounting for 43.5 per cent of the Creative Industries GVA [Gross Value Added].

Although software is regarded as a creative industry in many countries' national statistics, its customer relationships are not always the same as those in areas such as advertising, design and media. Customer relationships can place constraints on the adoption of some creative design practices.

Evolving creative design briefs (that are often presentations rather than documents) can track dynamic understandings of problems alongside solutions. This makes problem-solution co-evolution a meaningful reality, rather than an imagined ideal. Such briefs are evidenced via, and supported by, a range of explicit representations such as sketches, with a range of formats from rough to highly finished. Sketching is fundamental to creative design practice [31]. Sketching can be practiced in ways that both co-evolve and integrate problem and solution spaces. While sketches (e.g., wireframes) and prototypes are used in agile practices, the key point here is that in creative design they typically develop the understanding of the problem as well as the solution. To benefit fully from the creative potential of sketching, it must not be restricted to refining solutions.

As already stated, requirements are the essential wall between problem analysis and solution synthesis in rational engineering, but this wall constrains the ways in which problem and solution spaces can be integrated and overlapped. The question thus arises about the nature of requirements in a context of co-evolving problem and solution spaces. The answer is that requirements have a limited role, if any, in such contexts. Instead, an evolving brief tracks both problem and solution spaces, with no need for a wall in between:

- What we believe we should be trying to achieve?
- What we intend to develop as a solution?

Either of these can be considered as the requirements, i.e., what must be achieved or what will be developed. User stories in agile methodologies can bridge between both, but only if roles and goals/desires are present and valid. Creative design briefs have the advantage of maintaining coherent understandings of problem and solution spaces, whereas user stories fragment the latter and may delete the former from view.

Sketches and related documentation and presentations support *argumentation*. Rittel and Webber advocated 'second generation' design methods based on argumentation rather than rational planning [2]. Argumentation is essential given the unique nature of wicked problems, which have to be understood and resolved within their specific contexts. Argumentation can deliver *Design Rationales* through conversations between people and the materials of a design situation [32]. This leads into the second key insight from research *into* creative design (Design Materials Talk Back). Before turning to this second insight, the complex discussion of co-evolving problem and solution spaces above is now summarised:

- Rational engineering needs requirements to form a wall between problem analysis and solution synthesis.

- SUCD has a limited role in formation and use of requirements, despite its rational philosophy. SUCD both depends on, and is disempowered by, rational engineering design.
- In creative design, problem analysis and solution synthesis co-evolve. Studies of design work indicate that much design work is creative. Only 'tame problems' are amenable to rational design.
- Evolving briefs (largely) replace requirements in creative design. Developing the brief is one of the most critical activities in creative design. Evolving briefs maintain coherent understandings of both problem and solution spaces.
- The appropriate balance of efforts for problem analysis and solution synthesis is project specific. Methodologies should not impose specific balances of activities, especially ones that focus overly on problem analysis or solution synthesis.
- Popular agile practices are overly focused on the solution space, perhaps exclusively so. Agile practices retain many features of rational engineering design, constraining co-evolution of problem and solution spaces.
- Making room for the co-existence of engineering, creative and UCD must allow co-evolution of problem and solution spaces and their continuous integration. Rational engineering blocks this via requirements specifications, which close down opportunities for integrating problem analysis and solution synthesis.

Co-evolution of problem and solution spaces is the fundamental characteristic of creative design work. It inevitably requires complex analysis, which further complicates the relationships between creative practices, engineering and UCD. However, engaging with this complexity is necessary to provide a foundation for balancing and integrating three distinct approaches to design work (i.e., engineering, UCD and creative practices). The other two key insights into the nature of creative design are more straightforward.

11.2.2 Design Materials Talk Back

The rationality of normative engineering design makes it very attractive, and it is thus defended vigorously by its advocates (e.g., Meyer's defense of 'upfront tasks' [7], and Gould and colleagues' inability to acknowledge the value of creative opportunistic actions over planned rational ones [16]). The rapid demise of the Design Methods movement did not influence Herb Simon until his third edition of his *Sciences of the Artificial* [33], 24 years after Rittel and Webber [2]. By then, Simon embraced the possibility of goal-less designing, which occurs for solution-led co-evolution in creative design (e.g., [34]). Before that, frustration with the tenacity of the idea of rational design had already led Donald Schön to confront Simon and other rationalists with the realities of creative reflective professional work [35].

Schön's *Reflective Practitioner* [35] extended known opportunistic behaviours in creative design to a range of professions (hence two educational references for this chapter: [36, 37]). In contrast to Rittel and Webber's conceptualization of design as *argumentation* [2], Schön conceptualised design as reflective *conversation with the materials of a design situation* [32]. Argumentation is externally oriented, whereas reflection is internally oriented. Reflection happens at different points in design work. Reflection *during* design activities (e.g., sketching) is reflection *in* action. Reflection *at the end* of a block of design work is reflection *on* action.

Studies of sketching show repeatedly that they are not simply mute passive externalisations of possible design solutions, but instead 'talk-back' to the designer [25]. Far from simply recording ideas, sketches typically lead to new idea generation. During sketching, designers can reflect *in* action on either the solution space, the problem space, or both. This nudges forward the co-evolution of problem and solution framing.

Schön [32] generalised beyond sketching to any materials of a design situation. Any artefact formed during design work is capable of talking back, and in this sense, they are not wasteful (especially rough sketchy ones), even when customers never see them (working sketches get tidied up and 'rationalized' for presentations).

Popular agile methodologies value working code as the main material of their design situations. Code can undoubtedly 'talk back' (especially when it does not work), but conversations here are expected to remain within the solution space. This is due to an expectation that problems with interpretations of a relevant requirements should not arise once coding is underway, as 'requirements must be straight before coding' starts [27]). Once working code is in customer use, the code cannot talk back directly, but is instead mediated by customer use and feedback. This introduces a distance between the software designer and the main material of their design situation. Such distance is often helpful, prompting both Schön's reflection *on* action [35], and the later extension to reflection *for* action [36]. However, the quality of software released to the customer can be much improved through continuous reflection *in* action. A UCD mindset here is likely to improve that of software developers who are exclusively focused on the internal quality [1] of their work. This again raises issues with the Agile manifesto [14] and its valuing of 'individuals and interactions over processes and tools'. In the absence of UCD experts within an agile team, UCD processes and tools can help software developers to focus on external quality [1]. Again, processes and tools that are not (fully) present are not (really) valued, so the test of the Agile manifesto's recognition of value in the latter ('processes and tools') is their manifestation in design work. What is clear here is that, in Schön's terms, popular agile methodologies have restricted the materials of their default design situations, by limiting documentation and other non-code resources. This restricts the range of conversations that are possible within agile design work to ones with code, wireframes and similar informal representations, plus whatever reflection on action occurs within *retrospectives* [7]. Refactoring often results from retrospectives, but is largely restricted to code, whereas many other design materials could also be profitably refactored after a run of sprints (e.g., personas).

UCD methods clearly add materials to design situations, such as personas, scenarios and user test results, all of which could extend the range of possible design team conversations. However, quality standards for UCD materials typically reflect human science values, reporting facts about users, tasks and user experiences. Such materials can 'talk at' rather than 'talk back' unless software developers have been involved in creating them, since materials primarily talk back to their (co-)creators.

In summary, popular agile methodologies constrain the range of materials for a design situation, and UCD can limit their ability to talk back. This raises two questions:

1. What design materials, are needed to support creative reflection in, on and for action [35, 36], in addition to code and resources from valuable UCD practices?
2. How can broad agile teams be involved in the creation and use of design materials in ways that maximize their 'backtalk' (talking back) across the whole team.

To answer the first of these questions, John Heskett identified four sources of design outcomes in his introductory overview on design [38]:

> The forms and structures of the immediate world we inhabit are overwhelmingly the outcome of human design. ... The human factor is present in decisions taken at all levels in design. ... Choice implies alternatives in how ends can be achieved, for what purposes, and for whose advantage. ... also ... by what means we can evaluate their effect or benefit.

The four sources of design outcomes in the above are:

1. *artefacts* ("how ends can be achieved"),
2. *purpose* ("ends"),
3. *beneficiaries* ("for whose advantage"),
4. *evaluations* ("by what means we can evaluate their effect or benefit").

Each of these four sources of design outcome above is a *design arena* that contributes specific materials to a design situation. In the most popular agile methods, the artefact is simply working code and the beneficiary is simply the customer. However, neither purpose nor evaluation are well represented as design arenas. At best, purpose will be scattered across dozens of user stories as disparate goals or desires. Software testing is not evaluation, nor is quality assessment. Neither agile nor UCD have well focused comprehensive approaches to evaluation [15], since they do not e-valu-ate, i.e., identify achieved value. Instead they typically identify flaws in software artefacts or usage. By inserting hyphens in the word e-valu-ate, we make it clear that e-valu-ation must focus on value, and not just defects or correctness.

In terms of design arenas, agile development does well with *artefacts*. UCD does well with *beneficiaries*. UCD and agile development include basic *evaluation*. Neither are strong on *purpose*, a design arena where creative design can excel. This leads into the third key insight from research *into* creative design (The Best Design Work is Generous in Scope and Intent, see below), but before turning to this, we will consider initial answers to the two questions.

1. What design materials, are needed to support creative reflection in, on and for action, in addition to code and resources from valuable UCD practices?
2. How can broad agile teams be involved in the creation and use of design materials in ways that maximize their 'backtalk' (talking back) across the whole team.

In answer to the first, the design materials required must span all four design arenas, i.e., artefacts, beneficiaries, purpose and evaluations. They must span these in such a way that the achieved balance is appropriate for a specific project. Together, the materials and practices across these four design arenas are genuinely *things* in the sense of *assemblies* (as in Old Norse: *þing* [thing]) a sense used extensively in Binder and colleagues' [39] conceptualization of design situations as *Design Things*.

Conversations with all design materials should be possible, and referring back to the second question above, agile team members need to be involved in their creation and use in ways that maximize their 'backtalk' across the whole team. To achieve this, team members' competences should be broad enough to engage in worthwhile conversations with a broad enough range of design materials. Scrum's origins in Takeuchi and Nonaka's "new new product development game" [3] are relevant here. An example from Epson in [3] shared an expectation that team members be well versed in two technological fields (e.g., mechanical and electronics) and two functional areas (e.g., marketing and design). Scrum's three roles are not configured to achieve such breadth, and thus Scrum misses some key guidance in the paper where it found its name.

11.2.3 The Best Design Work Is Generous in Scope and Intent

Agile development and UCD assume respectively that customers and users will be the main source of requirements and constraints. As with all engineering work, the aim is to deliver an optimal solution that best meets specified requirements. Failure can take several forms, such as total failure (delivering nothing), exceeding budget, or not meeting requirements (excessive change of scope, unsatisfactory solution delivered). For the latter, meeting requirements optimally is the best outcome possible. Cross [25] reveals how different creative design practice is here, quoting the architect Sir Dennis Lasdun, for whom an architect's job was to give the client (in the gendered language of his day):

> Not what he wants but what he never dreamed that he wanted; and when he gets it, he recognizes it as something he wanted all the time.

Cross further demonstrates the importance of designers' *generosity* with the example of Kenneth Grange, founding partner of the renowned interdisciplinary design consultancy Pentagram (before SUCD existed). When given a brief to restyle the top of the range Frister and Rossman sewing machine, he also independently redesigned it for use (1970/1). Grange reasoned through the usage issues with the sewing machine and added his own alternative brief to the one from the client, Maruzen Sewing Machine Co. (Osaka [25]). With considerable hesitation, he presented his design responses to both briefs ("restyling" and "for use") and his uncommissioned design was enthusiastically accepted.

What distinguishes creative design from rational engineering here is the urge to always exceed requirements, enabling goals and meeting desires that customers and users may never have been able to articulate. The best creative design work delights and surprises, delivering value that cannot even be imagined until an outstanding solution is presented. It extends the envisaged scope of a project, at acceptable additional cost, beyond all original intentions.

Simply meeting the requirements of others, even optimally, is a mark of failure in creative design. It indicates laziness and indifference in problem framing, by never moving beyond customers' requirements once they become clear enough for a design team to proceed.

It is generosity rather than creativity that results in the best design work. Creativity is a means to an end, and not an end in itself. A unique selling point (USP) sells by being valuable, not by being unique (the latter only creates attractiveness relative to the competitors). True ends have to be valuable in their own right, and not just as means to ends. 'Creativity' is a word that is not often heard in creative design contexts. Creativity as a concept postdates the Second World War, with origins in psychometrics. Much loved by innovation coaches with their 'creativity methods', it is overly associated with the generation of ideas ('ideation') within the design arena of artefacts. Focusing creativity techniques on requirements can produce improvements for agile teams (e.g., [40]), but this will not make full use of creative design practice across a project.

Ideation is understood (often tacitly) to be required in all design arenas. The relationship between *generosity* and creative practices lies within the design arena of purpose. Development processes have to make room for this and not limit creative work to the design arena of artefacts. Innovation in all design arenas, and in their integration, is required for innovative digital products and services. Thus innovation can result from new creative approaches to not only artefacts and purpose, but also to the design arenas of beneficiaries and evaluations.

To summarise this third key insight from creative design research:

- Generosity is the designer's creative expansion of design purpose, and is the mark of the best design (by increasing achieved value beyond expected value).
- Popular agile practices restrict design purpose to requirements from customers and users that are accepted as user stories in project backlogs.
- UCD restricts design purpose to empirically validated user needs and wants.

Generosity is a subjective biased first person phenomenon. Ideally, agile practices and UCD requirements are objective real third person phenomena. Seasoned software developers may understand that this is not the case, and expect requirements to be contested, but will nevertheless prefer to work to the objective requirements of others. Rational values guide us to prefer objective requirements, but delivering what was asked for can result in customer disbelief and be seen as neglectful (when it has been clear that a solution will be inadequate, even if it delivers on its specifications). Disbelief and neglect are high prices to pay for objectivity. Generous design purpose replaces neglect with care, and disbelief with delight. It is outcomes that matter, not inputs. If bias and subjectivity are the price to pay for outstanding design, then so be it.

11.3   Revisiting the Agile Manifesto

Rittel and Webber [2] broke free from the constraints of rational engineering design almost three decades before agile methods moved less far in the same direction. The last decade of design research has witnessed consolidation and syntheses within design research that were not widely available when the Agile Manifesto was drawn up [14]. The three key insights from creative design research introduced and discussed in Sect. 11.2 in relation to agile and UCD expose limitations for the Agile Manifesto's 12 principles. These limitations will now be discussed, with principles referred to using numbers based on their order of presentation in http://www.agilemanifesto.org/principles.html, e.g. "Simplicity – the art of maximizing the amount of work not done – is essential" is the tenth principle listed.

11.3.1   Creative Design Work Co-evolves Problem and Solution Spaces

Principles 2 and 11 in the Agile Manifesto [14] are relevant to this first key insight.

- Welcome changing requirements, even late in development. Agile processes harness change for the customer's competitive advantage (Principle 2).
- The best architectures, requirements, and designs emerge from self-organizing teams (Principle 11).

With respect to Principle 2, changing requirements are inevitable when problem and solution spaces co-evolve. However, requirements remain rooted in rational engineering design in the sense that they create a wall between problem and solution spaces. Creative design can and does do without requirements, opening up a much wide space for design work through briefs. This is not to say that there are no goals, imperatives or constraints in creative design, but these are simply aspects of the problem space that shape the solution space. Generalizing goals, imperatives and constraints to 'requirements' does not add value, nor does it improve a designer's understanding of their work. Rather than 'solve problems', creative designers are more likely to exploit new opportunities for solutions or reframe problems. Dorst [41] has shown through extensive analyses of innovation case studies that generous problem (re)framing is a key driver in innovation. Solving other people's problems is rarely innovative, and an innovative solution by definition has to provide more customer value than solving 'tame problems' [2].

Takeuchi and Nonaka associated their "new new product development" [3], which inspired Scrum, with six characteristics. One is *overlapping development phases* [3], which is more general than simply being open to changing requirements. It is a much broader basis that allows problem and solution spaces to co-evolve. As with Rittel and Webber [2], Takeuchi and Nonaka [3] were directly critical of NASA-style Phased Project Planning. No agile methodology has yet fully endorsed concurrent work across all four design arenas (chopping out early 'upfront' phases is not enough here, nor is it wise). Takeuchi and Nonaka's important characteristic of "new new product development" [3] is thus ignored.

In contrast, a second of the six characteristics in [3], *self-organizing project teams*, is not ignored in the Agile manifesto. It is directly included in Principle 11, which is wholly focused on the solution space, and can only include aspects of a problem space when requirements are expressed by rich user stories (i.e., not "user wants <feature>"). However, other characteristics from [3] constrain the scope for a team's self-organisation. A third characteristic, *multilearning*, has to apply to innovative multifunctional teams [3], requiring multiple expertise for each team member. A multifunctional team is not formed of members with identical skills, but instead has the range of expertise required for all aspects of product development. Any agile methodology with only three team roles (e.g., Scrum) inevitably constrains the possibilities for multilearning unless team members are developed to become appropriately multifunctional. Multilearning requires all four design arenas to be regularly in focus. Simplicity is not a virtue in this context. A fourth of Takeuchi and Nonaka's characteristics [3], *built-in instability*, also constrains the scope for a team's self-organization. Paraphrasing Karl Marx (The Eighteenth Brumaire of Louis Bonaparte[1]):

> teams organize themselves, but they do not self-organise as they please; they do not self-organise under self-selected circumstances, but under circumstances formed around them

The overall verdict for Principles 2 and 11 that arises from design research on problem-solution co-evolution (and also arising from [3]) is that agile methodologies have yet to fully embrace co-evolution of problem and solution spaces and the multiple expertise that this requires. UCD is better on multiple expertise, but not good enough. User perspectives are necessary for design success, but not sufficient. Users are not the only beneficiaries: customers also need to be understood. Principles 2 and 11 thus need to be revised e.g. as:

- (2) Welcome more generous innovations, even late in development. Agile processes harness generosity for the customer's competitive advantage.
- (11) The most worthwhile software results from highly capable multifunctional teams who challenge themselves more than their customers ever can.

---

[1]"Men make their own history, but they do not make it as they please; they do not make it under self-selected circumstances, but under circumstances existing already."

11.3.2   Design Materials Talk Back

Five principles in the Agile Manifesto [14] are relevant to this second key insight.

- Deliver working software frequently, from a couple of weeks to a couple of months, with a preference to the shorter timescale (Principle 3).
- Business people and developers must work together daily throughout the project (Principle 4).
- The most efficient and effective method of conveying information to and within a development team is face-to-face conversation (Principle 6).
- Continuous attention to technical excellence and good design enhances agility (Principle 9).
- At regular intervals, the team reflects on how to become more effective, then tunes and adjusts its behavior accordingly (Principle 12).

With respect to Principle 3, frequent delivery of software enables frequent field evaluation for UCD, but when the closed window principle [7] applies, this can restrict how design materials talk back (which will impede co-evolution of problem and solution spaces). To reduce delay on acting on new insights or feedback, sprints need to be short: long delays before acting on new insights or feedback will result in some combination of wasteful development activity, loss of insights, or poor organizational memory as the nature and implications of feedback fade.

With respect to Principle 4, only XP [7] has committed to attempting this (although DSDM [42] supports it in a more nuanced way), and it has not been effective. However, it will not favour co-evolution of problem and solution spaces if the value of input coming on a daily basis from customers and product owners is reduced by delays that result in loss of organizational memory (Principle 3 above). The closed window rule would create delays here when the 'pigs and chickens' principle[2] applies (the language has changed in Scrum, but not the principle [43]). Scrum team members are 'pigs' who are 'committed to the project', whereas no-one else is: the 'chickens' here are only 'simply involved'. Daily input here is not expected to change the course of a sprint, or even the burn down order for a backlog. Unless all stakeholders can 'talk back', be listened to and respond, then neither UCD nor creative design can contribute fully to agile development. The author's experience on commercial UCD led work is that daily changes to software and websites are possible in immediate response to user testing. The key words in Principle 4 are 'work together' (i.e., not 'work for'), so self-organizing teams. (Principle 11) should be generous with who is and is not in the team.

Another shortcoming of Principle 4 is its constraints on multilearning [3] through its restriction to business and developer roles. With additional roles to support UCD and creative design work, more valuable use of daily customer and product owner

---

[2]The Chicken and the Pig business tale is about commitment to a project. To make ham and eggs, a pig is sacrificed to provide ham and a chicken provides eggs, but survives: the pig is fully committed, while the chicken is only partially involved, yet both are needed.

time is possible, e.g., through paper prototyping by a visual designer or co-design with a UCD expert.

Principle 6 is wrong. If it were true, then humans would never have developed writing or imagery. The effectiveness of a communication medium depends on context [44]. Conveying information is often not enough. It has to be understood, remembered, recalled and acted on. There are a whole range of design materials, such as personas, scenarios and user test feedback from UCD, that have to be read and discussed. The quality of backtalk will typically be higher with persistent materials, in comparison to ephemeral conversation, where focused sustained reflection is not possible [44]. The expression "conveying information" indicates too simple an understanding of design, ignoring the need for argumentation and conversation:

> The successful completion of most tasks involving more than one individual requires both conveyance and convergence processes, thus communication performance will be improved when individuals use a variety of media to perform a task, rather than just one medium [44].

Interaction Design reference materials such as Style Guides (e.g., iOS, Windows, Android) cannot be replaced by face-to-face conversation. Project goals, imperatives or constraints also need to be documented and referred to on a regular basis.

Principle 9 begs the question of what agile practices would be without technical excellence and good design. As with creativity above, there is a confusion between means and ends here. Agility and technical excellence should be means to good design, and both only have value in so far as they do result in good design. This begs a further question of what constitutes 'good design'. The current consensus from creative design practice is often summarized as 'design thinking' [24, 25, 45]. There are various accounts of what this involves. Brown [24] presents a compact set of principles:

1. Hit the streets
2. Recruit T-shaped people
3. Build to think
4. The prototype tells a story
5. Design is never done

The last design thinking principle here relates to the co-evolution of problem and solution spaces. The other four all enrich design materials beyond code and associated Scrum artefacts such as task boards. The first two refer to knowledge and expertise relevant to the design arenas of beneficiaries and purpose. The second requires team members with a primary upright of expertise and a cross bar that allows them to work effectively with other experts (the upright and cross bar form a 'T'). This relates to multilearning [3], since T-Shaped people can learn more because by definition they know and understand more: new learning has to be grafted onto existing knowledge. The third and fourth design thinking principles require materials other than code, such as paper or card prototypes, or video envisionment. The resulting conversations with materials here advance both problem and solution spaces. No agile methodology explicitly promotes any of the design thinking principles above.

The first principle, *Hit the streets*, could be regarded as a source of upfront waste. If Scrum's three roles are enough, then *T-shaped people* are unnecessary (Scrum Masters can glue the crossbar of the Product Owner to an upright of developers). There is no need to Build to think, because no-one codes to work out requirements [27]. Prototypes in agile development may be primarily seen as a way to firm up requirements, not to tell stories about envisaged experiences. Lastly, design is done in agile development, by definition!

Principle 12 in the Agile manifesto is compatible with reflective activities, as advocated by Schön [35]. However, the focus should not only be on becoming more effective at completing sprints, but should also address design quality and the achievement of design purpose.

Overall, consideration of these five Agile manifesto [14] principles that are relevant to conversations with the materials of a design situation reinforce agile's practices imbalance across design arenas, which result from an excessive focus on implementation at the expense of innovative design and evaluation of achieved worth [18]. The result is a narrow range of team roles and design materials, which can only limit the achievable quality from an agile development process. Principles 3, 4, 6, 9 and 12 thus need to be revised, e.g., as:

- (3) Deliver demonstrably worthwhile software frequently, from a couple of weeks to a couple of months, with a preference for shorter timescales.
- (4) A multifunctional team, with the appropriate range of expertise for the project, must work together regularly throughout the project.
- (6) Use face-to-face conversation when it is the most efficient and effective method of conveying information to and within a development team: otherwise complement it with appropriate persistent communication media.
- (9) 'Good design' and technical excellence are means to the higher end of demonstrably worthwhile software. Both are wasteful if they do not deliver demonstrable worth.
- (12) At regular intervals, teams reflect on how to become more effective at demonstrating worth, tune and adjust their behaviour accordingly, and commit to developing further critical creative resources required for generous innovation.

11.3.3   The Best Design Work Is Generous in Scope and Intent

Five principles in the Agile Manifesto are relevant to this third key insight.

- Our highest priority is to satisfy the customer through early and continuous delivery of valuable software (Principle 1).
- Build projects around motivated individuals. Give them the environment and support they need, and trust them to get the job done (Principle 5).
- Working software is the primary measure of progress (Principle 7).

- Agile processes promote sustainable development. The sponsors, developers, and users should be able to maintain a constant pace indefinitely (Principle 8).
- Simplicity – the art of maximizing the amount of work not done – is essential (Principle 10).

Principle 1 begs the question of what 'valuable' means here. There are no agile practices that explicitly address value, so the assumption must be that understanding and communicating the nature of relevant 'business' value is a task for customers or product owners. Support from mainstream software engineering for value foci is limited and mostly postdates the Agile Manifesto (e.g., [46]). However, within HCI, there has been work on value-sensitive design for two decades [47]. The initial ethical focus here has widened, and broader worth-focused approaches have developed in the intersection between HCI and creative design research [48]. Agile methodologies however were ahead of both SUCD and software engineering in recognizing the primacy of value in software quality. To deliver on this insight however, problem framing activities need to be properly resourced and focused on value, as do evaluation activities [15]. SUCD evaluation has been overly focused on quality in use criteria, without reference to the value that is achieved in relation to user effort expended. With respect to the Principle 7, 'working' must mean more than passing tests for functional correctness. Achieved value must be demonstrated in use, which is the proper context for every 'definition of done'. Better still, worth, as the balance of achieved benefits over actual costs and risks [48], should be demonstrated. Both positive and negative value need to be considered.

Principle 5 begs another question, that of what individuals are motivated to do and what 'get the job done' means here. To be consistent with the best creative design, doing the job is not enough. Individuals need to be motivated to delight and surprise, not just deliver. Takeuchi and Nonaka [3] identified a fifth characteristic of "new new product development", *subtle control* that is used by senior management to motivate and direct teams in the right direction, steering them to add value beyond explicit requirements from customers.

Related to this, Principle 8 is also wishful thinking. Delivering value is often time sensitive [3, 7]. Teams can still prepare time estimates, but this does not rule out periods of unsustainable development effort. Some sprints will really have to sprint [7].

Lastly, Principle 10 introduces the risks of lost opportunities. There is no inherent virtue in simplicity, so here again means are treated as ends. Generous design does not avoid work. Waste results from the unnecessary, not the additional, as captured by Anontine de Saint Exupéry [49]:

Il semble que la perfection soit atteinte non quand il n'y a plus rien à ajouter, mais quand il n'y a plus rien à retrancher
  ... perfection is finally attained not when there is no longer anything to add, but when there is no longer anything to take away. (Lewis Galantière's translation).

Overall, consideration of the five Agile manifesto principles that are relevant to generosity in design again highlight agile practices' excessive focus on team comfort and implementation at the expense of innovative design. While Principle

1's focus on value was innovative at the time for software, agile methodologies largely rely on customers and product owners both to define value and to assess its achievement. Principles 1, 5, 7, 8 and 10 thus need to be revised, e.g., as:

- (1) Our highest priority is to satisfy all target beneficiaries through early and continuous delivery of demonstrably worthwhile software innovations.
- (5) Build projects around motivated competent multiskilled individuals. Give them the resources that they need, and trust them to delight and surprise.
- (7) Achieved worth is the primary measure of progress
- (8) Development pace should be appropriate for customer needs and available affordable resources.
- (9) Generosity – the drive to maximize unexpected worth – is essential.

11.3.4   Agile as a Stepping Stone to BIG Design

Issues with popular agile methodologies are so extensive that they are unlikely to survive in their minimal forms. The realities of software development force teams to augment and adapt all 'textbook' practices, agile or otherwise. This introduces the risk of teams reinventing the wheel. If the bulk of the work in getting agile methodologies to work happens outside of the methodology, then public resources can better support this adaptation work.

Difficulties in integrating UCD within agile development are not the only issue with agile methods, nor are they necessarily the most important. The most popular agile methods currently are those that are most focused on implementation and most hostile to upfront tasks. As a result, *all* inputs to a design process are obstructed by the most popular agile methods, and not just UCD inputs from user studies and evaluations. The way forward is thus to loosen up popular agile practices to all design inputs, and not just to UCD. Richard Banks [50] has stressed the openness of creative design practice:

> I'm a strong believer that inspiration comes from many sources, any of which can lead to strong ideas.

Truly empowered self-organizing teams can decide which inputs to design are relevant for their projects, without obstruction from a narrowly defined sprint structure. The primary measure of progress is how these inputs influence and shape design moves that result in worthwhile software innovations.

The main value of agile development is that it has abandoned some core principles of engineering design as rationalized by NASA and others into waterfall process stages, which has opened up software design to more creative design practices, including those covered in accounts of Design Thinking [24, 45]. If this opportunity can be seized, then appropriate room will be also made for UCD (subject to design and engineering values, rather than to human science values) alongside other design inputs such as respectful ethics, sustainability, business goals, participative design and new technological opportunities and creative trends. Following [3], the only way to efficiently achieve this is to allow overlapping activities [18] that accelerate the co-evolution of problem framing and solution development. This follows because as the activities across design arenas expand, it becomes absolutely infeasible to manage them within separate sequential waterfall process stages.

The potential chaos of concurrent development activities can be managed through the ideas of design arenas, which distill Heskett's [38] understanding of the sources of design outcomes. Four design arenas result, two primarily in the problem space (purpose and beneficiaries) and two primarily in the solution space (artefacts and evaluations). Integration is achieved when elements of one design arena inhabit both problem and solution spaces, for example:

- *Evaluation* criteria derived from design *purpose*
- *Artefact* features based on users' (*beneficiaries*) preferences and capabilities
- *Evaluation* results causally related to *artefact* features and qualities
- Design *purpose* grounded in stakeholder (*beneficiary*) goals

There is an opportunity here to move Agile even further away from rational engineering design by incorporating all four design arenas distilled from Heskett [38] into the work of sprints. The motivation here is that Agile has not abandoned enough of the constraints of rational engineering design. Embracing creative design practices would move Agile from tacit and partially understood understandings of creative design to explicit and expert exploitation of their potential.

Design arenas can be used to balance and extend agile development by maintaining backlogs for all four design arenas, with commitment made to burn down from one or more in each sprint, especially for cross arena connections. For examples, backlogs for purpose and beneficiaries can be related to uncertainties due to ungrounded assumptions (as in Lean UX [51]). Grounding of these assumptions, and proof of any associated hypotheses, provides a 'definition of done' for purpose and beneficiary design arenas. Just as code has to be designed and implemented, so too do evaluation studies. Interim 'definitions of done' are needed for the design and scheduling of evaluation and beneficiary studies. All UCD studies can have their own associated backlogs. However, the final 'definition of done' needs to be reserved for successful integration of design inputs with the current artefact. Some activities here will never meet this final 'definition of done', but this needs to be accepted as a cost of creative design. Activity level waste needs to be offset against the overall gain from all activities within a design arena. It is inevitable in creative work that many activities will not fully deliver on expectations. The value of work on design inputs thus needs to be assessed holistically. Gains from successful activities need to offset the costs of ones that turn out to only result in waste.

All agile activities need to be extended in principle to cover all four design arenas, for example definitions of done, sprint planning, task boards, sprint activities, burndown, delivery to the customer and retrospectives. The last activity here is of particular importance for meeting final 'definitions of done', as the whole team needs to be involved in identifying and tying up loose ends here. Conversations and argumentation, supported by appropriate integrating materials such as worth maps and sketches [48] are key to maximizing meeting final 'definitions of done'.

Refactoring also has to extend beyond the artefact to all four design arenas. If resources within a sprint can be dedicated to restructuring code, for example to reduce adverse feature interactions or to improve run-time performance, then resources with a sprint can also be dedicated to rethinking understandings of beneficiaries and purpose, and also to improving evaluation approaches.

By adopting the values of creative design, a balanced extension to agile development will be *generous* as long as the four design arenas are well integrated. The principles for this broader and more inclusive post-agile practice are simply Balance, Integration and Generosity, giving us the name of BIG Design [18] for software development that can fully respond to Takeuchi and Nonaka's [3] agenda for product innovation.

11.4 Making Room for Everyone

Agile development, especially in its most popular guises, will not be fixed simply by adding UCD or creativity. There are extensive issues with agile methodologies [7] that need to be addressed across all potential design inputs, and not just user-centred studies and evaluations. By making room for all potential design inputs that are needed for a specific project, new contexts will be formed for UCD practices. This will not be where Gould and Lewis [10] or ISO [11] locate them, in protected phases of analysis and testing.

Recent agile extensions such as Lean UX [51] offer new process structures and philosophies by combining business and design approaches across all four design arenas. Lean UX's *Learning loops* (build – measure – learn) combine design led empirical hypothesis testing cycles with reflection. Business concerns shape design purpose and derive related evaluation measures. Design thinking shapes idea generation and reflection on action.

Lean UX's just in time approach to UCD activities reflects its influences from design practice and research, abandoning the impossibility of "meaningfully searching for information without the orientation of a solution concept" [2]. By basing user research and evaluation on hypothesis statements that combine complete user stories with evaluation criteria, Lean UX supports appropriate timing of UCD activities within an agile context (Kanban also has promise here [52]). However, Lean UX does not explicitly encourage generous design, and it is not clear how it would manage balance and integration for full BIG design [18]. Even so, as with agile development, Lean UX needs to be given credit for further breaking out of the constraints of rational engineering design and balancing design and business inputs. What remains for BIG design is to further ease these constraints to allow balances of creative, engineering and UCD practices that are appropriate for a specific project, and to provide new approaches to managing the above mentioned four design arenas simultaneously, rather than moving sequentially from one to the next as in ISO

9241-210 [11]. We also need to find ways to encourage generosity (and not just creativity) across the whole project team. Lastly, we need to support planning, tracking, balancing, integration and refactoring across the four design arenas.

There are BIG challenges here, but meeting them will be very worthwhile. We should be generous with our aims here for research *through* and *for* design, aiming to maximize flexibility in extended agile practices.

Acknowledgments My understanding of design arenas has its roots in a UK NESTA Fellowship on Value-Centered Design (2005–2008), and was further developed during the TwinTide COST Action (2008–2013). My understanding of agile practices developed during TwinTide through collaborations with Igor Garnik and Marcin Sikorski [53] and with Marta Lárusdóttir and Åsa Cajander [54]. Joe Dumas' invitation to write an editorial [17] for the *Journal of Usability Studies* gave me a valuable opportunity to apply the results of creative design research to rethinking UCD practice.

References

1. Gram C, Cockton G (1996) Design principles for interactive software. Chapman and Hall, London
2. Rittel HWJ, Webber MM (1973) Dilemmas in a general theory of planning. Policy Sci 4:155–169
3. Takeuchi H, Nonaka I (1986) The new new product development game. Harv Bus Rev 64(1):137–146
4. University of Cincinnati (2016) Science and engineering expo, https://www.research.uc.edu/sciencefair/participants/student-grades-6-12.aspx
5. Dym CL (1994) Engineering design: a synthesis of views. Cambridge University Press, Cambridge, MA
6. Dym CL, Little P (2009) Engineering design: a project based introduction, 3rd edn. Wiley, New York
7. Meyer B (2014) Agile! the good, the hype and the ugly. Springer, Switzerland
8. Boehm B, Turner R (2003) Balancing agility and discipline: a guide for the perplexed. Addison-Wesley, Boston
9. VersionOne (2015) State of Agile™ Survey. www.versionone.com/pdf/state-of-agile-development-survey-ninth.pdf
10. Gould J, Lewis C (1985) Designing for usability: key principles and what designers think. CACM 28(3):300–311
11. ISO (2010) ISO 9241-210:2010. Ergonomics of human-system interaction – part 210: human-centred design process for interactive systems. International Organisation for Standardization
12. McNeill T, Gero JS, Warren J (1998) Understanding conceptual electronic design using protocol analysis. Res Eng Des 10(3):129–140
13. Guindon R (1990) Designing the design process: exploiting opportunistic thoughts. Hum Comput Interact 5(2):305–344
14. Beck K, Beedle M, Van Bennekum A, Cockburn A, Cunningham W and 12 other authors (2001) Manifesto for Agile Software Development. http://www.agilemanifesto.org/
15. Cockton G (2007) Make evaluation poverty history. alt.chi paper, CHI 2007. Available from https://www.academia.edu/1906725/Make_Evaluation_Poverty_History
16. Cockton G (2008) Revisiting usability's three key principles. In: Czerwinski M, Lund AM, Tan DS (eds) CHI 2008 extended abstracts, pp 2473–2484

17. Cockton G (2013) A critical, creative UX community: CLUF. J Usability Stud 10(1):1–16. Invited Editorial, uxpajournal https://www.org/a-critical-creative-ux-community-cluf/
18. Cockton G (2013) Design isn't a shape and it hasn't got a centre: thinking BIG about post-centric interaction design. In: Proceedings of MIDI'13. ACM, Article 2, 16 pages. doi:10.1145/2500342.2500344
19. Brennecke A, Keil-Slawik R (eds) (1996) Position papers for Dagstuhl seminar 9635 on history of software engineering. http://www.dagstuhl.de/Reports/96/9635.pdf
20. Jones JC, Thornley DG (eds) (1963) Conference on design methods. Pergamon Press, Oxford
21. Frayling C (1993) Research in art and design. R C Art Res Pap 1(1):1–5
22. Cross N (2007) Designerly ways of knowing. Birkhauser, Basel
23. Cross N (1982) Designerly ways of knowing. Des Stud 3(4):221–227
24. Brown T (2005) Strategy by design, fast company. June 2005. http://www.fastcompany.com/52795/strategy-design
25. Cross N (2011) Design thinking: understanding how designers think and work. Berg, Oxford
26. Dorst K, Cross N (2001) Creativity in the design process: co-evolution of problem–solution. Des Stud 22(5):425–437
27. Sutherland J (2003) SCRUM: get your requirements straight before Coding. https://www.scruminc.com/scrum-get-your-requirements-straight/
28. Cohn M (2004) User stories applied. Addison-Wesley Professional, Boston
29. Kaczor K (2011) 5 common mistakes we make writing user stories. Scrum Alliance Member Article. https://www.scrumalliance.org/community/articles/2011/august/5-common-mistakes-we-make-writing-user-stories
30. Department for Culture, Media and Sport (2016) Creative industries economic estimates.https://www.gov.uk/government/uploads/system/uploads/attachment_data/file/494927/Creative_Industries_Economic_Estimates_-_January_2016.pdf
31. Buxton B (2010) Sketching user experiences. Getting the design right and the right design. Morgan Kaufmann, San Francisco
32. Schön DA (1992) Designing as reflective conversation with the materials of a design situation. Res Eng Des 3(1):131–147
33. Simon HA (1969) The sciences of the artificial, 1st edn. MIT Press, Cambridge, MA (2nd edn 1981, 3rd edn 1997)
34. Darke J (1979) The primary generator and the design process. Des Stud 1(1):36–44
35. Schön DA (1983) The reflective practitioner: how professionals think in action. Basic Books, New York
36. Killion JP, Todnem GR (1991) A process of personal theory building. Educ Leadersh 48(6):14–17
37. Go JC (2012) Teaching as goal-less and reflective design: a conversation with Herbert A. Simon and Donald Schön. Teach Teach 18(5):513–515
38. Heskett J (2005) Design: a very short introduction. Oxford University Press, Oxford
39. Telier A (Thomas Binder, Giorgio De Michelis, Pelle Ehn, Giulio Jacucci, Per Linde and Ina Wagner) (2011) Design things. MIT Press, Cambridge, MA
40. Hollis B, Maiden N (2013) Extending agile processes with creativity techniques. IEEE Softw 30(5):78–84
41. Dorst K (2015) Frame innovation: create new thinking by design. MIT Press, Cambridge, MA. ISBN 978-0-262-32431-1
42. DSDM Consortium with Jennifer Stapleton (2002) Business focused development. Addison Wesley, London
43. Porter S (2011) Chickens and pigs, Scrum.org Community Publications, Article 90, https://www.scrum.org/About/All-Articles/articleType/ArticleView/articleId/90/Chickens-and-Pigs
44. Dennis AR, Fuller R, Valacich JS (2008) Media, tasks, and communication processes: a theory of media synchronicity. MIS Q 32(3):575–600
45. Brown T (2009) Change by design: how design thinking transforms organizations and inspires innovation. Harper Business, New York

46. Biffl S, Aurum A, Boehm B, Erdogmus H, Grünbacher P (eds) (2005) Value-based software engineering. Springer, Berlin
47. Friedman B (1996) Value-sensitive design. Interactions 3(6):16–23, ACM
48. Cockton G (2008) Designing worth: connecting preferred means with probable ends. Interactions 15(4):54–55, ACM
49. de Saint Exupéry A (1972) Terre des Hommes. Gallimard (reprint of original 1939 book)
50. Banks B (2008) A sort of philosophy. rb.log, www.richardbanks.com/?p=1497
51. Gothelf J with Seiden J (2013) Lean UX: applying lean principles to improve user experience. O'Reilly Media
52. Law EL-C, Lárusdóttir MK (2015) Whose experience do we care about? analysis of the fitness of Scrum and Kanban to user experience. Int J Hum Comput Interact 31(9):584–602
53. Garnik I, Sikorski M, Cockton G (2014) Creative sprints: an unplanned broad agile evaluation and redesign process. In: Proceedings of NordiCHI'14. ACM, pp 1125–1130
54. Lárusdóttir M, Cajander Å, Gulliksen J, Cockton G, Gregory P, Salah D (2014) On the integration of user centred design in agile development. In: Proceedings of NordiCHI'14. ACM, pp 817–820

Printed in the United States
By Bookmasters